# Hidden Horrors

# Transitions: Asia and Asian America

Series Editor, *Mark Selden*

# Hidden Horrors

## Japanese War Crimes in World War II

**YUKI TANAKA**

with a Foreword by
John W. Dower

WestviewPress
*A Division of HarperCollinsPublishers*

Copyright © 1996 by Westview Press, A Division of HarperCollins Publishers, Inc.

Published in 1996 in the United States of America by Westview Press, 5500 Central Avenue, Boulder, Colorado 80301-2877, and in the United Kingdom by Westview Press, 12 Hid's Copse Road, Cumnor Hill, Oxford OX2 9JJ

First published in 1993 in Japan by Otsuki Shoten (in Japanese) as Shirarezaru Senso Hanzai [Unknown war crimes: What Japanese forces did to Australians]

A CIP catalog record for this book is available from the Library of Congress.
ISBN 0-8133-2717-2.   ISBN 0-8133-2718-0 (if published as a paperback)

The paper used in this publication meets the requirements of the American National Standard for Permanence of Paper for Printed Library Materials Z39.48-1984.

10    9    8    7    6    5    4    3    2    1

For Tom Uren, former Japanese POW
and good friend of the Japanese people,
who says: *There's no progress in hate.*

# Contents

# Illustrations

# Foreword
*John W. Dower*

The fiftieth anniversary of the end of World War II, commemorated throughout the world in 1995, was a doubly sobering occasion. It was sobering, of course, to confront again the scenes of atrocity and rampant destruction that characterized that merciless conflict. We reencountered a world gone murderously mad. At the same time, and of a different order, it also was sobering to observe how the war was recalled in most countries. Everywhere, people tended to excavate particularistic shards of memory from the wartime experience, to dwell on their own sacrifice and victimization, to localize and personalize the murder and mayhem that engulfed the world. Such intimate recollections, often intensely moving, tended to remain compartmentalized. The fragmentary nature of this mosaic of memory made clear that, even after half a century, our ability to fully comprehend the war—to truly imagine its extraordinary breadth and grasp its tangled imperatives and psychopathologies—remains rudimentary.

Even some of the most elemental and brutal aspects of the war, such as conventional war crimes and atrocities committed by the forces of Imperial Japan, remain incompletely comprehended. At first glance, this might seem implausible. The barbarous behavior of Japanese fighting men, epitomized at an early date in the Rape of Nanking, received worldwide condemnation beginning in 1937, when Japan launched its all-out war of aggression against China. Japanese brutalization of Allied prisoners of war, initially withheld from public knowledge in the West, became widely publicized in the English-speaking countries beginning in 1944. The ferocious Rape of Manila that accompanied the death throes of the emperor's military machine early in 1945 was made known to the world in shocking black-and-white photos and documentary footage taken by the U.S. forces that liberated the Philippines. From mid-1946 to the end of 1948, the "Class A" war crimes trials conducted by the victorious Allied powers in Tokyo—the Japanese counterpart to the Nuremberg trials of German leaders—provided a forum for exposing the "crimes against peace" and "crimes against humanity" allegedly committed or abetted by top Japanese leaders. Simultaneously, as Yuki Tanaka reminds us, in scores of locales throughout Asia the victors brought to trial thousands of generally low-level Japanese accused of more conventional "Class B" and "Class C" war crimes.

Surely, one might think, more than a decade of such relentless exposure and denunciation of Japanese atrocities, from the late 1930s to late 1940s, should have provided an ample and enduring perspective on at least this atrocious aspect of the war in Asia. In fact, it did not; and the reasons why tell us something about the political and ideological construction of our popular "memories." In the postwar milieu, where defeated Japan was immediately subordinated to U.S. authority and soon thereafter resuscitated as America's rearmed and preeminent cold-war ally in Asia, sanitizing the Japanese past quickly became a collaborative Japanese-American undertaking. Certain egregious Japanese war crimes were covered up to serve American interests. These involved, most notoriously, a murderous program of "medical" experiments pertinent to the development of an advanced biological-warfare capability and the forced enlistment of several hundred thousand non-Japanese young women to provide sexual services for the emperor's soldiers and sailors. As the cold war replaced the old war, policies of forgetting rather than remembering soon became promoted bilaterally, since dwelling on Japan's recent aggression and atrocious war conduct was hardly conducive to eliciting support for its remilitarization. Consideration of war crimes and war responsibility became inseparable from cold war polemics. Within Japan itself, for example, academics and public figures who continued to call attention to Japan's war record commonly were aligned with the political left; their persistent critique of Japan's recent past was inseparable from their opposition to Japanese rearmament under the bilateral U.S.-Japan military relationship. Even when the issue of Japanese war crimes was faced squarely, moreover, Japanese as well as non-Japanese commentators tended to fall into a discourse about Japanese "peculiarity" that contributed little to understanding why our modern world has been so horribly scarred, almost everywhere one looks, by atrocious behavior.

This present study, originally published in a shorter Japanese version under the title *Shirarezaru Sensō Hanzai* (Unknown war crimes), breaks from the postwar and cold war mold in several ways. It addresses the issue of "ordinary" Japanese war crimes through a series of excruciatingly detailed case studies. There have been few such new accounts in English since the late 1940s, and very few indeed of an academic nature. At the same time—in contrast to the bulk of critical Japanese writings on these matters, which tend to focus on the Japanese victimization of other Asians—the atrocities analyzed here involve captured Caucasians. Race and ethnicity constitute a ground bass in most wartime atrocities; certainly racist contempt must be taken into account when we try to explain the callous behavior of Japanese fighting men vis-à-vis other Asians. In the present case studies of Japanese brutality against "white " prisoners, however, we confront the racial hatreds of World War II in Asia in their starkest form.

Yuki Tanaka's signal accomplishment, however, lies not merely in reconstructing these events but rather in trying to comprehend *why*, in an earlier generation, his countrymen performed such atrocious deeds. Such probing, self-critical consciousness makes this an exemplary "post-1995" book. *Hidden Horrors* dwells not on victimization but on victimizing. It seeks to understand the atrocities of ordinary fighting men not in popular mythic terms of abiding "cultural" legacies (such as *bushidō*) but rather in more precise historical, political, sociological, and psychological terms. The implications of such an approach are far-reaching, for ultimately one moves from the concrete atrocities themselves to the peculiar circumstances and socialization that fostered such behavior—and from this, in turn, to a broader understanding of how and why atrocities accompany war everywhere.

By placing the criminal acts of his Japanese protagonists firmly in the context of the post–World War I "emperor system" ideology that militarists and civilian ideologues drilled into the populace, for example, Yuki Tanaka not only reminds us of the *modernity* of Japan's emperor worship but also prompts us to think more generally about the political uses of "tradition" and ideological manipulation of "culture" and "history" in all societies. In observing that the Japanese victimizers of others often were simultaneously victims themselves—low-level links in a "transfer of oppression" that extended from top to bottom domestically in Imperial Japan's rigidly hierarchical society (and was replicated with particular harshness within the military)—he calls our attention to a pecking order of brutalization and dehumanization that had distinctive Japanese characteristics but that ultimately was hardly peculiar to Japan.

Few recent books have been as relentless as this in recreating the horror of Japanese war crimes. For many readers, however, the greatest shock may lie in discovering that many of the individuals who committed these atrocities were simply ordinary men in extraordinary circumstances—manipulated by their leaders and dehumanized by the very nature of war itself. Their acts become all the more horrible when we no longer can regard them as having been committed by people utterly unlike ourselves.

# Acknowledgments

Throughout the writing of this book, I constantly received valuable advice and moral support from various people. I appreciate particularly the many supporting letters from those people in various countries whom I have never met but who apparently came to know of my research through media reports on my work. Disappointingly, media reports have often distorted not only the content but also the intention of my research, thus causing ill feelings in certain circles. To receive such warm-hearted letters was therefore particularly encouraging when I encountered criticisms, most of which were based upon misunderstanding.

I thank many Japanese, Taiwanese, and Australian veterans who provided me with much indispensable information. At the same time, I apologize for frequently making difficult requests to them to recollect and talk about traumatic war experiences that they probably wanted to forget forever. These interviews gave me the valuable opportunity to contemplate human behavior and consequently deepened my knowledge of the nature of human beings considerably.

The draft of Chapters 1 and 2 led to the production of a television documentary film, *Return to Sandakan*. I am grateful to Ray Quint and Julian Leatherdale, who read an early draft and subsequently used this as the backbone for their excellent film.

The draft of Chapter 3, which I presented at a Japanese studies conference held at Australian National University in September 1993, caused a tremendous controversy in Australia that I had never expected. My reference to the misconduct in Hiroshima by some members of the Australian occupation forces soon after the war upset some Australians. As a result, I was bombarded with criticism not only by concerned people but also by some Australian media. However, this nationwide controversy suddenly ended when a former Australian soldier of the occupation forces, Allan Clifton, publicly supported my statement by quoting his own memoirs. Allan Clifton passed away in July 1995. Regrettably, I missed the opportunity to meet him and to express my gratitude.

However, I had a delightful experience, too. During my research I came across many interrogation reports prepared by an investigator named Albert Klestadt of the Australian War Crimes Section. I was curious about this person with a German name who apparently spoke good Japanese. Eventually I found that he lives only a few kilometers away from my home here in Melbourne. Fortuitously, I was able to meet him and to ask him to read the draft of Chapter 6 on the war crimes case that he investigated nearly 50 years ago. I thank him for his assurance on the accuracy of my historical analysis of this crime case.

I offer my thanks also to the many other individuals with specialized knowledge who were extremely helpful: David Barrett, Tim Bowden, Michael Dutton, Hugh Clarke, Syd Crawcour, Sheila Jeffrey, Peter Lisowski, Ian Maddocks, Hank Nelson, Tilman Ruff, Arthur Stockwin, Don Wall, Awaya Kentarō, Fujiwara Akira, Gotō Kenichi, Hanasaki Kōhei, Hayashi Hirofumi, Ienaga Saburō, Igarashi Kenichi, Irokawa Daikichi, Nakagawa Sadamu, Oda Makoto, Sugimoto Yoshio, Takemae Eiichi, Tsuneishi Keiichi, Utsumi Aiko, Yoshida Yutaka, and Yoshimi Yoshiaki. Special thanks are due to Mark Selden who gave me the most detailed comments on my draft manuscripts. Without his help and encouragement, I could not have finished this book. I wish also to thank John Dower for his most articulate and informative Foreword. Finally, I extend my sincere gratitude to my long-standing friends Gavan and Fusako McCormack for their continuous support and friendship.

For help in searching archival documents, photos, and pictures, I thank Esta Carey of the Melbourne branch of the Australian National Archives; Moira Smythe of the same Archives in Canberra; all the staff of the Australian War Memorial, in particular, Ian Afflex, George Imasheve, and Elena Rench; Rick Boyland of the U.S. National Archives, Suitland; and Aijima Hiroshi and Hoshi Kenichi of the Japanese Diet Library. I also thank the Australian War Memorial for the research grant I received between 1994 and 1995. I also wish to express my gratitude to Sakaguchi Eiko and Aoki Hidekazu for obtaining relevant Japanese books for me.

For help with refining my English writing, I thank Bill King, Guy Rundle, and Anita Punton.

Finally and most of all, thanks to my wife, Jo, who did the final editing work. The moral support I received from Jo and our daughters, Mika and Alisa, made the completion of this project possible.

*Yuki Tanaka*

# Author's Note

All Japanese names, including authors of Japanese texts, have been cited in traditional Japanese order with the surname first. All dates and times are cited according to the date and time west of the International Date Line, unless otherwise indicated. For instance, although in the United States the attack on Pearl Harbor is referred to as having taken place on December 7, 1941, in this book I use the date December 8.

*Y. T.*

# Introduction

"Why open Pandora's box?" "What do you hope to achieve by revealing the painful and horrifying events of the past?" Such are the questions that, as a historian specializing in the study of war crimes committed by Japanese troops during the Asia-Pacific War, I frequently encounter not only from incredulous Japanese people but also from citizens of former Allied nations against whose soldiers various atrocities were committed by Japanese forces.

"To master the past"—what the Germans call *Vergangenheitsbewälti-gung*—is, I believe, the most appropriate answer to such questions. This does not mean simply to comprehend events of the past intellectually but also to exercise *moral imagination*. Moral imagination requires us to take responsibility for past wrongdoings and at the same time stimulates us to project our thoughts toward the future through the creative examination of our past. My aim in investigating the war crimes and atrocities committed by the Japanese is therefore to master the past. To this end I will begin with a general analysis of the war crimes tribunals conducted by the Allied nations.

After World War II, the Allied nations prosecuted Japanese and German military personnel and civilian collaborators who were alleged to have committed war crimes against Allied soldiers and noncombatants. Three types of war crime categories were established. The A Class consisted of "crimes against peace," and those who were prosecuted included military leaders and politicians who had instigated the war against the Allied nations and bore final responsibility for the various war crimes committed by their own forces. The B Class encompassed more "conventional" war crimes—those committed by soldiers in the field against either enemy soldiers or civilians of enemy countries. The C Class, which covered "crimes against humanity," consisted of crimes against civilians of any nationality. This last category was specially created in order to prosecute Nazi war criminals who had committed crimes against their own citizens, most notably Jews, Gypsies, homosexuals, the mentally ill, and communists. In this sense, C Class was a "nonconventional" supplement to the B Class conventional war crimes. However, because in the Japanese case the difference between the B and C categories was not always clear, they were usually combined to form a single B and C Class for the purposes of prosecution.[1]

On May 3, 1946, the International Military Tribunal for the Far East (usually known as the Tokyo War Crimes Tribunal) was convened in Tokyo to prosecute A Class war criminals. On November 12, 1948, the judgment of the court was handed down. Of 28 war leaders charged with war crimes, 25 were found guilty, 1 was declared insane, and the remaining 2 died before completion of the trial. Among these 25, 7—including General Tōjō Hideki, the commander in chief of Japanese imperial forces—were sentenced to death and hanged on December 23, 1948.[2]

Tribunals for B and C Class war criminals were conducted between October 1945 and April 1951 by seven Allied nations—the United States, Britain, Australia, Holland, France, the Philippines, and China (Taipei government)—in 49 locations in the Asia-Pacific region. The locations of the tribunals included Singapore, Rabaul, Manila, Hong Kong, and Yokohama. A total of 5,379 Japanese, 173 Formosans, and 148 Koreans were tried. Of these, 984 were sentenced to death. A further 475 were sentenced to life imprisonment, and 2,944 were sentenced to various terms of imprisonment.[3]

Whether the Tokyo War Crimes Tribunal and the B and C Class tribunals were completely impartial remains an open question.[4] What cannot be doubted from the results of them, however, is that the Japanese were responsible for many war crimes throughout the Asia-Pacific region. Seventy-three percent of those prosecuted at the B and C Class tribunals were found to have committed war crimes, as defined by the Hague and Geneva Conventions, including ill-treatment and murder, against Allied prisoners of war.[5] This figure alone indicates the degree of cruelty exercised by the Japanese on POWs during the Asia-Pacific War. Of the estimated 350,000 prisoners under the Japanese during the war, 210,000 were captured in the first three months after the outbreak of war in the Pacific, and 290,000 were captured in the first six months.[6] Therefore most of the POWs who survived had endured an arduous and painful internment of more than three years. According to the findings of the Tokyo War Crimes Tribunal, of the 350,000 POWs, 132,134 were from Britain, the Netherlands, Australia, the United States, Canada, and New Zealand, and 35,756 died while detained, a death rate of about 27 percent.[7] (For details of the breakdown of POWs by nation, see Table I.1.) In contrast, deaths among the 235,473 Allied POWs interned by Germans and Italians reached 9,348, a rate of 4 percent.[8] In other words, the death rate for POWs under the Japanese was seven times that of POWs under the Germans and Italians. Moreover, the postwar death rate among surviving POWs of the Japanese was also higher. For example, from 1945 to 1959, the death rate among former Australian POWs who had been detained by the Japanese was

TABLE I.1    Number of Allied POWs and Death Rate Under the Japanese

| Country | Number of POWs | Number of Deaths | Death Rate (percent) |
|---|---|---|---|
| Australia | 21,726 | 7,412 | 34.1 |
| Britain | 50,016 | 12,433 | 24.8 |
| Canada | 1,691 | 273 | 16.1 |
| New Zealand | 121 | 31 | 25.6 |
| United States | 21,580 | 7,107 | 32.9 |
| Holland | 37,000 | 8,500 | 22.9 |
| Total | 132,134 | 35,756 | |
| Average death rate | | | 27.1 |

*Source*: Based on data in "Horyo Saishū Ronkoku Fuzoku-sho 'B,'" Kykutō Kokusai Gunji Saiben No. 337, February 19, 1948.

four times the rate among Australian POWs imprisoned by German and Italian forces,[9] although many of the latter had been held longer than those imprisoned by the Japanese because the war in Europe started earlier.

The Allied nations found the Japanese treatment of POWs in places like the Burma-Thailand railway almost beyond comprehension.[10] The postwar trials built on and strengthened the widely held belief that the Japanese were a peculiar people, particularly in their propensity to cruelty, a belief that took root in the Allied nations during the war and has persisted since. This is one of the foundations of the current dominant image of the Japanese as peculiarly group-oriented and cooperative among themselves yet extremely aggressive in pursuing their own interests externally, particularly economic interests.

Many Japanese have also continued to hold on to the notion that they are "different." This thinking can even be seen in the work of critical Japanese historians who have attempted to come to terms with Japan's role in the Asia-Pacific War. They too have persistently assumed that Japan is a special case. This can be seen in recent work on the "comfort women" issue in Japan.[11] Critical historians, who have severely criticized Japanese government policies on military prostitution, have unfortunately approached the issue of the wartime exploitation of women as if it was peculiar to the Japanese armed forces at the time. Needless to say, it is the responsibility of Japanese intellectuals to face up to the issue of Japanese war crimes and critically examine the specific events. Important contributions have been made in bringing to light the inhuman treatment of comfort women and other victims of Japanese aggression. Yet virtually all of these studies, whether by Japanese, by authors from the countries occupied by Japan during the war, or by Western authors, have treated Japanese war crimes as if they are unique.

Japanese historians in general and historians of the Asia-Pacific War in particular rarely write comparatively, partly because they presuppose that Japanese war crimes are a special case. In the absence of studies of war crimes of other nations, Japanese scholars have reinforced beliefs in Japan's uniqueness, including a unique proclivity to torture, violence, and inhumanity.

Much analysis of Japanese culture by foreign Japanologists and historians has been based on the belief in this uniqueness—both as a blameworthy trait and one to be celebrated. For example, Ezra Vogel's *Japan as Number One* (the epitomy of celebratory Japanology) and Karel von Wolferen's *The Enigma of Japanese Power*[12] (representative of the highly critical revisionist Japanology), though ostensibly presenting opposing views of Japan, share an underlying image of Japan as a peculiar nation and the Japanese as a peculiar people. These works, together with much other recent Japanology, present a more sophisticated picture than World War II Allied propaganda. But they remain propaganda nonetheless. These works, some of which have been best-sellers both in the West and in Japan, have reinforced images of the Japanese as "different." In short, both ithin and outside Japan, and regardless of whether the intent is to celebrate or criticize, Japan and the Japanese are frequently represented as peculiar or, at least, "different."

Gavan Daws's recent book, *Prisoners of the Japanese,*[13] is undoubtedly a masterpiece in the sense that no other books hitherto have presented such a detailed account of the treatment of POWs by the Japanese during the Asia-Pacific War. His meticulous analysis of extensive information that he obtained from a vast number of interviews conducted with former POWs over a ten-year period gives us a real picture of the cruelty that the Japanese inflicted upon their captives and the traumatic legacy thus engraved on the minds of surviving POWs. Yet because of the absence of any explanation as to *why* the Japanese were capable of committing such cruelty, his book unfortunately also gives readers the strong impression of the Japanese as a people with "unique characteristics."

In this book I focus on specific instances of Japanese war crimes and attempt to explain the cause of these in a way that challenges culturally based notions of Japanese uniqueness. Comparative historical methods offer a sound basis for achieving this aim. War crimes are *not* a uniquely Japanese phenomenon. By documenting and analyzing the historical roots of Japanese war crimes, I am seeking to illuminate the specific dynamics of Japanese culture and society during the Asia-Pacific War but within the context of a broader analysis of the universal problem of wartime hatreds and war crimes. Japanese war crimes, rather than deriv-

ing from a peculiar Japaneseness or national character, must be understood in relation to the specific conditions of Japanese society in general
and the Japanese military in particular both during the Asia-Pacific War
and in the years leading up to it. Unfortunately, Japanese historians have
failed to strike an appropriate balance between specificity and universality when dealing with war crimes, although recently some Western ana-
lysts such as John Dower and Mark Selden have successfully made comparative analyses of the war crimes committed by Americans with those
committed by the Japanese.[14]

The consequences of this scholarship of the "unique" have been profound in shaping images of Japan at home and abroad. Although critical
Japanese historians have readily acknowledged past wrongs and even
war crimes, they have failed to find the cultural taproot of war crimes and
thus have been unable to contribute to an understanding that might help
prevent future war crimes. Although rightly criticizing Japanese war
crimes and calling for appropriate recompense, they have failed to see
that Japan's dark past is far from unique. Specific features are of great importance, but war crimes were and are the monopoly of no people or nation. Their study, if appropriately framed in a comparative perspective,
can provide valuable lessons for everyone.

Comparing Japanese war crimes with those of the Nazis or the Allies
during World War II or even with those of more recent wars, such as in
Vietnam, Iraq, the former Yugoslavia, and Rwanda, highlights the universality of this phenomenon. It is this possibility that makes past crimes
worth remembering, even after all victims and perpetrators have died.
Unless we have an eye to the present and future as well as the past, facing
up to the past is of little value. It is the relevance of what has happened in
the past to what is happening right now or what might happen in the future that matters most. Past wrongs have already occurred, but perhaps
the study of the past can help prevent future wrongs and atrocities.

The study of Japanese war crimes by Japanese scholars frequently suf-
fers from a fundamental lack of methodological rigor, most clearly seen in
the complacent attitude of mainstream nationalist Japanese historians.
Nationalist historians in Japan have consistently played up the fact that
the Japanese were victims as well as perpetrators of war crimes, often to
the point of being concerned only with Japan's role as victim. It is undoubtedly true that the Japanese were victims as well as aggressors, but
nationalist historians have systematically glossed over the specificities of
Japanese war crimes.[15] Their goal has been to exculpate Japan by rendering it morally equivalent to every other nation and by seeing universal responsibility as equivalent to no one's responsibility.

A truly universal account must deal honestly and critically with the war
crimes of every participating nation—and that means paying attention to

specificities. Critical Japanese historians have effectively demolished the self-serving analyses of the nationalist,[16] but the effect of their critiques has been limited by an inability to analyze effectively both specific and universal elements. Caught up in a polar opposition with the conservatives, they have tended to focus exclusively on the unique and timeless features of Japanese aggression and inhumanity. Critical historians have thus far failed to place their detailed knowledge about specific cases of Japanese war crimes in an appropriate interpretive context. Sometimes they have even unwittingly distanced themselves from the problem by rendering war criminals as an "other" with which they share nothing, including responsibility.

Those who fought in the Asia-Pacific War were in reality mostly ordinary Japanese men. They were our fathers and grandfathers. We need to face up to the fact that we could easily become this "other" ourselves in changed circumstances. What then would prevent us from committing crimes comparable to those committed on the Burma-Thailand railway or at Nanjing?[17] The extraordinary events of war crimes have a closer connection with the everyday life of ordinary people than we might want to acknowledge. In closely studying the history of specific Japanese war crimes so as to understand how they could have been committed by ordinary people, we can gain a sense of how they remain our problem to this day.

In contrast to the Japanese, German war historians, influenced by *Alltagsgeschichte* (history of everyday life), have made repeated efforts to examine German war crimes critically and understand how intimately they were connected with the everyday life of ordinary people.[18] We Japanese, too, need to reexperience the crimes of our fathers and grandfathers as deeply and as viscerally as the Germans have reexperienced their past. It is not enough for us to gain a purely intellectual understanding of them. In so doing, though, it is important to understand that crimes of war were not unique to Japan and to ask the question: Under what circumstances did (and do) human beings conduct themselves as war criminals?

Historical analysis of everyday life is not without its pitfalls, however, and we must take care not to be trapped in them. In examining particular cases there is a tendency to place all responsibility on the individual and to neglect the political and social context in which those individuals acted. In focusing, for example, on the perpetrator of a rape or murder, there is a danger of neglecting the responsibility of the military and the state. When dealing with the individual cases of B and C Class war crimes, we must always maintain an awareness of the interrelationship between the actions and responsibilities of individuals and the structure of power of the Japanese military and state. To overlook this need leads invariably to a confrontationist stalemate between specificity and universality. The approach of this study is from the bottom upward, from individuals to social structures, but with the aim always to maintain a link between the two levels.

The insights provided by Oda Makoto, a well-known Japanese novelist, social critic, and activist, are also useful here. Oda sought to explore issues of responsibility in both aggressors and victims. From this angle we can see that most perpetrators of war crimes were themselves victims who were subject to the orders of superiors and that many of them committed crimes unwillingly. This is particularly obvious in the case of Taiwanese and Koreans, many of whom were conscripted to serve in low-ranking POW guard positions with the Japanese forces. Many war criminals were thus no more masters of their own fate than were their victims. Every soldier is a victim of the state that drafts him, sends him to war, and demands that he kill the enemy. However, at the same time, this soldier still bears responsibility for his actions as an aggressor or war criminal. For Oda, the way to rescue the soldier from the simultaneous and intertwined fate as victim and aggressor is to establish a principle higher than the state—one that resides in the recognition by the soldier that he is not the state and that he has no right to kill others. Oda called this the principle of "absolute peace."[19]

So far we Japanese have not adequately examined ourselves as aggressors and as victims at the same time. The view of most Japanese on the Asia-Pacific War is overwhelmingly inclined toward seeing ourselves only as the victim. There are several reasons for this myopia, such as the fact that we were victims of the world's only nuclear holocaust; that, unlike in Germany, the Japanese committed no racial genocide within their own country or abroad; that we were threatened by economic and political advancement of Western powers into Asia; and that Japan's national ethos specific to its fascist ideology was based upon the emperor ideology. This national ethos prevented us Japanese from perceiving ourselves as the aggressors that we were. I will discuss this issue further in the Conclusion.

The general feeling of the Japanese people immediately after the war—that we had been deceived by the state or that the state bore responsibility for the war—gave us the opportunity to realize that we were a separate entity from the state. Yet this way of thinking obscured our own responsibility for collaborating with the state, even if in many instances it was unwillingly. Consequently, we Japanese have failed to recognize ourselves as aggressors, still less as perpetrators of war crimes. Moreover, because of the widespread perception of ourselves as the victims of war, the notion of "victim" gradually expanded even to the point that the Japanese state was also seen as a victim of war.

Nonetheless, because of this strong self-perception as victims of war, the majority of Japanese welcomed Article 9 of their new U.S.-imposed postwar constitution, which refers to the "renunciation of war." Now, after 50 years, this "victim" consciousness is rapidly disappearing, along with the consciousness of having been an aggressor. This is clearly indicated in recent newspaper polls that reflect the popular attitude toward Japan's military roles in world political affairs, despite people's awareness that such military activities outside Japanese territory are clearly in breach of Article 9 of the constitution.[20] Now many Japanese, especially the young, regard Article 9 as no longer relevant to the political situation in Japan.

Recently, some Japanese political leaders have made public statements about the nation's war crimes and have even apologized to the citizens of those countries that suffered. However, these official apologies seem perfunctory in the light of Oda's "principle of absolute peace." Their real motivation seems more likely to be found in the realm of international politics: to make amends with these nations to improve economic and trading terms.[21] Indeed the majority of Japanese politicians lack a clear recognition of Japan's war responsibility. In August 1995 at the fiftieth anniversary of the end of World War II, then Prime Minister Murayama Tomiichi tried to issue an official apology as the head of the Japanese government. However, because of political pressure from the conservative members of the coalitionist Liberal Democratic Party, he was forced to apologize as an individual rather than in his official capacity of prime minister.

The aim in this book is to examine closely the specific cases of war crimes committed by the Japanese forces from the viewpoint of perpetrators and of victims concurrently. At the same time, I will attempt to focus on fundamental characteristics of war in general: the dehumanization of the "other" and the brutalization of the "self" as a result.

Chapters 1 and 2 deal with the massacre of prisoners in Sandakan POW camp in North Borneo. More than 2,500 POWs—most of them Australian soldiers—were held in this camp. Only six survived the depredation of forced labor, starvation, mass execution, lack of medical treatment, and two death marches in which prisoners were forced to walk 260 kilometers. Why did Japanese forces eliminate these POWs in such a gratuitous manner? Answers are sought in an analysis of the particular power structures and goals of the Japanese military.

In Chapter 3 I examine the massacre of 21 Australian military nurses on Banka Island in Indonesia and the attempt to coerce 32 other nurses into prostitution for the Japanese officers. What were the reasons for this massacre of noncombatants who had already surrendered? In this chapter I examine the links between this incident and the more general phenomenon of rape and enforced prostitution in wartime. I also consider the degree to which this was unique to the Japanese military in the Asia-Pacific War.

My focus in Chapter 4 is on the widespread cannibalism by Japanese soldiers in New Guinea. The Australian military forces gathered extensive information on Japanese cannibalism committed against many Australian soldiers, Asian POWs, and New Guinean locals. Yet despite such extensive evidence, Australia did not present this case to the Tokyo War Crimes Tribunal and chose instead to pursue prosecutions for this crime only at the lower-level B and C Class tribunals. Who made the decision to take this course of action, and what were the reasons behind it? Why did the Japanese forces commit such grotesque crimes?

In Chapter 5 I analyze the Japanese forces' plan for bacteriological warfare in the Pacific War as well as the medical experiments carried out on POWs in the Southwest Pacific. Japanese medical officers conducted various experiments on POWs in order to discover how to combat tropical disease and starvation. Why was no one prosecuted, despite the fact that the Australian War Crimes Section collected ample evidence of such experiments? In this chapter, I undertake comparative analysis between Japanese medical doctors involved in the experiments and Nazi doctors who conducted equally horrific experiments on their prisoners.

The massacre of German missionaries and Allied civilians in the Southwest Pacific by Japanese naval forces is discussed in Chapter 6. Why were these noncombatants massacred, despite the fact that they offered no threat to the Japanese? I examine not only the lack of knowledge of international law among the Japanese officers and soldiers but also how the Japanese wartime belief in *gyokusai* ("glorious self-annihilation") contributed to the disregard for basic human rights. I highlight the typical example of the Japanese forces committing suicide in the face of defeat and the psychological effect this intention had on their behavior.

In the Conclusion, I argue that inhumane treatment of POWs by the Japanese was a specific phenomenon occurring between the so-called China incident (Japan's invasion of China) in 1937 and the end of World War II in 1945 and that Japanese POW policy prior to the China incident was quite the opposite. I explore a possible explanation as to why the Japanese POW policy was corrupted by analyzing the changes that occurred in Japanese political culture from 1910 onward. My basic argument is that the brutality of the Japanese forces during the Asia-Pacific War did not derive from an inherently peculiar Japaneseness but was an inevitable product of the emperor ideology based upon the "family-state" concept, which was gradually strengthened in the late Meiji and Taishō periods.

Through this study of Japanese war crimes, we can learn how easily a person, regardless of nationality, can be trapped by the psychology of brutality when involved in war. Such brutality is often caused by hatred of others, as is clearly illustrated in acts of racism. The most fundamental problem we must address when dealing with any war crime is the profound fear of death that soldiers experience. In order to overcome fear during war, people tend to rely upon violence, which in turn degrades their morals and manifests itself as an outbreak of brutality. War is the most unproductive human activity, and death in war is thus the most unproductive death possible. Therefore violence and brutality as exemplified by war crimes are probably the most negative manifestations of a human being's desire to live.

# 1

# The Sandakan POW Camp and the Geneva Convention

## The Forgotten POW Camp

What images does the name "Sandakan" evoke for the Japanese? Many know of it as a place somewhere on Borneo, yet few know of its exact location. Some know of it through Yamazaki Tomoko's novel *Sandakan Hachiban Shōkan* (*Sandakan Brothel Number Eight*), a story (also made into a film) about the military brothels located there and the Japanese women—the *karayuki-san*, or "women travelers"—who worked there. In World War II, Sandakan was a key strategic point that linked the oil fields of the east coast of Borneo to the Philippines and to the whole of the Japanese-occupied Asia-Pacific. It also contained a large POW camp.

Few people outside Japan are familiar with the name "Sandakan," and even in Australia fewer still know of the extraordinary events that occurred there. By September 1943 Sandakan POW camp held about 2,000 Australian POWs and 500 British POWs; only 6 survived to the end of the war—a survival rate of 0.24 percent. At Ambon POW camp 123 out of a total of 528 Australian POWs survived;[1] in this case the survival rate was 23 percent. A total of 60,500 POWs worked on the construction of the Burma-Thailand railroad; about 12,000 died, a survival rate of more than 80 percent. Of the 9,500 Australian POWs who worked there, the survival rate was 72 percent—2,646 died.[2] Of course, comparison of the survival rates should not overshadow the raw figures.

Construction of the Burma-Thailand railway and other such incidents have remained vivid memories in Australian history, yet Sandakan has been forgotten. Why is this so? It may be that the relatively large number of survivors of the more notorious incidents has ensured that many stories, memories, and publications circulated through the Australian community in the postwar years. The survivors of Sandakan were so few, and their experience was so extreme, that in some respects it is beyond telling. The psychological legacy is so overpowering that the remaining survivors find it difficult to talk about their experience at all. It was only in the early 1980s—when interviews were recorded with the survivors for an ABC (Australian Broadcasting Corporation) radio program—that the name of Sandakan began to be heard.

Sandakan is similarly forgotten in Japan, though for a different reason. All of the guards at the Sandakan camp were Formosans (Taiwanese), under the command of Japanese officers, so there were few returnees to Japan who had any knowledge of the incident. And all documents relating to the camp were burned sometime toward the end of the war.

I conducted several interviews with surviving former Japanese military officers, soldiers, and Formosan guards who dealt with POWs in Sandakan. However, it was quite difficult to obtain honest accounts of their wartime experiences because of the nature of their inhumane acts against the POWs as well as the stigma attached to the label "war criminal." In particular, Formosans are extremely reluctant to tell of their ordeal, first because of the shame about their own conduct in dealing with the POWs and second because of a deep mistrust of the Japanese, including me. These former Formosan guards regard themselves as victims rather than perpetrators of war crimes, much more so than the Japanese do. This seems to be quite natural since they did not voluntarily become POW guards but were forced to work for the Japanese forces. As a result, the amount of valuable information obtained through the interviews with the Japanese and Formosans was quite limited.

Yet the Sandakan incident provides the clearest picture possible of the relationship between the power structure of the Japanese army and the occurrence of war crimes. Warrant Officer William Stiepewich, one of the survivors of Sandakan, gave evidence at the Tokyo War Crimes Tribunal about the ill-treatment and ultimate massacre of POWs there. Stiepewich's testimony, together with an affidavit from another survivor, Keith Botterill, ran to 109 pages.[3] This testimony, the documents and transcripts from the B and C Class trials, and the interviews recorded for the ABC give us a fairly clear picture of the three-year ordeal of those who lived and died in Sandakan.[4]

## Establishment of the Camp and the Labor Issue

Prior to World War II Borneo was divided into two regions, Northwest Borneo, occupied by the British, and Southeast Borneo, which was a Dutch colony. The conquest of Borneo, Java, and Sumatra was a high priority for the Japanese forces, as the area had a number of major oil fields—Tarakan, Sangasanga, and Balikpapan on the east coast and Seria (now Brunei) and Miri on the west coast (Map 1.1). The destruction of Pearl Harbor and the siege of Singapore in late 1941 made it possible for an invasion force sailing from China to take these islands without fear of being outflanked by British Commonwealth forces, the South China Sea already being under the firm control of the Japanese forces. Seria and Miri oil fields and the refinery in Lutong were captured in mid-December, and on January 11, 1942, Japanese paratroops attacked Menado. Tarakan was taken on the fourteenth, Balikpapan on the twenty-third, and Pontianak, the largest city on the west coast, on the twenty-ninth. By the end of the month the whole of Borneo was in Japanese hands. The invasion force was followed in by the Oil Corps, a division of the Army composed of drafted engineers, who took over the operation of the oil fields and refineries from British and Dutch operators.[5]

The distance between the Philippines and Singapore (both of which had fallen to Japanese forces by early 1942) was too great for Japanese aircraft to fly in one stretch, and so it was decided there should be an airfield at Sandakan to provide a refueling point. The Sandakan airfield would also serve as a refueling point for aircraft en route to islands to the south, such as Java, the Celebes, and Timor.[6] It was clear to the planners that construction of this airfield would require an enormous amount of forced labor. However, the Japanese forces had difficulty in gaining local laborers because most of them were mobilized for the construction of essential roads and military facilities in the Sandakan area at that time. Therefore, a POW camp was established at Sandakan for the purpose of exploiting the labor force of POWs. The Sandakan camp was established as a branch of the larger Kuching POW camp, the center of the Borneo POW camp network.

The notorious Changi camp in Singapore was used as a pool from which to draw POW labor. Changi held more than 50,000 prisoners, most of them British, Australian, and Indian men who had been captured in Singapore, Malaya, and Timor. From these prisoners a number of labor groups were formed. The first, A Force, consisting of 3,000 Australian POWs, was sent to South Burma in May 1942 and was mobilized to build an airfield there. These men were later sent to work on the Burma-Thailand railway. B Force, consisting of 1,494 POWs (145 officers, 312 NCOs, and 1,037 enlisted men) was sent to Sandakan.[7] Some prisoners were conscripted into B Force by the Japanese, but the majority were prisoners who had volunteered for a work detail. They were not told by the Japanese what sort of work they would be given, but they were told that they would receive better rations and be located in a healthier environment than those who remained at Changi. B Force was moved from Changi in July 1942. By this time a number of Japanese war crimes had

14

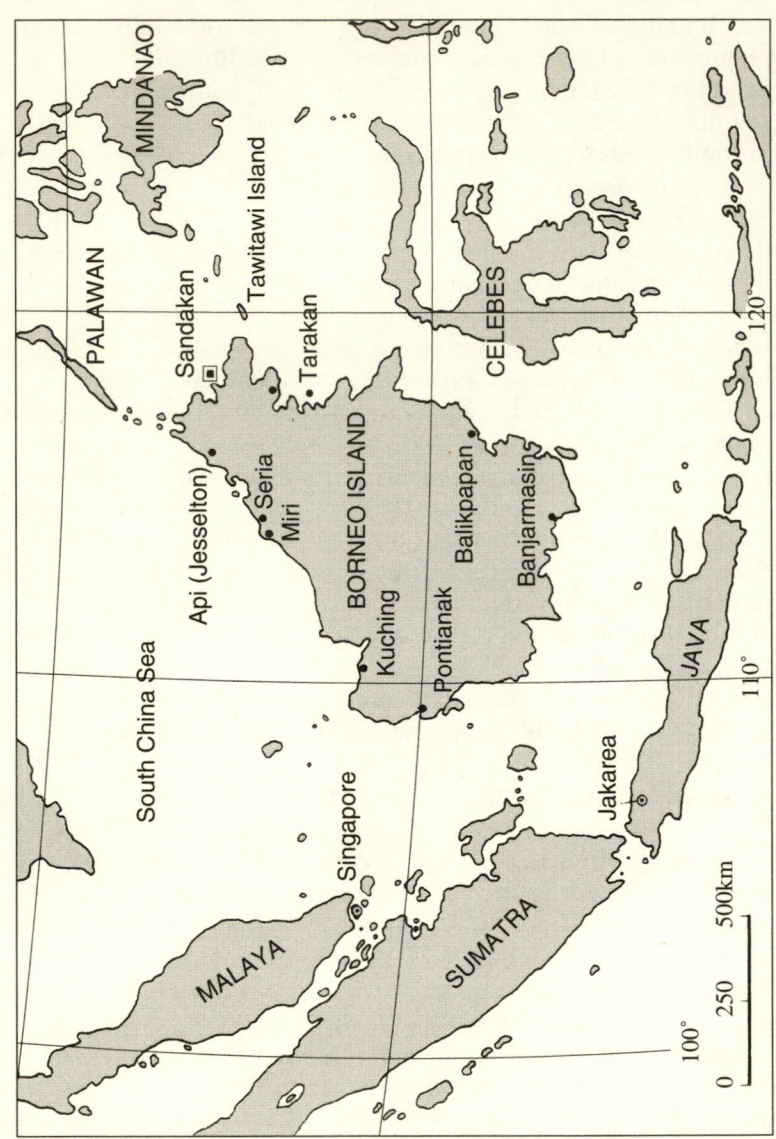

Map 1.1  *Borneo.*

already been committed against Allied POWs in other parts of the occupied Asia-Pacific. An example is the Bataan death march, which occurred in April 1942. About 16,000 Filipino and 2,000 American POWs, who had been captured during the fall of the Philippines, died after being forced to march 100 kilometers with little food and water.[8] A Force had already commenced work in the extremely harsh conditions that were to become standard for POW labor, yet the prospective members of B Force knew nothing of these events.

POWs in all of the camps located in the Singapore area were obliged to take part in work details, but the work was not excessive and the treatment of prisoners by Japanese guards was relatively humane. (At this stage, prison guards were all Japanese. Conscripted Korean and Formosan guards were not used before May 1942.) But there were 50,000 prisoners in Changi, and they often went hungry. The opportunity to join a work detail, in which promised rations were relatively generous, must have been the major attraction for many.

Others might also have believed that their chances for escape would be greater in a smaller and more remote prison camp. Many found the atmosphere of Singapore—the city as well as the camps around it—extremely depressing. An air of humiliation and shame hung about the place. There were other, grisly reminders of death and defeat, such as the decapitated heads of Chinese and Indian civilians who had resisted Japanese rule, which were on display in the streets of the city and often seen by the prisoners when they were trucked from place to place on work details.[9]

The 1,500 members of B Force left Singapore in the 3,000-metric-ton *Ubi Maru* on July 7, 1942.[10] Conditions were extremely uncomfortable. The *Ubi Maru* was a cargo ship, and the prisoners were camped on deck with no space to move around. They were also given little food and water throughout the journey. The ship took 10 days to reach Sandakan, sailing via Miri. During the voyage many of the prisoners noticed that the *Ubi Maru* had no naval escort and that relatively few guards or sailors were on board. This led to discussion of the possibility of taking over the ship by sheer force of numbers. Ultimately, however, it was decided by the ranking officers in B Force that it was "too early" to take over the ship and that the force should wait for a better opportunity for a mass escape to present itself. Subsequently, they were informed that a Japanese submarine had been following the ship at all times.[11]

B Force arrived in Sandakan on July 17 and was held 13 kilometers inland from the port, in what had previously been a British experimental farm. An internment camp had been built there by the British for Japanese residents of Borneo at the outbreak of the Pacific War. It had internment quarters with an intended holding capacity of 200, in which all

1,500 members of B Force were held. However, aside from the overcrowding, conditions were relatively good at first. The healthy POWs walked the 13 kilometers, and the POWs who were ill were ferried from the port to the camp by truck together with all heavy equipment.[12]

Several weeks after arrival in Sandakan, B Force was mobilized to build the airfield and the road that would be used to connect the airfield and the town. The original plan called for two landing strips each 850 meters long and 50 meters wide, which were completed in the first three months. But in order that large bomber-type planes could land, airstrips had to be extended to 1,400 meters long. Both ends of the 850-meter airstrips were valleys, and thus the extension work of filling up the valley was extremely hard.[13] The prisoners left camp at 7:30 every morning and walked to the construction site eight kilometers away. They worked until 5:00 in the evening with a lunchbreak and even special rations, such as coffee, for those who had worked hard. There was no work on Sunday, so the prisoners usually held entertainment functions, such as a concert or a boxing match, on Saturday night. Prisoners received a small amount of pay, and there was a camp canteen from which they could purchase coconuts, turtle eggs, bananas, tobacco, and other goods.[14] They also set up vegetable gardens within the camp. Thus, although the rations could not be said to be plentiful, they were at least sufficient for basic good health. Colonel Suga Tatsuji, the head of the POW camps in Borneo, appears to have been a relatively humane officer, as a number of events show. On the occasions when he visited the Sandakan camp, the prisoners' rations would be improved (although they usually reverted to normal on his departure) by the prison officers, who must have presumed Suga would be impressed that the POWs were receiving relatively good rations (rather than the reverse). On another occasion he granted prisoners a three-day holiday, an extremely unusual act for a camp commandant. When he visited the civilian camp at Kuching, he would bring biscuits and other gifts and play with the children of the interned Commonwealth and Dutch families.[15]

It was not a war crime to put POWs to work, so long as they were paid. Article VI of an annex to the Hague Convention of 1907 (which was ratified by Japan) states that

The state may utilise the labour of prisoners of war. . . . Work done for the state is paid at the rates in force for work of similar kind done by soldiers of the national army, or, if there are none in force, at a rate according to the work executed. When work is for other branches of the public services, or for private persons, the conditions are settled in agreement with the military authorities.[16]

This article was further developed in Section 3 of the Geneva Convention (1929) governing work by prisoners of war. The Japanese government had signed the Geneva Convention but never ratified it because of strong opposition from the Japanese military.[17] Soon after the Pacific War began, the Allied nations demanded that the Japanese government make a commitment to abide by the convention, a demand to which the Japanese government agreed.[18] In accordance, the Japanese government enacted a regulation regarding POW wages in February 1942, which guaranteed wages for working POWs along the lines suggested by the convention. Further regulations of this sort were enacted regarding transport of POW labor (October 1942), treatment of POWs (April 1943), and work by POWs (May 1943). Overall, the content of these regulations was in line with the conditions set down by the two conventions.[19]

But one clause present in the convention articles regarding work by POWs was conspicuously absent from the Japanese regulations of 1943: the clause that prohibits putting POWs to work on projects directly connected to "the operations of war." Furthermore, in May 1943 the Japanese government amended the October 1942 regulation regarding transport of POW labor to specify that the military was prepared to receive requests from vital industries—such as munitions or aircraft factories—for the supply of POWs as labor.[20] The Japanese government went to great lengths to obscure the degree to which POWs were being used for war work. Yet the amendment cited clearly demonstrates that the use of POWs for war work was part of official policy.

Because of the discrepancy with the Geneva Convention and the complicated nature of the official Japanese position in relation to the convention, there was immediate conflict between the Allied POW officers and the Japanese camp commandants as to the legality of putting prisoners to work on the airfield. Australian officers complained to Captain Hoshijima Susumu, the commandant of Sandakan POW camp, and to Colonel Suga that putting prisoners to work on the airfield was a breach of international law. Both commandants told the Australians, untruthfully, that the airfield would be purely for commercial use.[21] This lie was to become a major point of contention at the B and C Class trials held in Labuan after the war. However, both Hoshijima and Suga were caught in a bind, for the Japanese government did not formalize its guidelines for treatment of prisoners until the enactment of the 1943 regulations on POWs and work.[22]

In August 1942, when work on the airfield began, existing Japanese regulations contained no guide as to what types of work, if any, could not be undertaken with POW labor. Furthermore, individual initiative was not a highly regarded virtue within Japanese military culture, and middle-range Japanese officers were expected to follow closely and enact orders from higher authorities. It would have been completely out of military character for them to make their own interpretation of Japan's relation to the Geneva Convention over and above the carrying out of their explicit military duty. In fact, the use of POWs as labor on military projects was not merely a common occurrence during the war; it was an important part of the overall war strategy and was explicitly ordered by Minister of Army General Tōjō Hideki in his July 1942 address to newly appointed POW camp commandants.[23] Therefore, the final responsibility for this problem lies with the Japanese war leaders who refused to make explicit their divergence from the Geneva Convention on this matter or to create regulations that acknowledged their clear intention to use prisoners for military work. Instead they left a gray area, where the military imperative to use prisoners for war work was clear, but the regulatory framework within which this could legally occur remained obscure.

Of course, Australian POWs were always aware that the Sandakan aerodrome would be for military use and that the commandants were lying, but they let the matter drop quite quickly and continued to work on the airfield. The somewhat half-hearted nature of the officers' resistance to enforced military work stemmed not only from their powerlessness as POWs but also perhaps from their privileged position in relation to enlisted men who were POWs. Both the Hague and Geneva Conventions state that officer POWs should not have to engage in work, although they may volunteer for such. However, the conventions also state that even officers who refused work were to be paid, and their pay was to be the same amount as that of officers of comparable rank of the army that had captured them.[24] At first the Japanese respected this division between officers and enlisted POWs. The officers were given comfortable quarters in solidly built wooden huts, and the enlisted men were housed in thatched barracks. Officers were paid and could shop at a special officers-only canteen in the camp. Whether the work being performed by the enlisted men was in accordance with the Geneva Convention had, at best, less direct impact on the officers because they were not obliged to take part in it, and this may well have been one reason their resistance to the use of POWs for war work was so weak. One must look not only at the Japanese military hierarchy but also at the Geneva Convention with its assumptions and values in order to gain an understanding of how this work came to be performed.

## Escapes and Nonescape Contracts

At first, when food was adequate and brutal treatment of prisoners had not yet occurred, there were relatively few attempts to escape from Sandakan. The camp was surrounded by a barbed-wire fence, but initially the perimeter guard detail was very low-key; at one stage it consisted of a single guard standing at the front gate. A number of POWs took advantage of this one night, crawled under the fence, and went for an evening walk, returning to camp when they had taken sufficient night air. Nine days after arrival at the camp, two POWs made an escape; a few days later, another four escaped. After a few weeks, five more escaped. At morning roll calls their absence was concealed by other prisoners for a time.[25]

All of these groups of POWs were hiding in the jungle. Their plan was to make contact with the local people and to get food, supplies, and a boat in which to sail back to Australia via a large number of short hops between islands. They had almost no chance of success, for they had no maps or navigation instruments, and at this early stage of the Pacific War, the entire region was under secure Japanese control. All were eventually recaptured. Only the group of five actually made it as far as putting to sea. They had made contact with some Malay Chinese, among whom anti-Japanese sentiment was strong, and had been given supplies and a boat. They made a hut and lived in the jungle for several months, waiting for the end of the monsoon season, after which they put to sea, and were recaptured by the Japanese while still in Sandakan Bay.[26]

The two POWs who had been the first to escape—Herb Trackson and Matt Carr—were recaptured six weeks after escape, at the end of August 1942, and brought back to Sandakan. They were interrogated at the Sandakan jail. They told the Japanese that their commanding officers—Major G.N. Campbell and Captain J.H. Scribner—had ordered them to take any possible opportunity to escape. These two officers were also arrested and interrogated by members of the Kempeitai (the Japanese Army police force, the Japanese equivalent of the Gestapo) in Sandakan and again in Kuching. At the same time the POW commander of B Force, Colonel A.W. Walsh, was also interrogated. Walsh told the Kempeitai that under Australian Army regulations it was a POW's duty to take any reasonable opportunity to escape and that consequently he had no authority to order prisoners not to attempt to escape. The Kempeitai became concerned that the prisoners would attempt a mass escape and notified the 37th Army (the Borneo Garrison) headquarters in Kuching of this danger. The barbed-wire perimeter fence was secured, and the guard detail increased.[27]

In August 1942 camp commandant Hoshijima was instructed by headquarters to confiscate all writing materials from POWs and to order them to sign a nonescape contract—a pledge that they would not attempt to escape. On September 2 Hoshijima gathered all POWs together and ordered Colonel Walsh to read and sign the contract. The contract contained three demands:

1. We will attempt to accomplish any order given by the Japanese.
2. We will not attempt to escape.
3. We are aware that we will be shot if we attempt to escape.

Walsh read the contract and then told Hoshijima that he could not sign it because it was in breach of the Geneva Convention. Hoshijima became very angry and instructed guards to tie Walsh's hands behind his back and take him outside the barbed-wire fence. A machine gun was then set up facing him. The other POWs were also surrounded by guards with guns. There was silence.

One of the prisoners, Major J. Workman, believed that the contract would be invalid because it would be signed under duress, and he there-fore urged his fellow prisoners to sign it and thus avoid bloodshed. But he stipulated one condition: that the wording of the contract would have to be changed from "we" to "I" and that each prisoner would have to sign an individual contract. Workman argued that it was not possible for the representative of a group of people to sign a contract on their behalf. With a fair degree of audacity—given that he did not regard the contract as valid in any way—he argued that each soldier would have to sign his own contract in order for it to be binding. Hoshijima agreed to individual signatures and—not lacking in audacity himself and unwilling to create a thousand copies of the document—changed the wording of the contract from "we" to "we individuals" and asked all prisoners to sign on the one sheet of paper! Both of these performances were topped by the large number of prisoners who signed themselves as "Ned Kelly" (a famous Australian "bushranger" and something of a Robin Hood figure in Aus-tralian folklore) or as any one of a number of movie stars. Thus the pris-oners overcame the first crisis of their time at Sandakan.[28]

The contract incident highlighted the distinction between Japanese and Western attitudes to law and the contradictions between the Geneva Con-vention and the principles of Japanese military law. The Geneva Conven-tion did not make it illegal for armies to punish POWs who attempted to escape, but it also recognized a POW's right to attempt to escape and specified that the maximum possible punishment that could be applied to a POW who had unsuccessfully attempted to escape was 30 days in soli-tary confinement.[29] Thus the Australian Army regulations, which specifi-cally obliged an Australian POW to attempt to escape at any reasonable opportunity, were not in contravention of the Geneva Convention. How-ever, the contract that Hoshijima was asking the POWs to sign was, for it tried to remove their right to attempt to escape and to have them consent to being executed by firing squad if recaptured.

The seventh article of the Japanese law on punishment of prisoners states that the leader of a group of prisoners who had been captured while attempting to escape would be punishable by death or between 10 years and life imprisonment and all other members of the group by im-prisonment for a minimum of one year. The regulation on the treatment of POWs stipulates that POWs must sign a contract promising not to escape and that any prisoner who did not sign such a contract would have thereby expressed an intention to attempt to escape and therefore be subject to heavier surveillance.[30] If a prisoner did sign such an oath and subsequently attempted to escape, he would also be subject to a minimum sentence of one year's imprisonment.[31] These laws and regulations—which are in clear contravention of the Geneva Convention—were ratified and brought into force after Japan had agreed to abide by the rules of war set out in the convention. (The law on punishment of prisoners dated from 1905 and was reconfirmed and modified in March 1943, and the regulation on treatment of POWs was formulated in April 1943. The Japanese government had made a commitment to the Allies to apply to the Geneva Convention on January 29, 1942.) A Japanese law dating from 1904 gave Japanese prison guards the right to shoot at escaping prisoners when such action was necessary to prevent the prisoner from successfully escaping.[32] However, the law gave no explicit guidance as to what constituted "necessity" in such a case.

Obviously any contract signed under duress would be invalid under any reasonable conception of contract law, but this was not the belief of the Japanese at Sandakan. Once the contracts were signed, the Japanese were satisfied that the prisoners had made a firm commitment not to escape. Consequently, those prisoners who did attempt to escape but failed were usually shot, either in the escape attempt or by firing squad on recapture. They were regarded as criminals by Hoshijima and denied the dignity of a graveyard burial accorded to prisoners who had died of illness. Instead they were buried on a patch of land close to the place where work was being carried out on the airfield, as a warning to the other prisoners.

Virtually all Japanese POW guards at other camps would shoot prisoners who made unsuccessful escape attempts, despite the Geneva Convention and the regulations of both the Japanese military and the armies of the POWs. Virtually all prisoners who were captured while attempting to escape were shot or died while being tortured. The case of Private G.A. Arbin serves as an example of this practice. Arbin was an Australian POW in the Orio camp in Fukuoka. Unable to stand prison life, he escaped in August 1943, despite the fact that he had absolutely no chance of reaching friendly territory. He was recaptured three days later and complied fully with the interrogation by the military police. Despite these circumstances he was taken out and shot after interrogation, without trial. The documents relating to his case were then falsified to suggest that he had attempted a second escape, which according to Japanese practice at the time would have made it permissible to shoot him.[33] Falsification of events was a common practice in these cases.

In many cases the commandants and guards of the prison camps were unaware of the contents or even the existence of the Geneva Convention

and of Japan's relation to it. Major General Saitō Masazumi, who was appointed commandant of the Java POW camp in July 1942, attended a
briefing for all new POW camp commandants at Army Headquarters in
Tokyo during that month. In his testimony to the Tokyo War Crimes Tribunal after the war, he stated that the issue of international law in relation
to POWs was never raised at that meeting, that he personally had no
knowledge at the time of the international law relevant to POWs, and that
he did not ask about it.[34] Lieutenant Colonel Yanagida Shōichi, commandant of a POW work camp on the Burma-Thailand railway, also testified
that he had no knowledge of the Geneva Convention.[35] Thus it is quite
possible that Hoshijima—who was a conscripted officer (he was a chemical engineer by profession) rather than a professional soldier—had very
little knowledge about either the Geneva Convention or the specifics of
Japanese military law. Nor did he feel any need to pay serious attention to
the protocols of international military law. Protests by POW officers that
treatment of prisoners was against the Geneva Convention were met with
the response that the Geneva Convention was of no importance to him
and that his principal duty was to Japanese military law. The overriding
importance of unquestioning obedience to both the overall Imperial Code
and the Field Service Code was impressed upon all Japanese soldiers,
whether professional or conscripted, from the day they began military
service.

Hoshijima's firm stand on the issue of the nonescape contracts was in
startling contrast to his more conciliatory position in relation to earlier
protests by prisoners that the content of their work (the construction of
the airfield) was in contravention of the Geneva Convention article forbidding the use of POWs for military work. But in that situation the
Japanese military law was ambiguous, and he had been obliged to make
an independent decision. On the issue of the nonescape contracts, the law
was explicit, and Hoshijima's duty was clear. It is also possible that he
was under pressure from the Kempeitai to tighten security around the
POWs. Hoshijima's personality may also be a factor in these events. He
was a typical "organization man"—proud and continually insistent about
his university degrees and civilian qualifications, arrogant in his treatment of those under his command, yet sycophantic and deferential to his
superiors. There is little doubt that he would have been fearful of Kempeitai officials and eager to do everything necessary to maintain their approval of him.

However, Hoshijima cannot be held solely to blame for the conditions
at the prison camp at this stage; he was but one of a number of culpable
figures. Without exculpating Hoshijima in any way, it is important to understand how he would have seen his role. He was sent to Sandakan in
his capacity as an engineer to oversee construction of the airfield, and he

had no expectation of being made camp commandant.[36] His position as commandant of the POW camp was an additional duty, and he left much of the day-to-day running of the camp to his subordinates. His principal task was the construction of the airfield, and the POWs were the raw material with which he was to complete that task. Their welfare was doubtless a secondary issue for him.

Indeed, the responsibility for what occurred at Sandakan could be taken higher, to Lieutenant General Maeda Toshitame, the commandant of the Borneo defense forces (he died in September 1942 in an airplane accident and was replaced by Lieutenant General Yamawaki Masataka). It was Maeda who appointed Hoshijima as both commandant of the POW camp and officer in charge of the construction of the airfield. These two tasks made contradictory demands on Hoshijima, as the imperatives for the construction of the airfield were often against the best interests of the prisoners and their welfare.

## The Sandakan Incident and the Kempeitai

For a period of time after the signing of the nonescape contracts, there were no major incidents at Sandakan camp. Outside Borneo, however, the Pacific War had escalated. In August 1942 U.S. forces landed at Guadalcanal Island, and from September onward there was fierce island-to-island fighting in the surrounding region. By the end of 1942 the Japanese force in this area was near starvation. There were 31,400 soldiers garrisoned at Guadalcanal; 20,748 perished, 70 percent of these from disease and starvation. In New Guinea the Kokoda battle began in July 1942, and Japanese casualties were heavy. By the end of November the Japanese forces were pushed back to Gona and Buna. In this battle the Japanese lost 12,000 of their 18,000 men. By January 1943 Japan had been driven back to the north of New Guinea. On April 18, 1943, Admiral Yamamoto Isoroku, the commander of the Japanese fleet, died when his plane was shot down over the Bougainville Islands. On May 29 the Japanese force at Attu Island was defeated.[37]

As these conflicts were occurring, the POWs at Sandakan meanwhile began to suffer significantly from the spread of tropical diseases: malaria, dysentery, beriberi, and tropical ulcers. Although the Japanese Army had adequate supplies of medicine for its own men, it did not provide the POWs with sufficient medicine to treat these diseases. Illness thus significantly depleted the labor force, and the construction of the airfield fell behind schedule. In March 1943, 750 British POWs were brought in from Kuching, and in April, another 500 POWs (E Force) were brought in from Changi. They were held on Bahara Island in Sandakan Bay until additional huts were completed in June. The original Sandakan labor force was housed in Camp No. 1, the British in Camp No. 2, and E Force in Camp No. 3. Sandakan had become a large POW camp holding 2,750 prisoners. It was now compulsory for officer POWs to work on the airfield, and those who refused were to be denied rations. Nobody refused.[38]

When B Force had first arrived at Sandakan in July 1942, Captain Lionel Matthews had formed a group of about 20 officers and NCOs in order to gather intelligence about the region. These men volunteered to work in the vegetable garden (which was located outside the camp) on the pretext that they needed the exercise. Security was lax for a time, and Matthews managed to make contact with a native Malaysian, Dick Maginal, who was employed by the Japanese as a gardener in the vegetable garden and who was sympathetic to the Allies. From Maginal, Matthews obtained information that about 90 British civilians who had lived in Sandakan before the war were being detained on Bahara Island, guarded by local police officers and a small contingent of Japanese soldiers. Maginal managed to arrange a meeting between Matthews and the local police officer, Ahbin (a member of the Dasan tribe), who visited the Sandakan camp and Bahara Island camp regularly, and an information link between the two camps was thus established.[39] A number of Allied civilians—most of them doctors and dentists—had not been interned at Bahara and had been given permission to remain in the Sandakan township. Again through Ahbin, Matthews managed to make contact with an Australian doctor, J.P. Taylor.[40] Taylor arranged to smuggle essential medical supplies to the POWs; these supplies would be left at a cache in the jungle and picked up by POWs who had been sent out on a work detail to collect wood for cooking and for the electricity-generating boiler. These wood-gathering parties were led by a Lieutenant Rod Wells, a member of the intelligence group organized by Matthews. Taylor also supplied regular information on Japanese troop movements via the same method.[41]

The traffic of information and supplies between the Sandakan camp and the town community even extended to the provision of parts for a radio receiver—supplied by local Chinese merchants and workers whose anti-Japanese sentiments stemmed largely from the fact that the Japanese forces had destroyed their highly protected and profitable stranglehold on local business activity. Some prisoners had already smuggled in radio parts when B Force was initially transferred from Singapore. Two prisoners who had a knowledge of radio mechanics—Lieutenant Weynton and Corporal Richards—used these and additional parts supplied by the Chinese civilians to construct a radio receiver, which was completed by November 1942.[42] However, in order to operate this radio, they required a good electricity supply. The wood-fired electricity generator was located some distance from the POW barracks and was operated by four civilians. Lieutenant Wells made an arrangement with the foreman of this group—a Chinese civilian named Ah Ping—whereby Wells would supply them with extra wood, in order for them to increase the amount of power generated at ten o'clock each night, which would then be used to run the radio receiver. To secure this arrangement, Wells arranged for Ah Ping to make a request for additional manpower to operate the generator, a request that was granted. Another member of Matthew's intelligence group—one Sergeant Stevens—was assigned to the generator shed to assist the four locals in maintaining the electricity supply. From this point he could also pass information between Wells and Ah Ping.[43]

The intelligence group began radio reception on November 4, 1942, with the increased power supply they had obtained. They picked up BBC and American news reports and gathered the information contained in these—which unsurprisingly differed greatly from the war reports offered by the Japanese military—into a weekly written bulletin that was passed on to Dr. Taylor and the interned civilian population by the police officer, Ahbin.

Matthews had always believed that obtaining arms and smuggling them into camp were high-priority tasks for the intelligence group. He was confident that the Allies would attempt to recapture Borneo at some stage and that such a landing would offer an opportunity for the Sandakan prisoners to launch an armed uprising within the prison. The news the radio brought him of Japanese losses and setbacks in the wider Pacific War made such a project all the more imperative. He had already obtained a pistol, some ammunition, and a map of North Borneo from a Chinese collaborator, Alex Funk. Through Funk, Matthews also made contact with anti-Japanese guerrillas operating in the southern Philippines, and these guerrillas arranged for the supply of 2 machine guns, 27 rifles, and 2,500 rounds of ammunition to the POWs. These were hidden in a cache 24 kilometers from the town of Sandakan.[44]

In May 1943 the Matthews group decided to build a radio transmitter. They received some radio parts that had been smuggled in by E Force, which had arrived the previous month, and once again they attempted to obtain the remainder from sympathetic Chinese civilians. But this time disaster struck. One of the sympathetic Chinese—a local worker named Joe Ming—was caught assisting the POWs by one of his coworkers, an Indian named Dominic Koh. Koh attempted to blackmail Ming and gain money and further information about the extent of contact between POWs and civilians. When Ming refused to cooperate, Koh passed on such information as he had to a Chinese civilian, Jackie Lo, who was acting as a Japanese spy at the camp.[45]

Lo informed the Japanese, who arrested Ming and his father and tortured them until they gave names of other Chinese collaborators, including Alex Funk, who were also tortured and gave details of all those involved in the attempt to build a radio transmitter. All members of the Matthews intelligence group as well as Dr. Taylor and the police officer Ahbin were subsequently arrested by the Kempeitai. On July 22 the camp was searched, and two pistols, some maps, and a note from Lieutenant Wells to Ahbin (hidden in Wells's boots) were found. The radio was not detected. On July 24 a second search was made, and this time a list of the radio parts smuggled into camp was discovered. Hoshijima showed the list of parts to Lieutenant Wells and demanded he tell where the radio was hidden. After interrogation and torture Wells decided to hand over the half-completed transmitter in an attempt to convince the Japanese that this was all they possessed and to keep the receiver undetected. But his interrogators were not fooled and continued to torture Wells and other members of Matthews's group. Eventually one of them confessed and the receiver was discovered. The torture and interrogation continued for three months, and the initial refusal of civilians and POWs to talk was eventually broken down.[46] The Kempeitai called this episode the "Sandakan incident."

The Kempeitai was a military police force established in 1881 for the purpose of maintaining discipline within the armed forces. In the late 1920s, as the Japanese government strengthened its anticommunist policies, the Kempeitai established a division known as the Tokkō-ka, or Special Service. The purpose of the Special Service was to maintain surveillance of the labor movement, farmers' groups, student organizations, and other radical bodies. The power of the Kempeitai was thus stretched far beyond the field of purely military matters, and its role became increasingly political. In the 1930s Kempeitai branches were established throughout Japan proper, in its colonies such as Korea and Taiwan, and in territories such as the Philippines and Borneo captured during the first stages of the war. The original purpose for which the Kempeitai was created—the maintenance of military discipline—gradually was displaced by the more important task of political surveillance. Operatives' antisubversive actions became increasingly drastic and eventually included the torture, murder, and detention without trial of suspected radicals or enemies of the imperial government and armed forces. They were known as the "devil's Kempeitai" and had few qualms about using the most extreme forms of torture in the extraction of confessions and information.[47]

A branch of the Kempeitai was established in Sandakan soon after the Japanese occupation of Borneo was completed. By the time of the Sandakan incident, there were 15 Kempeitai operatives stationed at the city under the command of Warrant Officer Murakami Seisaku.[48] The Kempeitai had a number of different methods of torture, among them the notorious "water torture," in which the victim's face would be covered with a cloth mask and then doused repeatedly with water. The wet cloth over the mouth and nose would make it impossible to breathe and force the victim to inhale huge amounts of water. When the victim's stomach was full to bursting, a Kempeitai officer would jump on him from the top of a chair. Another common torture was the "rice torture," in which the victim would be starved for several days and then have a large amount of un-cooked rice forced down his throat. A hose would then be put in the vic-tim's mouth and he would swallow a large amount of water, which caused the rice to expand. This would cause excruciating pain as the stomach stretched to its limit, and the pain would often continue for days as the rice was digested. The resulting stress on the digestive tract would also cause internal and rectal bleeding. Beatings were made more painful and terrifying by the use of wet sand, which was smeared over the victim and was pressed into the skin when he was beaten with a wooden sandal. This abraded the skin and made the whole beaten area red, raw, and bleeding. All these methods of torture were used on those interrogated in the aftermath of the Sandakan incident.[49]

Why did Kempeitai members use such horrific and bizarre methods of torture in their interrogations? In order to answer this question we must look at the structure within which such violence occurs and the nature of the power relations therein. Such an analysis may shed some light on the causes of violence and brutality in the Japanese military as a whole as well as in the Kempeitai in particular. It will also be valuable to examine the political situation that existed in Borneo at the time.

One of the crucial events of this period is what is known as the "Haga incident." In June 1942—one month before the Sandakan incident—oper-atives of the Kempeitai raided the house of an Indonesian radio me-chanic in Banjarmasin and discovered a radio transmitter that was being operated from there. The Kempeitai claimed that the radio was being used by the local resistance to communicate with the Allied forces. The Kempeitai operatives also claimed that they found arms and ammunition at another house in the Banjarmasin area. They then arrested Dr. B.J. Haga, who had been the Dutch governor of East and West Kalimantan provinces, and accused him of being a leader of the Indonesian anti-Japanese resistance. During the next few months more than 257 people were tortured and murdered in the course of this investigation, including Haga and his wife. In September, while the investigation of the Sandakan incident and the torture and interrogation of the Matthews group were continuing, a groundless rumor spread that resistance fighters connected with the Haga group were now operating a radio and planning an armed overthrow at Pontianak, in southwest Borneo. At the time the Navy rather than the Army was stationed at Pontianak, and the naval equiva-lent of the Kempeitai—the Naval Special Police Force—began to arrest suspects and torture them in an attempt to extract confessions. More than

1,500 civilians were arrested—Indonesians, Chinese, and Indians—and the vast majority were eventually tortured and killed.[50]

There was, however, one real event that contributed to the belief among Kempeitai members that they were facing a major uprising. In October 1943, as the investigation into the Sandakan incident was drawing to a close, a large-scale uprising occurred in Api (known as Jesselton by the British and now known as Kota Kinabalu). This uprising was led by a young Chinese man named Guo Hengnan, who was trained in the southern Philippines as a spy by U.S. intelligence officers. He was dropped near Api by submarine and began organizing a resistance force there. On October 10 he led about 100 locals in attacking Japanese trading company offices, Kempeitai branch offices, police stations, military inns, and warehouses. About 60 Japanese and Taiwanese residents were killed. It took the Japanese three months to crush this group and arrest Guo Hengnan and the other ringleaders.[51]

Because of these events as well as the Sandakan incident, the Kempeitai began to lose confidence in its ability to maintain security within occupied Borneo. The war was beginning to go very badly for the Japanese, and news of Allied victories began to circulate among the civilian population. The Japanese setbacks and the possibility that the Allies might attempt to recapture Borneo lowered morale among the Japanese forces. It made both regular troops and the Kempeitai increasingly suspicious, aggressive, and paranoid in their relations with the local population. Surveillance, arrests, and torture increased. Yet in cases such as the Pontianak and the Haga incidents, the real threat to Japanese security was either small or nonexistent. Kempeitai members were projecting their fears onto the local population and thus constantly "discovering" new conspiracies. They were usually convinced of the guilt of those arrested before any interrogation had taken place. The confessions they extracted after days, weeks, or even months of torture were usually given by victims who would confess to anything, even crimes punishable by death, in order to end their ordeal. Those named in such confessions would also be arrested and tortured, so the circle of false confession and torture would widen and fuel the paranoia of Kempeitai operatives, who became increasingly convinced that they had uncovered a comprehensive network of resistance activity. This merging of fantasy and reality was doubtless a factor in the investigation of the Sandakan incident. The Matthews group had not intended to begin an armed uprising until such time as there was an Allied invasion of Japanese-occupied Borneo. Yet Kempeitai officials were convinced that such an uprising was imminent when the radio and weapons had been discovered. Eventually they tortured out of the members of the Matthews group the confessions they wanted to hear.

The torture of Allied POWs may also have given some psychological satisfaction to the Kempeitai. The war was going badly, and the Allies were rapidly regaining dominance over the region that the Japanese had only recently wrested from them. Torture functioned as a sort of revenge for this reversal of fortune and maintained the illusion of dominance over the enemy. It may also have helped to relieve the fear felt by the security officers facing an anticipated Allied invasion of Borneo. The worse the news of Allied victories and Japanese defeats, the greater the need to derive satisfaction from torture became. This "therapeutic" use of torture is common to many armies experiencing setbacks or defeats; for instance, members of the Australian Army used the water torture during the Vietnam War. This torture was used to extract information from suspected Viet Cong sympathizers, but its use increased when units were surrounded by enemy forces, thus making its psychological motivation clear.[52]

## The System and Purpose of *Gunritsu Kaigi*

On October 25, 1943, after more than three months of torture, the 20 or so members of the Matthews group and some other POWs and more than 50 civilians who had assisted them were taken by boat to Kuching and held in a military jail there while awaiting their trials. On arrival at Kuching several of the POWs were discharged and relocated to Kuching prison camp.[53] The remainder were divided into three groups, and each group was tried separately. All of the accused were found guilty. Dr. Taylor was tried on February 3, 1944, and sentenced to 15 years' imprisonment, and the rest of the ringleaders were tried on March 2, 1944. Matthews, Ahbin, Alex Funk, Joe Ming, and five others were sentenced to death by firing squad and executed immediately after the trial. Wells was sentenced to 12 years' imprisonment. The remainder were sentenced to prison terms ranging from 6 months to 15 years. Four of the civilians and three of the POWs died in prison before the end of the war, their health broken by the ordeals of torture and imprisonment.[54]

Colonel Suga, commandant of the Borneo POW camp system, was present at the trial and made an open plea to the judges in the courtroom. He asked them to give the accused prisoners and civilians a fair trial in accordance with international law and to be merciful in their sentencing.[55] This would have been an uncommon act even in a court-martial of Japanese soldiers; in a trial of enemy prisoners it was extremely unusual and courageous. Clearly Suga was aware that the trial of POWs by a Japanese military court was, to say the least, in potential conflict with the rules of international law.

Japanese military law provided for two different types of court-martial. One, *gumpō kaigi,* is equivalent to a Western court-martial: the trial of members of the armed forces according to a specific military law. The other, *gunritsu kaigi,* is the trial by a military court of civilians and POWs charged with crimes in an occupied area subject to martial law. The *gunritsu kaigi* is an application of the rules governing *gumpō kaigi* and especially of the rules governing the *tokusetsu gumpō kaigi* (special court-martial), in which the defendant is not permitted legal representation and has no right of appeal.[56]

There were five types of *gumpō kaigi* (court-martial hereafter). In descending order of authority, these were the high, army, division, provost, and field court-martials. The former three were permanent institutions within the military structure; the latter two were temporary and incidental. There were seven army court-martial jurisdictions: four in Japan proper and one each in Taiwan, Manchukuo, and Korea. Within each of these jurisdictions there were a number of division court-martial jurisdictions, and the court-martial at which a member of the armed forces charged would be tried depended on rank, with the higher ranks tried at an army court-martial. There was the right of appeal directly to the high court-martial from either of the lesser permanent court-martials, and there was provision for the trials of very high-ranking officers to go directly to a high court-martial. There was no right of appeal from a provost or field court-martial.

A case presented to one of the three permanent court-martials would be heard before five officers from fighting units acting as judges. At the high court-martial, it was necessary for two of the five officers to be military lawyers. At an army or division court-martial only one of the five was required to be a military lawyer. In principle it was necessary for the prosecutor at all such cases to be a military lawyer. The permanent court-martials were apparently just and liberal in their manner of conduct, with an open court, the right of the accused to be represented by a lawyer, and the right of appeal. But in practice this was little more than a sham. The judges had the right to hear a case in camera when the details of it involved confidential military matters, and this power was often abused by judges who wished to keep public knowledge of military matters to a minimum. Defense representatives were invariably junior officers who were often deterred from making real efforts for their clients by implicit or explicit threats to their military careers. The judges had the right to exclude anyone from the proceedings of the trial. This rule could even be applied to a defendant's representative, who would thus have been effectively fired by the judges. The defendant would have no choice but to make the firing official and to request a new representative. Consequently, defense lawyers would make efforts to avoid offending or antagonizing the judges, and this would often make it impossible for them to defend clients effectively.

Because those judges with legal expertise were always in a minority in any of these court-martials, an acquittal was all but impossible to obtain on the grounds of technicalities or points of law, as the judges without a legal background always constituted a de facto majority. Even those judges who were legal specialists were unlikely to be sympathetic to a fully legalistic interpretation of military law: Court-martial trial judges were required to have had experience as either court-martial prosecutors or as governors of military prisons and thus to have displayed a commitment to the heavy discipline of Japanese military law.

The court-martial system was designed to protect officers—especially those who were graduates of the military college—and to enforce the discipline of officers on enlisted men. The administering of justice was a minor consideration in such a system. Prosecutors, who were frequently junior officers, were given no dispensation from the general rule that they were obliged to obey orders, and thus any investigation of senior officers was all but impossible. Furthermore, senior officers could stonewall investigation of their junior officers if they so wished. Prosecutors could not direct members of the Kempeitai to investigate officers, and this left them without the opportunity to gather evidence and build a case. It was rare indeed that an officer above the rank of major would ever appear before a court-martial; when such cases did occur, the punishment was almost invariably minor. By contrast, the punishments for enlisted men were always severe, even for fairly minor offenses. One example shows a typical pattern: A soldier in the Kwantung (Kantō) Army based in Manchuria, when summoned by his officer, said to him, "What the hell are you talking about?" He was court-martialed and given three months' imprisonment.[57]

The special court-martial was even more draconian in its process and its judgments. It was designed to be applied in the field and in occupied areas where iron discipline was believed to be particularly necessary. Because of the likelihood that such a trial would take place under battlefield conditions, the process was simplified to an extreme degree. There were only three judges, and only one was required to be a legal specialist. The accused had no right to representation or appeal to a higher court, and the trial was held in camera. In the standard court-martial the judgment of the court was required to be authorized by the Minister of the Army. In the special court-martial the field commander of the unit in question was empowered to authorize the judgment. All of the conditions that excepted officers from the rule of the general court-martial were present in the special court-martial.

The primary purpose of the special court-martial was to maintain discipline on the front line and to stamp out acts of individual disobedience and insubordination before they became more general acts of mutiny. Obedience was mandatory, no matter how absurd or dangerous the orders of an officer were, and the punishments for disobedience included everything from long prison sentences to execution. There were many officers who murdered or summarily executed soldiers in the field without the benefit of any sort of trial, and these officers were never prosecuted for any offense. Soldiers who assaulted officers or even who merely disobeyed an order were invariably heavily punished, no matter what mitigating circumstances there might have been.

The *gunritsu kaigi* (civilian court-martial) was the direct application of the special court-martial to POWs and civilians. It was designed to enforce discipline in occupied areas and to minimize the possibility and spread of resistance activity and sabotage by the subjugated population in those areas. The principles of natural justice were of no consideration in its application. It was used to make an example of those civilians who had engaged in anti-Japanese activity—or even those who were merely suspected of having done so.[58]

After the war, Lieutenant Wells, who had been sentenced to twelve years' imprisonment for his part in the Sandakan incident, made a report of the trial to the Australian War Crimes Section. He argued that the trial was clearly in breach of international law as the accused had had no intention of starting a revolt in the prison. He claimed that the evidence had been distorted by prosecutors, that the defendants had no opportunity for legal representation, and that, as a result, nine people had been unjustly executed.[59] However, the War Crimes Section did not prosecute the one surviving judge, Captain Tsutsui Yōichi (the other two had died during the war). The prosecutor, Captain Watanabe Haruo, and the officer who authorized the executions, Lieutenant General Yamawaki Masataka, were tried but acquitted.[60]

Another civilian court-martial held in Kuching by the Borneo garrison involved POWs who were tried and executed. Between February and March 1944, several groups of Australian soldiers were landed in the northeast of Borneo to gather information about Japanese troop movements. A member of one of the intelligence parties, Sergeant William Brandeis, became lost in the jungle and wandered for some time. He lost most of his clothes and was nearly naked when he was captured by Japanese soldiers. Brandeis surrendered immediately, handed his captors his pistol, which he was wearing openly, and volunteered his name, rank, and serial number. Two other soldiers from these parties—Lieutenant Alfred Rudwick and Sergeant Donald McKenzie—were also captured by the Japanese. They too were clearly identifiable as Australian soldiers when they surrendered. The Geneva Convention provides that a man who is captured in uniform and with unconcealed weapons should be treated as a captured soldier and not as a spy, no matter in which region the capture took place. Despite their insistence that they were entitled to be regarded as soldier POWs in line with the Geneva Convention, the three Australians were tried as spies and executed.[61] In this case also, the two surviving judges, the prosecutor, and Yamawaki were tried and acquitted of war crimes charges. The judges who presided over these trials also placed gag orders on the proceedings, forbidding the Australian press from reporting on either their conduct or the verdicts.[62]

Article 61 of the Geneva Convention prohibits the judgment and sentencing of POWs who are not given the opportunity to defend themselves, Article 62 gives POWs a right to representation, and Article 64 stipulates that the accused must have the right of appeal to a higher court. Clearly the civilian court-martial flew in the face of the Geneva Convention, yet the Australian military forces, who in general were harsh to Japanese war criminals, were inclined to be lenient in the case of those who had participated in civilian court-martials that were in effect war crimes. Furthermore, there is considerable evidence of situations in which the Australian military authorities were prepared to regard Japanese court-martials as legitimate.

In September 1945, less than one month after V-J Day, Japanese POWs from the Bougainville garrison, detained on nearby Tauno Island, held a court-martial of some of their own soldiers, who had allegedly either disobeyed orders or deserted. Toward the end of the war, many of the South Pacific islands had their supplies cut off by the higher command, and the men stationed there were literally starving to death. Soldiers who left the front line to hunt for food in the jungle were often rounded up by the Kempeitai, charged with desertion, and summarily executed (as was the standard Japanese Army punishment for that crime). Many others, however, simply left the front line and hid in the jungle, emerging only when the war concluded, and there were so many of these soldiers that the Allied forces dropped pamphlets in the jungle announcing the end of the war. These men, after surrendering, were interned in the same camps as troops who were still at their posts when the war ended. Enlisted men and officers were also imprisoned together, and some of the enlisted men saw an opportunity to take revenge on officers they felt had treated them badly. They presumed—wrongly—that the officers would no longer hold legitimate authority or command obedience. The officers held a series of special court-martials and punished the offending troops with either solitary confinement or execution. Australian detention camp authorities not only gave their tacit consent to the conduct of such trials but also, incredibly, loaned weapons to the Japanese officers in order that the death sentences might be carried out.[63]

These camp court-martials were ostensibly conducted in line with Japanese military law as authorized by the Japanese constitution, but this law granted no jurisdiction over the inmates of the detention camps.

According to international law, these camps and all their inhabitants were under the jurisdiction of Australian military law. Nor could the camp be in any way regarded as Japanese territory, in the manner of an embassy or consulate. In many cases there was no commandant of a sufficient rank to authorize an execution within a camp, yet executions took place nevertheless, so the whole process was illegal even under principles of Japanese military law, which the officers were erroneously applying. Clearly, the camp court-martials were illegal in every respect.[64]

Why, then, did the Australian military forces tacitly and actively support the conduct of these trials? Presumably, the Australian officers experienced a kind of solidarity with the Japanese officers and a shared commitment to the maintenance of military discipline—a fellow feeling directed against enlisted men of whatever nationality. The specific nature of military law might differ from nation to nation, but maintenance of discipline within an army is universally seen as the primary function of military law, with the administering of justice a secondary consideration. This shared view would have been widely held among officers. It might also help explain why those Japanese officers who had presided over special court-martials and passed death sentences on Australian POWs and "spies" were acquitted by the officers acting as judges in the B and C Class trials.[65]

## Mistreatment of POWs and the Formosan Guards

About one week after the POWs charged over the Sandakan incident were transported to Kuching, 230 officers from the Sandakan camp also were transferred to the Kuching POW camp. Only about a dozen officers, most of them Australians, remained in Sandakan, and four of them were military doctors. This move was undoubtedly an attempt to break the organized resistance of the POWs. The Japanese believed that enlisted men would be more or less incapable of mounting any active resistance without leadership.[66] By November 1943, after these removals and the death of 24 POWs from illness, the number of prisoners in Sandakan was reduced to about 2,470.[67]

After the Sandakan incident, the treatment of POWs by the Japanese dramatically worsened. Wages were no longer paid, camp canteens were closed down, and weekend leisure activity ceased. Incidents of physical maltreatment increased and were crueler than they had been previously. Physical maltreatment on the airfield construction site had been worsening even before the Sandakan incident, largely because the Japanese guards gradually realized the prisoners were on a "go slow"—work was proceeding at a snail's pace and with a great deal of pretense, and there was low-level sabotage.

When E Force arrived in Sandakan in April 1943, new guards came with them to augment the total number of guards at the camp. Eight guards were formed into a special squad whose main purpose was to administer punishment to disobedient prisoners at the airfield site. Each of these guards was armed with an ax handle or a club, and with these they would patrol the airfield site during working hours. If a prisoner was judged to be working too slowly, the punishment unit would round up the whole of his detail (a unit of about 40 or 50 men) and they would all be severely beaten. Other punishments included being made to stand with arms outstretched (sometimes holding a heavy log) and staring at the sun for 20–30 minutes or to hold a push-up position for the same amount of time. If the prisoner closed his eyes, dropped the log, or collapsed, he would be beaten, and the punishment would continue. Each day several groups of POWs would be punished in this fashion, and many prisoners lost consciousness or suffered broken limbs. Prisoners who attempted to stop the beating of a fellow POW were themselves beaten. One prisoner was beaten with the stock of a gun and lost several teeth. In another incident a prisoner was taken to the camp hospital after being kicked in the testicles, and when the POW doctor complained to the guard responsible, the guard kicked him in the testicles.[68]

As time passed many POWs became sick with tropical ulcers and beriberi. These men were given lighter duties in the camp vegetable garden, but the lack of shoes and the use of human excrement as fertilizer aggravated their tropical ulcers, especially those around their feet and legs. In order to ascertain whether a prisoner with bandaged legs was genuinely sick or merely malingering, the guards would kick the infected area, causing great pain. In September 1944 even these light duties were abolished as the labor force at the airfield shrank because of the increasingly high mortality rate, and sick prisoners were put back to work there.[69]

The summary punishment for minor acts of disobedience and insubordination also increased, with prisoners spending longer periods in the punishment cage. The maximum punishment period was 30 days according to camp regulations, which were based on the same regulations as applied to the punishment of Japanese soldiers under military law.[70] The Sandakan cage measured 1.8 by 1.5 by 1.2 meters. The floor and the roof were made of wood. It was located outside the guardhouse and was to all intents and purposes a large dog kennel. The cage was originally intended for Japanese soldiers who had committed minor crimes, but it was never used for that purpose. It was exclusively employed for punishing POWs and became used so frequently that two additional cages had to be built in June 1943 (of 2.7 by 2.1 by 1.5 meters) and October 1944 (4.5 by 2.7 by 2.7 meters) in order for all punishments to be carried out. The second and third cages were larger because prisoners were by then being punished in groups.[71]

A typical example of a victim of the cages was a sapper (army engineer) named Hinchcliffe, who was initially punished at the airfield construction site after he was caught trying to barter some personal effects with the locals in exchange for food. (POWs had relied on contact with the locals in order to supplement their meager camp diet and acquire essential medicine, since wages and canteen access had been discontinued in mid-1943). Hinchcliffe was made to stand in a squatting position, with sharp-edged lengths of wood jammed behind and under his knees, his arms outstretched and facing into the sun for one hour. Every 10 minutes, the punishment squad would come and beat him. He was then taken to the punishment cage and confined for seven days without food.[72]

One POW, Keith Botterill, endured three separate periods of detention in the punishment cage, the longest of which lasted 40 days, thus exceeding the 30-day limit prescribed by the Japanese military regulations. The following is his testimony:

Forty days. The first seven days got no food. No water for the first three days. And then they forced you to drink until you were sick on the third night. . . . Every evening you would be—a bashing. Hit with sticks and fists and kicking. . . . No wash in that forty days—I was in forty days and never had a wash. . . . I was just in a G string, covered with lice, crabs, scabies. . . . The time I was in for 40 days, there [were] 17 of us in there. . . . Not allowed to talk, we used to whisper. We had to kneel down all day, there wasn't room to lay down of a night, we'd all lay side by side, squashed up, and had to sit up again at dawn and kneel up—kneel down.[73]

A number of other testimonies exist about time in the punishment cage, but all are similar to Botterill's. No food was provided in the first week, and the water torture was usually conducted on the third or fourth day. Prisoners were permitted to go to the toilet only twice a day, once in the morning and once in the afternoon. At "exercise" time once a day, the prisoner was severely beaten by the guards. The prisoners wore only loincloths or shorts, and neither blankets nor mosquito nets were provided. The constant exposure to mosquitos made sleep difficult and was also a cause of malaria. Because the prisoners were suffering from malnutrition and the effects of forced labor, they were in poor health, and their condition rapidly deteriorated while in the cage. The psychological states of many of the men punished in the cage also deteriorated, as can easily be understood. When Hoshijima was interrogated about these regimes, he claimed that only one prisoner had died (of malaria) while in the cage.[74] This was technically true because many succumbed to disease or malnutrition afterward in the hospital, but the severity of the punishments obviously contributed to the deaths of these men.

The majority of POWs confined in the cage were those who had stolen food from the camp vegetable garden, although they had done this in most cases from sheer hunger. The Geneva Convention mandates adequate care of POWs, and thus responsibility for such crimes must lie with the camp administration. The convention permits the punishment of POWs for misbehavior; however, the prisoner being punished must be allowed two hours exercise per day and given access to reading and writing materials and medical care.[75] The punishment-cage regime violated not only the Geneva Convention but also Japanese regulations governing punishment of prisoners, including the provision limiting the maximum confinement to 30 days. The regulations also required that proper food and bedding be provided at least once every three days and that the bedding be suited to the climate (such as extra blankets or mosquito netting).[76] Although Hoshijima was aware of the conditions and nature of the punishment, he did not constantly supervise the situation. He was more concerned with the progress of work on the airfield and left administration of punishment to his junior officers.

The breach of regulations by Japanese forces was compounded by the extraordinary degree of wanton cruelty displayed by many of the Formosan guards and the toleration of and consent to such behavior by many Japanese officers. For example, one Formosan guard commanded a POW to wash the guard's loincloth in the pot used by the POWs for cooking. When the POW refused, he was severely beaten.[77] Another POW, Captain Piccone, an army surgeon, had rigged up a high-strength light using lights taken from POW barracks and bound together, in order to be able to perform an operation. This makeshift light was discovered by guards, and Piccone was severely beaten and forced to stand for two hours.[78] These two examples clearly illustrate that guards were not in fact punishing POWs for infringements of regulations in such cases but merely harassing and tormenting them to satisfy their sadistic impulses. Such harassment worsened as the war continued.

In October 1942 there were 2 Japanese officers, 4 NCOs, and about 50 guards at the Sandakan POW camp. In April 1943, as new groups of POWs arrived, more guards were added. Although the final figures are unclear, available evidence indicates that there were around 100 guards at Sandakan between April 1943 and the end of 1944. All of the guards were Formosan, as was the case throughout the Borneo prison camp system.

Borneo was not the only garrison that used non-Japanese soldiers as prison guards. The majority of guards in Japanese POW camps across the occupied territories were young men drawn from places such as Korea and Formosa (now Taiwan) who were press-ganged into service. On May

5, 1942, after the Japanese army had made the decision to employ Formosans and Koreans as POW camp guards, an instruction entitled "Outline for Dealing With POWs" was sent to the chief of staff for the Japanese forces occupying Formosa, Higuchi Keishichirō. The outline detailed two principal reasons for the use of non-Japanese guards in prison camps. One reason was to destroy the lingering sense of superiority attached to white people by many Asian societies that had been colonized and consequently to elevate the Japanese as "white substitutes." By having Koreans and Formosans guard white prisoners under Japanese command, the Japanese military hoped that the old "pecking order" would be reversed—that non-Japanese Asians would come to see whites as inferior, subjugated people and the Japanese as the "natural" leaders of Asia. The other, more mundane purpose was to free up more Japanese men to be sent to the front line. On May 15, 1942, 10 days after the outline had been distributed, the recruitment of Korean and Formosan guards began.[79]

Unfortunately, no documents exist that detail the methods involved in the training and indoctrination of Formosan guards. However, Utsumi Aiko of Keisen University, Japan, conducted extensive research on Korean POW guards and found that more than 3,000 young Korean men were "recruited" (that is, press-ganged or otherwise forced to "volunteer") for the prison guard corps. Many of these men feared they would be shipped to Japan as indentured servants if they did not join the corps. Others were perhaps attracted by the high pay rates offered—50 yen per month, a large amount at the time. Those who served in the guard corps were classified as civilian employees rather than members of the military, and many hoped this status would prevent their transfer to the front line and would allow them to be demobilized when their two-year contract was concluded. However, on joining, the new recruits were issued with uniforms, and their basic training was very much military in character, including weapons training. Despite the difference between the promise and the reality of the guard corps, few deserted, possibly because potential deserters were threatened with court-martial.[80]

There is no reason to presume that the situation would have been any different in Formosa. On April 1, 1942, military leaders had introduced a special "volunteer" system designed to recruit soldiers who would be sent to the front line after six months of training. Once again, the word "volunteer" is a nominal one; local police were set a quota for such volunteers and obliged to fill it by any means necessary. Many young Formosans undoubtedly found service in the prison corps a more attractive alternative than the front line. Conscription was introduced to Formosa in September 1943, and by the end of the war more than 200,000 Formosans had been pressed into service. More than 30,000 died. The majority were sent to the Pacific rather than the Manchukuo theater of war on the grounds that Formosans were better suited to the heat than the Japanese.[81]

The Koreans were trained in Japanese and forbidden to use their native language. They were also given Japanese names instead of Korean ones. They were instructed to treat POWs as animals as a way of ensuring their fear and respect. They were trained primarily in the Japanese Field Service Code, and they were frequently beaten by Japanese officers, for no justifiable reason. The Geneva Convention was never mentioned. In other words, they were trained as de facto Japanese soldiers, yet their rank of *kanshi-hei* (guard) was lower than that of a private, and there was no possibility of promotion. Clearly the Korean guards (and the situation presumably was no different for Formosans) were treated as second-class soldiers within the forces, bound by the same iron discipline yet enjoying none of the prestige accorded to Japanese soldiers. Indeed, one of their unstated functions within the forces was to give the Japanese soldiers someone to look down on, thus strengthening a sense of ethnic solidarity among the Japanese and minimizing the resentment felt by Japanese troops toward their officers. The Koreans were "boundary-crossers," neither fully inside nor fully outside the military forces—inside insofar as the rules to which they were subject, outside insofar as the treatment they were accorded.[82]

The guards' duties were more than merely to prevent the escape of prisoners. One of their most important tasks was to provide sufficient POW workers each day for the airfield, no matter how many of the prisoners were too sick or unwilling to work. The guards were also responsible for maintaining a sufficiently high rate of work and for administering punishment when work fell short of expectations. Contact between Japanese and POWs was relatively uncommon, whereas the Formosan guards were in daily contact with the POWs. Although the POWs continually complained to the guards about the lack of adequate food, shelter, and medical supplies, the guards were unable to do anything about this situation, subject as they were to Japanese military POW policy. The Formosans were in the unenviable position of being caught between the demands of the POWs and the rule of the Japanese officers. However, they were unlikely to take the demands of the POWs to the Japanese officers, not only because such an act would be seen as softness and failing in their duty but because they might themselves become liable for punishment. When Hoshijima did venture out to inspect the progress on the airfield, the guards' treatment of the prisoners was routinely worse. On one occasion (according to evidence of one witness) a Corporal Peters was beaten about the head with a baton and blinded in one eye in the presence of Hoshijima.[83] However, the POWs made little distinction between the

Formosan guards and their Japanese masters and had no sympathy for the guards' plight.

Thus the frustration of the guards became more intense as the war went on, and it was inevitable that they would turn that frustration on the POWs, the only people over whom they had any power. This was frequently expressed through the administering of beatings on POWs. Beating was a standard disciplinary and "character-building" tool of the Japanese military, and the Formosan guards themselves had been routinely beaten as part of their training. The ethical seriousness of physical assault had thus been greatly diminished in their minds, and they saw the POWs as fair game. As the war turned against the Japanese, the officers began to draw vicarious pleasure from watching the beatings of the POWs by the guards and would also relieve their own frustrations by maltreating the guards, who would then take those new frustrations out on the POWs in a sadistic multiplier effect. It is therefore no coincidence that both the Korean guards on the Burma-Thailand railway and the Formosan guards in Borneo were capable of great cruelty; it was an effect of the power structure that operated within the prison camp system.

Despite the general effectiveness of such a system in encouraging guards to transfer their rage and frustration to the POWs, a few Formosans evidently felt a greater solidarity with the POWs than with the Japanese officers. One, about whom there is a record, was a guard who was called "Toyoda Kōkichi" in Japanese. Toyoda was regularly in charge of the wood-collecting detail, a group of 35–40 POWs who went into the jungle every day to collect firewood with no officer supervising. Toyoda would allow the POWs in this detail to take it easy and work at their own pace. He would also cook chicken, fish, and rice meals for them with supplies he had purchased from local villagers out of his own money. He became particularly friendly with one or two POWs, giving them whisky and, on one occasion, lending money to a prisoner who had lost heavily at gambling.[84] After the war, Toyoda was sentenced to 12 years' imprisonment at the War Crimes Tribunal for his part in the execution of sick and injured POWs during the evacuation of the Sandakan camp. However, one of the six survivors of Sandakan, Keith Botterill, made a submission to the tribunal detailing Toyoda's generosity, and his sentence was consequently commuted to two years. Botterill had been a member of the wood-collecting party, and he testified that he had never seen Toyoda beating POWs.[85] Another guard, "Nakamura," took yet more extreme actions; after the death march from Sandakan (see Chapter 2), he shot and killed a Japanese officer, wounded two more, then shot himself. Apparently he found the maltreatment he was suffering at the hands of the officers intolerable. However, Toyoda and Nakamura were exceptions. The majority of prison guards routinely maltreated POWs.

By September 1944 the Sandakan airfield had almost been completed. More than 250 POWs had died from illness, maltreatment, or execution or had been transferred in the 10-month construction period, and the number of POWs in the camp had fallen to 2,250. As the death toll indicates, the treatment of POWs steadily worsened over this period, although this was often in the form of indirect maltreatment, such as inadequate medical supplies or poor rations.

When construction of the airfield commenced in August 1942, the provision of rations had been adequate if frugal. POWs engaged in heavy labor were given 750 grams of rice and 600 grams of mixed vegetables per day; those on light duties were given 550 grams of rice and 400 grams of vegetables. Meat and fish were rarely supplied; however, as has been mentioned, POWs could purchase goods such as turtle eggs and bananas at the canteen with the wages they were paid for their work. With the profits from these sales, the POWs who ran the canteen purchased and slaughtered yak (a type of cattle) and distributed the meat to the POWs. The canteen was closed in mid-1943, and in June 1944 rations were drastically reduced: POWs on heavy labor were henceforth given 400 grams of rice per day, and those on light duties only 300 grams. Tapioca and sweet potato were provided to supplement the meager rice ration.[86]

In July 1944 Saipan Island fell to U.S. forces, and Guam, Peleliu, and the Morotai Islands fell in August. The Morotai garrison withdrew to Borneo, and the commanders of the Borneo garrison began to worry that they had insufficient troops to mount a proper defense. The Sandakan defense force was increased in September 1944. The expanded troop numbers placed a higher demand on local food supplies, and Sandakan POWs were then denied permission to purchase food from the local villagers.[87] Supplies of rice also became scarce because these were imported from Sarawak and the advance of U.S. forces had made regular supply difficult. In response to this pressure, the Japanese began to stockpile rice, making supplies to low-priority groups—such as POWs—even more scarce. After the war, the Japanese claimed that working POWs were given 300 grams of rice and sick POWs 200 grams. But surviving POWs claimed they were given only 100 grams of rice per day plus a small amount of tapioca, sweet potato, and other vegetables. Whichever amount is correct, the POWs' rations were clearly inadequate. By the end of 1944 all POWs were suffering from malnutrition and most from some form of tropical disease as well. The weight of one POW who arrived in August 1942 dropped from 70 kilograms to 40 kilograms by the end of 1944. His case is typical.[88]

On October 14, 1944, Sandakan was attacked by the U.S. Army Air Force for the first time. Bombing attacks continued twice a day nearly every day thereafter.[89] Heavy damage to crops in the Sandakan area contributed to the food supply problem. The POWs' vegetable garden was also damaged by the bombing, and the bulk of the reduced supply of vegetables was commandeered by the Japanese. According to the post-war testimony of one Formosan guard, the Japanese officers and NCOs had lived relatively well before the commencement of the bombing, regularly dining on fish, meat, tinned salmon, eggs, milk, pineapples, and bananas. The rice ration for Japanese officers and NCOs was one-third higher than that for Formosan guards.[90] Not surprisingly, many POWs tried to steal food from the officers' supplies. Those caught were punished with a term in the punishment cage. For example, in December 1944 eight POWs broke into the camp store one night to steal food for sick POWs. They were caught and sentenced to 28 days in the cage. All died within a few days of the conclusion of their punishment.[91]

The decision to reduce the POW rations was made not by Hoshijima or Suga but by the Kuching headquarters of the Borneo defense forces. The purpose of this decision—aside from the obvious preference given to supplying guards and troops with an adequate diet—was to keep the POWs so weak that they would be unable to revolt when the Allied force landed. The Sandakan POWs were regarded as especially dangerous, largely because of the Sandakan incident, and the reduction of their rations was much more severe than the reduction of rations at Kuching. Other measures were taken to head off effective rebellion; for instance, all knives and scissors were confiscated from POWs at the end of 1944. Airfield construction continued throughout the bombing, and POWs were also put to work on bomb disposal. By this time, however, half of them were too sick to work.[92]

Medical supplies for POWs were always scarce, although at the beginning they were given access to aspirin and quinine. Prior to the Sandakan incident, the major supply came free from Dr. Taylor, and sick prisoners were often treated in the Sandakan hospital. After the incident and the removal of Taylor, the prisoners had to barter rings, watches, and other valuables in order to gain necessary supplies, and the Kempeitai ordered that all POWs be treated in camp. POWs made many written requests to Hoshijima for medical supplies, and Hoshijima repeatedly claimed to be "considering" these requests, although they never eventuated. In the latter half of 1944, William Stiepewich (one of the survivors of Sandakan) was doing some carpentry work in the offices of the camp and saw Formosan guards opening a large number of Red Cross packages—about 30 in all. However, the POWs received only three of the packages, and these contained little apart from gauze bandages.[93]

According to Japanese regulations, each POW camp was required to have at least one doctor. But Sandakan camp was established as a branch of the larger Kuching camp, and the camp doctor was permanently located there.[94] Two doctors visited Sandakan sometime in 1944, but they brought no medical supplies with them and treated none of the sick POWs. They merely made an inspection of conditions, then departed.[95] The last consignment of medical supplies sent to Sandakan from Kuching was in July 1944. The shipping route between Sandakan and Kuching was closed in October 1944 because of continual bombing and submarine attacks. The last doctor to visit Sandakan camp was a Dr. Yamamoto, who made two visits by plane in October 1944 and February 1945. He brought large amounts of quinine and atabrine (another antimalarial drug), but it is not known whether the drugs were distributed to POWs.[96]

After the reduction of the food ration in June 1944, the mortality rate jumped, largely as a result of malnutrition and disease. Until this time POWs had been buried in coffins, but the increasingly high death rate made it impossible to continue this practice. By the end of 1944, POW numbers were down to 1,850; more than 400 prisoners had died in the space of four months. Of the 1,850, only 700 were fit for work.[97] Yet, despite the supply difficulties created by Allied bombing and submarine activity, there was no real shortage of food or medical supplies in the Sandakan area. By March 1945 the Japanese had stockpiled huge quantities of food and medical supplies in preparation for the expected Allied invasion. Presumably these stockpiles were intended only for Japanese personnel. The storage room beneath Commandant Hoshijima's house contained more than 90 metric tons of rice and 160,000 quinine tablets. After the war, Allied forces found other stockpiles in the Sandakan area containing more than 786,000 quinine tablets, 19,600 Vitamin A and D tablets, large numbers of Vitamin B and C tablets, and a great deal of medical and surgical equipment. Nothing from these stockpiles was supplied to POWs, nor would the camp command have been permitted to do this even had they wished to.[98] Responsibility for the many POW deaths from malnutrition and illness must lie in large part with the higher command of the Borneo garrison and Lieutenant General Yamawaki Masataka and Major General Manaki Takanobu in particular, who seem to have made the decision deliberately to weaken POWs to death or close to it.

Whatever the deprivations experienced by the prisoners at the Sandakan POW camp until this time, much worse was to come when, on two occasions, they were marched from Sandakan to a place called Ranau, some 260 kilometers away. The Sandakan death marches and the massacres of the remaining prisoners at Sandakan are discussed in the next chapter. At the end of 1944, however, the POWs at Sandakan never imagined that their malnutrition and disease were but the prelude to the real tragedy of the following year.

# 2

# The Sandakan Death Marches and the Elimination of POWs

## The First Death March

Continuous bombing by Allied aircraft rendered Sandakan airfield unusable almost as soon as it was completed. At first the Japanese used the POWs to repair the airfield after each attack, but on January 10, 1945, they discontinued this practice, and therefore POWs were no longer required to perform physical labor. By this stage Palawan Island, to the northwest of Borneo, had been taken by the Americans, and the Japanese feared the Americans would use Palawan as a launching point for the attempted recapture of Borneo with a landing at Brunei. Consequently, commanders of the 37th Army (the renamed Borneo Defense Force) decided upon a major reorganization of the island's defenses. They ordered three of the five battalions in Tawao to march to Brunei (transport by ship was now impossible) and two battalions from Tawi Tawi as well as two of the three battalions from Sandakan to march to a place on the west coast near Api. At the same time they decided to use 500 relatively healthy POWs as carriers on the march and then to relocate them at a new prison camp at Tuaran, 35 kilometers north of Api.[1]

There was no proper road between Sandakan and Api, and throughout the occupation of Borneo, the Japanese had relied heavily on shipping routes around the northern cape of the island. Construction of a road linking the east and west coasts had been commenced during the occupation, and a rudimentary path between Sandakan and Api had been completed by August 1944. The most difficult part of the path to construct had been a 260-kilometer section between Sandakan and Ranau, an area of dense jungle. Unsure of the terrain, the Japanese had sought advice on the best route from a chief of the Dasan tribe named Kulang. However, Kulang was strongly anti-Japanese, and he deliberately mapped out a route that presented every conceivable obstacle to road construction, with

steep hills and valleys and swamps (Map 2.1). Unfortunately, his inge-
nious deception was to have tragic consequences.[2]

The first march from Sandakan began on January 29, 1945, under the
command of Captain Yamamoto Shōichi of the second battalion of the
25th Independent Mixed Regiment. The Yamamoto battalion had been
transferred to Borneo from Manchukuo in October 1944 and had been
engaged in construction of various defense emplacements around Sandakan since that time.[3] The 500 POWs were divided into a number of
smaller groups, each under the guard of a platoon from Yamamoto's battalion, and it was intended that one group would depart each day. POWs
were to be given four days' rations on departure, which were to be replenished at five rest points along the way. Yamamoto was required to ensure that all marching groups complete the trek to Ranau within 12 days,
at which point Captain Nagai would take over and march the groups
from Ranau to Api. Both commanders were instructed that all POWs
must complete the march, no matter how sick or exhausted they became.
Yamamoto realized it would be all but impossible to complete the march
within the allotted time, and he requested that a longer period be set. He
also requested an increase in the number of rest points along the way. Yamamoto believed the march to Ranau would take at least three weeks, although he did not mention this estimate to his superiors. In fact, three
weeks was the period his superiors had set for the entire 400-kilometer
march to Tuaran, and Yamamoto was informed that the urgency of the
transfer was such that no extra time could be allowed.[4]

Commandant Hoshijima was required by the authorities to hand over
500 prisoners to Yamamoto for the march, but he provided only 470 (of
which 370 were Australians and 100 British). The reasons for the shortfall
are not recorded, although it is possible that Hoshijima was unwilling to
hand over prisoners too sick to survive the march. The airfield had been
abandoned and Hoshijima was no longer responsible for its construction
or maintenance; he was possibly quite prepared to take a more lenient attitude to the POWs. Whether this stemmed from humanitarian motives or
concern about his future should Japan lose the war (as by then must have
seemed certain) is an interesting matter for speculation. Prior to the commencement of the march, Hoshijima gave the 470 POWs who were to be
transferred a horse to be slaughtered and eaten.[5] They were given no details of their destination but were told merely that they were being transferred somewhere with good food and medicine, from where they would
eventually be repatriated. They were also told that sick POWs would be
transported to the same place at a later stage. Many POWs believed these
assurances, and some sick POWs even volunteered to join the march, des-
perately clinging to the hope offered by Hoshijima's promise that they
would be delivered from their terrible conditions at Sandakan.[6]

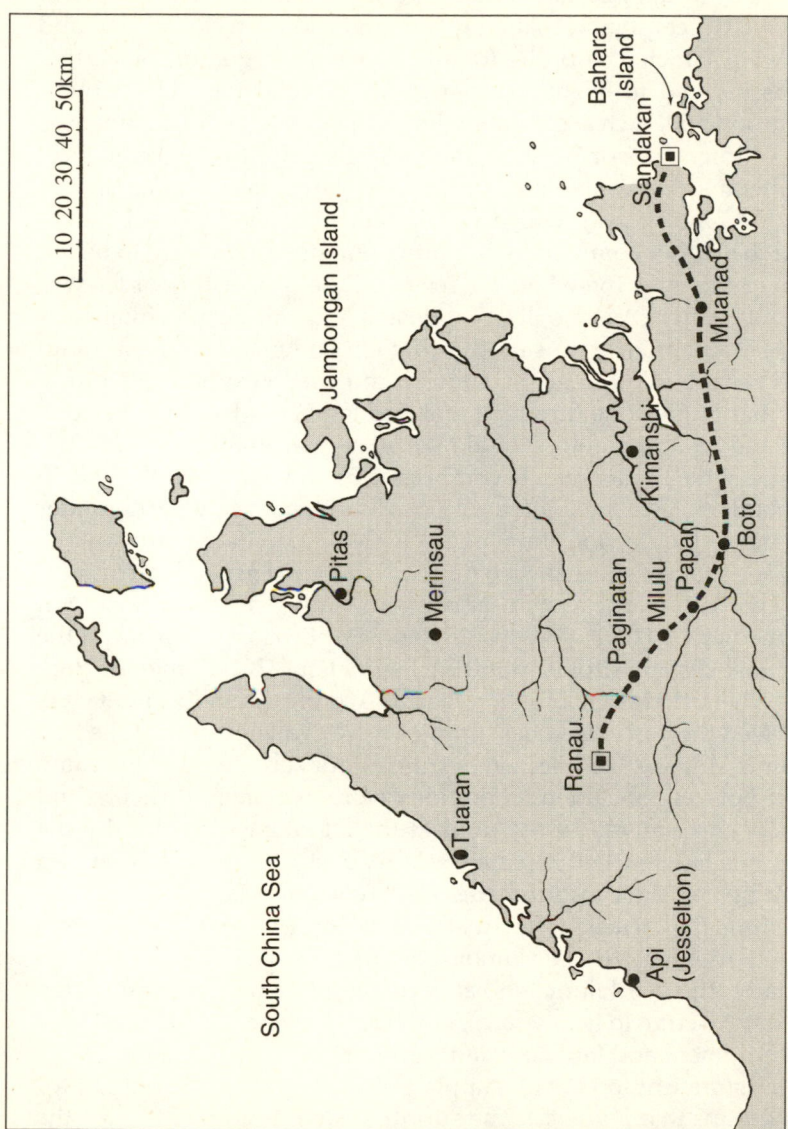

The reason for relatively short distances between the supply points located along the path from Boto to Ranau (indicated by ●) was probably the rough mountain terrain that took longer to traverse.

Map 2.1 *Sandakan-to-Ranau route.*

Yamamoto wished to delay the commencement of the march for as long as possible. Quartermaster corps soldiers had gone ahead to establish the rest points and food drops, and they needed time to reach their destinations. Yamamoto also wanted to wait out the rainy season, which was due to conclude in February. In late January he was probably skeptical about assurances by the command that all rest points had been established and that there were sufficient supplies for all prisoners and guards. Nevertheless he was ordered to begin the march. He divided the POWs into 9 groups of around 50, each accompanied by a platoon of about 40 Japanese soldiers, 1 officer, and 1 or 2 NCOs. Immediately prior to the commencement of the march, Yamamoto summoned all platoon commanders (except of the ninth group, which would leave last) and passed on the order from the higher command stipulating that no POWs were to be left behind along the way, for whatever reason.[7] The gist of this order was presumably that all POWs too ill or exhausted to continue marching were to be killed. Yamamoto then saw the platoon commander of the ninth group, Lieutenant Abe Kazuo, separately and made explicit this order: All POWs that groups one through eight had left behind were to be "disposed of," and he, Yamamoto, would take all responsibility.[8]

Group one of the Ranau march, comprising 55 Australian POWs and 40 Japanese soldiers, left Sandakan at 6:00 A.M. on January 29, 1945, under the command of Lieutenant Iino Shigeru with Yamamoto accompanying. After this, one group departed each day, with the final group leaving Sandakan on February 6. The system of rest and supply points broke down almost immediately. There were insufficient supplies for group one at the fifth and most distant supply point at Paginatan, 220 kilometers from Sandakan, where Iino was obliged to barter two pigs from local villagers in order to feed the party. Medical supplies were available only at the first supply point, Muanad, 78 kilometers from Sandakan. Because the rainy season had not yet concluded, conditions were extremely difficult, and the marchers encountered heavy mud at the 50-kilometer point. By the time group one had reached Muanad, 1 POW and 1 Japanese soldier had died. By Paginatan the death toll was 11 POWs and 4 Japanese soldiers, and by the time they reached Ranau at 4:00 P.M. on February 12, 15 POWs had died, the vast majority succumbing to malaria or beriberi. It took 15 days to march the 260 kilometers, an average of 18.6 kilometers a day (with one day lost due to heavy rain), with each prisoner carrying 30 kilograms of equipment and Japanese ammunition.[9]

There was sufficient food at all supply points for group one but not for any of the groups that followed. The supply system was chaotic from the start, with the supply units taking insufficient food to the supply points along the road. On January 29, the day group one left Sandakan, the supply units realized they did not have sufficient food for the nine groups.

They must have communicated this to officers at headquarters, who instructed the Yamamoto units in Sandakan to stretch their four-day ration to last eight days. However, this order was not communicated to the second and third groups (the first group had already departed before the order arrived), and they consumed their rations within the allotted time, fully expecting to be replenished at the prearranged supply points. When group two reached Muanad there was no food for them, and the group commander, Lieutenant Hirano Yukihiko, instructed the supply point soldiers to share their rations with the group. When the men reached Boto, the second supply point, all that could be provided was 300 grams of rice and a smaller amount of vegetables for the several days' travel to the next point. Another planned supply point along the route was not there at all; there were no traces of quartermaster soldiers and certainly no food. Group two started the march with 50 POWs and 49 soldiers. After 17 days, 15 POWs had died, 5 had escaped (and presumably died in the jungle, as they were never traced), and 10 soldiers had died.[10]

Not surprisingly, each new group found the food situation a little worse than the one that had preceded it. The commander of the third group, Lieutenant Toyohara, sent his NCO, Corporal Gotanda, several days ahead of the main group to reconnoiter the food situation and supplement any lack of army supplies with livestock bartered from the surrounding villages using blankets and personal belongings confiscated from POWs. But by the time the final groups began their march, even the local villages were running out of food available for barter. The situation became so desperate that Japanese soldiers resorted to stealing rations from POWs. After the war Japanese officers and NCOs testified to the War Crimes Tribunal that rations had been shared equally between Japanese soldiers and POWs. However, Keith Botterill testified that POWs had received only a third of the rations allotted to the Japanese. The true state of affairs has never been resolved.[11]

Lack of food was not the only problem. Yamamoto had been right about the effects of the rainy season. One officer testified that his group had to walk through a path 20 centimeters deep in mud for two days.[12] Very few POWs had shoes of any description. The Japanese provided the POWs with light rubber footwear halfway between sneakers and thick socks, known as *jikatabi*, but these were usually much too small for the feet of the POWs and too slippery for jungle conditions. Many of the POWs suffered from tropical ulcers, a condition considerably worsened by the march. There were also a number of dangerous reptiles and insects—cobras, crocodiles, and huge brown leeches. The leeches were a particular problem because there were so many of them and because they were so difficult to remove once they attached themselves. The loss of blood from leech bites further weakened the POWs; because of the long period of poor nutrition they had suffered, their blood often failed to clot. Very few POWs had blankets, and they could do nothing to protect themselves against the night rains except cover themselves with leaves. Much of the march was through mountainous terrain, and the POWs carried not only their own equipment but also that of the Japanese officers. In one case, the officer of group eight had several boxes of equipment that were carried by a group of POWs acting as bearers. In light of these conditions, it is hardly surprising that many succumbed to malaria so swiftly.[13]

POWs who were already weak or ill had little chance of surviving the march. Each group would march for a stretch lasting between 40 minutes and an hour and then take a break to allow stragglers to catch up to the main body of the group. However, the group would set off again as soon as the last stragglers reached the rest spot. The result was that those who were already weak were denied rest and weakened further. Each morning there were a number of POWs who were too exhausted or ill to get up. Those still fit to walk were marched off, and a small detail of Japanese guards was left with the exhausted, who were never seen again. After the war the officers of groups one through eight claimed that they had never ordered their soldiers to shoot sick or exhausted POWs, that these POWs had been carried either by other POWs or by Japanese soldiers, and that all POWs who died were properly buried. However, Keith Botterill's testimony gives a very different story:

There were men about one or two left behind every second or third day. Of a morning those who were too sick to move would tell our Australian officer in charge that they could not move with the party and the Japanese sergeant or officer would count us and move us off, and we would get along the road about a half mile and we would hear shots. The Japanese officer would tell our officers that they had to shoot the men who were left behind. At times when we were marching along the road, and the men were too weak to keep up and they dropped behind the Japanese would shoot them. . . . I can remember going up a big mountain at Boto and we lost five men. They were shot and I myself saw a Japanese corporal shoot two of them.[14]

Dick Moxham, another survivor who was in the seventh group, gave similar testimony. He also saw many dead bodies along the road—many of whom were mere skin and bone—as well as one POW who was still alive and in agony.[15] It is possible that only some of the POWs were shot and that others were left behind to die. Captain Yamamoto never gave an explicit order that POWs were to be shot; it was unnecessary. His officers understood, as well as he had, the implicit meaning of the order from headquarters in Kuching that "no prisoners were to be left behind." Furthermore, in each group between three and 10 Japanese soldiers died of malaria and other tropical diseases; they were clearly at the point of exhaustion themselves. It would have been all but impossible for the soldiers to carry sick POWs along the Ranau path. In a few cases sick POWs asked soldiers to shoot them. In one case a Japanese officer found himself incapable of shooting a sick POW and loaned his gun to an English officer to do the job.[16]

Group nine of the first march left Sandakan on February 6 and reached Paginatan on February 21. By this point, out of a group of 50 POWs and about the same number of Japanese soldiers, 18 POWs and 7 Japanese soldiers had died.[17] It is not clear how many of the 18 were shot and how many were merely left to die. The following is testimony by a Private Endō, who was one of two privates (the other was a Private Satō) ordered to shoot POWs by Lieutenant Abe. He ordered the two to walk at the end of the group and shoot those POWs who could not go on. He also assigned a Sergeant Major Satō to ensure that these orders were carried out. According to Endō:

Those of them that were too ill to travel at all we were instructed by Lieutenant Abe to kill. This order was given directly to Satō and myself by Lieutenant Abe . . . when we reached Boto S/M Satō of my unit was waiting for us. He had apparently received the same orders from Lieutenant Abe as we had. Shortly after leaving Boto another one of the POWs became too ill to continue the march. Private Satō and myself under the orders of S/M Satō then took the POW into the jungle at the side of the track and shot him. Between Boto and Paginatan a further nine POWs died. The first four were left with Private Satō and then later I was left with a party of five. These five men were very sick and suffering a great deal. Although my orders from Lieutenant Abe were to kill them I did not have the heart to do such a thing, and so left them behind, without food and water, to die. I believe that Private Satō did the same thing. On these occasions there were no officers or NCOs present to see that we carried out the orders. Looking back now and remembering how ill the POWs were I feel it might have been more humane to have killed them and buried them before going on.[18]

From all this evidence one can safely assume that the combination of shooting POWs and leaving them to die was common to all groups on the march.

Because of the total lack of food from the beginning, the last four groups on the march were forced to eat anything they could forage, including frogs, snails, and fern leaves. By the time they reached Paginatan, both POWs and guards were so weak that they were ordered to stay there and rest for a month. These four groups arrived at Paginatan between February 17 and 21. Forty of the two hundred POWs had died. Those who had survived were so sick that they continued to die at the rate of four or five a day while at Paginatan, despite the fact that their diet had improved with a supply of rice from Ranau. By the time they left Paginatan for Ranau, another 100 had died.[19]

Groups one through five reached Ranau between February 12 and 19. More than 70 out of a total of 270 of these POWs died. All of these POWs were extremely weakened, and most were suffering from either beriberi or malaria. It was impossible to continue the march to Api. The Kuching headquarters, realizing that the POWs would be unable to transport equipment, ordered that they be kept at Ranau under the guard of a unit based there while Yamamoto's unit continued on to Api. Thus the POWs were handed over to Major Watanabe Yoshio. The POWs were given two weeks' rest, but the food supply was as bad as at Sandakan, and no medical supplies were made available. After two weeks they were put to work on a number of day-to-day tasks—thatching huts, carrying water and equipment, gathering wood, and so forth. Those who had been seriously weakened by the march were killed off by the demands that such work made on their bodies. Within one month, more than half of the 200 or so POWs at Ranau had died.[20]

Despite the discontinuation of the march to Api, POWs continued to die. The task of rice carrying contributed to the mortality rate. The Ranau POWs were required to transport rice to the POWs and soldiers at Paginatan, and 60 of the fittest (least exhausted) POWs were chosen for this task. Each rice carrier took a 20-kilogram rice bag the 45 kilometers to Paginatan. The round-trip took five days, three days there and two days back, and those few POWs who had the physical strength for the task were used more than once. Keith Botterill made the journey five times. Those who fell and could not get up again were either bayoneted or shot, their bodies left in the jungle and their load of rice transferred to other POWs. Botterill described one trip in which 20 POWs started out on a rice run to Paginatan and only 5 returned. Presumably, the bulk of the rice went to Japanese soldiers and relatively little to POWs. The POWs at Paginatan were moved to Ranau at the end of March. However, of the 60 who had survived to that time, only 30 were able to march. The remainder probably were shot or left to die. When all surviving POWs from the first march were assembled at Ranau in early April, there were about 150. By the end of June, 6 were still alive.[21]

## The Second Death March

In Sandakan, meanwhile, the bombing had continued throughout February while the first march was on the path to Ranau. Hoshijima ordered that a "POW" sign be made in the camp compound, with each letter 10 meters high and wide. However, there were other military targets around Sandakan, and the camp was frequently hit by accident. By the end of April 1945, 30 POWs had been killed or seriously injured by American bombs. At that time commanders in Kuching ordered Hoshijima to remove the sign, and Hoshijima—whose personal quarters were very near to the camp—reluctantly complied.[22] Another time one of the wood-gathering parties was attacked by U.S. planes whose pilots presumably mistook the men for a group of Japanese soldiers. Twenty POWs and a number of guards were killed. At the beginning of April, in the middle of all of this, the camp was overrun by rats, whose previous food supplies had been disrupted by the bombing. The rats were particularly concentrated in the camp hospital, where the 400 seriously ill POWs were too weak to fight them off.[23] By March the drastic reductions in the rice ration, which had occurred in January, were beginning to take their toll, and each day 10 to 12 POWs were dying of exhaustion or disease. The supply of rice and water to POWs ceased completely at the beginning of April, and they had to survive on rice they had saved from previous rations, such wild vegetables as they could gather, and swamp water that they boiled. By this stage, the Japanese were no longer trying merely to weaken the POWs to prevent them from revolting; they were prepared to leave the POWs to die through starvation and thirst. When the first march left Sandakan in early February, 1,300 POWs remained in Sandakan. By the end of May their numbers had been reduced to less than 830.[24]

On May 20, 1945, Hoshijima was transferred from Sandakan and replaced by Captain Takakuwa Takuo, whose primary task was to remove the remaining prisoners from the camp.[25] The reasons for Hoshijima's transfer are not recorded. It is probable that 37th Army Headquarters deemed Takakuwa, who was a field officer, more suitable for the task than Hoshijima, who was originally commanding officer of the Engineering Battalion. This time there was no limit on the duration of the march, although the order was to complete it as soon as possible.[26] Takakuwa thought it was impossible to remove all POWs, most of whom were extremely weak. He therefore sent a telegram to headquarters seeking permission to select only relatively healthy POWs for the march. Lieutenant Colonel Iwahashi Manabu testified to the War Crimes Tribunal that he replied to Takakuwa's request on May 26, granting the request. However, Takakuwa did not receive this telegram.[27] On May 27 Sandakan was bombarded by Allied warships for the first time, in addition to the ongoing air raids. The Japanese defense force moved five kilometers inland from the Sandakan camp, presuming that the Allies would land in the very near future. The withdrawal left as few as 1,500 defenders at Sandakan. Takakuwa became very concerned about the vulnerability of the camp and decided to take all POWs who could walk to Ranau. Of 824 POWs held at Sandakan at the time, Takakuwa believed 439 Australian and 97 British POWs (536 in total) were fit to walk.[28]

Just after 9:00 A.M. on May 29, the buildings of the second and third POW camps were burned down. These buildings had not been used since the first march left Sandakan. The ammunition depots were also exploded, and five pigs were given to the remaining POWs. The POWs, seeing such unusual behavior, thought the Japanese were providing the food because they knew the landing of the Allied forces was imminent. Thus the POWs' hopes for rescue were raised.[29] At 11:00 A.M. Takakuwa came to see the POWs in the first camp and ordered them to remove all sick POWs to outside the camp buildings and to set fire to those buildings. At 6:00 P.M. the 536 POWs who could walk were gathered in the parade ground and divided into 11 groups. Each group consisted of around 50 POWs, as with the first march, and each was guarded by about 12 soldiers. There were 147 guards in all. Not all of them were Formosan. There were also Japanese soldiers sent from the Okuyama battalion to assist Takakuwa. However, unlike for the first march, there were very few Japanese officers or NCOs to command them. Therefore these 11 groups were combined into three parties. The first party was led by Second Lieutenant Suzuki from the Okuyama battalion, the second by Lieutenant Watanabe Genzō, and the last by Staff Sergeant Tsuji.[30]

As with the first march, the prisoners were told that they were being removed to a nearby place where there would be plenty of food. The prisoners, who expected the landing of the Allied forces to occur very soon, complained about the transfer, although they had no choice but to obey the order. Thus the second march to Ranau began at 7:00 P.M. on May 29.[31] One probable reason Takakuwa began the march at nightfall was his belief that the Allied landing was imminent. He might well have wanted to get as far from Sandakan as possible by the time he expected the Allies to arrive. Another possible reason is that he might have been afraid of detection by U.S. aircraft if the march commenced in daylight hours.

As soon as the prisoners left the camp, all but a few buildings used by the camp staff were burned down. At 11:00 that night, after the marchers were 20 kilometers from the town of Sandakan, each group was provided with two 45-kilogram bags of rice. This amounted to 1.8 kilograms per prisoner for the first 10 days of the march before the first supply point at Muanad was reached. In fact, there were 50 metric tons of rice hidden at this 20-kilometer point, but it was intended for the use of the Japanese forces after the Allied landing. There were many other food caches in the area around Sandakan. However, none of this food was intended for POWs. The march continued throughout the night, with only a two-hour rest in the morning, and lasted until 3:00 P.M. on May 30.[32]

Most of the POWs were sick and very weak by this time, so there were many who were unable to continue the march even a few kilometers after it began. For example, group seven, which had Warrant Officer William Stiepewich as POW leader, lost six men in the first seven kilometers. The guards kicked and beat the POWs with sticks and rifle butts if they fell by the wayside, forcing them to continue marching. As a consequence, a long distance opened between those at the front and the stragglers at the rear. Although the first and second parties reached the resting point at 3:00 P.M. on May 30, the third party did not reach it until sometime that night.[33] As would be expected, many of the prisoners who were beaten by the guards for straggling became yet weaker and unable to walk. These men were driven into the jungle by the guards and beaten to death or shot. Unlike on the first march, there were orders given by Takakuwa to the Japanese soldiers and Formosan guards at the beginning of the march to kill any POWs who either attempted to escape or could not continue to march. During the evening of May 30, one of the Japanese soldiers in charge of the third party, Corporal Katayama, together with two camp guards, drove seven prisoners into the jungle by kicking and beating them, then shot them.[34] There was little chance of survival for prisoners who attempted escape; they were barely strong enough to continue walking. Running off into the jungle and hiding there, avoiding recapture, would require more strength than virtually any of them could muster, although two men did manage to escape and survive until they were rescued months later. Escape became ever more difficult as the march progressed; the more time passed and the more the POW numbers decreased, the easier the guards' task became.

On the third day after leaving Sandakan, Takakuwa ordered that the departure times of the parties be altered, presumably to give the first party an extra hour's rest. The departure times set were 6:30, 7:00 and 7:30 A.M. and thereafter were rotated daily. The first party to leave each day was always led by Second Lieutenant Suzuki. The second party was led by Takakuwa himself. Tsuji always brought up the rear. Takakuwa formed two small groups of guards, one led by Watanabe and the other led by Tsuji, with the task of "disposing" of those POWs who could not continue marching. Every morning at 9:00 (one and a half hours after the last POW group left the resting point) Watanabe's group departed the resting point and attempted to force any POWs they came across to continue marching. If these men could not be made to continue, they were left under guard until Tsuji's group (which followed one hour behind Watanabe's) came along. Tsuji's group then shot those POWs. In this way, the prisoners who could not continue were eliminated. As was the case for all POW guards at Sandakan, the groups led by Tsuji and Watanabe consisted entirely of Formosan guards. The personnel in these groups were constantly rotated.[35] According to testimony two of these guards gave Australian military authorities at the end of the war, none of the killings were carried out by Japanese:

[I] was detailed to Tsuji's party three times. On the first occasion I do not know how many were killed and the second time I killed one out of a total of one but none on the first occasion. This killing was done on the orders of Tsuji. I have never seen Tsuji kill a POW nor has Fukushima killed any to my knowledge, as the latter simply took down the names. I have never seen Takakuwa and Watanabe kill any, but with the exception of a few sick [men], every Formosan guard had to take his turn.[36]

On the way over from Sandakan to Ranau I had to take my turn in Tsuji's party once or twice only and the first day 2 or 3 were shot, and about the same next time. I had to shoot one of them the first time. Capt Takakuwa was present and said "Shoot that man." We then went on leaving the bodies behind. Tsuji and Fukushima took the names of the men. I do not think they were buried. There were a few of the Formosans who did not kill POWs on the way over but very few. Takakuwa forced us all to kill.[37]

As is clear from the testimony, Takakuwa often joined Tsuji's party, presumably to make sure his orders were being obeyed.

As with the first march, after the day's march had commenced and all prisoners who could continue had left, those who could no longer move were taken into the jungle by Tsuji's group and shot. The following is testimony given by a guard who participated in the killings:

I was in the early morning killing party once and fired once. I remember the day when the rest of the POWs in the 110 1/2 mile camp were killed. We took the POWs about 400 metres along the Tambunan road, stopped and the POWs were allowed to smoke; we all had our rifles loaded. After resting S/M Tsuji told us the POWs were to be killed that day. He went away to select a position where we were told to bring one POW escorted by two guards. This place was 20 or 30 metres away. I took one POW with me to S/M Tsuji who was waiting and on his orders I was ordered to shoot.[38]

Thus the reason Tsuji's group stayed at the resting point for two hours after the others had departed was not only to follow those marchers who straggled and to drive them on but also to kill those who were unable to begin marching at all each day. At the War Crimes Tribunal, the Australian prosecutor claimed that by rotating the membership of Tsuji's party, the Japanese officers made sure that all of the bloodthirsty Formosan guards had an opportunity to kill POWs.[39] This seems a sensational claim. The most likely reason Takakuwa created such a system was to put equal pressure and equal responsibility on all of the guards.

The prisoners who left their comrades behind heard the sound of shooting after they had marched around two kilometers each morning. In this way, every prisoner soon became aware of his fate should he be unable to continue. The POWs also saw the decomposed remains of men who had been killed or otherwise perished during the first march and thus became aware of the fate of many of those who had left Sandakan five months previously. When a prisoner fell by the wayside during the day's march, his comrades would silently shake hands with him before moving on. After the war, the Australian forces collected the remains of about 280 men along the first 160 kilometers of the track, most of whom had been killed in the jungle about 15 to 20 meters from the path. The skulls of 80 percent of these showed severe damage, presumably from either gunshots or beatings.[40]

Although the rainy season should have been over, it rained very hard during the first few days of the march, and the mud added to the prisoners' ordeals. As on the first march, very few had any footwear. The march began on a tarred road but soon moved onto a rough jungle path, the first 45 kilometers of which was swampy and difficult to traverse even with good footwear. The swampy terrain then gave way to 60 kilometers of mountainous country with steep rises. Although the prisoners were not forced to carry ammunition, as they had been on the first march, their physical condition was much worse than that of those on the first march. It is scarcely surprising that so many men were unable to continue the march, even knowing they would be shot.[41]

Although it was planned that there would be five food supply points, the prisoners were given only 85 grams of rice each day, and that meager ration ran out before the march was completed. They were forced to gather anything that was possibly edible from the jungle, such as frogs and fern fronds. Takakuwa was clearly aware that there would be very little food at the five supply points, so he sent his junior, Ichikawa, two days' march ahead to get food from the local people by bartering.[42] However, the amount of food gained in this way was negligible and completely insufficient for the needs of the already malnourished prisoners. In contrast with the prisoners, the Japanese officers and the Formosan guards had more than enough food, unlike during the first march when the officers and guards also had inadequate rations. To add insult to injury, many of the prisoners were forced to carry the rations of the Japanese officers. Owen Campbell, a survivor of the second march, testified that the rations bag he was forced to carry included dried fish and soya bean powder. The officers and guards also had medical supplies, but those for the POWs were negligible.[43] When the march finally reached Ranau on June 25, there were only 183 surviving POWs out of the 536 who began. At most, one of the Japanese or Formosans died during the march from malaria.[44]

Evidence from the proceedings of the War Crimes Tribunal supports the following conclusions regarding the second march. Takakuwa knew how difficult the march would be, as he knew exactly what problems Yamamoto had faced on the first march. He was particularly aware of the food supply problems during the first march and therefore made sure that the POWs carried enough food and medicine for the soldiers and guards. Sending an NCO ahead to gather food for the POWs had also occurred with most groups of the first march. However, successfully obtaining food for the POWs and keeping them alive while transferring them to Ranau were, for Takakuwa, secondary to the task of getting there as quickly as possible. He knew that many Japanese soldiers died during the first march and believed that the danger to the Japanese and Formosan men in his charge would be minimized if the march were as brief as possible. The physical condition of the POWs in the second march was worse than that of those who undertook the first march; therefore (all else being equal) the second march would be slower than the first. Knowing this, Takakuwa was willing to take drastic measures in order to ensure the safety of the Japanese and Formosans under his command. Minimizing the duration of the march became Takakuwa's overriding concern, even though the orders he was given did not specify a time limit.

Furthermore, although Takakuwa took the same measures as Yamamoto in killing prisoners who were unable to continue marching, he went a step further in systematic planning. In the case of the first march, it was probably tacitly understood by the officers responsible for each group that prisoners who could not continue marching would be killed, and in the first stages, the killings seemed more random than systematic. As the first march progressed, however, a pattern emerged, and the killings clearly became more systematic. Moreover, in the earlier stages of the first march, some POWs were left to die rather than being shot; in the second march, all POWs who could not continue marching were killed by the guards. At the War Crimes Tribunal, Takakuwa's plans for killing prisoners thus became the major issue in the hearings concerning the second Sandakan death march.

The 37th Army commanders at Kuching did not give a direct order to kill POWs, either before the first march or the second one. The specific order before the first march was that no POWs should be left behind along the route of the march. The specific order before the second march was that all POWs had to be removed from Sandakan and taken to Ranau. However, in mid-April 1945, Lieutenant Colonel Takayama Hikoichi of the 37th Army command had visited Sandakan to investigate the physical condition of the POWs.[45] From his report, 37th Army commanders must have known that the orders were impossible to comply with unless prisoners were killed. They also knew, of course, how many prisoners and soldiers had died during the first march. Therefore, final responsibility for what happened during the second march must lie with those 37th Army officers who gave the orders. Both Takakuwa and Yamamoto clearly understood the real intention of the orders, and both (but Takakuwa especially) showed by their actions that they were willing to carry them out. In January 1945, the intention of the 37th Army commanders was to remove healthy POWs to the west coast of Borneo and to exploit their labor for carrying ammunition and equipment. As we have seen, this plan met with complete failure. However, by April 1945 the plans changed completely. As can be seen from the fact that food supplies to Sandakan were cut off completely, the commanders had evidently decided to eliminate POWs rather than attempt to use them for the war effort. To force malnourished and sick POWs to walk 260 kilometers in harsh terrain fits well with a secret plan to eliminate them.

## The Elimination and Crucifixion of POWs

After the second march left Sandakan, there were 288 prisoners remaining at Sandakan, most of them too weak to have undertaken the march, as well as a few relatively healthy men who had stayed to tend to the sick. Because the camp buildings had been burned down, the prisoners were forced to improvise huts from whatever materials were at hand. These huts were without walls, and the roofs, made of leaves and blankets, offered little protection from the often heavy rains. At this time, apart from the prisoners, there remained one Japanese soldier, Staff Sergeant Murozumi Hisao, 16 Formosan guards, a few Javanese laborers, and five Chinese kitchen staff. The remaining POWs had not been supplied with any food or medicine since sometime before the march departed and had been subsisting mainly on wild cabbages they gathered from the swamp and, occasionally, on scraps the guards threw out.[46]

On the first of June, three days after the second march left Sandakan, Lieutenant Moritake returned to Sandakan from a 10-day trip to the town of Kimanshi. There is no record available to clarify why Moritake went there, but it is probable that Takakuwa sent him to explain to Takakuwa's superiors why it would be impossible to carry out the orders he had been given. (At this time it was no longer possible to make radio contact between Sandakan and the headquarters at Kuching.) Moritake seems to have returned with the orders to remove all POWs. On June 9, Moritake selected 75 POWs and gave them to Second Lieutenant Iwashita of Okuyama Battalion.[47] Iwashita, along with 37 Japanese soldiers, departed for Ranau with these men. It was, from the beginning, an impossible task for these POWs to complete the 260-kilometer march to Ranau. All of the POWs and all but one Japanese soldier perished in the jungle. No details of their fate are known; the survivor may have been interrogated but there are no available records. All that is known is that all of the POWs died or were killed within the first 50 kilometers of the march.[48] From what is known about the first two marches, we can guess how these men met their deaths.

After these 75 POWs were taken away, there were 185 POWs remaining at Sandakan. By July 12 the number had dwindled to 50.[49] Probably Moritake was waiting for all of them to die of disease and starvation; the journey to Ranau would then be easier for the remaining soldiers and guards. A few days before July 12, Moritake received an order from Takakuwa to leave for Ranau as soon as possible and to dispose of the POWs along the way.[50] Takakuwa was concerned for the safety of his men because most of the Japanese fighting forces had left the Sandakan area by that time. Moritake selected 23 POWs he considered relatively healthy. He believed the deaths of the other 27 were imminent. Rather than take these 23 POWs on the march, Moritake decided to execute them immediately.

At this time Moritake was suffering from malaria so passed the task of executing the POWs to Staff Sergeant Murozumi Hisao. Moritake ordered Murozumi to take the men to an air-raid shelter trench near the airfield and to shoot them. On July 13, at around 6:00 P.M., 12 Formosan guards took the 23 men to the airfield, where they were lined up beside the trench and shot. Many of the Formosan guards objected to Murozumi's order, but he threatened to shoot them too if they disobeyed. Murozumi even had a pistol aimed at the Formosan guards while they shot the prisoners. After all of the prisoners were shot, their bodies were thrown into the trench and buried.[51]

Moritake died of malaria on July 17, and Murozumi took charge at Sandakan. However, some of the 27 men Moritake had expected to die survived him. Murozumi testified at the War Crimes Tribunal that the last two of these men died on August 14 or 15.[52] Murozumi's testimony is, however, questionable, as will become apparent later.

Meanwhile in Ranau at the end of June there were 189 POWs who had survived the marches from Sandakan, 6 from the first march and 183 from the second. Just before the 6 survivors of the first march joined the survivors of the second, another 10 survivors of the first march had been shot.[53] By this time every surviving POW was suffering from severe malnutrition and tropical disease. Another 19 men who had survived the second march died within a few days of arriving in Ranau.[54] Food supplies in Ranau were meager; prisoners had 70–75 grams of rice per day and almost no meat or vegetables. The POWs were given no rest after arriving in Ranau in order to recover. They were immediately put to work building thatched huts for the Japanese officers as well as for themselves. Takakuwa decided to set up a "POW camp" in the jungle 10 kilometers from Ranau, as Ranau had also been bombed by the Allies. The POWs were again used as labor for this task and for carrying provisions from the camp at Ranau to the new camp in the jungle. Carrying 20-kilogram food bags through the jungle, often several times over, took its toll on the POWs, and yet more of them died as a consequence. Other POWs were given the task of carrying water from a stream in the valley below the jungle camp. Those who fell while climbing the hill or spilled water were beaten by the guards, and many died as a result.[55]

At around 5:00 P.M. on July 4 a Formosan guard called "Nakamura" suddenly entered the hut in which four Japanese officers, including Takakuwa, were housed. He fired shots at them and threw a hand grenade before turning his gun on himself. The hand grenade did not explode, but one of the officers, Second Lieutenant Suzuki, died, and Takakuwa and an unnamed NCO were injured. Nakamura evidently could no longer bear the ill-treatment dealt out to the Formosan guards by the Japanese officers. A few days before, he had been severely beaten by Takakuwa for not cleaning his gun. On the following day, Second Lieutenant Watanabe, on Takakuwa's orders, assembled all of the Formosan guards and berated them for over 40 minutes. The brutality of the guards toward the POWs increased as a result.[56]

A few days before Nakamura attacked the officers and then committed suicide, he told William Stiepewich that Takakuwa was planning to kill all of the POWs in the near future. About the same time, Keith Botterill was informed by other guards of Takakuwa's plans and told by them to run away as soon as possible. Stiepewich did not decide to run away at this stage, but Botterill, Moxham, Short, and Anderson escaped from the camp on July 7. Anderson died while they were on the run in the jungle; the other three made contact with an Australian soldier, a member of a reconnaissance party, with the help of local people on August 1. Because of their poor physical condition, the men were unable to join the reconnaissance party and march to the Australian front line at Merinsau, north of Ranau. They were forced to remain in hiding in the jungle in a hut some of the local people built for them. Before they were finally rescued in mid-August, they had a number of close shaves with the Japanese.[57]

On July 7 when the Botterill group escaped, there were about 100 other POWs still alive. The building of the jungle camp was completed on July 18, and the 72 surviving POWs, who until then had been camped in the open air, were moved into a single hut, 9 meters long and 5 meters wide, with a thatched roof and raised floor but no walls. The POWs suffering from dysentery had to sleep on the ground underneath the floor of this hut. There were 38 POWs housed on the floor and 34 below it. Even those not suffering from dysentery were very weak, so nobody was able to give a proper burial to those who died each day. Even the strongest of the men could do no more than drag the bodies of the dead to the graveyard and cover them in dirt. On July 20 the POWs officially ceased work, although by this stage none of them would have been capable of working anyway.[58]

Thus the new Ranau POW camp was in reality little more than a hiding place for Takakuwa and his men. It seems that Takakuwa exploited the POWs' labor to set up a hiding place for himself and his men with the full intention of killing the prisoners as soon as the work was completed. On July 26 William Stiepewich was told by a guard about a plan to dispose of all POWs, and he then decided it was time to make his escape. On the following day the number of guards around the POWs' hut was doubled. Stiepewich discussed his plan to escape with others, but few were physically capable by this time. On the night of July 28, Stiepewich and another man, Reither, managed to escape into the jungle. They met up with local people who hid them away, but Reither died on August 1. Stiepewich was rescued by the Australian forces in mid-August.[59]

These four survivors of the two escapes from the jungle camp near Ranau account for most of the survivors of the Sandakan camp. There were two others, Campbell and Braithwaite, who on separate occasions ran into the jungle during the second march to Ranau and managed to survive. They were later rescued by U.S. forces, again with the help of local people.

There were 38 POWs remaining in the camp after Stiepewich and Reither escaped. Of these, 12 could just walk, but the others were incapable of moving and 8 of them were comatose.[60] On the morning of August 1, Takakuwa decided to kill all of the remaining POWs. There were 33 prisoners still alive then. Takakuwa gathered all the NCOs and ordered them to kill all the prisoners, giving instructions as to how the prisoners should be killed in each case. He divided the 33 POWs into three groups. The task of disposing of the 17 POWs who were most ill was given to Lieutenant Watanabe Genzō and Sergeant Okada. Nine guards were assigned to shoot these POWs at the graveyard. Two of these 17 men could walk; the others were made to crawl or were carried by the guards on stretchers. Two large holes had been dug at the graveyard, and the prisoners were laid down at the edge of them, then shot all at once and their bodies thrown in. Sergeant Tsuji was given the task of disposing of 11 POWs who could still walk. He, together with 12 guards, took these POWs about 500 meters into the jungle and told them they were about to be shot. They were each given a cigarette, then taken away one at a time and shot. Their bodies were dumped in a single large hole. The remaining

5 POWs were 2 officers and 3 military doctors. Sergeant Beppu and 8 guards were given the task of killing them. They were taken into the jungle and shot, then buried in two holes. All of this occurred between 10:00 A.M. and 1:00 P.M. on August 1.[61]

The events described so far in this chapter have been reconstructed from documents prepared by Australian military authorities for the War Crimes Tribunal and from the proceedings of the tribunal. The tribunal completed its hearings concerning the Sandakan death marches by May 1946, by which time the entire picture seemed clear. However, almost a year later, in April 1947, a new witness appeared. He was a Chinese boy named Wong Hiong, who was a cook for the Japanese and Taiwanese staff at Sandakan between October 1944 and August 1945. At the time he gave evidence, Hiong was only 19 years old. Hiong had been unable to tell his story for so long because the events he had witnessed were so horrific. It is not precisely clear when the events recounted by Hiong happened, but it is likely that they occurred sometime between early June 1945, when the second march left Sandakan, and early July, when Moritake died.

According to Hiong's testimony, early one morning, while walking back from the latrines, he saw a prisoner being dragged away by two guards, "Hinata" and "Fukuta." An officer Hiong called "Moditake" followed them, carrying a hammer in his hand. There was no guard called Hinata at Sandakan at this time. A guard called Hinata had been at Sandakan previously but had left. Hiong probably confused Hinata with a guard called Hirota, who was at Sandakan at the time. Presumably, the man Hiong called Fukuta was a guard called Fukuda Nobuo, and the man he called Moditake was Moritake. Hiong followed behind secretly and hid under an unused hut that had not been burned down. He saw the POW dragged over to a large timber cross about 80 meters away from where he was hiding. The following is Hiong's testimony:

The prisoner was made to stand with his back to the cross and was supported in this position by Hinata. I then heard the Jap officer give a shout, whereupon a Jap soldier by name Nishikawa emerged from the administration office carrying a stool and a knife with a blade about 8" long. Nishikawa took the stool and knife to the Jap officer who was standing near the cross with the prisoner. Nishikawa then returned to the office.

The Jap officer then stood on the stool with the hammer in his right hand. He then raised the prisoner's left arm and driving a nail through the palm of the left hand fixed it to the left arm of the cross which was the height of the prisoner's shoulders. When the officer commenced to pierce the palm of the prisoner's left hand with a nail the prisoner tried to wriggle and scream, whereupon Hinata held the body of the prisoner against the upright post of the cross and put a piece of cloth into the prisoner's mouth. The Jap officer then placed the stool towards the prisoner's right and nailed the prisoner's right hand to the cross in the same manner by standing on the stool. He then put the stool aside and nailed both of the feet of the prisoner with two nails to a horizontal wooden board on which the prisoner was standing. Thereafter the Jap officer again stood on the stool and fixed the prisoner's head to the cross by driving a large sized nail through the prisoner's forehead. The Jap officer then took the knife and first cut a piece of flesh from the left side of the prisoner's stomach and placed the flesh on a wooden board nearby. He then cut another piece of flesh from the right side of the prisoner's stomach and also placed it on the board. He then put a rubber glove on his right hand and pulled out the intestines of the prisoner which were also placed on the board. Taking the knife again, the officer then proceeded to cut bits of flesh from the prisoner's left and right thighs, both arms and neck, all of which were placed on the same wooden board.[62]

About half an hour later, Nishikawa brought two more prisoners to this place. Moritake ordered them to carry back to the camp the board on which the remains of the crucified prisoner had been placed. The prisoners were lined up in the parade ground, and Moritake told them something (which Hiong was unable to hear from his hiding place) while gesturing to the remains on the wooden board. The body of the POW who had been crucified was left to rot on the cross until just before the remaining staff left for Ranau, at which time they burned down the cross.[63]

Why did such a brutal murder happen? Hiong testified about another incident that seems to be closely linked with this murder. According to Hiong's testimony, the staff had many pigs at the time, intended for their own consumption. One day Nishikawa realized that one of the pigs was missing. He looked for the missing pig without success, but eventually found pork in the bowls of some of the prisoners. One of the prisoners confessed under interrogation that he had stolen the pig and cooked it. This incident happened sometime soon before the crucifixion occurred.[64] It is known that there was very little food left for the prisoners remaining in the camp after the second march departed, so taking the pig would have been a desperate measure by this man to keep himself and his comrades fed. Moritake, who was informed by Nishikawa of the theft of the pig, evidently decided to execute the POW as an example to the others. Moritake most probably told the assembled prisoners after the crucifixion that if they stole pigs to eat, they too would end up as meat.

How could Moritake have done such a thing? As has been explained previously, Moritake traveled to Kimanshi to explain how difficult it would be to transfer all prisoners to Ranau. It is probable that he returned to Sandakan with strict orders to remove all prisoners to Ranau. On the way back to Sandakan, Moritake lost his junior, a prison guard, to malaria. Moritake himself was suffering from malaria at the time he returned and was in a state of exhaustion. In addition, there were virtually no Japanese forces remaining in the Sandakan area, and Moritake must have felt an overwhelming fear about his impending death. His psychological state at the time almost certainly contributed to his inhumane conduct.

Moritake's probable psychological condition was by no means peculiar to him. Toward the end of the war, at both Sandakan and Ranau, Japanese officers and Formosan guards viciously beat prisoners daily for the most trivial of offenses. For ordinary people in ordinary situations, it is extremely difficult to comprehend such behavior as beating sick and starving prisoners. The guards and officers, however, were not in an ordinary situation: They had been ordered to fight until the end, even though most of the Japanese armed forces had been routed by this time and the situation seemed hopeless. Therefore these men were doubtless experiencing such intense frustration that they had no means other than violence to release it. This violence was directed toward a concrete "enemy," the prisoners, seen by the Japanese and Formosans as the real cause of their frustrations. In this situation, no matter how weak and ill the prisoners were, they were bound to be treated as threatening enemies. It seems that the Japanese and Formosans were able to gain some release from fear of their own deaths by killing others. Therefore, the deeper the fear they were experiencing, the more brutally they would act toward others. Moritake's extraordinarily brutal act was thus that of a man who was in an extraordinary situation and had been for a long time.

The POW who was crucified was probably a British marine officer, given Hiong's description. However, by the time this incident came to the attention of the authorities, Moritake was already dead and Hirota and Fukuda had both returned to Taiwan, as they were not known to have been involved in any other crimes against POWs and had not been put on trial. Nishikawa was in prison at that time, serving a 12-year sentence for his involvement in the massacre of POWs at Sandakan airfield. He was interrogated but denied that the incident had ever happened. Other prison guards who were known to have been at Sandakan at the time of the crucifixion and were subsequently imprisoned for war crimes were interrogated and also denied that such an event had ever happened.

However, in August 1947 the graveyard unit of the Australian forces dug up the spot where Hiong claimed the cross had been. They found human remains, some wire, four nails 15 centimeters long, and four 7.5 centimeters long. The human remains were too decomposed to provide any evidence of crucifixion, so only the existence of the nails provides substantial verification of Hiong's testimony.[65]

Hiong also claimed that there was another murder of a POW that had not previously been brought to the attention of the tribunal. This was the murder of the last remaining prisoner at Sandakan, who was killed on either August 14 or 15, 1945. At the Labuan War Crimes Tribunal in January 1946, Murozumi testified that the 27 POWs who had not been massacred on July 13 all died, one after another, of illness and starvation between then and August 15. Hiong's testimony, however, differs from Murozumi's:

[After the second march departed] the PW camp was then burned down by the Japs. There were only 28 PW alive after the 23 were shot. Twenty-seven of them died through sickness, starvation and exposure. The PW slept under a shelter of blankets on sticks in the open. The one surviving PW came from No 3 Camp (Aust). His legs were covered in ulcers. He was a tall dark man with a long face and was naked except for a loin cloth.

One morning at 7 am I saw him taken to a place where there was a trench like a drain. I climbed up a rubber tree and saw what happened. Mirojumi was with the man and fifteen Japs with spades were already at the spot. Mirojumi made the man kneel down and tied a black cloth over his eyes. He did not say anything or make any protest. He was so weak that his hands were not tied. Mirojumi cut his head off with one sword stroke. Mirojumi pushed the body into the drain with his feet. The head dropped into the drain. The other Japs threw in some dirt, covered the remains and returned to the camp. The Japs went away the next day and that was the finish of my job.[66]

The man Hiong called Mirojumi was doubtless Murozumi. Whereas Murozumi testified that there were 27 remaining POWs after the massacre at the airfield, Hiong testified that there were 28. It is possible that Murozumi testified there were 27 in an attempt to hide the fact that he had murdered the last remaining POW. The Australian graveyard unit also dug up the site where Hiong claimed that this POW was murdered and found a body with the skull situated between the thigh and shin bones.[67] This strongly suggests that the head had been cut off before the body was buried. Murozumi was already serving a life sentence at Rabaul. He was interrogated about the incident but denied that it had happened. Some prison guards who were serving sentences at that time were also interrogated. They also denied that the murder alleged by Hiong had taken place.[68]

Hiong was thus the only witness who testified to the two murders. Other local people had been employed at the Sandakan camp, but all of them had been told not to go anywhere near the POWs and were threatened with being shot if they disobeyed. Therefore none of them ventured near POWs unless they were specifically instructed to do so.[69] About 130 pages of documents were prepared by the War Crimes Section of the Australian military concerning these two incidents, but there is no evidence of any prosecutions as a result of the preliminary investigations. It is presumed that the Australians decided not to prosecute any Japanese or Taiwanese for these crimes because, in the first case, Moritake was already dead and, in the second case, Murozumi was already serving a life sentence. With only one witness and relatively little forensic evidence, the cases might well have been considered too weak to make successful prosecution a likely outcome.

## Responsibility for Maltreatment and Massacre of POWs

At the B and C Class war crimes tribunal, Captain Hoshijima Susumu, who was commandant at Sandakan until May 1945, was sentenced to death by hanging. He was found guilty of ordering the ill-treatment of POWs, thus causing their deaths, as well as forcing sick POWs to work at the airfield and failing to provide sufficient food and medicine for them. Captain Yamamoto Shōichi, the officer in charge of the first march, was sentenced to death by hanging because he had ordered the murder of POWs. All nine officers responsible for each group in the first march were sentenced to death. In the end, only Lieutenant Abe, who was responsible for the rear group of the first march, was executed by firing squad. The other eight had their sentences commuted to terms of imprisonment. Captain Takakuwa Takuo, who was in charge of the second march and ordered the shooting of POWs, and his immediate junior, Lieutenant Watanabe Genzō, were both sentenced to death, Takakuwa by hanging and Watanabe by firing squad. Staff Sergeant Murozumi Hisao was sentenced to life imprisonment for carrying out the execution of 23 POWs at Sandakan airfield under the orders of Lieutenant Moritake. Most Formosan prison guards received sentences of between 12 and 15 years for their roles in the ill-treatment and execution of prisoners; only four of them received death sentences.[70]

Colonel Suga Tatsuji, who was the chief commandant of all Borneo POW camps, never went to trial. He committed suicide on September 16, 1945, at the Labuan POW camp, where the Allies were holding Japanese POWs. Colonel Suga was apparently a good-natured man, who evidently showed more respect for the rights of POWs than did his junior officers. However, Suga's indirect role in the ill-treatment of POWs in Borneo would probably have earned him a death sentence. Suga gave orders to Hoshijima and Takakuwa to put prisoners to work on the airfield, to reduce their rations, and to remove them from Sandakan to Ranau. However, these orders would have originated with 37th Army commanders, so Suga was conveying these orders rather than formulating them. Nonetheless, even in conveying these orders, Suga was culpable and must bear a share of the responsibility for the war crimes against POWs that occurred in Borneo. The responsibility of Suga and others for war crimes must, however, be understood in the context of the Japanese military system, which required absolute obedience to those higher in the chain of command.

The Australian War Crimes Section found that the orders to commit criminal acts originated from the 37th Army command, then were conveyed through POW headquarters at Kuching to Sandakan. Thus the War Crimes Section concurred that responsibility for war crimes principally lay at the highest levels of the chain of command. Lieutenant General Baba Masarō, who was commanding officer at 37th Army headquarters when the war ended, was sentenced to death by hanging for giving the orders for the Sandakan death marches.[71] Baba's role in ordering the second march was regarded by the tribunal as his most serious crime because he knew of the deaths that occurred in the first march and thus the likely fate of the second one. In addition, in mid-April 1945, Baba had sent Colonel Takayama Hikoichi to Sandakan to investigate the physical condition of the POWs.[72] Unless Takayama made a false report, which is unlikely, Baba should have known that the prisoners were in even poorer condition than those who had undertaken the first march and that it would be all but impossible for them to undertake the 260-kilometer march. As soon as he realized that Takakuwa had not taken all prisoners from Sandakan, Baba ordered that the remaining POWs be removed. Because 75 prisoners were made to march following this order and all of them died or were shot within a few days, Baba clearly bore considerable responsibility for the deaths of these men. All evidence shows that the 37th Army commanders were committed to removing all prisoners from Sandakan, regardless of how this was achieved. What was the real intention of those at the top of the chain of command?

The 37th Army commanders seem to have been attempting to remove all evidence of the existence of the Sandakan camp in order to prevent the Allies from learning about the atrocities that occurred there. This would explain why they were so persistent in giving orders to remove all POWs from the camp and also in ordering that no POWs be allowed to fall behind in the marches. Knowing that many of the POWs could not possibly survive the march from Sandakan to Ranau, the officers must have intended to dispose of all the POWs, although one would expect such plans to remain secret. The marches were a pretext for carrying out these plans. The cutting of rations and the order to remove the POW sign from the Sandakan parade ground are also consistent with such plans. It is possible that the plans to dispose of all POWs existed, at least in a vague form, as far back as late 1944 when Allied air raids on Sandakan began. As time passed and the war turned further against the Japanese, the plans probably became more clearly formulated.

Indeed, according to Yamada Masaharu, a former staff officer at Kuching headquarters who conveyed the orders to Yamamoto and Takakuwa to remove the POWs from Sandakan, the officers at headquarters were aware that considerable numbers of POWs would die and some of them would have to be disposed of. But they expected that the officers and soldiers who were given the task of removing the POWs would dispose of them even though there were no such instructions from headquarters.[73]

In an interview, Yamada also claimed that the order to move Japanese forces and POWs from the east coast to the west coast of North Borneo did not originate from 37th Army commanders but from Imperial Headquarters in Tokyo, in October 1944. He was critical that this decision was made by young staff officers at Imperial Headquarters who were familiar only with the geographical conditions of Manchukuo and knew nothing about the situation in North Borneo. He also argued that the officers in Kuching, including Commander Yamawaki and the chief of staff, Manaki, were strongly against such a plan.[74] However, it is doubtful the Kuching officers understood how difficult it was for their own soldiers and POWs to march through dense jungle and steep mountains with extremely meager provisions and within a limited period of time.

The officers' strict and insistent orders to eight of the 10 battalions and POWs to undertake the east-west march caused a tragedy not only for the POWs but also for the Japanese forces. During this march, about 8,500 Japanese soldiers perished in the jungle of North Borneo. Deaths were particularly high among the Okumura Battalion, which was forced to make an 800-kilometer return trip from Api to Sandakan because of mismanagement of the operational plans by staff in Kuching, and the Iemura Battalion, which was forced to walk 600 kilometers from Tawao to Api. The Okumura battalion lost 889 out of 1,025 members, and the Iemura Battalion lost 1,226 of its 2,150-strong force. The fact that only half of the soldiers who reached the west coast still had the strength to carry their own rifles clearly indicates the degree of the difficulty of this march.[75]

Thus it is unfair to place responsibility for the war crimes at Sandakan as well as for a large number of deaths of the Japanese soldiers entirely on the shoulders of Lieutenant General Baba Masarō, the commander of the 37th Army at the end of the war. Baba was posted to this position in December 1944. A new chief of staff, Major General Kuroda Shigeru, was also posted at this time. Prior to being sent to Kuching, Baba was commander of the Fourth Division of the Japanese Army. He did not arrive in Kuching until January 21, 1945. Until that time Lieutenant General

Yamawaki Masataka was in command at Kuching, and Major General Manaki Takanobu was chief of staff of the 37th Army.[76] These men, not Baba, decided to transfer most Japanese troops from the east coast of North Borneo to the west coast and to use POW labor for that purpose. Indeed, Yamawaki was in command when the order for the first march was given. It was also the decision of Yamawaki and Manaki to remove the POW sign from Sandakan and to reduce POWs' rations dramatically in June 1944.

Lieutenant Colonel Douglas MacBain of the Australian War Crimes Section was clearly aware that Yamawaki and Manaki, rather than Baba and Kuroda, had issued these orders. MacBain therefore recommended that Colonel Takayama Hikoichi and Lieutenant Colonel Iwahashi Manabu be interrogated to determine the role of Yamawaki and Manaki in the Sandakan war crimes.[77] However, there is no evidence that Takayama and Iwahashi were actually interrogated or that Yamawaki was tried for the Sandakan death marches. It is not clear why Yamawaki was not tried for these crimes. Similarly, it is unclear why the War Crimes Tribunal found him not guilty of illegally executing prisoners following the Sandakan incident. As has been mentioned previously, the tribunal proceedings concerning the Sandakan incident were permanently suppressed (although Freedom of Information legislation enacted in 1977 in Australia subsequently made them available to the public). It may well be that there is a connection between decisions made about Yamawaki's role in the Sandakan incident and his role in later war crimes. If Yamawaki was to be tried for these later crimes, doubt might be cast on the tribunal's findings concerning the Sandakan incident. Thus, Yamawaki, who arguably had the most personal responsibility for the Sandakan war crimes, was tried only for the Sandakan incident; his juniors who carried out his orders, Hoshijima, Yamamoto, and Takakuwa, were all tried and later executed.

## Japanese POW Policy

Responsibility for these crimes cannot be seen solely in individual terms. Individuals were always acting within the context of Japanese POW policy, which was not in accord with the Geneva Convention. Therefore it is necessary to examine the POW policies of the Japanese military. According to the proceedings of the Tokyo War Crimes Tribunal, there were 132,134 Allied POWs held by the Japanese during World War II. Of these, 35,756 died, a death rate of 27 percent. By way of contrast, the German and Italian forces held 235,473 Allied POWs and 9,348 of them died, a death rate of 4 percent.[78] Clearly the death rate of POWs held by the

Japanese was extremely high. According to Australian figures, of 22,376 Australian POWs held by the Japanese, 8,031 died, a death rate of 36 percent.[79] That more than a third of the Australians in Japanese hands died shows how badly the Japanese treated POWs. Therefore it is not surprising that 73 percent of Japanese POWs who were tried by the B and C Class war crimes tribunals were tried concerning crimes committed against POWs (for murder, ill-treatment, and theft of POWs' personal effects).[80] As was mentioned in the previous chapter, at the outbreak of hostilities, Japanese forces informed Allied nations that they would apply the Geneva Convention, even though they had not ratified it. Within a year, however, they implemented plans to exploit POWs for military labor, even though this contravened the convention. The Japanese forces effectively treated POWs as equivalent to military supplies, in much the same way as they treated the "comfort women." The crimes committed against the Sandakan POWs were thus by no means peculiar to the 37th Army. They are but one example of systematic ill-treatment of POWs by the Japanese military.

Immediately after Japan surrendered to the Allies, the Japanese Ministry for the Army instructed those in charge of POW camps to destroy all documents. The ministry destroyed all important documents it held as well as those held by the POW Information Bureau (which was set up, in accordance with the Geneva Convention, for the purpose of information exchange with the Allies).[81] The documents concerning the comfort women were also destroyed at this time. The ministry must have been acutely aware of its responsibility for the treatment of POWs and comfort women. The leaders of the military forces attempted to cover up their responsibility by destroying documents and also tried to put the blame on Korean and Formosan guards whenever possible. For example, about a month after surrender, on September 17, 1945, the minister for the army, Shimomura Sadashi, conveyed a message to all relevant battalions to instruct their men to tell interrogators that ill-treatment of POWs happened because of language and cultural problems as well as the structural problem created by using Koreans and Formosans as prison camp guards.[82] Thus the exploitation of Koreans and Formosans by the Japanese continued even after their defeat.

In some cases the Japanese may have planned to massacre prison guards as well as POWs. According to the memoirs of a Korean prison guard, Hon Jun-Muk, from the No. 4 POW camp on the Burma-Thailand railway, all 800 Korean guards in the region were gathered at a place called Songraburi in the mountains under the pretense of assembling a suicide force for a last-ditch battle against the Allies. In fact, according to Hon Jun-Muk, the Japanese were intending to execute these men. The

Koreans were to be gathered in a dugout and explosives thrown into it. At the last moment an order came from headquarters preventing the massacre.[83]

At this point I briefly consider the broader context of military policy on prisoners of war and the changes that occurred in policy in the period leading up to the Asia-Pacific War. I then examine the psychology of cruelty and how individual acts of cruelty toward prisoners of war took place within a context of military policy that did much to encourage them.

The most important historical lesson to learn is that the Japanese armed forces have not always acted toward their prisoners in a brutal manner. Their attitude was much harsher during the Asia-Pacific War than it had been at previous times.

The first war waged by the modern Japanese state was the Sino-Japanese War of August 1894 to April 1895. The Imperial Proclamation of War clearly stated that Japanese soldiers should make every effort to win the war without violating international law. Indeed, the Japanese forces immediately released all 1,790 Chinese prisoners after demanding they sign an agreement not to take up arms against the Japanese state again. Upon signing this agreement, the prisoners were released on the battlefield without first being held in detention camps. At the time, the Brussels Declaration, which was signed by 12 European nations, was the only international agreement governing humane treatment of POWs. Japan was not a signatory, but it did make an effort to abide by the declaration.[84]

In the Russo-Japanese War, which was waged between September 1904 and February 1905, Japanese POW policy was based on the Regulation Respecting the Laws and Customs of War on Land (a precursor of the Hague Convention). The Japanese government this time made an even greater effort to comply with international law than it had during the Sino-Japanese War. At Imperial Headquarters, law scholars and diplomats advised the military in the application of international law. At each army command office, a law scholar specializing in international law was employed as an adviser. Immediately after the outbreak of the war, the army produced regulations concerning the treatment of POWs. Article two of these regulations clearly stated that POWs must be treated altruistically and should not be despised or ill-treated. The Japanese military wisely assumed that there would be language and cultural problems with Russian prisoners and therefore produced an information pamphlet in Russian. During the war 79,367 Russians were taken prisoner. They were detained in 29 POW camps throughout Japan and were well treated. Russian officers at the Kanazawa camp were even taken to an inn for entertainment. The Hague Convention was later to stipulate that POWs should be paid a salary equivalent to that of soldiers of the same rank in the forces of the country that was holding them. During the Russo-Japanese War, the Russian prisoners were paid double the amount paid to Japanese soldiers. After the war ended, all of the POWs were safely returned to Russia.[85]

In World War I, Japan maintained its policy of humane treatment of POWs. Japan declared war against Germany in accordance with the Anglo-Japanese alliance and sent 50,000 soldiers to Tsingtao, which then was a German colony. The Japanese captured 4,600 German soldiers, who were taken to Japan and held there from 1919 until 1920. These prisoners were also well treated and even developed friendships with the local people, in particular through their musical activities. These POWs formed an orchestra with some local Japanese amateur musicians in Bandō, Shikoku Island, where the camp was set up. The favorite music played by this orchestra was Beethoven's Symphony no. 9, which later became one of the most popular pieces of classical music in Japan and now is played throughout the country toward the end of each year. Another legacy left by these German POWs was bread making and beer brewing, traditions that were also adopted by the locals in Shikoku.[86]

However, over the next decade or so, the attitude of the Japanese government toward international law changed dramatically. In July 1929 Japan signed the Geneva Convention, but when the ratification period elapsed in 1934, military leaders were strongly against ratification, primarily because they did not expect Japanese forces to surrender and become POWs of foreign forces.[87] For the Japanese forces, to be taken prisoner was shameful, and it was expected that soldiers would commit suicide rather than surrender. This creed was first formulated by Lieutenant General Yamagata Aritomo during the 1894–1895 Sino-Japanese War.[88] As the Japanese military leaders saw it in 1934, ratification of the Geneva Convention would place obligations on Japan but bring nothing in return to members of its forces, as they should never become prisoners of war. However, there must have been more to the thinking of Japanese military leaders at this time. Although the Japanese military forces treated their own men very harshly and the creed that being taken prisoner was shameful was a long-standing one, Japan had clearly treated POWs very well in the wars it fought prior to the 1920s. Further, Japan had ratified the Hague Convention in 1912.

In 1937, in order to cover up the fact that it had unlawfully invaded China, the Japanese military referred to the invasion as the "China Incident" (a somewhat similar situation to U.S. involvement in the Vietnam War in that the United States never officially declared war on North Vietnam). The Japanese argued that because they were not waging a war, they did not need to obey international law in their treatment of Chinese prisoners.[89] In the Imperial Proclamation of the Pacific War, issued on

December 8, 1941 (December 7 in the United States), Japan did not refer to international law in any respect, unlike during the Sino-Japanese War and the Russo-Japanese War when it was clearly stated that Japan would abide by international law.

This background is needed in order to interpret individual acts of cruelty toward prisoners of war. I shall now turn to the psychology of cruelty and how the broader social setting helped make individual acts of cruelty possible.

## The Psychology of Cruelty

The ill-treatment and massacres of POWs at Sandakan and the Sandakan death marches were made possible in large part by the new Japanese military ideology and the training procedures that arose from it. Men were trained to follow orders habitually and unquestioningly, and the training evidently worked. Captain Yamamoto Shōichi and Captain Takakuwa Takuo apparently never questioned the orders they were given by their superiors. Their primary concern was how they could carry out their orders, and this thinking led them to commit war crimes. It is insufficient to attribute responsibility to these individuals, however, without placing their behavior within the context of Japanese military ideology.

I am not suggesting we should place the cause of Japanese war crimes with Japanese military ideology alone. According to research conducted by John Dower, during the course of the Pacific War, the Allied forces became increasingly less likely to take Japanese soldiers prisoner. Eventually, the Japanese effectively had no choice but to fight to the death. Soon after the outbreak of the war, the unofficial principles of the Allies were no mercy, no surrender, and no POWs. The military ideology of the Allies thus also reflected brutalization. There was doubtless an element of revenge against the increasing brutality of the Allies in the ill-treatment of POWs by the Japanese. In the early stages of the Pacific War, the Allied forces had humiliating experiences with mass surrenders of their troops, especially in the Philippines and Singapore. However, after these initial mass surrenders, there were very few voluntary surrenders of either Allied or Japanese troops. As Dower put it, the Pacific War rapidly became a war in which one could either kill or be killed. Therefore the decision to surrender and live or to fight on and die rapidly became a meaningless one.[90]

It should be noted too that routine obedience to orders is hardly unique to the Japanese military during World War II. Obedience to orders has been a primary principle of virtually all armed forces at all times. Therefore the attitudes of blindly obeying superiors and despising prisoners do not seem sufficient in themselves to explain why the Japanese committed such horrific war crimes against POWs. The Nazis made very similar demands for obedience from their men, who readily committed mass murders against Jews, Gypsies, and other groups they despised. The Nazis rarely, however, massacred POWs, although there is no doubt that they treated them harshly. It should also be noted that the Allies were not immune from ill-treating POWs. According to research, the Allied occupation forces treated German POWs more harshly in the period immediately after the Allied victory than the Germans had treated Allied POWs during the war. For instance, at the Remargen POW camp in the Rhine valley, around 150,000 German POWs were held in the open air, without sufficient food and water, for a long period. As a result of their harsh treatment, 1,200 of these men died from disease and malnutrition within the first few months. It has been claimed that 50,000 POWs died throughout Germany from malnutrition and disease.[91]

There have also been numerous reports of Australian military forces mistreating Japanese POWs. At Torokina on Bougainville Island, in the Southwest Pacific, 4,500 Japanese soldiers were held for a few months prior to repatriation. According to some sources, they were given inadequate rations and no medicine during this period, and as a result, 1,000 of them died, mostly of malaria. Suspected war criminals among the prisoners were given 40 percent lower rations than the other men and were made to do heavy labor, often into the night.[92] Violence against Japanese prisoners was common everywhere. Another source revealed that a group of Japanese soldiers at Torokina were marched at bayonet point for three and a half hours in the midday sun—a revenge act for the Sandakan death marches. Three of these men died as a result, and a large number received bayonet wounds.[93] At Labuan in Borneo, Murozumi Hisao (who was at the time being interrogated about the execution of the last remaining POWs at Sandakan—a crime for which he was later given a life sentence) was constantly bashed and kicked by his captors and was made to sleep without a blanket or mosquito net. He became critically ill as a result.[94] Many other Japanese POWs have made similar claims, especially those who were held by Soviet forces in Siberia.[95]

There have been more recent examples of ill-treatment of POWs. In the 1990 Gulf War, the Iraqis coerced Allied POWs into appearing on television denouncing the conduct of the Allied nations. In the Balkans conflict, prisoners have been held in appalling conditions that match anything meted out during World War II; indeed, certain militias have even openly claimed that they do not take prisoners and that they kill all captured enemies instead. These examples show that ill-treatment of POWs occurs in many different societies. To explain Japanese ill-treatment of POWs by focusing only on what was peculiar to Japanese society during World War II is not only to exaggerate that peculiarity but also to ignore important causes that cross national and cultural boundaries. The focus instead should be on universal questions about why *any* soldiers could be capable of ill-treating and massacring POWs.

Why do soldiers ill-treat POWs who obviously have little or no means to fight back against their captors? Why do ordinary men with ordinary lives, including loved ones they care for, become capable of such brutality when they become soldiers? In ordinary life these men would be incapable of killing animals let alone other people. Everything changes, however, when certain other people become enemies. John Dower cast some light on how this happens:

The dehumanisation of the Other contributed immensely to the psychological distancing that facilitates killing, not only on the battlefield but also in the plans adopted by strategists far removed from the actual scene of combat. Such dehumanisation, for example, surely facilitated the decisions to make civilian populations the targets of concentrated attack, whether by conventional or nuclear weapons. In countless ways, war words and race words came together in a manner which did not just reflect the savagery of the war, but contributed to it by reinforcing the impression of a truly Manichaean struggle between completely incompatible antagonists. The natural response to such a vision was an obsession with extermination on both sides—a war without mercy.[96]

War is inevitably accompanied by ideologies that thoroughly dehumanize the enemy. Those on the battlefield are usually in situations where they must kill or be killed. The enemy is seen as brutal in order to be capable of posing such a threat. For those on both sides, it is all but impossible to see the enemy as anything other than brutal and inhuman. Thus, what Dower called the struggle between completely incompatible antagonists develops very quickly. Because of this dichotomy, hatred toward the enemy results in brutal actions toward the enemy, with the consequent retaliation serving to further that hatred in a vicious circle. This explains how brutality on both sides usually escalates rapidly after war breaks out. A striking example of this process can be seen in the Balkans conflict, in which Serbs, Croats, and Moslems, who had for many years coexisted peacefully in the same villages, suddenly became capable of unbridled cruelty to each other.

Once both sides become trapped in this vicious circle of dehumanization, even those who pose no real threat, such as POWs, are a target for hatred because they are identifiable as the enemy and thus as a "psychological" threat. Dehumanization involves a psychological distancing process whereby it becomes possible to act aggressively toward a weaker person without feeling the remorse that would occur in more normal circumstances. Unless soldiers have a real commitment to a moral code that demands respect for one's opponents, such as *bushidō* (which I shall discuss in the Conclusion) or chivalry, or have strong religious beliefs that make the same demand, they are all too easily trapped into dehumanizing their enemies and acting brutally toward them.

When dehumanization of the enemy reaches its extremes, normally unthinkable acts such as the massacre of POWs become possible. In the situation at Sandakan, the Japanese believed they were under such threat from an Allied invasion that there was no hope for them; they were destined to dehumanize prisoners and act brutally toward them.

Robert Lifton noted that U.S. forces in Vietnam also fell prey to the feeling that the situation was hopeless. This led them to what Lifton called a "malignant obsession" with the numbers of Viet Cong killed and even to falsify figures in a vain attempt to hold on to the illusion of a "noble battle."[97] At Sandakan the enemy bodies that could be counted were those of dead prisoners rather than enemy combatants, but the officers at Sandakan shared the same malignant obsession with counting the dead. The Japanese, partly out of the overwhelming anxiety that they were about to meet their own deaths, felt driven to kill prisoners and then, perversely, were able to use the numbers of dead to reduce their anxiety.

Extreme violence can provide an instant and apparently total solution to the psychological pressure of fear. As war situations become yet more complicated, soldiers become ever more reliant on violence as a way of coping. This response can be clearly seen in the testimony of a U.S. Vietnam veteran:

As anyone who has fired a bazooka or an M60 machine gun knows, there is something to that power in your finger, the soft, seductive touch of the trigger. It's like the magic sword, a grunt's Excalibur: all you do is move that finger so imperceptibly, just a wish flashing across your mind like a shadow, not even a full brain synapse, and poof! in a blast of sound and energy and light a truck or a house or even people disappear, everything flying and settling back into dust.[98]

In short, there is no need to think at all; a violent response is so simple.

What needs to be examined here as a fundamental problem is the specifically male propensity to violence. As Virginia Woolf put it, "To fight has always been the man's habit, not woman's."[99] It seems that many men love to fight, and war provides them with both opportunities and justifications. The same Vietnam veteran noted that hatred of war coexists with love of it:

War is ugly, horrible, evil, and it is reasonable for men to hate all that. But I believe that most men who have been to war would have to admit, if they are honest, that somewhere inside themselves they loved it too, loved it as much as anything that has happened to them before or since. And how do you explain that to your wife, your children, your parents, or your friends?[100]

The ill-treatment and massacres of POWs at Sandakan cannot be explained completely in terms of a specific group of men who had been brainwashed by Japanese military ideology. The propensity to violence is already widespread among ordinary men; brainwashing might make violence more likely, but there is no need to invoke brainwashing to explain how it can occur at all. Soldiers are almost always ordinary men, perhaps with wives and children, but through their extraordinary experiences they find they love war as much as they hate it. More light can be cast on this paradox by approaching male violence from another angle. In the next chapter I focus on women's experience of male violence during wartime.

# 3

# Rape and War:
# The Japanese Experience

## Rape and the Tokyo War Crimes Tribunal

Until very recently in Japan, the term "war crimes" conjured up images of the inhumane treatment or murder of enemy soldiers, especially prisoners of war. By describing and perceiving women during war as civilians who held the "home front" during the war, commentators seem to have perpetuated the belief that women were not the direct victims of war. However, the eruption of the "comfort-women" issue has created an awareness throughout Japan that such an idea is both discriminatory and unrealistic. Despite the existence of many books and articles documenting the ordeal of the comfort women, only in the 1990s has the matter become a subject of nationwide debate. It is now necessary for the Japanese people as a whole to question not only why and how these crimes were committed but also why it took so long for knowledge of the crimes to become public.

Two important ideological structures that are fundamental to the Japanese nationalist mentality underlie the comfort-women issue. The first of these is xenophobia, which is closely related to the Japanese emperor ideology. The second is the contempt with which women are held in Japanese society and the exploitation of their sexuality by Japanese men. The comfort-women issue did not initially gain the attention of the Japanese public because the Japanese tend to avoid confronting these two nationwide discriminatory attitudes. The recent change in awareness may be related to the fact not only that the women's movement in Japan is gaining strength, but also that the whole society, through its increased internationalization, is becoming less insular and more aware of the impact Japanese actions have on other cultures.

However, to see the comfort-women affair as a crime committed uniquely by the Japanese is to risk dismissing such acts as aberrations and not recognizing their full significance as part of a larger pattern of how war makes women victims. By analyzing how all wars affect women, the Japanese people can provide some scholarly and intellectual foundations for the study of war and thereby contribute to the establishment and maintenance of peace.

The necessary materials for such an exercise can be found among the large number of testimonies and evidence presented at the Tokyo War Crimes Tribunal held immediately after the Asia-Pacific War. The most significant case among these was the rape and massacre of Chinese women by the Japanese 10th Army and 16th Division in Nanjing in December 1937. Although in Japan this incident is known as the "Nanjing Massacre," it is often referred to by non-Japanese as the "rape of Nanjing," a more accurate description of the rape and massacre of numerous Chinese women. The event was described by American missionary James McCallum in his diary, which was presented in evidence at the Tokyo War Crimes Tribunal:

Never have I heard or read of such brutality. Rape! Rape! Rape! We estimate at least 1,000 cases a night, and many by day. In case of resistance . . . there is a bayonet stab or bullet. We could write up hundreds of cases a day.[1]

Other evidence presented to the tribunal was a report prepared by a British resident in Nanjing, Iver Mackay, which contains the following information:

On the night of December 15 a number of Japanese soldiers entered the University of Nanking buildings at Tao Yuen and raped 30 women on the spot, some by six men. . . . At 4 P.M. on December 16 Japanese soldiers entered the residence at 11 Mokan Road and raped the women there. On December 17 Japanese soldiers went into Lo Kia Lu No. 5, raped four women and took one bicycle, bedding and other things. . . . On December 17 near Judicial Yuan a young girl after being raped was stabbed by a bayonet in her abdomen. On December 17 at Sian Fu Wua a woman of 40 was taken away and raped. On December 17 in the neighbourhood of Kyih San Yuin Lu two girls were raped by a number of soldiers. From a primary school at Wu Tai Shan many women were taken away and raped for the whole night and released the next morning, December 17.[2]

Numerous concrete examples of horrific rape and massacre in Nanjing were recorded in the proceedings of the tribunal. Evidence that Filipinas and Dutch women presented at the Tokyo War Crimes Tribunal is also valuable documentation.[3]

However, the incidents of rape and massacre of civilian women by Japanese soldiers, especially in the Nanjing case, have been substantially investigated in numerous books and articles, and a clear general picture of the event has emerged.[4] The purpose of this chapter is to focus upon a number of events that have hitherto been neglected, such as the fate of the military nurses. By comparing the experience of military nurses in war with the experience of civilian women in war, we can gain a clearer picture of the effect of war upon women in general. A few instances in which the nurses of the Allied forces became victims of war crimes committed by the Japanese forces were presented at the Tokyo War Crimes Tribunal. The most significant case among them seems to have been the massacre of Australian military nurses at Banka Island, the only survivor of which—Vivian Bullwinkel—testified at the tribunal. The record of the proceedings of this case runs to more than 23 pages.[5] In addition, over 200 pages of records of investigations and interrogations by the Australian military forces are now available. To examine this incident, I have used these documents as well as a number of Japanese secondary sources.

## The Massacre of Nurses at Banka Island

The most important strategic objective of the Japanese in the Pacific War was to secure natural resources in Asia, especially the oil in the then Dutch colony of Indonesia. In order to secure Indonesia, it was vital to seize Singapore, which was not only the base of the British eastern naval fleet but also the key to Britain's commercial and financial dominance of the region. At 2:15 on the morning of December 8, 1941, advance troops of the 25th Army, led by General Yamashita Hirofumi, landed at Kota Bharu (on the east coast of the Malay Peninsula) for the purpose of seizing Singapore. This landing was an hour and 20 minutes before the attack on Pearl Harbor (and so, strictly speaking, marks the beginning of the Pacific War). At an unknown time on the same day, the main force of the 25th Army advanced to Singora in Thailand, in the northern part of the Malay Peninsula. Another group of troops started advancing from Patani in Thailand, in the middle of the Malay Peninsula, toward Singapore. The Japanese forces had a plan to attack Singapore on three flanks and by traversing 1,100 kilometers down the British colony of the Malay Peninsula. This enabled them to approach Singapore from the north and well away from the British large-bore artillery defending Singapore from attack via the Straits of Malacca.[6]

The Japanese troops numbered 20,000; the defending troops consisted of 88,000 British, Australian, and Indian soldiers and Malay volunteers. Despite the fact that the British forces had a far greater advantage in numbers, Singapore fell relatively quickly. The British underestimated the ability of the Japanese forces, were insufficiently trained in jungle warfare, and lacked adequate communication among their different forces.

The British lost one battle after another. The Jitra fortress, near the Thai border, which they had anticipated they could maintain for three months, fell to Japanese forces in one day. On January 31, 1942, 55 days after the landing on the Malay Peninsula, Japanese forces occupied British Malaya and reached Johore Bahru—the southernmost point of the Malay Peninsula—which faces Singapore over the Johore Strait. On the morning of February 8, the Japanese began shelling Singapore from Johore Bahru, and 4,000 Japanese troops landed on the northwest coast of Singapore. In the following two weeks, the battle raged fiercely, day and night, all over Singapore. On the evening of February 15, Lieutenant General A.E. Percival of the Commonwealth forces offered the unconditional surrender of Singapore.[7]

When the Japanese forces invaded the Malay Peninsula in December 1941, 15,000 Australian soldiers of the 8th Division of the Australian military forces were stationed there, mainly in the role of defending the southwest coastal area between Johore Bahru and Malacca. At the same time, there were 140 Australian military nurses in this region who were divided into three groups working for the 2/10th Australian General Hospital in Malacca, the 2/4th Casualty Clearing Section in Kluang, and the 2/13th Australian General Hospital in Tamping. Because of the rapid advance of the Japanese forces, all nurses, together with hospital materials and patients, were evacuated to Singapore on January 10, 1942, and divided into two groups. One group was moved into St. Patrick's School on the southeast coast of Singapore; the other was moved to Oldham Hall, a school in the northern suburbs of Singapore city. The two schools were converted into hospitals as an emergency measure. Six hundred beds were brought into St Patrick's and 1,200 to Oldham. The nurses were divided between these two emergency hospitals. Between December 8, when the Japanese invasion began, and February 15, the day Singapore fell, 1,789 Australian soldiers died on the battlefield and 1,306 were nonfatally injured. As a result, the nurses were fully occupied.[8]

At the end of 1941 the Australian nurses in Singapore had received grave news regarding their British colleagues in Hong Kong. On the night of December 25, Japanese soldiers from the main invasion force of Hong Kong had forced their way into the emergency hospital set up at Stanley College, killed two doctors, and raped British nurses.[9] A report of this incident was prepared by the British forces after the war and presented to Allied Forces GHQ.[10] According to this report, Dr. Black, the British director of the hospital (which was at the time flying a Red Cross flag), tried to explain to Japanese soldiers that the building was a hospital. He was shot at the entrance. The Japanese then threw grenades into the hospital, killing injured soldiers. Those patients still alive were bayoneted. The Japanese then forced British and Chinese nurses as well as Chinese volunteers into one room and gang-raped them throughout the night. Two women among them were later killed by decapitation on the tennis court of the school. The rape and murder of these women continued even after 7:00 P.M. on December 25 (now known as Black Christmas) when the governor of Hong Kong, Sir Mark Young, and the commander of the British forces, Maltby, officially offered surrender. Australian nurses must have been shocked by the news that Allied forces had been massacred and fellow Commonwealth nurses raped. One British officer stationed in Singapore at that time advised the Australian nurses that if they faced a similar situation, it would be better to be shot by friendly soldiers than to become the victims of Japanese soldiers.[11]

When the New Year came, the nurses were in the dangerous situation of having to tend injured soldiers throughout daily air raids. Therefore, on January 20, the senior Australian medical officer, Colonel Alfred Durham, requested that the Australian forces withdraw all military nurses from Singapore. However, probably because of the large number of injured soldiers, the order for all nurses to evacuate Singapore was not issued until just before the city fell. On February 11, four days before the fall, the first group of Australian nurses left Singapore for Australia on the *Empire Star*. The following day, the remaining 65 nurses departed on a small ship of 1,669 tons, the *Vyner Brooke*. The *Empire Star* managed to evade the Japanese air attack and reached Australia via Batavia.[12]

The *Vyner Brooke*, however, departed too late because the nurses had to take shelter frequently from air attacks on their way to the wharf and were late in arriving. When they reached the wharf, they were put aboard the small ship (which already held 300 civilian passengers). The overcrowding meant that many women and children were forced to camp on the deck. Because it was dangerous to travel in daylight, the ship departed Singapore at 8 o'clock at night and sailed throughout the night, anchoring early each morning near a small island and thus avoiding detection. However, even during the night, progress was impeded by the need to avoid Japanese naval searchlights. On the morning of February 14, while the ship was anchored near tiny Tojon Island, Japanese planes flew within sight several times. Assuming the ship had been detected, the captain of the *Vyner Brooke* decided it would be wise to sail at full speed toward Banka Island rather than wait to be attacked.

The ship departed Tojon Island at 10:00 A.M. but was bombed by nine Japanese planes just after 1:00 P.M. and sank at about 1:40. There were six lifeboats on board with a combined capacity for 140 people, but only two were serviceable. The rest had been destroyed by the bombing. Thus most of the passengers were forced to take to the water and save themselves by whatever means they could. The ship went down between Sumatra and Banka Island at a spot relatively near Banka Island (approximately 16 kilometers away) but in the treacherous northern opening to the Banka Strait.[13] As a result, many people drowned, including 12 of the 65 Australian nurses. One group of women floated all day on the sea and were eventually rescued by a Japanese landing boat. But most of the passengers had to swim to shore, and some floated for three or four days until they reached Banka.[14]

On the night of February 14, the two lifeboats landed on Radjik beach (Map 3.1). Aboard were 22 Australian nurses and about 30 civilian passengers (most of them women and children), some of whom were injured. A group of the nurses went to a village nearby and asked for help, but the villagers, afraid of punishment by the Japanese forces, refused. Because the whole island was occupied by the Japanese, the villagers suggested the women should surrender.

That night, the women observed ships being attacked by the Japanese in Banka Strait and built a signal fire to help survivors find their way to shore. Approximately two hours later about 20 British soldiers landed in a lifeboat and joined the group. Some of these soldiers were injured, and it was necessary to treat them as soon as possible. Early the following morning (February 16) they considered their situation and concluded that because it was virtually impossible to escape from the island because of the number of children and injured, they should surrender. To this end, one of the crew of the *Vyner Brooke* set out to walk to Muntock, the island's center, and inform the Japanese forces of their intention. Not long after the sailor left for Muntock, Matron Drummond suggested that the civilian women and children start walking toward Muntock while the nurses stayed with the injured soldiers. So a group of civilians, led by a Chinese doctor, departed, leaving behind the British soldiers, 10 of whom were on stretchers, and the Australian nurses. At about 10:00 A.M. the crew member who had walked to Muntock returned with a troop of 15 Japanese soldiers led by an officer. The nurses and the British soldiers were no doubt relieved to see them, as they anticipated that medical treatment, food, and water would be provided.[15]

The details of what followed have been gathered from the account given by Vivian Bullwinkel (the sole survivor of the 22 nurses) and documents produced by the Australian military after the war.[16] It is clear that the Japanese soldiers separated men from women and able from disabled and further divided the able men into two groups. The crew member who had brought the Japanese soldiers from Muntock complained to the Japanese officer that they should be treated fairly as prisoners of war, but he was ignored completely. One group of British soldiers was taken behind the cliff—about 100 meters away from the beach and out of sight of the remaining prisoners. They were apparently bayoneted. About 10 minutes later these Japanese soldiers returned and took another group of men to the

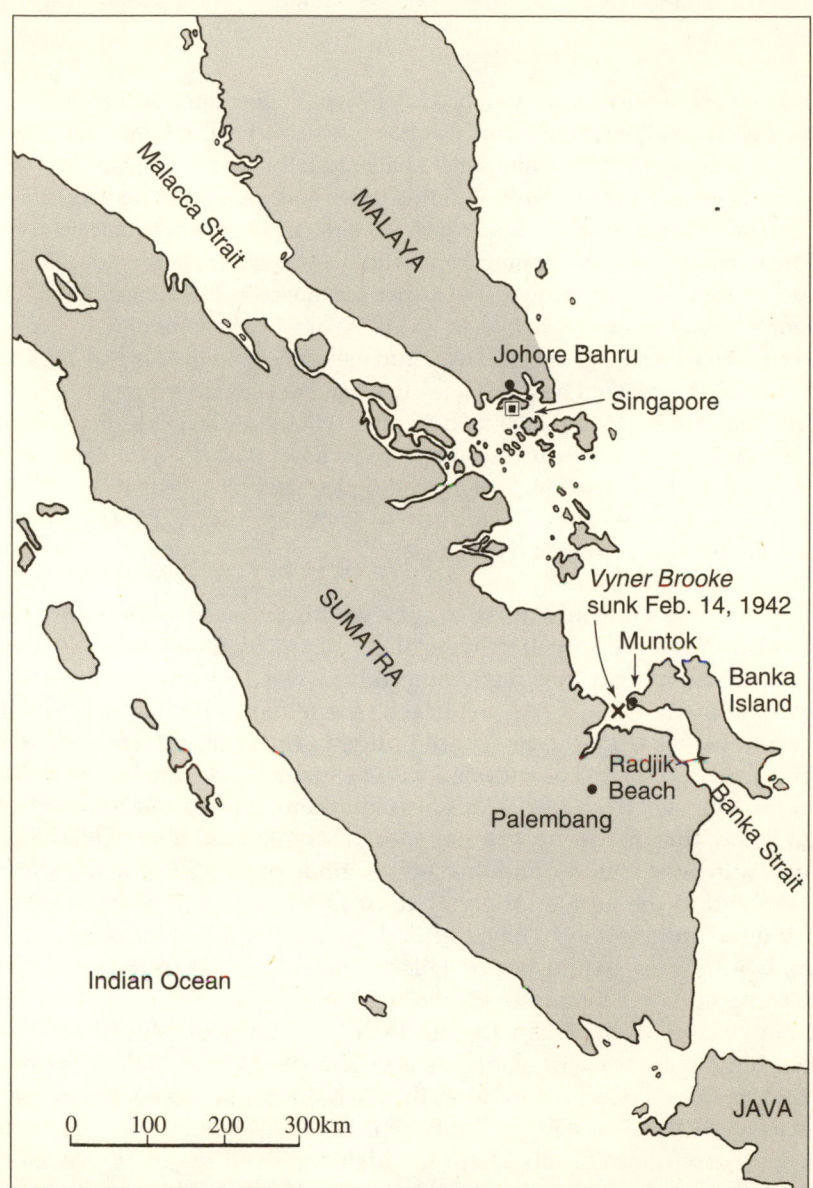

Map 3.1   *Location of Banka Island.*

same place. This time, the nurses heard a few gunshots that were the result of two British soldiers' attempts to escape. After the second group was bayoneted, the Japanese returned to the nurses. Vivian Bullwinkel gave the following account:

They came back and we knew what had happened . . . they came back wiping their bayonets. We realised what was going to happen. I can remember one of the girls saying, "Two things that I hate most, the sea and the Japs, and I've got them both." We were all sitting down and we were ordered up, and then told to march into the sea. Which we did. As we got to about waist level they started machine-gunning from behind. I was hit just at the side of the back. The bullet came through, but I wasn't aware of it at the time. I thought that once you were shot you'd had it. What with the force of the bullet and the waves I was knocked over into the water. And in doing so, I swallowed a lot of water. I became violently ill, and as I stood I realised I was very much alive. Next thing I thought, they will see me heaving. So I tried to stop and I just lay there. I wouldn't know how long. When I did venture to sit up, there was nothing. All my colleagues had been swept away and there were no Japs on the beach. There was nothing. Just me. I got up, crossed the beach, and went into the jungle.[17]

Bullwinkel was the only nurse to survive this massacre. Afterward, the injured British on the stretchers were also bayoneted. One soldier, Private Kingsley, miraculously survived, although he was severely wounded; as Bullwinkel made her way up the beach, she failed to notice he was still alive. A few days later, the two, both hiding in the jungle, eventually met up. Bullwinkel collected abandoned water canteens from the beach, made a bed for Kingsley from life jackets also left there, and bound his original wound and that made by the bayonet with coconut fibers. Her own wound was less serious and healed as time passed. Bullwinkel and Kingsley hid in the jungle for about 10 days but realized they could not stay hidden indefinitely. They decided to contact the Japanese forces again, hoping they would not be killed. They went out to the road and were picked up by a Japanese naval officer and a soldier in a car, and this time they were safely taken to the detention camp in Muntock. Bullwinkel hid her injury with canteens and Kingsley wore a less damaged shirt taken from a dead comrade so they would not be suspected of having survived the massacre on the beach. Both Bullwinkel and Kingsley were very careful not to talk about the incident, even to fellow prisoners in the detention camp, because they believed they would be in danger if the Japanese discovered they had witnessed the massacre. Therefore, very few people among the POWs knew of this incident during the war.[18]

Bullwinkel's account also makes the following clear. At the time of the massacre all nurses were in the uniform of the Australian Military Nursing Service and wearing Red Cross armbands. When they reached the Radjik beach, they also raised the Red Cross flag, thus clearly indicating they were noncombatants.[19] There were about 20 British soldiers among this group, but the fact that one of the men went to the Japanese forces to indicate their desire to surrender makes it clear that they had no intention of fighting against the Japanese forces. The Japanese clearly saw that there were injured soldiers among these men, and it was obvious the British showed no indication of challenging them when they were forced to walk behind the cliff. Despite all this, Japanese soldiers massacred both the British soldiers and the nurses. Of particular note is that men and women were separated and that men's bodies were left on the beach after they were bayoneted individually, whereas the nurses were driven into the sea and machine-gunned as a group. It seems the Japanese made sure that evidence of the women's bodies would not be left behind. What does this different method of killing signify?

There are two possible answers. The first is that the officer of this Japanese group was clearly aware that assault and murder of POWs and nurses violated the Geneva Convention and thus he took steps to destroy any evidence by disposing of the nurses' bodies in the sea. Why then did Japanese soldiers kill the nurses in spite of knowing this international law? Possibly they were bewildered by the unfamiliar sight of more than 20 women in military uniform; traditional male ideology holds that war is absolutely and exclusively a male activity. In this front line of the war, a group of women in military-style uniform suddenly appeared in front of these Japanese men, who murdered the women perhaps as a spontaneous reaction to this bewildering incongruity. It could be said that the massacre of the nurses at Radjik beach was a typical example of the massacre of women by soldiers in war. In contrast, the fact that the Japanese soldiers bayoneted the British soldiers was possibly a result of a male ideology that war is the exclusive realm of men fighting men and therefore even POWs who have "lost" in war deserve to be killed. Furthermore, there lies in this ideology the belief that a man must fight another man and kill him individually to demonstrate his personal power.

The second possible answer is that the Japanese soldiers separated men and women because from the beginning they intended to rape and kill the women after they had massacred the men. Is it too unrealistic to assume that Bullwinkel tried to save her dead colleagues from the disgrace of being known as victims of rape? It seems that such an interpretation is not impossible from the various documents of the investigation of this incident. Immediately after the war, the Australian military tried to find the perpetrators through a thorough investigation of Japanese activities on Banka Island at that time. Although there were attempts by the Japanese to create a cover-up, the investigators eventually found that this crime was probably committed by some soldiers of O Battalion under the command of Lieutenant O.M., who was attached to the 229th Regiment.[20] So that they could interrogate O.M., the Australian military requested that the war crimes committee of the Allied forces in Tokyo locate this officer. It was discovered that he had been in Manchuria when the war ended and had become a POW of the Soviet Union and was still in a Siberian prison camp.[21] Quite separately, the British forces were investigating the massacre of nurses in Hong Kong by Japanese soldiers and found that the same battalion, under the command of Lieutenant O.M., had participated in the invasion of Hong Kong before heading to Banka Island. British forces were also trying to locate him, believing he was one of the perpetrators of the atrocity.[22]

Lieutenant O.M. was released and returned to Japan in June 1948, but he was arrested by the representative of the Australian forces in Tokyo and detained in Sugamo prison. However, on September 13, before the interrogation had begun, he committed suicide by slashing a blood vessel in his neck with a glass-cutting tool he had smuggled into his cell from the prisoners' workshop.[23] Because of his death and because most of the soldiers of O Battalion died during the war, the Australian forces were unable to build a sufficient case around the incident and did not prosecute anyone over it. However, the documents of both the British and Australian investigations raise the distinct possibility that the soldiers who massacred the Australian nurses on Banka Island were the same soldiers who had raped and murdered the British nurses in Hong Kong two months before.

The crucial issue is not whether the Australian nurses were raped but rather that they were massacred as a group and killed in a very different manner from the British soldiers at the same place. Therefore, it seems clear that the Japanese intended to eliminate these women from the battlefield. Because of this, the soldiers' (male) ideology of the need to eliminate women should be critically examined in relation to the rape of women by men in war. This point is taken up later in this chapter.

## The Threat of Prostitution

The women massacred on Radjik beach were not the only nurses to survive the sinking of the *Vyner Brooke*. A number of passengers on the ship eventually reached Banka Island at different times and in different places, though many drowned. Of the original 65 nurses, 12 drowned and 21 were massacred, but 32 survived. Within a few days of the ship's going down, not only the *Vyner Brooke* passengers but also the many civilians and military personnel from about 70 Allied vessels, which were attacked by the Japanese forces, were arrested and detained in camps in Muntock, on Banka Island. Altogether, more than 600 people were detained in the camps. Those suffering severe injuries were tended by the nurses.

The detention camp on Banka had once been the living quarters of Chinese coolie laborers, and therefore facilities were limited. The nurses had to sleep on the concrete without bedding or blankets. There was s single water tap for drinking, and meals were provided only twice a day: at lunchtime and at four o'clock in the afternoon. At lunchtime they received a small quantity of cooked rice; the afternoon meal was cooked rice and a small quantity of vegetable or potato. As a result they were always near starvation. At night the Japanese guards wandered around the camp and prevented sleep by bashing the women's legs with their torches. The most degrading experience for the women was using the toilet facilities, which consisted of nothing but a concrete pit in the open around which Japanese guards would suddenly appear and stare and laugh at the women. Already, early in their detention, they were being treated as sexual objects.[24]

At 3:00 A.M. on March 2, 1942, they were suddenly wakened and ordered to prepare for a trip. The nurses, together with civilians, were transferred to the former Dutch settlement of Bukit Besar, a suburb of Palembang in southern Sumatra. The arduous trip took two days. In the settlement men and women were separated, and the 32 nurses were accommodated in two houses that had once been used by Dutch colonialists. Some comfortable furniture and foodstuffs had been left behind in the houses, and for a time the nurses ate well and lived in relative comfort. The first week passed without incident. In the second week Japanese officers intruded frequently in the houses without warning, on the pretext of making an inspection. On some occasions they even came into the bathroom while nurses were showering.[25]

On the weekend of the second week, the women were ordered to vacate the houses because they were to be used for the purpose of leisure. The nurses became suspicious and asked the Japanese authorities to allocate them two houses at the other end of the street as new living quarters. This request was rejected, and they were ordered to move into the two houses immediately next to the original two. They were also ordered to clean the houses they vacated and arrange new furniture that the Japanese forces brought in. They were informed that these two houses would be used as an officers' club. The other female civilians who had been housed in six houses not far away were also ordered to vacate so that the premises could be used as "comfort houses" (military brothels). Naturally, the nurses feared they would be used as prostitutes for the Japanese officers. At first the Japanese adopted a policy of persuasion by using a British woman to recruit the Australian nurses for comfort-women duties. She told the women of all the advantages they would receive if they complied, but the nurses refused.[26]

When this attempt at persuasion failed, the Japanese officers issued an order to the Australian nurses to attend the opening night of the officers' club. That afternoon the nurses discussed strategy to avoid becoming prostitutes. They left behind the most physically attractive nurse with the excuse that she had to look after three sick nurses. The remainder of the nurses did attend, but they endeavored to make themselves as unattractive as possible. They wore their khaki uniforms with football or army boots. At the officers' club they pretended not to understand the English spoken by the Japanese officers, and when they had to respond they spoke as quickly as possible so that the Japanese could not understand them. As agreed among themselves, they refused any alcohol, in spite of the Japanese insistence. One of the officers asked, "What do Australian women drink then?" The nurse responded, "We do not drink anything but milk," hoping they would be offered milk, rich in the vitamins they had lacked for a long time. Unfortunately no milk was offered. However, their strategy was successful, and most of the nurses were released a few hours later. Four were ordered to stay on at the club and were subject to continuous demands by the Japanese officers that they become prostitutes. They were threatened with starvation if they did not comply, but all refused, saying they would prefer starvation to life as comfort women.[27]

The attempt to threaten the four women as a group failed, and the next day the Japanese officers tried a new strategy. They summoned four other nurses and put each in a different room. In each room there were three Japanese officers who repeatedly demanded that the nurses become comfort women. They were also asked to choose between starvation and prostitution. One of the women was given a document written in English and ordered to read it. The document said the Japanese military required women for the purpose of comforting soldiers and these women must work for this purpose. Again, all four refused and said they would choose starvation. On the following day the nurses complained through a Dutch doctor to the Japanese governor of Palembang, who had final responsibility for management of the detention camp. It is unknown whether the governor sent any instructions to the officers, but their requests ceased. However, immediately after this incident the amount of food provided was considerably reduced, and the nurses had to face chronic starvation for the rest of their internment. Soon after this, they were transferred to a different camp that had been a slum area in Palembang, and their living conditions became worse still.[28]

From this evidence it seems that the Japanese military forces in Palembang had a meticulous plan to exploit the Australian nurses as prostitutes. First, they demoralized the women with appalling living conditions and deprived them of sleep and food. In the next stage, they provided the nurses with relatively comfortable housing and sufficient food. They used a British woman as an intermediary to try to persuade the nurses that there would be considerable improvement in their conditions if they complied. When this persuasion did not work, the officers employed the threat of starvation. Even this tactic failed, and the poor conditions were reimposed.

Even after these refusals the Japanese officers did not give up. In late 1942 they used deception. They claimed that British and Dutch POWs working at the Pladjoe oil field required attention from Western nurses and asked the Australian nurses to go. However, the nurses became suspicious and decided not to comply with the request until it was thoroughly investigated. The nurses suggested to the Japanese that two Allied doctors and one Australian officer be allowed to visit the oil field on their behalf and investigate the situation. There was no reply from the Japanese side, and the request was not repeated. Immediately after the war the nurses met Dutch POWs who had been working at the oil field and found they had not made any such request; it had indeed been a ruse to lure them into prostitution.[29]

Nurses from other Allied countries also faced such risks. An Australian nurse described an indicative event in her autobiography. Four British nurses and the wife of a Dutch doctor detained at the same camp were taken out to Palembang under the pretense of attending the sick. When they returned to the detention camp in February 1944 after more than one and a half years' absence, the disturbed appearance of these women made it obvious that they had been severely affected by their ordeal. For reasons that are not clear, these five women had been placed in solitary confinement for almost six months, were forced to sit on a concrete floor day after day, and were not allowed to read or write. In the last few weeks they were placed in two small cells and had to live in extremely cramped quarters.[30] It is probable the women had to undergo these conditions because they refused to become prostitutes.

Fortunately, the Japanese officers did not rape the Australian nurses. There are a number of possible reasons for this. One could be the strong solidarity among the nurses, which afforded them protection and gave them the courage to refuse requests and threats. It would have been psychologically difficult for the Japanese officers to rape these women and so break the bond among them. This situation—quite different from that of civilian women detained at the camp—worked to the nurses' advantage. Second, among the civilian women who were in more vulnerable positions, there were some who started cooperating with the Japanese in return for food and the safety of their children and themselves. The existence of these other women made it unnecessary to force the nurses to become prostitutes by raping them. In their testimonies and autobiographies, nurses often disparagingly used the phrase "Japs' free girlfriends" in describing women who collaborated.[31] But these civilian women seem to have become "girlfriends" because of the pressures brought to bear on them; it is unlikely that they complied with any willingness. In other words, the "Japs' free girlfriends" can also be seen as victims of rape, and this too should be seen as a war crime. Nurses despised these "girlfriends" yet were often protected directly by them; there were occasions when these women intervened on the nurses' behalf to stop the Japanese guards from inflicting corporal punishment upon them.[32] Thus, in some cases the nurses owed their safety to these civilian women.

## The Establishment of Comfort Houses

The detention camp near Palembang, where Australian nurses were detained, also held a number of Dutch civilian women, but there are no documents detailing how these women were treated or whether they were forced to become prostitutes. However, in Java, which lies close to Sumatra, some Dutch civilian women became the victims of Japanese forces. In July 1992 the newspaper *Asahi Shimbun* published portions of Dutch wartime documents from the Dutch national archives that described how Dutch women at Semarang detention camp were taken to the military brothel in the city and forced to work there.

According to this source, in late February 1944 Japanese military forces took 35 Dutch women ages 16 to 26 from five women's detention camps and put them into four brothels (the Officers' Club, the Semarang Club, the Hinomaru Club, and the Seiun-sō). In order to avoid legal problems, the military forced these women to sign an agreement. But here, too, the Japanese forces used various tactics, ranging from deception to threat, to force women into prostitution. Some of these women were told that they would work as waitresses in the coffee shop in the Officers' Club, but when they arrived they were ordered to work as prostitutes. When they refused they were threatened with torture and death for themselves and their families. One girl tried to commit suicide but was revived. Testimony also revealed that Indonesian, Korean, and Vietnamese women were working at different brothels nearby. The four brothels were closed two months later under the instruction of military headquarters in Tokyo. Presumably, the Japanese authorities were afraid of international criticism if reports of the exploitation of civilian women, including minors, became public. However, according to the proceedings of the war crimes court at Batavia in Indonesia, even after the closure of the brothels, 17 Dutch women were taken to the brothels on Flores Island where the Japanese airfield was under construction. They were detained there until the end of the war. This court report also revealed that each woman was given a daily quota: 20 enlisted men in the morning, two NCOs in the afternoon, and the senior officers at night.[33]

One Dutch woman who was forced to work in Semarang was Jeanne Ruff-O'Hearne, who moved to Adelaide, Australia, after the war. She was initially detained at Ambarawa camp together with her mother and her two younger sisters and was taken to the brothel with nine other girls in February 1944. What follows is her testimony:

We were forced into the trucks. We huddled together like frightened animals and drove through the hillside suburb of Semarang. The truck stopped in front of a large house. Seven girls were told to get out. I was one of them. We were made to understand that we were here for the sexual pleasure of the Japanese. In other words we found ourselves in a brothel. We were to obey at all times; we were not allowed to leave the house. In fact, the house was guarded and trying to escape was useless. We were in this house for only one purpose: for the Japanese to have sex with us. We were enslaved into enforced prostitution.

We protested loudly that we would never allow this to happen to us, that it was against all human rights, that we would rather die. The Japanese stood there laughing, saying that they were our captors and they could do with us as they liked, and if we did not obey our families would suffer.

Opening night arrived. We were all terrified and we huddled together in the dining room. We were all virgins and none of us knew anything about sex. We were all so innocent and we tried to find out from each other what to expect and what was going to happen to us.

I knew that the only thing that could help us now was prayer. I opened my prayer book and led the girls in prayer. As we were praying we could hear the arrival of more and more military to the house, the crude laughter and boots treading the floor.

We were ordered to each go to our rooms, but we refused, clinging to each other for safety. My whole body was burning up with fear. It is a feeling I can't possibly describe, a feeling I shall never forget and never lose. Even after almost 50 years I still experience this feeling of total fear going through my body and limbs, burning me up. It comes to me at the oddest moments; I wake up with it in nightmares and still feel it just lying in bed at night.

I hid under the dining room table. Eventually I was found and dragged out. A large Japanese officer stood in front of me, looking down at me, grinning at me. I kicked him in the shins. He just stood there laughing. My fighting, kicking, crying and protesting made no difference.

He had paid a lot of money for opening night, and he became extremely angry. He took his sword out of its scabbard and pointed it at me, threatening me with it. He was getting impatient by now and he threw me on the bed. He tore at my clothes and ripped them off. He threw himself on top of me, pinning me down under his heavy body.

I tried to fight him off, I kicked him, I scratched him, but he was too strong. The tears were streaming down my face as he raped me. I can find no words to describe this most inhuman and brutal rape. To me it was worse than dying.

Each evening I tried to hide in a different place, but I was always found, then dragged into my room after severe beatings. Every time the Japanese raped me I tried to fight them off. Never once did any Japanese rape me without a violent struggle and fight. Often they threatened to kill me, often they severely beat me.

I can't remember exactly how long we were kept in the Semarang brothel, but it was at least three months. I don't think I could have carried on any longer. During that time the Japanese had abused me and humiliated me. They had ruined my young life. They had stripped me of everything, my self-esteem, my dignity, my freedom, my possessions, my family.[34]

Javanese women from this area were also forced into prostitution. For example, Doug Davey, a member of the Australian 9th Regiment, which acted as the British-Borneo Civil Affairs Unit, was in Borneo in August 1945 and found some Indonesian women who had been transported there by the Japanese. They were living in the ruins of the Japanese brothels at Beaufort on the Padas River in the northwest. The Australian forces took them to a small island off the Borneo coast for the purposes of medical treatment and rehabilitation with the intention of sending them back to Indonesia. But the women were afraid of going home because of the shame associated with their experience; one committed suicide.[35] It is very difficult to gain a picture of activities of the Japanese military brothels in the Pacific region because most of the relevant documents were burned soon after the war. However, it can be presumed that a large number of Asian women, such as these Javanese, were sent far away from their homes and into prostitution.

The comfort houses were first established in Shanghai before World War II, possibly as early as 1932. During the Shanghai incident in January 1932, Japanese soldiers raped many Chinese women, and the deputy chief of the general staff in Shanghai, Okamura Teiji, set up a brothel in order to prevent further rape.[36] In 1938, after the Nanjing massacre, the Japanese forces adopted the general policy of setting up military brothels in various places in occupied China and "recruiting" comfort women to staff them, not because of their concern for the Chinese victims of rape by Japanese soldiers but because of their fear of creating antagonism among the Chinese civilians. Thus many so-called military leisure houses were established where Japanese forces were stationed.[37] The word "recruit" is, of course, an official euphemism; in reality many women were forcibly pressed into prostitution. It is now widely known from various testimonies that the Japanese military forces were directly involved in procuring large numbers of women for prostitution. One man, Yoshida Seiji, confessed that he was one of the officers responsible for this action.[38] Many Korean women were also exploited in this way and later spoke of their ordeals. It is also clear from the autobiography of Nogi Harumichi, the captain of the Ambon naval police force, that military police, who were supposed to prevent such military crimes, collaborated to procure women for prostitution.[39]

There were three different types of comfort houses: those run directly by the Japanese Army; those ostensibly privately owned and run but in reality under tight control of the Army and only for the use of military personnel; and those privately owned and frequented by civilians but operating under an agreement with the Army to provide "special services" for military personnel. The second type was the most common, and these houses were usually located next to military supply bases or in the center of towns in which soldiers were stationed. Units located in more remote places usually had comfort houses directly attached to the barracks. If the unit moved, its comfort house would move with it. Smaller units, which did not have comfort houses, would often have comfort women sent to them for short periods from the larger comfort houses in the towns. The buildings for the comfort houses were provided by the Army, which also took charge of such matters as hygienic measures, hourly rates for "services," and designation of days on which members of particular units were permitted to visit.[40]

There seem to be four major reasons the Japanese military decided that comfort houses were necessary. As I have mentioned previously, Japanese military leaders were very concerned about the rape of civilians by members of the Japanese armed forces but not out of concern for those civilians. For good strategic reasons, they believed that the antagonism of civilians in occupied territories toward their conquerors was exacerbated by such behavior. They also believed that a ready supply of women for the armed forces would help to reduce the incidence of rape of civilians.[41] What the military leaders apparently did not consider was the possibility that the highly oppressive culture of their armed forces might be contributing to the problem and that at least part of the solution would thus be to reform the military structure.

The military leaders also believed that the provision of comfort women was a good means of providing their men with some kind of leisure. Unlike Allied soldiers, the rank and file of the Japanese armed forces did not have designated leave periods or limited tours of duty. The military leaders had been advised by senior staff that they should make greater provision for both the health and well-being of their men, including such measures as extended leave back home. However, most of those suggested measures were never implemented. The notable exception was the provision of comfort women.[42]

Another concern the leaders had was the incidence of venereal disease among the armed forces. They believed that venereal disease threatened to undermine the strength of their men (and hence their fighting ability) and that it could also potentially create massive public health problems back in Japan once the war was over.[43] The leaders believed that a regulated system, such as the comfort houses, would enable them to take effective preventive health measures. It must be said that the measures they employed were thorough even if not completely effective. Those "recruited" were mostly young, unmarried women because it was believed they were the least likely to be carrying venereal diseases. Army doctors regularly checked the health of the comfort women to ensure that they had not contracted a venereal disease and also provided condoms for the men to use. According to the Centre for Research and Documentation on Japan's War Responsibility, during the war the Army Accounts Department and the Supply Headquarters were responsible for sending condoms to forces stationed overseas, and officials ensured a ready supply. In 1942, for example, 32.1 million condoms were sent to units stationed outside Japan.[44] Records suggest a similar thoroughness with medical examinations of comfort women; most of them were examined for venereal disease every 10 days. However, such measures could not prevent venereal disease, even if they went some way toward reducing its incidence. For instance, according to a report by medical officers of the 15th Division in northern China in 1942 and 1943, 15 to 20 percent of comfort women were found to be suffering from venereal disease each month. Evidence from former comfort women suggests the figure could have been much higher.[45]

The fourth concern the leaders had was security. They believed that private brothels could be infiltrated by spies easily. Alternatively, it was thought that the prostitutes working in them could easily be recruited as spies by the Allies. Kempeitai members were frequent visitors to comfort houses and kept close tabs on the women to ensure that no spies were among them.[46]

Why were most comfort women almost invariably from Korea, Taiwan, China, or various places in Southeast Asia? This might seem odd at first, given that the Japanese were notoriously racially prejudiced against the peoples of these countries. However, racial prejudice provides part of the answer to the question because that very racism helped make these women suitable for the role of comfort women.

There were Japanese prostitutes during the war, but most were in a different position from the comfort women. The Japanese prostitutes mainly worked in brothels that served high-ranking officers, and they experienced much better conditions than the comfort women. The Japanese military forces did not believe Japanese women should be in that role because they were supposed to be bearing good Japanese children who would grow up to be loyal subjects of the emperor rather than being the means for men to satisfy their sexual urges. The Japanese military government took its lead from Nazi eugenic ideology and policy in these matters. In 1940 the National Eugenic Law was proclaimed. The purposes of the law were to prevent miscegenation and the reproduction of the "unfit," such as those with mental illnesses that were believed to be inherited.[47]

Another reason non-Japanese were used as comfort women can be found in international law. In 1910 the law suppressing trade in women for the purposes of prostitution was proclaimed in Paris following an agreement by a number of European nations. Japan later became a signatory. In 1921 a similar international law banned trade in women and children. Once again, Japan became a signatory. In February 1938 the Japanese Ministry of Home Affairs issued orders to the governors of each prefecture to ensure that only prostitutes over age 21 were issued with authorizations to ply their trade. However, officials believed these laws were not applicable to Japan's colonies, and this, combined with the belief in the superiority of Japanese women and the suitability of women of other races for prostitution, cemented the decision to use women from colonies and occupied territories as comfort women. Young unmarried women in the colonies and occupied territories were thus treated by the Japanese as a resource for that purpose.[48]

It is impossible to deny that the Japanese military was directly involved in organizing comfort houses and recruiting women to work in them. Recently discovered documents and the recent testimony of former comfort women, who only now feel able to speak freely about their ordeals, have added details about what happened. However, the Japanese government is still withholding pertinent documents that could give a clearer picture, especially about who should bear individual responsibility in the lines of command.

However, it appears from the available evidence that orders to recruit women for comfort houses directly controlled by the military army came from the headquarters of each dispatched army—that is, from the chiefs of staff of each army. Those orders would then have been conveyed to staff officers in various divisions and carried out by the Kempeitai. The Kempeitai usually operated by forcing the elders of villages in the occupied territories to round up all of the young women.[49]

As for the putatively private brothels, the owners were assisted by the Kempeitai in the task of recruiting local women. Most of these women were forcibly taken to the brothels from their villages. Some women, however, were led to believe that they were going to do some other kind of job, such as working in a factory, only to find out too late that they had been deceived.[50]

In January 1942 the minister for foreign affairs, Tōgō Shigenori, instructed his staff that comfort women should be issued with military travel documents. After that time, comfort women did not require a passport for overseas travel.[51] This indicates that involvement in decision-making about comfort women went all the way to the top levels of government. Other documents reveal a similar picture about high-level involvement. In March 1942 the headquarters of the South Area Army made plans to set up comfort houses throughout the Asia-Pacific region. One recovered document shows that orders were issued to Taiwan headquarters to recruit 70 comfort women and send them to Borneo. The commander in Taiwan, Lieutenant General Andō Rikichi, and the chief of staff, Major General Higuchi Keishichirō, instructed the Kempeitai to select three brothel owners to assist them in the task of gathering the comfort women. Seventy women were in fact sent to Borneo from Taiwan; all carried military travel documents with the seal of the head of general affairs of the Ministry for the Army, Tanaka Ryūkichi, and his junior, Kawara Naoichi. Because the minister of the army at this time was Prime Minister Tōjō Hideki, he therefore bore final responsibility for the ordeals of the comfort women.[52]

Comfort women were transported to the front lines in Army ships or on Army railways or trucks. On a few occasions comfort women were even flown by Army planes to the front lines. The head of Army supplies was responsible for controlling transport and must have been ultimately responsible for decisions made about transport of the women.[53]

Less evidence is available about the role of the Navy in the exploitation of "comfort women" than about the role of the Army. However, according to documents written by Rear Admiral Nagaoka Takasumi, head of general affairs of the Ministry for the Navy, on May 30, 1942, the Navy was to dispatch comfort women to various naval bases throughout Southeast Asia. For instance, 45 women were to be dispatched to the Celebes, 40 to Balikpapan in Borneo, 50 to Penan, and 30 to Surabaya. This was the second dispatch of comfort women to these bases. These documents were sent to Rear Admiral Nakamura Toshihisa, chief of staff of the Southwest Area Fleet. As with the Army, Navy involvement went to the very top ranks. Admiral Shimada Shigetarō, the minister for the Navy, can therefore also be held responsible for the ordeals of the comfort women.[54]

The available evidence thus gives a clear picture that the very top ranks of both the Army and the Navy were directly involved in decisionmaking concerning the comfort women and that other arms of government, such as the Ministry of Foreign Affairs, collaborated with them, also with high-level involvement. The comfort-women case could well be historically unprecedented as an instance of state-controlled criminal activity involving the sexual exploitation of women. The history of "camp followers" (military prostitutes) in European wars provides a strong contrast because evidence suggests that the relevant decisions were made by those on the ground and not back in the metropolitan corridors of power. We Japanese thus have a special responsibility to acknowledge the crimes of our forebears in subjecting the comfort women to their ordeals and, especially, a responsibility to demand that our government gives adequate compensation to the survivors.

The comfort women were treated as "military supplies," but relevant documents were either hidden or destroyed at the end of the war. Therefore it is impossible to know how many women were exploited; the best estimates range from 80,000 to 100,000. According to the Japanese military plan devised in July 1941, 20,000 comfort women were required for every 700,000 Japanese soldiers,[55] or 1 woman for every 35 soldiers. There were 3.5 million Japanese soldiers sent to China and Southeast Asia, and therefore an estimated 100,000 women were mobilized. Eighty percent of these women are believed to have been Koreans, but newly available evidence shows that many from Taiwan, China, and the Philippines were also used. Recent testimony by Malaysians indicates that the Japanese forces set up brothels in which local Malaysian women were housed.[56] Thus, it is clear that the Japanese forces exploited large numbers of Asian women as well as women from Allied nations under the excuse of preventing rape. Although this was the official justification for the program, it should not be forgotten that these estimated 100,000 women were themselves victims of rape. The following testimony by a former Korean comfort woman drives home the point:

I was nearly killed several times during my time as a "comfort woman." There were some military men who were drunk and were brandishing swords at me while making demands for perverted sex. They drove their swords into the tatami, then demanded sex from me. . . . Afterwards the tatami was full of holes from them driving their swords into it. . . . The threat they were making was obvious—if I didn't co-operate they would stab me.[57]

Was the exploitation of women in military brothels effective in preventing widespread random sexual violence by Japanese soldiers? General Okamura, the initiator of the Japanese military brothel, himself said of the Japanese invasion of Wuhan in 1938 that random sexual violence occurred despite the fact that the Japanese forces had groups of comfort women attached to them, and he admitted his scheme was a failure.[58] In

June 1939, Hayao Takeo, then a lieutenant in the Japanese military as well as a professor at the Kanazawa medical college, submitted to the authorities a secret report about particular battlefield problems and control measures. In one chapter he analyzed the cases of rape by Japanese soldiers and expressed the same opinion as General Okamura: that it was impossible to prevent rape by setting up military brothels and that many Chinese civilians, whenever they saw Japanese soldiers, feared being raped by them.[59] He also stated that the Japanese soldiers who did not rape women in Japan suddenly became very violent and considered themselves free to rape Chinese women. In addition, he said that commanding officers often turned a blind eye to rape, believing that rape was necessary to enhance soldiers' fighting spirits.[60] Thus Dr. Hayao clearly recognized the two essential issues regarding rape in war. First, on the battlefield in a foreign country, where soldiers are outside the jurisdiction of their own laws of rape, it is extremely difficult to prevent rape, regardless of the availability of prostitutes at military brothels. Second, many officers deem it necessary for their soldiers to rape women in order to stimulate aggression. This was also clear from the testimonies of former Japanese soldiers who said they were given condoms before embarkation, despite officers' instructions not to rape women.[61]

Dr. Hayao recognized the importance of these two factors. Yet after observing the Japanese soldiers' activities in China, he puzzled over why these soldiers had no control over their sexual desires and could not maintain their decency.[62] But was this behavior peculiar to soldiers of the Japanese forces? It is necessary to examine the actions of the military forces of other countries to analyze the universal effects of war on women.[63]

## The Universality of Rape in War

The most well-documented report on rape in World War II is that of the rape of Jewish women by German soldiers. From the day the Germans entered Poland in September 1939, mass rape—of Jewish women in particular—was an everyday occurrence. Such incidents had commenced before the war; many Jewish women were raped during Kristallnacht, the night in November 1938 when a new wave of violent attacks on Jewish people and property began.[64] This pattern—the looting and destruction of property, the rape and, in many cases, subsequent murder of women—was to be repeated throughout the war and was particularly directed against the Jews.

There are many reports of young Jewish women being taken from the ghettos and abused and raped. In Warsaw those women deemed the most beautiful were given work in factories packing mirrors; they would usually be raped at the completion of their shift.[65] In one incident 40 women were taken from the ghetto and forced to join a party at the quarters of some officers in a Warsaw mansion. They were made to drink, strip, and dance with the officers, after which they were raped and released at three o'clock in the morning.[66]

At the end of 1939 a plan was developed to establish a number of brothels in Warsaw to be staffed by Jewish women, with separate brothels for officers and enlisted men. The plan was never implemented, probably because of pressure from higher echelons.[67] It of course contravened Nazi ideology about race mixing, in particular the 1935 Nuremburg race laws that prohibited sexual intercourse between "Aryans" and Jews. The incidental rape of Jewish women was also in contravention of this law but was a widespread practice. In concentration camps many young Jewish women—especially virgins—were raped by guards. In Auschwitz a brothel was established and staffed by non-Jewish women prisoners.[68]

Not only Jewish women were the victims of rape by German soldiers. An interim report prepared in January 1942 and submitted to the governments of the Allied nations by Soviet foreign minister Molotov refers to the fact that many Russian women were raped by German soldiers. This report—the "Molotov note"—was later presented to the postwar Nuremburg War Crimes Tribunal as evidence.[69] It contains reports of hundreds of cases in which Russian women were raped and murdered, sometimes in front of their relatives. In Smolensk, for example, hundreds of Russian women were taken from their homes and sequestered in a hotel that had been turned into a brothel. Other evidence given to the Nuremburg tribunal included the case of French women raped by Germans, especially those who were members of or collaborators with the Resistance.[70]

There were also many cases of rape and murder by Allied soldiers in World War II, but these of course did not come before the Nuremburg tribunal. During the fall of Berlin, Red Army soldiers looted and raped through the whole of the city. Cornelius Ryan, a historian, collected a great deal of evidence in the 1960s,[71] which included interviews with many German women who were civilians during the fall of Berlin. Not only was rape found to be a common experience, but there were many reports of particularly atrocious and grotesque acts of rape, including the rape of pregnant women in maternity wards and women who had just given birth.[72] One woman who had been raped when caught hiding in an air-raid shelter said the rapist told her he and his fellow soldiers were taking revenge for what German soldiers had done to Russian women.[73]

Yet such a claim is at best only half true. When Russian forces invaded Manchukuo in 1945, they raped a large number of Japanese women despite the fact that Japanese soldiers had raped no Russian women, if only because they had not had the opportunity—Japan and Russia had not been at war until this time. The details of such acts and the numbers of victims are unknown because there was never a systematic investigation of these events. However, there are a number of isolated accounts, such as this one given by an orphan refugee, Yoshida Reiko:

We were told by senior Japanese officers that we had lost the war, and that now we had to get together and act as a group. We went into the aeroplane hangars at Beian airport. There were about a thousand people there—the families of Manchukuo rail workers, and civilians who worked for the Japanese forces. From then on it was hell. Russian soldiers came, and told our leaders that they had to provide women to the Russian troops, as the spoils of victory. We didn't go outside—we spread our straw mat on the floor, and slept there. Our food was very limited—we had some dried bread and rice. We had no drinking water, so we collected rainwater, and drank that. Everyday Russian soldiers would come in and take about ten girls. The women came back in the morning. Some women committed suicide, usually by hanging themselves—they said it was better to die, than to be taken away by the Russian soldiers. . . . The bodies of these women were buried in the field. The building was surrounded by logs, and the Russian soldiers told us that if no women came out, the whole hangar would be burnt to the ground, with all of us inside. So some women—mostly single women—stood up and went. At that time I didn't understand what was happening to these women, but I clearly remember that women with children (who remained) offered prayers for the women who did go out, in thanks for their sacrifice. Some women went out of the hangar, and never returned.[74]

Some of the Japanese military nurses who were working at the front line in northern Manchukuo were also raped by Russian soldiers. There were 75 nurses at the Sunwu military hospital at the time of surrender. Every day Russian soldiers would come and rape a group of them. Japanese officers made many official complaints to the Soviet military headquarters about these incidents but to no effect. In fact, the Soviet forces responded to these complaints by asking the Japanese officers to provide a number of nurses as prostitutes, as they believed this would minimize the number of rapes by Soviet soldiers.[75] A doctor at Beian was also ordered to provide nurses and women office workers to the Soviet headquarters for this purpose. He refused and was beaten. Eventually a few young nurses and a typist volunteered under duress to become prostitutes at the headquarters; in fact, the "typist" was a prostitute the Japanese officers had kept on the staff for their own pleasure during the war. For these comfort women, the end of the war did not mean the end of their suffering. For them, there were neither friendly nor unfriendly soldiers—all men were their enemies.[76]

There is no documentary evidence of mass rape by British, Commonwealth, or American soldiers during World War II. However, British forces established brothels in Tripoli during the North African campaigns, with different brothels set up for the different races and for officers and enlisted men. Among the prostitutes staffing these brothels were four Italian women. It appears these women were prostitutes brought to North Africa by Italian forces and then abandoned. They were subsequently pressed into service and exploited by the British forces in these brothels.[77] The British also established brothels for officers in Delhi, but these were later closed on orders from London.[78] At the time of America's entry into the war, General George Patterson had contemplated establishing official military brothels for the U.S. Army. In the end, however, he decided that the outcry from the American public would be too great and abandoned the plan. U.S. soldiers used the brothels established by the French government soon after the D-Day landing in June 1944, but these were closed after no more than three days because of pressure from Washington. Of course, U.S. soldiers made full use of the civilian brothels, which remained open.[79]

Although it is possible that some incidents have been censored or removed from the record of Allied conduct in World War II, it is clear that the conduct of British, American, and Commonwealth soldiers was relatively restrained during the war years.[80] This was not the case in the occupation of Japan in 1945. From the day they landed, U.S. soldiers engaged in the mass rape of Japanese women. The first reported case was at 1:00 P.M. on August 30, 1945. Two marines went into a civilian house in Yokosuka and raped a mother and daughter at gunpoint. The marines had landed three and a half hours earlier. There were four reported cases that day in Yokosuka alone.[81] On September 1 there were 11 rapes reported in Yokosuka and Yokohama. In one of these cases a woman was gang-raped by 27 U.S. soldiers and nearly died. After that the incidence of rape spiraled upward throughout the period of the occupation, and the standard atrocities began to occur: young girls raped in front of their parents, pregnant women raped in maternity wards, and so on. Over a period of 10 days (August 30–September 10) there were 1,336 reported cases of rape of Japanese women by U.S. soldiers in Kanagawa prefecture (where Yokosuka and Yokohama are situated) alone. If these figures are extrapolated to cover the whole of Japan—and if it is assumed that many rapes went unreported—then it is clear that the scale of rape by U.S. forces was comparable to that by any other force during the war. Yet according to an official U.S. report, only 247 U.S. soldiers were prosecuted for rape in the latter half of 1945, and these figures include prosecutions for rape in occupied Europe.[82] Clearly there were many soldier-rapists at large in the occupied areas who were not prosecuted.

U.S. forces occupied the bulk of Japan, but some areas such as Hiroshima were occupied by British Commonwealth occupation forces (BCOF) composed of Australian, New Zealand, and Indian soldiers under the command of British officers. These forces also participated in the rape of civilians. A Japanese prostitute made the following comment about Australian soldiers who landed at Kure (the port of Hiroshima) in November 1945:

> Most of the people in Kure stayed inside their houses, and pretended they knew nothing about the rape by occupation forces. The Australian soldiers were the worst. They dragged young women into their jeeps, took them to the mountain, and then raped them. I heard them screaming for help nearly every night. A policeman from the Hiroshima police station came to me, and asked me to work as a prostitute for the Australians—he wanted me and other prostitutes to act as a sort of "firebreak," so that young women wouldn't get raped. We agreed to do this, and contributed greatly.[83]

An Australian member of the BCOF, Allan Clifton, also claimed in his memoirs that crimes such as rape were committed by Australian members of BCOF and that black marketeering was particularly common.[84] Clifton described one of the women victims in Hiroshima who was raped by Australian soldiers:

> I stood beside a bed in a hospital. On it lay a girl, unconscious, her long, black hair in a wild tumult on the pillow. A doctor and two nurses were working to revive her. An hour before she had been raped by twenty soldiers. We found her where they had left her, on a piece of waste land.[85]

The Japanese government had discussed ways of dealing with the anticipated problem of mass rape by occupation forces in the week following surrender and before their arrival. On August 21, 1945, Prime Minister Prince Higashikuni Naruhiko called a meeting of several of his ministers to discuss the issue; attendees included the health, internal affairs, and foreign ministers and the attorney-general. This was dubbed the "comfort-women meeting." They decided to set up a Recreation and Amusement Association (RAA) for the occupation forces. A special government fund of 30 million yen was allocated to the project, and the head of the Japanese police force was ordered to take all measures necessary to assist such an organization.[86] In fact, the government had already taken the first steps toward establishing such an organization four days earlier. Governors and police chiefs of all prefectures had been instructed to procure women from geisha houses, brothels, and nightclubs in sufficient numbers to staff a nationwide organization of brothels. In Tokyo the chief of police summoned all owners of brothels and nightclubs and requested their cooperation in such a project.[87] The Japanese politicians who had procured tens of thousands of non-Japanese comfort women during the war now turned to the procurement of their own women for the benefit of soldiers who had recently been their enemies.

The RAA was disbanded on March 27, 1946, primarily in order to halt the rapid spread of venereal disease among the U.S. forces but also because it was contrary to the principles of the "new democracy" that General MacArthur was trying to establish in the Japanese polity. Of course, prostitution on a large scale continued but as a private business activity. More than 20,000 Japanese women were mobilized into the RAA by the end of 1945, according to an internal report. At its peak more than 70,000 women worked for the organization. As the demand for women to staff the organization outstripped the supply of professional prostitutes, geishas, and the like, other groups of women were drafted, including high school students (who had been put to work in munitions factories toward the end of the war) from Saitama, Hiroshima, and Kawasaki. These young women were not allowed to return home after the surrender and were forced to work in the brothels of the RAA.[88] The case of the girls from Hiroshima was particularly sad: They had been put to work in Kure and had thus survived the bombing of Hiroshima, in which their families had perished and their homes had been destroyed. They had nowhere to return to and were offered no alternative to service in the RAA. These young women were also victims of rape.

The first brothel the RAA established, named Komachien (which loosely translates as "The Babe Garden"), was in Ōmori, a suburb of Tokyo, and it opened on August 27, 1945. Hundreds were established soon after all over Japan. One of these brothels was managed by the mistress of General Ishii Shirō, who headed the notorious Unit 731, a Manchukuo unit that had developed biological weapons and tested them on more than 3,000 Chinese prisoners. The establishment of comfort-women brothels did little to minimize the incidence of mass rape by Japanese forces during the war; the same could be said of the RAA project during the occupation.

It is a harsh irony that while the accounts of mass rape and rape in the form of enforced prostitution committed by Japanese forces during the war were being heard in the Tokyo trials—and judgment and sentence being passed on the perpetrators—the same practice was continuing throughout occupied Japan with the active participation of Allied forces and the approval of the high command of the occupying forces.

## War, Rape, and Patriarchy

It is clear from the preceding accounts that mass rape and rape by enforced prostitution were practiced by forces of many nations and were not unique to the Japanese forces of the Asia-Pacific War. Although it is necessary for Japanese to examine critically the conduct of the Japanese military during World War II—especially given the huge scale of the comfort-women operation and the massive number of women who suffered from it—it is also necessary to examine the widespread occurrence of rape in wartime and the general features of such a phenomenon.

Why do soldiers rape? Further, why does mass rape routinely occur in large-scale military campaigns? Serious analysis of the phenomenon of military mass rape is rare, yet there is ample documentary evidence of it, both from World War II and from conflicts that have occurred since. In the early stages of the Vietnam War, while the Algerians were battling for independence, the French Army brought Algerian women into the battle zone and forced them to work as prostitutes.[89] U.S. forces in Vietnam also established military brothels inside a number of their camps.[90] Yet this did not prevent the rape of large numbers of Vietnamese women, most hideously in incidents such as the My Lai massacre.[91] In the Balkans conflict in 1993, Serbian soldiers used mass rape as a terror tactic in their campaign of "ethnic cleansing." It is estimated that between 30,000 and 50,000 Muslim women have been raped and many of them subsequently murdered in this war.[92]

It is perfectly understandable that soldiers should want to have sex, if only as a temporary escape from the horrors they encounter daily. That such a respite is positive is reflected in the following comment by a Vietnam veteran:

A man and a woman holding each other tight for one moment, finding in sex some escape from the terrible reality of the war. The intensity that war brings to sex, the "let us love now because there may be no tomorrow," is based on death. No matter what our weapons on the battlefield, love is finally our only weapon against death. Sex is the weapon of life, the shooting sperms sent like an army of guerrillas to penetrate the egg's defences—the only victory that really matters. Sex is a grappling hook that pulls you out, ends your isolation, makes you one with life again.[93]

However, it must be remembered that consensual sex and rape are dramatically different undertakings (even if the boundary gets blurred in some people's accounts of their actions), and it would be very wide of the mark to account for an act of rape as a distorted outlet for an individual's sex drive. Wartime rape is a collective act on a number of levels. As another returned soldier from Vietnam put it: "They only do it when there are a lot of guys around. You know, it makes them feel good. They show each other what they can do—'I can do it,' you know. They won't do it by themselves."[94]

Indeed, the majority of rapes in war are gang rapes. They serve as a sharing of the "spoils" of war and a strengthening of the exclusively male bonds among soldiers. Fierce combat forms strong and intimate links among soldiers, and gang rape is both a by-product of this and a means by which such bonds are maintained in noncombat situations. There is also strong psychological pressure on soldiers to be brave and prepared for immediate physical combat, and this is especially so in the presence of other soldiers. The need to dominate the "other," the enemy, is imperative in battle with other men. In a noncombat situation women readily become the "other" and the target of the desire for domination by groups of tightly bonded men. The violation of the bodies of women becomes the means by which such a sense of domination is affirmed and reaffirmed. In an extreme situation such as war, in which the killing of the enemy is regarded as an act worthy of praise, the moral basis for the condemnation of crimes such as rape falls away, and the moral codes adhered to by soldiers in peacetime lose their validity.[95]

The internal power relations of armies work on a strict class system, and enlisted soldiers are always subject to the orders of officers. This creates a contradiction whereby soldiers whose principal task is to dominate and subjugate the enemy must subordinate themselves to the unquestionable authority of their officers. This contradiction is intensified in the battlefield, where the imperative to dominate the enemy is literally a matter of life or death for the individual soldier, and the need for the officer class to dominate and have unquestioned authority over groups of soldiers becomes strategically imperative. Such a contradiction creates both a high degree of tension and a context in which violence is the standard mode for the release of tension. Consequently the rape of women perceived as being the "enemy" or "belonging to the enemy" becomes a frequently used form of release—a reprehensible behavior, escaping the disciplinary matrix, that is really the underbelly of the disciplinary system. Incidents in which women are raped in front of their families—especially in front of their fathers, husbands, or brothers—are common because the violence enacted on the women also serves to humiliate enemy men and to reinforce their subjection to the occupying force. The more absolute the relation of domination between officers and enlisted men within an army, the more heightened is the contradiction between their relations to the subjugated enemy and their situation within their own force. Consequently their behavior toward the enemy—soldiers, male civilians, and women—becomes more violent. This is one explanation for the comparatively large number of rapes committed by the Japanese and German armies in World War II.

Rape in war has a number of different effects. During periods of heavy fighting, it serves to perpetuate and intensify the aggressiveness of soldiers. After victory or in noncombat periods, it serves to maintain the sense of dominance and victory and is often viewed by soldiers as the legitimate spoils of war. The Japanese army is not the only force to have used or condoned rape as a device for maintaining the group aggressiveness of soldiers. In the Falklands War of 1982, British soldiers being transported to the war zone by ship were shown violent pornographic films as a way of stimulating their aggressiveness prior to battle. As seen in the Bosnian conflict, rape can be employed on the front line as one of a range of strategies. War and rape are fundamentally related. It is foolish to imagine that the provision of large numbers of involuntary prostitutes (which is itself a form of rape) could prevent the mass or gang rape that is a general feature of modern war.

Moreover, soldiers in battle cannot avoid a further—and irresolvable—contradiction. War is usually presented as an exclusively male activity, a masculine bonding ritual, an activity in which women have no place.[96] Yet this is a fantasy of war. The reality is that war and battles frequently occur in areas occupied by civilians and that women are usually present as civilians near the front line. War is presented as an activity that demands physical strength and toughness and is seen as an occasion for the exclusive celebration of these attributes as exclusively masculine virtues. Therefore the very existence of military forces is regarded as a living symbol of masculine dominance over the "weaker" sex. In such a patriarchal ideology, it is strongly believed that a woman's place is on the home front and not in battle. This ideology demands that women be absent from battle, but its maintenance also requires that such dominance be repeatedly reinforced, especially when women are in fact present in the male domain of the battlefield, either as implicated civilians or as military nurses. Thus women must be both present and absent at the same time. War as a masculine activity is a continuing attempt to resolve such a contradiction, and yet its very existence is founded on this contradiction. The final recourse in the face of such a contradiction is to eliminate women altogether—hence the frequency with which women are massacred after rape.

Historically, military nurses have been major victims of such violence, not only because they are in close proximity to the front line but also because their military status—signified most graphically by their presence in uniform—marks them as "boundary-crossers": women who are partially but not fully integrated into a male activity. This contradiction becomes particularly apparent and acute in noncombat periods or in periods after a military victory. This may explain the massacre of the nurses on Banka Island: It can be seen as an attempt by Japanese soldiers to resolve the contradiction of being brought face to face with women in uniform. It may also be the case that nurses were regarded by the victors as spoils of war much more so than would be the case with civilian women. Nurses may have been regarded as women who had belonged to the army of their nationality but who now belonged to the victors—hence the assumption on the part of the Japanese officers that such women would be easily persuaded to become prostitutes. This can also explain the attitude of the British officer in Singapore who expressed the view that nurses would be better off being shot by soldiers of their own nationality if the only alternative was to fall into the hands of the Japanese.

Nowadays nurses are not the only women in uniform. The militaries of many countries recruit women into all branches of the military and claim they are the equals of their male comrades. One might think that this development would be undermining the kind of male society I have described and consequently be working against those social forces that produce wartime rapists. That might indeed be the case. However, strongly in evidence is a backlash from many military men against what they perceive as an invasion of their domain by women. Many men want to maintain all-male workplaces, and they often respond to the "threat" of women being present by sexual harassment of those women. This seems to be a particularly common phenomenon in the military, and the kinds of sexual harassment that occur seem to be more extreme than in other workplaces. There have been many rape cases reported in the armed forces of a number of countries in recent times.[97]

War is an inherently patriarchal activity, and rape is the most extreme expression of the patriarchal drive toward dominance of the "other." In peacetime such tendencies are held in check by the rule of law and internalized moral codes. In war the rule of law is often absent, internalized moral codes disintegrate, and these normal checks on such activities are largely replaced by incentives. Rape is unique to human beings; it does not form part of animal behavior. Despite the fact that it is often characterized as an "animal" activity, rape is profoundly cultural and patriarchal. As Virginia Woolf indicated in *Three Guineas* (1938), war is not just a military problem but is a problem created by a male-dominated society, and therefore war is closely related to other traditionally male activities such as law and organized religion.[98] To prevent war requires first destroying the male-dominated culture that creates war and then creating a new culture that ensures real equality between men and women. The same could be said of rape in war.

The 11 (male) judges at the Tokyo War Crimes Tribunal who heard the cases of mass rapes by Japanese soldiers probably never thought that the crimes they were investigating were closely related to their own status in the preeminently patriarchal world of the law. Just as Freud failed to see male sexuality as a weapon against women,[99] the judges of the tribunal failed to see these crimes committed by Japanese forces as a general characteristic of patriarchy.

# ❀ Photographs ❀

An Australian POW in transit to a labor camp from Changi POW camp in Singapore. The drawing is by Murray Griffin, an Australian official war artist who became a POW in Singapore in 1942. From the Australian War Memorial collection; used by permission.

Improvised kitchen utensils used by POWs at Sandakan POW camp, found after the war in the remains of the burnt POW camp. From the Australian War Memorial collection; used by permission.

Australian soldiers walking through the mud on the Kokoda trail in New Guinea in 1942, showing typical jungle conditions. An abandoned Japanese bicycle can be seen in the mud. From the Australian War Memorial collection; used by permission.

Captain Hoshijima (back to camera), chief of staff of the 37th Army; Major General Manaki Takanobu (second from right, wearing glasses and holding sword); and other officers shown inspecting site for an airfield in Sandakan, May 1942. From the private collections of Mr. Yamada Masaharu, a former staff officer of the 37th Army; used by permission.

British and Australian officers inspect a Japanese POW camp in Kuching soon after the war. The short man with military boots is the camp commander, Colonel Suga Tatsuji. From the Australian War Memorial collection; used by permission.

Captain Lionel Matthews, a leader of the intelligence-gathering group at Sandakan POW camp. Matthews was executed in March 1944. Australian War Memorial photo 593584; used by permission.

Kulang, a chief of the Dasan tribe, who pretended to assist the Japanese forces in constructing a path between Sandakan and Ranau and who concealed his strong anti-Japanese sentiment. From the Australian War Memorial collection; used by permission.

Lieutenant General Yamawaki Masataka, commander of the 37th Army between October 1942 and December 1944. From the private collections of Mr. Yamada Masaharu, a former staff officer of the 37th Army; used by permission.

Part of destroyed Camp No. 1 of Sandakan POW camp. The photo was taken on January 18, 1947. From the Australian War Memorial collection; used by permission.

Members of the Australian Army inspect the graves of Allied POWs at Sandakan POW camp on October 23, 1945. A Japanese look-alike onlooker seems to be one of the POW guards. From the Australian War Memorial collection; used by permission.

Wong Hiong testifies to an Australian officer about the execution of the last POW at Sandakan camp. Wong Hiong is standing where the body was buried. The date of the photo is unknown. Australian Archives (Vic): MP375/14; Dec 1945–Aug 1949; used by permission.

Russian officers, POWs of the Japanese, are shown wearing Japanese kimonos and enjoying meals and sake at a Japanese inn in 1905. Published by permission of Mainichi Shimbun.

An orchestra formed by German POWs detained in Bando, Shikoku Island, during World War I. Published by permission of Mainichi Shimbun.

Australian soldiers observe Japanese POWs engaged in hard labor on New Ireland after Japan's surrender. Australian War Memorial photo 98507; used by permission.

Australian military nurses newly arrived in Singapore in February 1941. From the Australian War Memorial collection; used by permission.

Mrs. Vivian Bullwinkel, the sole survivor of the Banka Island Massacre, standing in front of her own portrait at the Australian War Memorial in June 1992. From the Australian War Memorial collection; used by permission.

A group of Korean "comfort women" captured by the American forces in Okinawa in 1945. U.S. National Archives collection photo 127-YW600.

Sir William Webb, president of the Tokyo War Crimes Tribunal, shown with his staff in his Tokyo office. Date of the photo is unknown. Australian Archives (ACT): A1066/1; H45/580/6/3; used by permission.

Indian POWs of the Japanese being treated by Australian soldiers in Rabaul after Japan's surrender. Australian War Memorial photo 096492; used by permission.

The port of Rabaul and Simpson Bay not long after the war. Australian War Memorial photo 98016; used by permission.

The entrance to a cave in Tunnel Hill near Rabaul, New Britain. Allied POWs were detained in caves like this one. Australian War Memorial photo 96485; used by permission.

A Japanese hideout in Tunnel Hill. The Japanese made extensive use of tunnel systems in the Rabaul area after aboveground installations were destroyed by Allied bombing. Australian War Memorial photos 97494 (left) and 97493 (right); used by permission.

The graves of Allied POWs whom the Japanese claimed died as a result of illness. Australian War Memorial photo 96511; used by permission.

Rear Admiral Tamura Ryūkichi (right) being interrogated by an Australian officer through an interpreter at Kavieng, New Ireland, after the Japanese surrender. Australian War Memorial photo 98442; used by permission.

Bombs bursting at the main Japanese base at Kavieng in March 1944. A floatplane is ablaze in the water beyond the town. Australian War Memorial photo 127664; used by permission.

A large camouflaged house in Kavieng that was used as Japanese officers' quarters. The photo was taken in March 1944. The house was destroyed by planes from the 5th U.S. Army Air Force. Australian War Memorial photo 127665; used by permission.

Kavieng wharf after it was destroyed by Allied bombing. Australian War Memorial photo 98451; used by permission.

Captain Sanagi Tsuyoshi, staff officer of the Southeast Fleet (second from left), being questioned by Allied officers on an Allied ship in Rabaul after the surrender. Australian War Memorial photo 95708; used by permission.

An Australian POW.

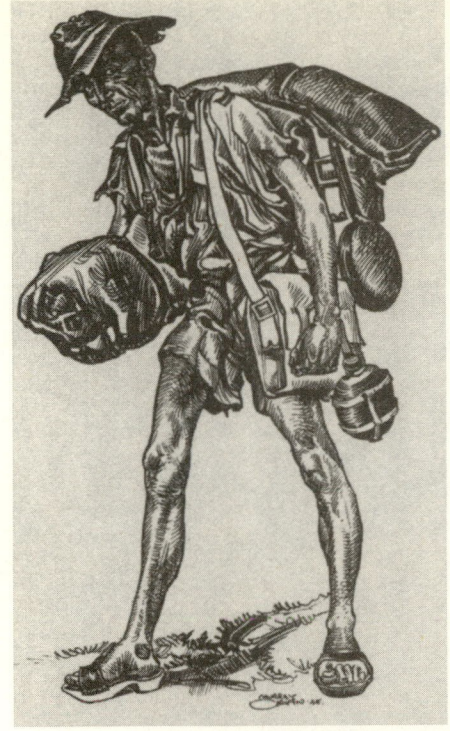

Improvised kitchen utensils
used by POWs.

Australian
soldiers on
Kokoda
trail.

Captain Hoshijima.

British and Australian officers inspect POW camp.

Captain Lionel Matthews.

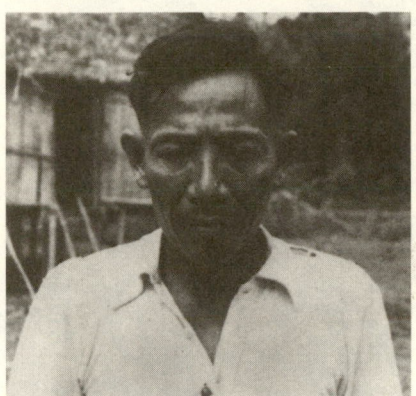

Kulang, chief of Dasan tribe.

Lieutenant General
Yamawaki Masataka.

Part of destroyed Camp No. 1 of Sandakan POW camp.

Members of the Australian Army inspect graves.

Wong Hiong.

Russian officers, POWs of the Japanese in 1905.

Orchestra formed by German POWs during World War I.

Australian soldiers observing Japanese POWs.

Australian military nurses in Singapore in 1941.

Mrs. Vivian Bullwinkel.

Korean "comfort women" in Okinawa, 1945.

Sir William Webb with his staff in Tokyo.

Indian POWs.

Port of Rabaul and Simpson Bay.

Entrance to cave in Tunnel Hill near Rabaul.

Japanese hideout in Tunnel Hill.

Graves of Allied POWs.

Rear Admiral Tamura Ryūkichi.

Bombs bursting at Kavieng in March 1944.

Camouflaged
house in Kavieng,
March 1944.

Kavieng wharf
destroyed by
Allied bombing.

Captain
Sanagi Tsuyoshi.

# 4

# Judge Webb and Japanese Cannibalism

## The Tokyo Tribunal and Cannibalism

On December 6, 1946, H.V. Evatt, Australia's minister for foreign affairs, sent a telegram to Judge William F. Webb, who was then in Tokyo for the International Military Tribunal for the Far East.[1] The telegram asked Webb to advise Evatt as to whether Australia should adopt the recent British decision regarding the B and C Class trials. Britain wanted to bring to these trials only those suspects who were charged with crimes punishable by either death or more than seven years' imprisonment. It was a matter of some importance for the Australian government to come to a decision on this matter. If the British and Australian governments adopted different policies for bringing suspected war criminals to trial, there would be the potential for a major political problem. The Australian government at this time was concentrating on the prosecution of major war crimes and was not actively prosecuting war crimes punishable by less than twelve months' imprisonment. Evatt wanted Webb to give his opinion as to whether Australia should also cease to prosecute "intermediate" war crimes for which prison sentences ranged between one and seven years.

Webb cabled his opinion to Evatt on December 10, 1946: "Your 388. Consider test of probable sentence unsatisfactory. Suggest all deliberate act or omissions causing, or likely to cause, death or grievous bodily harm. Also, *cannibalism* and torturing."[2] [Emphasis added.] It is clear from this cable that Webb was of the opinion that all those accused of war crimes in the B and C Class involving murder, grievous bodily harm, cannibalism, or torture should be taken to trial and that there should be no compromise. However, there is no evidence to suggest that Webb had actually brought the issue of cannibalism to the attention of the A Class tribunal, of which he was president.

During the war, as the chairman of the War Crimes Committee, Webb had viewed substantial numbers of documents and reports prepared by the Australian Army on the issue of cannibalism. In some cases he had personally interrogated witnesses to such crimes. Australia was the only member of the Allied nations to recognize cannibalism and mutilation of the dead as specific war crimes,[3] and this was probably because of the detailed investigations and reports gathered by Webb in the three reports on Japanese war crimes trials over which he had presided in the years 1944 to 1946. Nevertheless, it appears that Webb had no intention of revealing his knowledge of such crimes while participating in the A Class tribunals. Theoretically it was not possible for Webb, as a judge at these tribunals, to select which war crimes would come to trial. However, in practice Webb maintained close contact with the Australian prosecutors and was a close friend of the chief Australian prosecutor, A.J. Mansfield. It seems highly unlikely that they would not have discussed the issue of cannibalism at some stage of the proceedings. Australia brought the most representative cases of murder, grievous bodily harm, and torture to the A Class tribunal but not those of cannibalism. Why did Webb neglect to have this issue brought to the attention of the tribunal? Before this question is answered, it is necessary to analyze the actual occurrences of cannibalism committed by Japanese forces.

## Evidence of Japanese Cannibalism

There is a certain amount of Japanese writing suggesting that Japanese forces committed acts of cannibalism in the Philippines and New Guinea during the Asia-Pacific War (Map 4.1). A typical example is found in the novel *Fires on the Plane* by Ōoka Shōhei.[4] The 1987 Japanese documentary film *Yuki Yuki te Shingun* (Onward Holy Army) contains interviews with Japanese war veterans who confessed to engaging in cannibalism during the New Guinea campaign.[5] Several autobiographies by Japanese veterans of that campaign also make explicit references to cannibalism. For example, Ogawa Shōji mentioned incidents that occurred between December 1943 and March 1944 when Japanese forces were retreating through the Finisterre Mountains in north-central New Guinea.

Here I saw something genuinely horrible. There was the body of a soldier lying on the track, and a large part of his thigh had been hacked off. . . . Later I was walking along a track with Y when we were called by a group of four or five soldiers who were not in our troop. They had just finished a meal, and there were mess-tins nearby. They said that they had a large cut of snake meat and invited us to join them. But we didn't like the way they were smiling as they said it. We felt that they were not telling us something. It was as if they wanted us to be "partners in crime." There was something unusual about the way they were staring at us, as if they were waiting to see

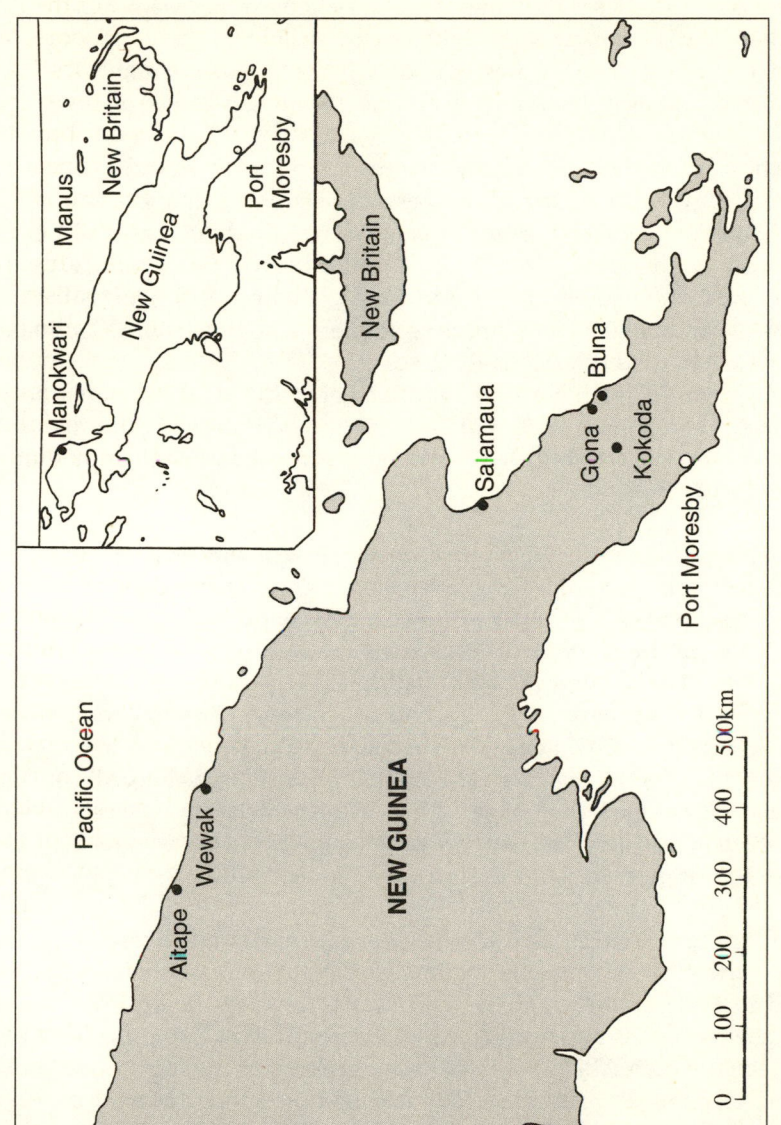

Map 4.1 *New Guinea.*

our reaction. Y felt the same way about the situation and said "no thanks; maybe some other time." The situation was very tense. We left hurriedly, but cautiously, scared that they might try to shoot us. After we had walked a while, Y said to me "It's very strange. What do you think they were doing? If that had been snake meat they would never have given any to us. Don't you think they were trying to drag us into the crime they had committed?" . . . In fact we saw many bodies which had had their thighs hacked off.[6]

In a book published in 1992, Ogawa reported that toward the end of the war he was witness to horrific conversations among Japanese soldiers in New Guinea along the lines of "so-and-so has died, let's go and get his body."[7] In another case a friend of his found human flesh in the mess tin of an officer who had become ill and died.[8] The impression left is that the victims of cannibalism were Japanese soldiers who had been killed in battle or who had died of various illnesses.

In his memoirs Nogi Harumichi, the chief of the Japanese naval police force in Ambon, mentioned incidents that occurred in the Philippines and that were reported to him by a Japanese army lieutenant immediately after the war.

Most of the Japanese forces who were retreating from mountain to mountain were looters. This is a terrible thing to remember. There was absolutely nothing to eat, and so we decided to draw lots. The one who lost would be killed and eaten. But the one who lost started to run away so we shot him. He was eaten. You probably think that many of us raped the local women. But women were not regarded as objects of sexual desire. They were regarded as the object of our hunger. We had no sexual appetite. To commit rape would have cost us too much energy, and we never wanted to. All we dreamt about was food. I met some soldiers in the mountains who were carrying baked human arms and legs. It was not guerillas but our own soldiers who we were frightened of. It was such a terrible condition.[9]

The Japanese sources give the impression that in most cases Japanese soldiers themselves were the victims of the acts of cannibalism that occurred in New Guinea and the Philippines toward the end of the war when their supplies had been completely cut off. However, incidents also occurred in which Allied soldiers and members of the local populations became victims. For example, Ogawa Shōji noted that toward the end of the war, Japanese soldiers referred to the Allies as "white pigs" and the local population as "black pigs."[10] But such honesty is rare, and so information about the widespread practice of cannibalism during the latter part of the war has long been confined to rumor. The only information on the practice available from the Japanese side has come from autobiographies and memoirs such as Ogawa's.

My recent discovery of extensive reports of the Australian War Crimes Section and records of war crime trials by the Australian military has made it possible to undertake a more comprehensive analysis of the practice of cannibalism committed by the Japanese in New Guinea. I also obtained U.S. National Archives documents that refer to Japanese cannibalism in New Guinea. However, the number of U.S. documents on this subject is very small, which is understandable because at the time the majority of Allied forces operating in this region were Australians.

The victims of cannibalism in the war can be divided into four groups: (1) Allied soldiers, the majority of whom were Australians; (2) Asian POWs who were brought to New Guinea as laborers; (3) the local population of New Guinea; (4) other Japanese soldiers. Not surprisingly, the Australian reports concentrate on incidents in which Australian soldiers were victims of cannibalism and refer only rarely or incidentally to incidents involving Japanese victims, although there is no evidence to suggest that Japanese were victims less frequently than other groups. Indeed, there is the evidence from a number of interviews I conducted with former Australian soldiers who gave eyewitness accounts of many mutilated bodies of Japanese soldiers. U.S. reports contain a number of cases in which Japanese soldiers were victims along with Australians and Americans, despite the overall small number of reports on this issue.

In the transcripts of the Australian War Crimes Section reports and the war crimes trials, the Australian National Archives and the Australian War Memorial have removed all references to the names of Australian victims of cannibalism, the places where the incidents occurred, and the dates of such incidents. This has not been done for incidents in which Asian POWs or members of the New Guinea population were victims. The names of the Japanese soldiers accused of the practice have also been retained in the reports. The U.S. documents contain all the names of the victims as well as suspected perpetrators. However, throughout this chapter, I will use only the initials of the accused, as the purpose of this analysis is to give a more systematic view of the practice of cannibalism and to move away from a focus on particular perpetrators. I do not disclose victims' names that appear in the U.S. documents for the sake of privacy of the victims and their relatives.

## Allied Victims of Cannibalism

Among the various reports on cannibalism prepared by the Australian military forces, the most detailed description of the condition of the bodies can be found in cases in which the victims were Australian soldiers. This is probably because the majority of eyewitnesses of such incidents were members of the same squad as the deceased, and they usually reported the incidents immediately after they occurred, when the details were still vivid in their memory. In some cases the bodies were inspected by army doctors, and these reports also contribute to the detailed description of such incidents. In cases in which the victims were Asian POWs or indigenous locals, the incidents were frequently reported by witnesses who did not speak English, and thus many of these reports are more perfunctory and contain much less detail than those of Australian victims.

The following is a typical example of a report on an Australian victim recorded on May 20, 1945:[11]

SX8064 WO II HUGO C of ——— Bn, being duly sworn, states:

On the morning of the ——— at 0900 hours, NX 79420 Cpl GRIFFIN, J, the late Sjt Sewell, and myself recovered the body of ——— who had been killed by enemy action on the ———. We found the body in the following condition:

(a)  all clothing had been removed
(b)  both arms had been cut off at the shoulder
(c)  the stomach had been cut out, and the heart, liver and other entrails had been removed
(d)  all fleshy parts of the body had been cut away, leaving the bones bare
(e)  the arms, heart, liver and entrails could not be found
(f)  the only parts of the body not touched were the head and feet.
A Japanese mess tin which appeared to contain human flesh was lying four to five yards from ———'s body between two dead Japanese soldiers.

(signed) C. HUGO WO II
SX 8064

The content of the U.S. reports is quite similar to that of the Australian documents. The following is an example from the U.S. files:[12]

1.  On January 24, 1943, Pfc. E.H. was killed in action in an attempt to capture a group of Japanese. The next day the body was recovered by Lieut. William C. Benson, Co. "G," 163rd Infantry Regiment, who certified that it was found in the following condition.

"The abdomen had been opened by two criss-cross slashes. Flesh had been removed from the thighs and buttocks."

The body was examined by Captain Henry C. Smith, M.C., 2nd Battalion Surgeon, 163rd Infantry Regiment, who certified to the following evidence of mutilation.

"A mid-line abdominal incision from the lower rib cage to the pubis. This incision was straight and clear with smooth edges. No examination was made of the abdominal content. A clean strip of skin tissue and muscle approximately 4 x 12 x 2 was removed from the lateral portion of the thigh."

2. Pvt. M.W., 163rd Infantry Regiment, was killed in action 24 January 1943, in an attempt to capture a group of Japanese. On 25 January 1943, the body was recovered by Lieut. William C. Benson, Co. "G," 163rd Infantry Regiment, who certified that flesh had been removed from both thighs.

3. Sgt. H.B. reported missing in action on 19 January 1943 was found in a mutilated condition on 23 January 1943. The body was identified and examined by Pfc. Other [sic] E. Dickson who swore that the body was found in the following condition.

"The flesh part of the thigh and each leg had been cut away. The abdominal cavity had been opened by cutting away the skin and flesh under each lower rib. The face had not been mutilated, thus making identification possible."

Pvt. Dickson further stated that a stew pot in a nearby Japanese bunker contained the heart and liver of approximate size of that [of a] human.

The above statement was also sworn by Cpl. Clinne C. Lamb, 36679399, Co. "F," 163rd Infantry Regiment, who was also a member of the searching party.

Many other cases refer to the fact that Japanese cannibalism extended to the entrails and the genitals of the victims; in some cases the brains were taken out, and therefore in such a case it was difficult to identify the soldier, as the face was disfigured beyond recognition. That intestines were cooked is confirmed by a report dated May 22, 1945, from which the following is an excerpt.[13] This report is about four separate incidents involving a total of six Australian victims. Each incident had between two and four witnesses.

NX14764 Lieut A B Carson being duly sworn states:

———, ———, and ———, were killed in an attack on enemy positions on the afternoon of ———. My section was sent in to endeavour to extricate the bodies that same afternoon, but accurate sniper's fire forced us to withdraw before reaching the spot where they were reported to have been killed. Enemy resistance made it impossible to get the bodies out before ———, on which day I was again sent out on patrol for this purpose. We found three sets of Aust web equipt, two pairs of boots, two sets of clothing and other odd items which were recognised as belonging to the victims.

Further search revealed scalp which was easily recognised as that of ———, by the ———. Entrails were strewn across a log and pieces of flesh which had been partially burnt were nearby whilst in one of our own basic pouches were pieces of what appeared to be liver. Evidence such [as] bloodstains and pieces of flesh which had definitely been cut with a sharp instrument, proved beyond doubt that bodies had been butchered, gutted and scalped.

Outside a hut 300 yards further along from this position were found the fresh bones of a burnt foot. Inside this hut we also found fragments of a right thigh bone which had obviously been cooked and broken for the marrow. The size of this bone indicated that it came from a body ———— feet in height presumably ————.

Outside another hut 100 yards away more leg, thigh and shoulder bone were found together with human flesh with ———— on it.

Outside yet another hut the head of ———— was recognised, and the body consisting only of a head which had been scalped and a spinal column lay on the ground. Besides these remains lay a wrist and hand which were charred and burned.

———— AAB 83 and atebring [sic] roll book were found inside the first mentioned hut.

In all cases the condition of the remains was such that there can be no doubt that the bodies had been dismembered and portions of flesh cooked.

The injuries sustained by these men were not due to high explosive from our arty [artillery] but by rifle fire. The MO of my Sqn examined certain of the above-mentioned remains and concurs fully with my statement. I am quite certain that the remains found were ————, ————, and ———— and the following witnesses will bear out this evidence, themselves assisting in the burial of the remains.

Signed. A.B. Carson

Signed before me. Signed. Nisbet Major.

The condition of the scalps indicates that the Japanese soldiers tried to remove the brains of the victims but were interrupted by the advance of the Australian forces. In the cases mentioned here there was neither time nor opportunity for the Japanese soldiers to hide the evidence of cannibalism. In fact, the vast majority of incidents in which Australian soldiers were victims had a similar pattern in that the Japanese soldiers had no time to dispose of the mutilated and cooked remains. The following U.S. report also seems to support such an interpretation:[14]

1st Lieut. H.F. was killed in action 8 January 1943. Statement made by Sgt. Roy G. Mikalson, 20929231, Co. "C", 163rd Infantry Regiment, and S/Sgt. Gordon F. Meager, 20220220, Co. "C", 163rd Infantry Regiment, state that they were within ten and two yards respectively of Lieut. F when he was killed by a Japanese bullet. These witnesses further stated that when the platoon withdrew, Lieut. F's body was not mutilated in any way. At that time it could not be removed as the enemy fire was too intense.

On 11 January 1943, the body was recovered. The left arm had been cut away and was not found with the body. Slices of flesh had been cut from the calves of the legs and the body had been disembowelled, the heart and liver being also missing.

Later, on 11 January, the bones of the left forearm were found in a Japanese perimeter 400 yards north east of the US perimeter Musket.

It seems clear that Japanese soldiers removed the bodies of Allied soldiers from the area in which fierce combat was occurring and carried them to a safe area to be cooked and consumed, while others held back the Allied forces in order to prevent them from recovering the bodies. This indicates that these incidents were not isolated or sporadic acts but part of an organized process.[15]

There also appears to have been incidents in which Australian POWs were victims of cannibalism, although there are no Australian eyewitness accounts of mutilated or cooked bodies. Australian military officials interrogated a number of Japanese soldiers after the war, but all denied any knowledge of or participation in the practice of cannibalism, and therefore it became very difficult to establish a reliable account of such incidents.

In November 1944 a Dutch POW, P.W. Wildemar, escaped from the POW camp in Wewak and lived in the jungle nearby. At some time in early 1945 he met a Japanese deserter, Corporal M.T., in this area, and they stayed together for some time. At this time M.T. told Wildemar that he had witnessed the murder and consumption of an Australian pilot POW by Japanese soldiers in January or February of 1945. Wildemar was rescued by the Australian forces, but M.T. stayed in the jungle. M.T. was a member of C Battalion. Toward the end of January 1945 two planes went down in this region, a Royal Australian Air Force (RAAF) Kittyhawk piloted by Warrant Officer R.K. and another RAAF plane piloted by a Corporal F.M. Both pilots were reported missing. Either (or both) of these men could have been the victim of this act.[16]

After the war, the Australian military followed up Wildemar's story and located M.T. in Japan. He was interrogated on June 2, 1947, but denied that he had witnessed the murder of the Australian pilot and claimed he had merely heard about the events secondhand. Australian officials also interrogated members of the Kempeitai stationed in this region and discovered that the Kempeitai had interrogated both of these pilots about troop movements and the like. The pilots had no useful information and were murdered by the police. However, the police denied that they had taken part in acts of cannibalism.[17]

Major H.S. Williams, who investigated this case in Tokyo, sent a letter to the headquarters of the Australian military stating that "as M.T. has been proved to be untruthful, it is proposed to re-open this investigation as soon as any additional leads can be obtained."[18] There is no further information about this case in archive files; presumably it proved impossible to establish a case for prosecution.

What is significant about this alleged incident is that, if true, it is an example of deliberate murder for the purpose of cannibalism rather than the cannibalism of soldiers or civilians who had died in battle or of illness. There are reports of other incidents of a similar nature in the files, but no prosecutions were launched.

## Cannibalism of Asian POWs

It is well known that many Allied POWs were forced to work in various parts of Japanese-occupied Southeast Asia during the war, mainly on large-scale construction projects such as the Burma-Thailand railway, where more than 60,000 Allied POWs and 270,000 Asian laborers were exploited.[19] A large number of Indian, Chinese, and Malaysian POWs and civilians were sent to New Guinea and neighboring small islands. Documents in the Australian War Crimes Section report suggest that many such forced laborers became victims of Japanese cannibalism. One of the most shocking cases is that concerning a number of Indian Muslims.

The Indian POWs working in New Guinea were divided into two types of work groups: construction companies and special transport companies in both the Army and the Navy. They were of various sizes; one mentioned in an interrogation consisted of 546 Indian POWs. There were 30 of these companies stationed in the New Guinea region.[20] Given that there were 5,570 Indian POW forced laborers on Rabaul and New Ireland at the end of the war, it can be estimated that there were between 8,000 and 10,000 in New Guinea proper.[21]

Most of these Indians were probably in the Indo-Pakistan forces that formed part of the larger Commonwealth forces and were taken prisoner when Singapore fell in February 1942. The following testimony was given by Hatam Ali, a Pakistani soldier taken prisoner on February 15. His company was mobilized into forced labor in various places in Malaysia, and attempts were made to recruit members of the company into the Indian National Army, a pro-Japanese force that had been established to benefit from Indian anti-British sentiment. Ali refused to join and was put into a laboring party of about 1,000 prisoners who were sent to Manokwari in New Guinea toward the end of 1943. Soon after they arrived, they were put to work on the construction of an airfield, and in April 1944, 206 prisoners were sent to a new site 300 miles from Manokwari under the supervision of S Unit, one of the construction units.[22] Ali was one of these.

I was included in this number. We were taken to a place about 300 miles away, we were employed for 12 hours daily on hard fatigues and were given very little to eat. There was no medical treatment and all prisoners who fell ill were immediately killed by the Japanese. Later, due to Allied attacks and activity, the Japs also ran out of rations. We prisoners were made to eat grass and leaves and due to starvation we even ate snakes, frogs and other insects. At this stage the Japanese started selecting prisoners and everyday 1 prisoner was taken out and killed and eaten by the Japanese. I personally saw this happen and about 100 prisoners were eaten at this place by the Japanese. The remainder of us were taken to another spot about 50 miles [away] where 10 prisoners died of sickness. At this place the Japanese again started selecting prisoners to eat. Those selected were taken to a hut where flesh was cut from their bodies while they were alive and they were then thrown into a ditch alive where they later died. When flesh was being cut from those selected terrible cries and shrieks came from them and also from the ditch where they were later thrown. These cries used to gradually dim down when the unfortunate individuals were dying. We were not allowed to go near this ditch, no earth was thrown on the bodies and the smell was terrible.[23]

Eventually Ali's turn came. He was escorted by two soldiers toward this hut, but he ran away. He was chased by a Japanese soldier and was injured in the left ankle, but he finally escaped. He spent the next 15 days wandering the jungle and was rescued by Australian forces. Investigators located no other witnesses to corroborate his story, but if true it raises certain questions. Why did the Japanese soldiers find it necessary to cut flesh from the POWs while they were still living?

In the first stage of cannibalism, the soldiers were killing prisoners and then consuming their flesh. But by the time they moved camp, the situation had become desperate. Prisoner numbers were down to less than 100, and there was no likelihood of a conventional food supply being reestablished. It is possible that the Japanese soldiers—faced with the problem of the rapid rate of putrefaction in the Tropics—cut the flesh from living prisoners as a way of ensuring that they would survive for a period and that their internal organs would then be available for later consumption. Hence the ditch in which these prisoners were dumped was not covered with earth. There seems to be no other explanation for the adoption of such hideously cruel methods, unless of course the whole business of systematic cannibalism had brutalized the Japanese soldiers to such an extent that an increasing degree of sadism became incorporated into the process.

This case is a horrifying example of a situation in which POWs were kept alive as a food source for the Japanese guards. However, such cases were comparatively rare. It was far more typical for soldiers to kill and consume POWs who had become ill. Such prisoners were usually shot;

however, there are cases in which army doctors would administer lethal injections to the sick prisoners. For example, on April 5, 1943, a Japanese army doctor T.T. administered lethal injections to two Indian army POWs and subsequently cut flesh from their thighs and removed their livers. He ordered another Indian POW—a cook, Rabi Lohar—to prepare the flesh and livers for consumption. But Lohar refused to do this, even after being beaten. Eventually, a Japanese soldier, N.Y., cooked the body parts.[24] In May 1943 another Indian POW was killed by the same method and for the same purpose. T.T. was tried and executed on May 3, 1946, and three Japanese soldiers who participated in the consumption of the Indian POWs were sentenced to ten years' imprisonment.[25]

It is known that a large number of Formosan laborers were also mobilized by the Japanese forces for the construction of military-related facilities in various places in the Pacific region. How many Formosans were sent to New Guinea is unknown, but at least two reports prepared by the U.S. forces clearly indicate that some Formosans also became victims of Japanese cannibalism in this region. One report refers to incidents on Biak Island in the northwest of New Guinea, the other to incidents on Manus Island in the Bismarck Sea, northeast of New Guinea. The following summaries of interrogations conducted on Formosan POWs appear in the Biak report:[26]

PW, JA(USA) 149583, <u>SON, Kei Zun</u>, a FORMOSAN civilian employee of 2 Co, 107 Airfield Survey and Construction Unit, surrendered to US troops at <u>BOROKI</u>, BIAK I, 28 Aug. '44.

<u>Cannibalism</u> 28 Aug. '44, while PW was foraging for food on BIAK I, he heard a rifle shot approx 100 meters away. From concealment he saw two JAP soldiers approach a dead FORMOSAN whom he thought was from 108 Fld Airfield Survey and Construction Unit. JAPS stripped body and used bayonet to hack off a leg. PW became frightened and immediately related incident to other FORMOSANS in his unit. Believing their lives were in jeopardy, they fled to US troops.

PW, JA(USA) 149579, <u>SHU, Kon Tsu</u>, a FORMOSAN civilian employee of 107 Airfield Survey and Construction Unit, surrendered to US troops at BOROKI, 28 Aug. '44.

<u>Cannibalism</u> BIAK I, Jul '44, PW heard from C.Z.R. that he saw JAPS collecting dead Formosans for their meat. 4 Aug '44, PW heard C was murdered by JAPS near WARDO for the same purpose.

14–15 Aug '44, approx six hours march from WARDO toward SORIDO, PW saw the remains of his hometown friend R.H.K. and two others at South agricultural field. Only the head and bones remained but PW noticed each victim had been slashed across the throat. He heard of 15 other FORMOSAN corpses having been stripped of the flesh.

JAP troops and FORMOSANS prepared their meals individually. JAPS always seemed to have meat but FORMOSANS had only the vegetables they grew and the little rice that was allotted them. FORMOSANS often traded with natives but could get meat only from JAPS. JAPS always claimed meat was dog meat but PW suspected it was human flesh, therefore, never bartered. He thought it impossible that there should be a daily supply of dog meat specially when he had rarely seen a dog on BIAK I.

Meat seen by PW had little skin or hair but he knew dog meat to have thick layer of skin and thick stubble of hair. He heard human flesh was too salty to eat if fried, and therefore had to be broiled.

PW, JA(USA) 149826, <u>CHO, Seki Ju</u>, a FORMOSAN civilian employee of 108 Fld Airfield Survey and Construction Unit, surrendered to US troops after reading ALLIED leaflet at WARDO, BIAK I, 7 Sep '44.

<u>Cannibalism</u> Jun '44, on BIAK I, PW and 13 other FORMOSANS decided to surrender to ALLIES after having read an ALLIED propaganda leaflet. En route, group was intercepted by approx 100 u/i JAP troops. Eight of the FORMOSANS were killed and PW felled by a bayonet. While feigning death, PW saw a JAP soldier take the intestines from a dead FORMOSAN and place it in his mess kit. PW did not see more as JAPS left.

Another interrogation summary of a Formosan POW refers to a scene similar to that described in Hatam Ali's testimony about flesh being hacked from live bodies:[27]

Prisoner of War RI, Shin Te (JA(USA) 149444); Formosan civilian employee of the 107 Airfield Survey and Construction Unit has established the probability of the following acts of cannibalism:

"During August 1944, prisoner of war saw many corpses lying around Biak with portions of flesh removed by knife, but did not witness such butchery. On 15 August 1944, prisoners of war came across three Formosan bodies that were not dead over few hours. They were lying in a pool of blood approximately 15 feet from a jungle path. Each was bayoneted through the chest and flesh was removed from thighs."

From these interrogation summaries it is almost certain that many Formosans, who were regarded as racially inferior to Japanese despite the fact that they were mobilized as "Japanese Army employees," also became the victims of murder and cannibalism.

## Cannibalism of the Indigenous Population

It seems that victims of cannibalism numbered as many among the indigenous population of New Guinea as among Australian or Commonwealth soldiers. Reports of such incidents based on the testimony of members of the local population were made to Australian military officials. In the majority of cases the victims were villagers who were known to be hostile to the Japanese forces and to have actively cooperated with the Australian forces. The following is a typical example of such an incident.

On April 12, 1945, a group of Japanese soldiers attacked a New Guinea village "T," ransacked the houses, and stole yams, copra, and other foods as well as cooking utensils. Most of the villagers hid in the jungle, but two failed to escape and were abducted by the soldiers. In order to rescue these two men, three villagers followed the Japanese soldiers. But when they reached the place where the Japanese soldiers had regrouped, "X," they were attacked by Japanese with submachine guns. The villagers defended themselves with hand grenades (which had been provided by Australian forces) and retreated. However, one was killed and another who was seriously injured later died in the jungle. The two villagers who had been captured made an escape; one was killed by submachine-gun fire. The Japanese remained at "X" for three days and then moved on. A party of villagers, including the two survivors of the earlier incident, returned to "X" some days later.[28] They found two mutilated bodies. One of the three villagers who had followed the Japanese soldiers after the raid gave the following testimony on May 10, 1945:

I found "W's" body. Flesh had been cut from the chest, thighs, calves, buttocks and back. His shoulders had been cut through and both forearms were missing. The viscera were intact. The top of the head had been cut off, and the brain removed. The flesh had been cut with some sharp instrument. The body of "S" had cuts on it but no flesh was missing. Near a small fire which the Japanese had used for cooking I found the bone from a man's forearm. It had been in a fire and shreds of cooked flesh were still adhering to it. There were scrapings of taro and yam around the same fire.[29]

The Australian forces took two other testimonies; one of the witnesses was the wife of victim "W." Because of the close-knit nature of New Guinean village society, it was common that the witnesses to such crimes were the close kin of the victim.

The second testimony was given by a Lieutenant F.M., who was interrogated on June 17, 1947, by the Australian War Crimes Section in Tokyo. F.M. had been the commander of a squad of 41 Japanese soldiers who surrendered to an Australian force in an area close to village "T" on May 3, 1945. F.M. claimed that the murder and consumption of the villagers had been committed by members of his squad, but he had not been aware of the incident at the time. He claimed he was informed only at a later stage and that he had then punished three soldiers involved by assigning them dangerous forward scouting and reconnaissance duties. These three soldiers died in the fighting that occurred prior to the surrender of the squad. F.M. also claimed that he could not remember the names of other soldiers who had taken part in the consumption of the villagers. The officer interrogating F.M. commented on his file "I know him to be the original 'Smart Alec' and constitutionally unable to speak the truth."[30] F.M.'s version of the cannibalism incident is, of course, false. A report by Captain David Feinberg, the Australian officer who captured this squad, stated that "these t[roo]ps were by no means starving and their discipline was excellent. It may be presumed that any atrocities were carried out with the consent and under the orders of the officers of the party."[31] Another report states that "the Japanese captured in 'W' area May 3, 1945, were found to be in good physical condition. This particularly applies to the officers. . . . The discipline maintained within the PW personnel was of the highest order. The officers had excellent control of men under their command."[32]

One category of crimes not covered in the report of the Australian War Crimes Section involved cannibalism inflicted upon soldiers of Papuan infantry battalions and the 1st, 2nd, and 3rd New Guinean Infantry battalions. These were units made up of members of the Papuan and New Guinean populations under Australian Army command. From July 1942 until the end of the war, more than 4,000 of these soldiers fought the Japanese on the mainland of Papua New Guinea and in New Britain and Bougainville under the command of 500 Australian officers and NCOs. They waged a guerrilla war against the occupying forces, and their familiarity with the jungle made it easy for them to conduct ambushes and lightning raids on enemy soldiers. The Japanese called them "Ryokuin" (green shadows), a nickname subsequently taken up by the Australian soldiers.[33]

According to one of the former officers of these battalions, Dick Collins, there were some instances in which the bodies of such soldiers killed in fighting could not be subsequently located. Squads who returned to the scenes of battles in these areas sometimes found human remains in Japanese mess tins.[34] However, there are no reports of such incidents in the testimony to the Australian War Crimes Section. It may be that they were not reported by the Australian officers in command of these troops or that such incidents were reported but not followed up by the War Crimes Section. Collins also noted the high level of discipline among Japanese soldiers who had been captured or who had surrendered, even when they were starving.[35]

## Starvation and Group Psychosis

It is clear from these reports that the widespread practice of cannibalism by Japanese soldiers in the Asia-Pacific War was something more than merely random incidents perpetrated by individuals or small groups subject to extreme conditions. The testimonies indicate that cannibalism was a systematic and organized military strategy, committed by whole squads or by specific soldiers working within the context of a larger squad. This is particularly so in the case of the Indian POWs and Formosan workers, who had outlived their usefulness as laborers and were now regarded by their captors as human cattle, as a food supply. The moral and psychological bearings of the Japanese soldiers and guards were transformed to such a degree that the act of cannibalism and even the murder of prisoners for the purpose of cannibalism became a normal occurrence rather than an extreme and grotesque activity. The fact that such activities were committed by whole groups, working within the normal military structures, resulted in a situation in which the act of cannibalism ceased to be horrific and became instead a part of everyday life. As was noted in the account of the cannibalistic consumption of Australian and American soldiers killed in battle, the gaining of bodies for this purpose was often carried out in the midst of battle, with one section of the Japanese squad continuing the fighting while another section removed the bodies from the battlefield to a safe area where they could be prepared for consumption. Sometimes such behavior more closely resembled that of animals on the hunt: The bodies were captured, mutilated, and consumed, and the cannibals then moved on.

Such "hunting parties" came to regard any corpse in an edible condition as "fair game," and the nationality or circumstances of death ceased to be of importance. Cannibalism is traditionally divided into two types: "exo-cannibalism," in which a group inflicts cannibalism on people outside the group, and "endo-cannibalism," in which members of the group become victims of the group's cannibalistic practices, usually as part of a religious or ritual ceremony.[36] In the cases described here, however, the cannibalism is neither exo- nor endo- but merely a sort of general "group-survival cannibalism," a practice driven by starvation and without the cultural meanings of the other types. As Ogawa Shōji remarked, "We took a deep breath and struggled to remain human, to not become wild animals."[37]

In such situations the distinction between the bodies of allies and enemies disappears. All become nothing more than a source of food—a situation well documented by the many reports to the Australian War Crimes

Section of discoveries of mutilated and partially consumed bodies of Japanese soldiers.[38] In some of these cases, those consumed were soldiers who had become ill and died, but other cases were similar to the incidents involving New Guinea villagers[39]—Japanese soldiers would kill other Japanese soldiers and consume them in a manner similar to that recounted in Nogi Harumichi's testimony excerpted earlier in the chapter. Indeed, one of the U.S. reports contains affidavits made by several U.S. soldiers who saw the mutilated body of a Japanese soldier, the condition of which clearly indicated that he was murdered by his comrades for the purpose of cannibalism. The following is one of those affidavits, presented by Felix Espinoza Jr., a member of Troop F 8th Cavalry:[40]

As a member of the patrol from Troop F 8th Cavalry, under the leadership of Sgt Aiello, I was a witness to the discovery of the butchered Jap. Our patrol was ordered by Captain Hickman to investigate a shot heard the previous night. Our patrol proceeded about 300 yards SE of Bohu Ai on Manus Island. We crossed a small creek and entered a clearing in which we counted several "lean to" and one shack. There was smoke rising from the Jap occupied shack. We knew there were Japs in the shack from their voices. We observed a Jap walking from a brush pile just outside the shack. We shot him and three others inside the shack. The former had blood on his hands which we found had come from a corpse lying under the brush pile. We lifted the brush and found a corpse of a Jap and it was crudely butchered. The flesh was cut from the legs from the knee to the hips. The calves of both legs were cut clear to the bone. The Jap had his hands tied and a rope around his waist. We checked the inside of the shack and found bloody mess gear and a bloody knife, the crude instrument used in the butchering. We reported back to camp. A small patrol was sent back under the control of Lt Miller to investigate further. [Emphasis added.]

Such instances have become models for the standard account of cannibalism by Japanese soldiers in World War II: an account in which cannibalism is held to be an extreme and unusual occurrence, a product of the chaos, disorganization, and starvation that occurred among the Japanese forces toward the end of the war. However, the reports of the Australian War Crimes Section clearly demonstrate that acts of cannibalism were not always the product of a collapse in morale and organization of Japanese forces. To the contrary, cannibalism was often a systematic activity conducted by whole squads and under the command of officers. Throughout periods of starvation and cannibalism, discipline was maintained to an astonishing degree.

There are repeated references in the testimony to the Australian War Crimes Section of the high level of discipline of captured squads of Japanese soldiers. The reports of Captain Feinberg to the War Crimes Section and of Dick Collins are two examples of this observation. Both reinforce the judgment that cannibalism occurred within a context in which discipline had been maintained rather than one in which discipline had collapsed. Thus there could be some cases in which Japanese soldiers who refused to participate in the group cannibalism committed by their squad or company became victims of this crime themselves because they were seen as potential traitors to the group's solidarity and discipline. In fact, the existence of such cases was implied in the film *Yuki Yuki te Shingun*.

It is undeniable that one of the principal reasons for the widespread occurrence of cannibalism in the Japanese-occupied areas was starvation caused by the lack of a food supply. Most incidents of cannibalism referred to in the War Crimes Section report occurred from mid-1944 to mid-1945, indicating that cannibalism was a desperate measure by Japanese soldiers whose supplies had been cut off. Yet many incidents cannot be explained in this way—for example, the incidence of cannibalism in the Kokoda campaign in the latter half of 1942.[41] The first victims of such incidents were Australian soldiers, but incidents in which the bodies of Japanese soldiers were mutilated in a cannibalistic fashion appear as early as February 1943.[42] How is it possible that such extreme behavior manifested itself at such an early stage, especially when the supply of rations to the Japanese soldiers was adequate, if not plentiful? Many Australian veterans of this campaign reported finding portions of rice and dried fish among the personal belongings of Japanese soldiers who were captured or killed in the same region that the acts of cannibalism occurred. These are clearly not cases of cannibalism brought on by starvation. Another explanation for such incidents must be found.

It is possible that the particular character of jungle warfare—in which the enemy is frequently invisible but at close range—created a degree of stress that rapidly became intolerable, and that such stress hastened the development of a sort of group madness in which acts of cannibalism and savagery took on a ritual dimension. It could be argued that gratuitous cannibalism took on different ritual meanings, depending on whether it was exogenous or endogenous. In cases of exogenous cannibalism (in which Japanese soldiers consumed Australian soldiers), the act of eating a slain enemy had a heroic aspect to it, the spoils of victory. In fact, one Japanese soldier who was tried after the war for cannibalism of an Australian soldier testified that he ate the human flesh because he hated Australian enemies.[43] Endogenous cannibalism (in which Japanese soldiers consumed their fallen comrades) probably served to reaffirm group solidarity, to create a bond between the living and the dead within the group.

Whatever the reasons for cannibalism, it was expressly forbidden within the Japanese Imperial Army, as was the act of murder for the purpose of cannibalism—whether of one's own troops or of enemy troops.

Both were regarded as the most serious war crimes. Despite this official position, high-level army officers were well aware that cannibalism was a frequent occurrence in the field of battle in the Southwest Pacific, but because it was so widespread, they had little choice but to turn a blind eye to its occurrence. Indeed, documents exist demonstrating that the Japanese command took steps to accommodate the practice of cannibalism. For example, a captured Japanese soldier interrogated by the Australian military forces in December 1944 stated that orders had been given making it a crime punishable by death to eat the flesh of other Japanese soldiers but permitting consumption of flesh of the enemy.[44] On December 31, 1944, Australian forces captured a secret order form that clearly supported the soldier's statement. The order, issued by Major General Aozu on November 18, 1944, stated that Japanese soldiers who knowingly consumed human flesh would be guilty of a crime punishable by execution; however, it was stated in parentheses that the consumption of enemy flesh was excepted.[45] In this order Major General Aozu stated that he had issued many similar orders but that such incidents continued to occur. It appears, then, that orders permitting cannibalism were given by troop leaders in order to accommodate practices they knew to be unpreventable, in direct contravention of the blanket ban on all acts of cannibalism issued by the high command.

## Responsibility and Reaction

The principal responsibility for the geographically widespread occurrence of cannibalism in the Southwest Pacific does not rest with individual troop commanders but with Japanese Imperial Headquarters and the strategies it employed in the prosecution of the war. Neither the Army nor the Navy undertook any serious studies of the geography, climate, or environment of New Guinea or the Pacific isles[46] and were consequently unprepared for the rigorous conditions their soldiers would face in these areas. The campaign to take Port Moresby (May–December 1942), for example, was planned purely "off the map" and took no account of particular local conditions and hazards. Consequently it was a disaster, with the entire Japanese contingent being forced back to Buna and Gona on the northeast coast of New Guinea. There were 18,000 soldiers committed to the campaign; 6,000 survived.[47] At this stage Imperial Headquarters ought to have reviewed its entire Pacific strategy. Indeed, several members of the general staff argued that the New Guinea campaign was unwinnable and that all Japanese forces should be withdrawn.[48] However, they were in a minority and their advice was not heeded. Headquarters continued with its haphazard and ad-hoc strategies, and the Japanese forces in New Guinea were driven further into the quagmire.

After the failure of the Port Moresby strategy in February 1943, Imperial Headquarters sent the 20th and 41st Divisions to Wewak on the north coast of New Guinea. In March the 51st Division was sent to Salamoa. The 20th Division came from Korea, the 41st from northern China, and the 51st from southern China. These divisions had no experience of jungle warfare and were given no training in such. The 20th and the 41st Divisions came from a harsh northern winter into a tropical climate and had no experience in dealing with tropical heat and disease.[49] By March 1943, the 51st Division's transport ships were completely destroyed, and it became extremely difficult to transport food and other supplies to Lae, the principal port in eastern New Guinea. In August Imperial Headquarters implemented a "self-sustaining policy" for eastern New Guinea.[50] This "self-sustaining policy" was fiction, of course: Imperial Headquarters—faced with the impossible task of maintaining supply lines with a seriously diminished transport fleet—had decided to abandon all Japanese forces in New Guinea. A total of 157,646 Japanese troops were sent to eastern New Guinea; only 10,072 survived to the end of the war, a mortality rate of 94 percent.[51] The majority of these deaths were from starvation and tropical disease. The widespread occurrence of cannibalism was by Japanese soldiers who had been abandoned by their commanders. Responsibility for these crimes must rest principally with Imperial Headquarters and its ill-considered and ad-hoc Southwest Pacific strategy.

Yet despite the fact that Australian military officials collected a vast body of evidence to link the actions of Japanese Imperial Headquarters to the occurrence of cannibalism, and despite the fact that Judge Webb and others involved in the War Crimes Tribunal were aware of such evidence, no attempt was made to lay charges for these crimes in the A Class war crimes trials. During the war, information about cannibalism in the Southwest Pacific was heavily censored within the military, and no information was released to the public about such incidents. When the Melbourne newspaper *The Argus* ran a report April 24, 1945, from a U.S. newspaper that gave details of the incidence of cannibalism in New Guinea—and of the fact that it extended to Japanese as well as Australian soldiers—the subject became a topic of intense interest throughout the city.[52] There was debate between the government and the military as to whether stricter censorship of civilian material should be enforced. E.G. Bonney, chief publicity censor of the Department of Information, was in favor of restricting the circulation of such "horror stories." He argued that "I would ban all horror stories affecting Australian troops on the grounds that the effect on relatives and on younger soldiers might be bad, and their publication would not, in my opinion, add an ounce to the war effort."[53] The commander in chief, General Thomas Blamey, on the other hand, was in favor of allowing such stories to be published, countering that "the effect on Australian troops generally of such occurrences is not one of demoralisation, but induces in them an even greater determination in the discharge of their duties."[54]

The debate was somewhat academic at least in relation to its effect on the soldiers. They were already well aware that cannibalism was occurring in New Guinea, and in reaction to this a tacit agreement of sorts had developed that they would take no prisoners. Although there is no explicit reference to this in official documents, certain expressions and turns of phrase indicate that the Australian high command was very likely aware that the no-prisoners unofficial rule was in place. Yet its members seem to have been relatively unconcerned with the effect that reports of cannibalism might have on the relatives of dead or missing Australian soldiers. Instead they took a narrow, purely professional approach and focused instead on the uses to which such information could be put, especially in the effort to maintain a fighting spirit among the soldiers in the latter part of the war.

## Aftermath of the Tribunal

Judge Webb was involved in three separate investigations of war crimes throughout the latter stages of the war. In the first two (March 1944 and October 1944) he acted alone, and in the last (1945–1946) he was one of three judges, participating until 1946 when he went to Tokyo as the president of the Tokyo War Crimes Tribunal.[55] Each investigation report contains many references to incidents of cannibalism, and there can be no doubt Webb was well aware that the phenomenon existed. It was probably because of his influence that this information was not released, despite the fact that the high command wanted to release it for propaganda purposes. Both in the latter stages of the war and at the Tokyo tribunal, it is probable that he wished to preserve the privacy of the victims and to avoid the undesirable psychological effects upon the relatives of the dead. Furthermore, the Tokyo tribunal of 1946 received an enormous amount of worldwide press attention, and he may well have wished to avoid the inevitable sensationalism that would accompany reports of such testimony as well as the upheaval that would occur in Australia when the news was reported. Thus there was no mention of cannibalism in the A Class war crimes tribunals, the high-profile trials that were receiving the majority of press attention.

In contrast, the B and C Class trials received scant media attention, except in the case of trials of top-level officers. The bulk of media attention on B and C Class trials was Australian, and it was probably easier to arrange a form of self-censorship in these situations. Thus Judge Webb took a different approach to these lower-level tribunals. However, the prosecution of many of these cases was difficult because the majority of those testifying had not witnessed actual murders or acts of cannibalism—they had merely seen the results, the mutilated or partially consumed bodies. In the majority of cases it was difficult even to locate the alleged perpetrators of the crimes. According to one Japanese source, there were only three cases of murder and cannibalism, one case of desecration of corpses and cannibalism, and one case of only cannibalism in the B and C Class trials. Of 15 Japanese soldiers prosecuted in total for these crimes, 2 were convicted and 13 were acquitted.[56]

Webb's effort to win convictions for cannibalism and associated crimes—at least in the B and C Class—failed. The real responsibility of the civilian and military leaders of Japanese Imperial Headquarters was never pursued. It was clearly a difficult decision for Webb to make, and there is little point in debating whether it was the correct decision. However, his course of action created at least two serious problems, especially for the Japanese.

The first problem is that this information was never made available to the public, and so the civilian public never became informed of the existence and degree of Japanese cannibalism. Yet many Australian soldiers had seen the evidence of cannibalism in the form of mutilated bodies, mess tins containing human flesh, and so on, and the existence of the practice was discussed throughout the armed forces. Inevitably this issue continued to be discussed after the war, and reports of it filtered back to the civilian population by word of mouth. However, people were not informed of the reasons cannibalism had occurred or of the responsibility of the Japanese high command for the abandonment of the New Guinea garrison. As a result, the Australian public fell easily into a belief that the Japanese people were animals devoid of a sense of normal morality and that all acts of cannibalism by Japanese forces had been gratuitous and sadistic.

The reports of cannibalism dovetailed easily with the picture of the Japanese developed in Australian propaganda during the war: that the Japanese were a Jekyll and Hyde–type people, capable in a stroke of switching from refined and civilized activity to savagery and barbarity.[57] In fact, such a wartime image of the Japanese is illustrated by a comment made by General Blamey:

Our enemy is a curious race cross between the human being and the ape. And like the ape, when he is cornered he knows how to die. . . . Fighting Japs is not like fighting normal human beings. The Jap is a little barbarian. . . . We are not dealing with humans as we know them. We are dealing with something primitive. Our troops have the right view of the Japs. They regard them as vermin.[58]

This view has carried over into the Australian image of the Japanese that has developed in response to the Japanese "economic miracle" in the postwar period. On the surface, Japan is seen as a society to emulate and to learn from, especially in its development of a highly successful business- and technology-oriented society with a consensus-based approach to industrial relations. Yet underneath there persists a belief that the Japanese are somehow "different" from other cultures and that they would have been easily capable of purely gratuitous cannibalism. In this sense there is little difference between the Jekyll-and-Hyde image of the war period and the more superficially positive image of the Japanese developed in the postwar period.

Therefore, it is necessary to dispel this widely held view of the Japanese and to show other examples of extreme situations in which people have resorted to or fallen into acts such as cannibalism. One example occurred in Cambodia in 1974 in Kompong Seila, a small town only 1 kilometer long and 500 meters wide located 115 kilometers southwest of Phnom Penh. In May 1974 it was completely surrounded by the Khmer Rouge. At that time the population of the town included 9,000 locals and 1,000 soldiers of the Lon Nol government stationed there. At first, attempts were made to airlift supplies into the town, but the target area was small and they frequently fell into enemy hands, so the government curtailed the airlifts and the town was cut off completely. In the next four months the 10,000 people in the village consumed all available sources of food, including dogs, cats, rats, lizards, and birds. By September they were starving and were suffering from severe protein deficiency. Several hunting teams of between four and 20 men were formed; these teams went out nearly every night. Their prey was the Khmer Rouge soldiers laying siege to the town. They would kill the Khmer Rouge out in the fields and bring the bodies back to the town for consumption. The body count varied; on one night they killed more than 30 of the enemy. All parts of the body were cooked and consumed—flesh, organs, limbs, and brains. The favored recipe was a soup, as this proved easy to distribute evenly among the villagers. In this manner they managed to survive for the next five months.[59] Other instances of survival cannibalism in Asia have been documented by Key Rey Chong in *Cannibalism in China*, in which he provided a convincing case that cannibalism has been a widespread practice in China during times of war or following natural disasters.[60]

The second problem that Judge Webb's actions created was that the Japanese people were never informed of the abandonment of the New Guinea garrison by Imperial Headquarters and the consequent death by starvation of more than 100,000 Japanese soldiers. Thus there was no opportunity at the Tokyo War Crimes Tribunal to explore the degree to which Imperial Headquarters was responsible both for these deaths and for the murder or mutilation of victims of cannibalism. In turn, the incidence of cannibalism was never revealed to the Japanese public as a whole but instead circulated as a series of rumors, anecdotes, and disconnected facts.

The Tokyo War Crimes Tribunal is often known as the "tribunal of the victors." At no stage did it even consider prosecuting Japanese war leaders for war crimes against their own people; indeed, there was no category for such charges. In this sense the tribunal was seriously flawed; the omission of any attempt to follow up the full responsibility for the acts of cannibalism was one of its greatest failings. Nor was there any structure within the Japanese legal-military framework that would have made such prosecution possible. The Japanese court-martial system was directed almost exclusively to the prosecution of enlisted men. Although it was formally possible for officers to be court-martialed, this very rarely occurred, especially if they were career officers who had graduated from the military college.[61] Thus the Japanese people had neither the evidence nor the structures within which prosecutions for the responsibility for the starvation of the New Guinea garrison soldiers and their acts of cannibalism would be feasible.

Those who are guilty of war crimes are often the victims of war crimes themselves. The case of cannibalism in the South Pacific clearly demonstrates that some Japanese soldiers were perpetrators of war crimes in their murder, mutilation, and cannibalism of enemy soldiers, POWs, and local civilians, but they also were victims of a war crime in that they were abandoned and starved by their high command. The same might be said of those Australian soldiers who decided to take revenge for such acts by instituting a no-prisoners rule. War creates situations in which the moral framework of peacetime ceases to be of any practical use. In looking at the acts of individuals caught up in such extreme situations, it is imperative to remember that guilt and innocence, the status of the perpetrator and that of the victim, are often indissolubly intertwined.

# 5

# Japanese Biological Warfare Plans and Experiments on POWs

## Unit 731 and Biological Warfare Plans

Unit 731 was the secret biological warfare unit set up in the northeast of China following the Japanese invasion; the headquarters were on the outskirts of Harbin in Manchukuo. Unit 731 researched, developed, produced, and tested biological weapons. As part of its research program, it experimented on humans and animals. The details of Unit 731's activities remained largely unknown until the mid-1980s, when a number of documents concerning its activities came to light. Many of these documents were produced by U.S. military organizations, such as G-2 (Intelligence) in the Office of the Assistant Chief of Staff and the Office of the Judge Advocate General. Substantial parts of these records were information seized by the U.S. occupation forces directly from former members of Unit 731 after the war, but these were never disclosed to the public, for reasons explained later in this chapter. Japanese historians also discovered some vital original documents prepared by members of Unit 731 that contained details of types of medical experiments that were conducted.[1]

In this chapter I analyze Japanese biological warfare plans for the Pacific region and the experiments conducted on Allied POWs who were held prisoner in the Pacific region. First I will outline the historical background of Unit 731.

In 1931 Japanese forces invaded the northeast of China, claiming that Chinese forces had destroyed the railway at Lake Liu near Mukden in southern Manchuria, although this had actually been done by the Japanese themselves to provide a pretext for the invasion. This marked the beginning of the so-called Manchurian incident. In 1932 the Japanese government annexed the northeast of China and set up the Manchukuo puppet state. In reality, Manchukuo was a Japanese colony and was governed by the Kwantung (Kantō) Army, the most powerful of the Japanese forces.

Ishii Shirō, a prominent physician and a graduate of Kyoto University, traveled to Europe in 1928 to investigate the situation concerning biological weapons. When Ishii returned to Japan in spring 1930, he urged the military leaders to provide a means for researching biological warfare and developing the capability to wage it. At that time, various Western nations were actively involved in research on biological weapons, although the United States had not yet started it. In 1932 Ishii set up the Epidemic Prevention Laboratory within the military medical school in Tokyo with the full support of the military. At the same time, Ishii set up in Manchukuo a small and secret subgroup, the Tōgō Unit, in the village of Bei-inho, 100 kilometers southeast of Harbin. Remote Manchukuo was chosen primarily because researchers wanted to conduct medical experiments on human beings, which were difficult to carry out in Japan. Experiments on humans using Chinese prisoners began as soon as the Tōgō Unit was established. Thus, research on defensive methods against biological weapons was conducted mainly in Tokyo, and research on offensive use and actual production of such weapons was carried out in Manchukuo.[2]

In 1925 the Geneva Convention prohibited the use of chemical and bacteriological weapons. Ishii obviously knew that his plans contravened the convention, but he also knew how effective biological weapons could be. The Ishii group sought out all bacteria and viruses that could prove useful as weapons and for which vaccines could be developed so as to protect the Japanese forces using them.

In 1936 the Tōgō Unit was reorganized and expanded into the Epidemic Prevention Department of the Kwantung Army (the Ishii Unit). A smaller section (the Wakamatsu Unit) concerned with combating animal diseases was set up by the Kwantung Army at Xinjing. Both units were set up with the approval of Japanese Imperial Headquarters. In 1938 a special military zone was declared at Pingfan, 25 kilometers southeast of Harbin, and the local residents were all evicted. Construction of a huge facility for the production of biological weapons began. On August 1, 1940, the Ishii Unit was renamed the Epidemic Prevention and Water Purification Department of the Kwantung Army (a description the very opposite of its real aims), although after 1941 it was more commonly referred to as Manchukuo Unit 731. Unit 731 was composed of four sections: research, experiments, antiepidemic, and water purification and production.[3]

After Unit 731 was set up in Pingfan, many faculty members of the military medical school were sent to Manchukuo and became involved in experimenting on humans to develop biological weapons. In fact, Ishii started recruiting young elite medical specialists from various Japanese universities a few years before the establishment of Unit 731 in 1936. Professors in the medical school of Kyoto University in particular assisted Ishii with this recruitment. Branch units were set up in Beijing, Nanjing, Guangdong, and Singapore; these units conducted experiments on weapons developed by Unit 731 and made plans for waging biological warfare within those regions. At this time Colonel Ishii had 3,000 staff in Unit 731 and as many as 20,000 staff under his command if all members from the branch units were totaled.[4]

Various methods were developed for dispersal of biological weapons. One was to introduce the pathogen to a local water supply or food supply. Another was to use airborne means, and Unit 731 developed a bomb specifically designed for dispersing pathogens from aircraft. In 1939, when Japanese and Russian forces clashed in the battle of Nomohan on the Mongolian-Manchurian border, Unit 731 introduced the typhoid-fever pathogen into rivers in the area. In 1940 and 1941 the unit used aircraft to spread cotton and rice husks contaminated with the black plague at Changde and Ningbo, in central China. About 100 people died from the black plague in Ningbo as a result. From the viewpoint of the Japanese, the casualties at Ningbo were insufficient, so they developed a bomb enabling more efficient dispersal from greater heights (thus making the process less hazardous for air crews, who would be subject to antiaircraft fire if required to fly low over an area in order to deliver their payload.) This bomb was not widely used, however, as it was not perfected until close to the end of the war.[5]

Unit 731 regarded fleas as the most useful vector for pathogens, especially the plague. The unit bred massive numbers of fleas and rats for producing the plague bacillus and tested whether fleas could survive being released from bombs dropped from aircraft. The unit also developed anthrax-bacillus bombs, which proved successful because the bacillus is heat resistant. Shrapnel from the bombs carrying the bacillus was highly efficient at infecting those hit by it. The anthrax bomb was tested many times on humans at Anta, 146 kilometers from Pingfan.[6]

The biological weapons developed by Unit 731 were widely used on the battlefield after September 1940, although they were used to a limited extent as early as 1939. In Zhejiang province, biological weapons were used six times between September 18 and October 7, 1940. A member of Unit 731, Tamura Yoshio, gave evidence after the war that he was engaged in the mass production of cholera, typhoid, and paratyphoid bacilli between early July and early November in 1940. He also reported that about 10 kilograms of typhoid bacillus were transported to Nanjing by plane in early September 1940. Around the same time 270 kilograms of typhoid, paratyphoid, cholera, and plague bacteria were sent to Nanjing and central China for use by Japanese battalions on the battlefield. Evidence from Tamura and other sources indicates that typhoid and cholera were the major biological weapons used by the Japanese in the period around 1940. As for the effects, reports suggest that casualties ranged from several dozen to several hundred on each occasion the weapons were used.[7]

After the outbreak of World War II, the Japanese continued to use biological weapons against the Chinese. They sprayed cholera, typhoid, plague, and dysentery pathogens in the Jinhua area of Zhejiang province in June and July 1942. This was done in retaliation for the first U.S. air raids on mainland Japan, in which Tokyo and Nagoya were bombed. After these raids, the Allied aircraft landed at airfields in China, and the Japanese took this as Chinese collaboration with the Allies. In the Jinhua pathogen attack, however, the Japanese also fell victim to the diseases, and large numbers of Japanese casualties occurred. According to one source, over 1,700 Japanese soldiers died.[8]

It is well known that Unit 731 used large numbers of Chinese people for experiments. Many Chinese who rebelled against the Japanese occupation were arrested and sent to Pingfan where they became guinea pigs for Unit 731; there is evidence that some Russian prisoners were also victims. The prisoners subjected to experiments were called "maruta" (literally "logs") by the Japanese. Every year the military police and the Manchukuo civilian police rounded up approximately 600 maruta to send to Pingfan. When they were being experimented on, the maruta were transferred from the main prison to individual cells where they were infected with particular pathogens by such means as injections or being given contaminated food or water. They would then be observed and their symptoms meticulously recorded, including the taking of blood and tissue samples. After succumbing to the disease, the prisoners were usually dissected, and their bodies were then cremated within the compound.[9]

Unit 731 also conducted frostbite experiments on the maruta. Frostbite was a severe problem for the Japanese forces in Manchukuo, where the winters are extremely cold. The prisoners were tied up outdoors in temperatures as cold as −20 degrees Celsius and parts of their bodies were sprayed with salt water in order to induce frostbite. Their arms were hit with hammers to determine whether they were frostbitten. They were then immersed in hot water of ranging temperatures in order to determine how recovery from frostbite could best be facilitated. In extreme cases, the prisoners' skin and muscles sloughed off in response to this treatment and the victims died immediately. As a result of the experiments, it was found that immersing frostbitten limbs in body-temperature water best facilitated recovery. It is said that General Ishii and his colleagues were particularly proud of this discovery.[10]

Maruta also were subjected to poisonous gas experiments. In one experiment conducted September 7–10, 1940, 16 Chinese prisoners were exposed to mustard gas in a simulated battle situation that employed a macabre form of experimental manipulation. The prisoners were positioned in various places, such as under a machine-gun cover or inside a building, and mustard gas shells were fired toward them. Some of the prisoners had gas masks and others did not, and they were also dressed in different types of clothes. Every few hours after the firings the condition of the prisoners was monitored. In another experiment, five prisoners were forced to drink a liquid form of mustard gas and their condition was then monitored for a five-day period.[11]

## Biological Warfare Plans in the Southwest Pacific

It is well known that the Japanese conducted biological and chemical warfare experiments on Chinese prisoners and used these weapons on the battlefield in China. What was not well known until the early 1990s is that the Japanese were also planning to use biological weapons against Allied forces in the Pacific War. Documents discovered in November 1993 revealed the plans of the chiefs of staff to use biological weapons on various occasions.[12] The earliest use planned for the Pacific theater was in March 1942. The plan was to attack U.S. and Philippine forces on Bataan Peninsula by releasing 1,000 kilograms of plague-infected fleas on each of 10 separate occasions. However, while the weapons were being prepared, the battle ended in early April with Japanese victory. The plans were therefore abandoned.[13]

Plans to use biological weapons against Allied forces continued, however. In April 1942 six regions were listed as possible targets for biological weapons: Kunming in the southwest of China; five cities in central and southern China (Lishui, Yushan, Quxian, Guilin, Nanning); Samoa (in the event of a Japanese withdrawal); Dutch Harbor, Alaska; major points in Australia; and Calcutta. It seems these plans were carried out only in certain cities in China. In November 1943 another plan was formulated to spread pathogens over Burma, India, Australia, New Guinea, and various islands throughout the Pacific. It was planned that 27 aircraft would be mobilized and that every two months 12 aircraft would conduct sorties.[14] Although the head of the strategic section of the chiefs of staff, General Hattori Takushirō, was keen to carry out this plan, there is no concrete evidence that any sorties were ever conducted.

During the battle of Saipan Island between June and July 1944, Japanese forces planned to attack U.S. forces with biological weapons. The chiefs of staff had already sent a ship carrying a biological warfare battalion to

Saipan in April 1944. Part of this battalion stayed on Saipan; the rest of the battalion was ordered to move on to Truk. However, the Japanese forces on Saipan were routed by the U.S. forces, and the Japanese were probably unable to carry out plans for biological warfare there. The other troops who had left Saipan were lost when their ship was sunk by a U.S. submarine on the way to Truk.[15] It is possible that these troops, had they reached Truk safely, would have been transferred to submarines and taken to Midway or Australia in order to conduct biological warfare operations.

The Allied forces had some knowledge about Japanese plans to use biological weapons in the Southwest Pacific. The British Bacteriological Warfare Intelligence Committee periodically conveyed its intelligence on both Japanese and German biological warfare planning and capability to the Australian military command.[16] One committee report dated September 7, 1944, contained a summary report on a Japanese bacteriological bomb based on information taken from captured Japanese documents:[17]

The reference in two recently captured documents to a Bacillus bomb is of considerable interest. The bomb is described as the Special Bomb, Mark 7, one report indicating a weight of 50–70 kg. (?)[sic].

The colour markings given are:

Green (or blue?)  nose
Purple            body or a band on body near nose
Grey              body or tail struts
Purple            tail or tail struts

Subsequent information indicates that the bomb is possibly the:

Special Bomb Mark 7, Experimental Type 13, 1 kg.

The probable letter markings being:
An Arsenal (KUSHO) type 13, Experimental, 1 kg. Mark 7.

Comment. The importance of the information lies not so much in the detail given, but in the fact that the Japanese have, apparently, designed a bomb for B.W. purposes. If the reports are reliable, and there is no reason to doubt the Japanese authors had some grounds for writing them, they represent the first definite indication of the point to which Japanese research on this subject has proceeded.

This report did not refer to where the Japanese documents were captured. However, another report issued by the Allied Translator and Interpreter Section, Southwest Pacific Area (ATIS-SPA), on July 24, 1944, referred to the same Japanese documents and noted that they were captured on Kwajalein.[18] The importance of these documents, as is made clear in the "comment," is that they showed Japan had a fully developed biological warfare capability. It is clear that the British intelligence committee was deeply concerned about Japan's capability and willingness to use it. An appendix to the report detailed Japanese biological warfare operations in China in November 1941 in which the plague was used as a weapon to devastating effect. This was a warning to the Australian command that it was facing a very serious threat.

In June 1945 another report by the British Bacteriological Warfare Intelligence Committee contained a 12-page summary of Japan's involvement in biological warfare. At this stage the committee had detailed knowledge about General Ishii and Unit 731 and their activities in China. This report also referred to captured documents relating to bacteriological warfare in the Philippines and the Southwest Pacific:[19]

(b) Captured and other documents relating to B.W. Offence

Document No. 14798 captured in Hollandis on 25.4.44 is a handwritten notebook concerning intelligence and fifth column activities in total war, undated, writer and unit not stated. The contents are presumably copied from a manual.

The collection of intelligence is considered an integral part of fifth column activities, which are defined. A suitable organization is described and general rules for subversive duties outlined. Actual methods for use against the person and against property are listed, and these include the use of pathogenic bacteria, harmful insects and poisons. (ATIS Enemy Pub. No. 271, 7.1.45)

"Manual on Raiding," Army Engineer School, dated April 1944, is presumed to have been captured on Saipan. The copy belonged to Kaminari 3200 Butai. Under "Execution of an Attack, Section I—Infiltration Manoeuvres" occurs "Reservoirs—Destroy the dam (sluice). Water pipes—try to destroy them at several places and at points where the damage will not easily be discovered. Another plan is to release bacteria." (CINCPAC-CINCPOA Trans. No. 15, 17.1.45)

Another document captured in Hollandis on 25.4.44 consists of 27 pages of handwritten notes, undated, owner and unit unknown, concerning demolitions and sabotage, from which it appears that the Japanese are teaching and are prepared to use sabotage methods which include bacterial agents.

Thus bacteria are noted for destroying food. Also:

"2. Note: It is important that the enemy does not find out your scheme.

(a) Arson: Wind, light. Spontaneous combustion scheme.

(b)  Bacteria: In fish and vegetable markets and kitchens use a contagious disease which has been prevalent.

Warehouses:
2.  Contaminate food with bacteria.

Destruction of watersheds:
2.  Spread bacteria around the watershed.

Cutting off water supply:
2.  Bacteria is futile because of chlorine disinfection."
(ATIS Rep. No.249, 20.12.44)

A bound mimeographed file entitled "NI Raiding Diversionary Tactics" classified "secret" was captured at Morotai on 24.9.44. It was issued by E 33rd Force, dated 1944, and belonged to 2nd Lt. Horiuchi, NI Force. This document gives details of the organization, functions and equipment of the "Raiding Diversionary Unit." It contains the following: "Great results can be obtained by contaminating their food and drink in kitchen by bacterial strategy." (AG 381, 6.10.44)

Document concerning the organization, equipment and duties of a "Five Man Raiding Party," captured in the Lungling region probably in early September 1944. The equipment listed appears to be normal until one arrives at that separately listed under Infiltration Equipment, the commander of the party being responsible for carrying the following:
　　　　"Luminous compass
　　　　Flashlight (with coloured lenses)
　　　　Watch
　　　　Climbing irons
　　　　Handflags
　　　　Special sword-stick
　　　　Luminous paint
　　　　Rope—30 metres
　　　　Bacteria—if necessary"
　　(JICA SN 9502, 21.11.44)

A photostat of the original document has been checked and the words "if necessary bacteria" are unquestionably present.

"Extract of KAKI Operation Order . . . containing information collecting plan for Northern Leyte Defence Unit . . . thirteen pages (fully translated by XXIV CAE, Translation II AE 194, Item 134)." "Special characteristics of terrain from the standpoint of bacillus tactics. Field sanitation, and sanitation in regard to animals used by the Army." (AG 385, 12.12.44)

These two groups of words are not sentences and have no meaning unless they are assumed to be headings of sections. In the latter event the details of the sections should make clear the meaning of the headings, but they are not given.

27 loose handwritten sheets containing notes on counter-intelligence, espionage and fifth column activity, undated, owner and unit not stated. Captured at Mongado, Luzon. The following occurs in the document:

<u>"C. Mass Fifth Column Work</u>

1. Poison—Community wells, springs.

2. Bacteria:
   a. Transport of uncultured bacteria.
   b. Culture of bacteria.
   c. Dissemination by airplane.
   d. Will be disseminated by avoiding sunlight—powdered form.
   e. Wells, rivers, springs, market goods.
   f. Prevent their theft.
   g. Prevent transport of uncultured bacteria.
   h. If not kept in the house during daylight, they are ineffective and they should be inspected from this standpoint."
(ATIS-SWPA Trans. No. 75, 27.2.45)

For details of captured documents relating to the Mark 7 Bacillus Bomb see below under 3 (a). Other captured documents containing accusations against the Allies of the use of B.W. are considered below under 4 (b).

<u>Comment:</u> These documents indicate that the Japanese are teaching and organizing sabotage by B.W. methods. Emphasis is laid on individual dissemination of bacteria for contaminating foodstuffs etc.

This document did not contain specifics about the process of making culture media, but another document captured in Butibum village on December 3, 1943, described the process in minute detail. This document was translated by ATIS and appeared in its report in March 1944.[20] According to this report, the document was prepared by Sasaki Section of Ko Force in June 1941. Unit 1855 of Ko Force was known as the Tiantan Central Epidemic Prevention Institute and was located in Beijing.[21] Sasaki Section was most probably Unit 1855 of Ko Force. The document gave details of how to culture cholera, typhoid, dysentery, and other pathogens used in biological warfare. The fact that it was in the possession of Japanese forces in the Southwest Pacific suggests that they were at least prepared to use biological weapons.

The documents compiled by British intelligence do not provide concrete evidence that the Japanese actually used biological weapons in the Pacific but do clearly show that Japanese forces there had received training in the use of these weapons. It is also important to note that documents concerning biological warfare were captured throughout the vast area of the Pacific theater.

Another interesting document providing evidence of Japanese biological warfare plans is the memoirs of Misaki Yōichi.[22] Major Misaki was commander of the Field Epidemic Prevention and Water Purification Department of the 8th Division. According to his resumé, he graduated from the medical school of Ōsaka Imperial University in 1934. In August 1936 he began a year at the military medical school, where he trained as a military surgeon. Between 1937 and 1940 he served in China and Korea. He returned to the military medical school in August 1940 and became involved in research on black fever in the Epidemic Prevention Laboratory under the command of Ishii. The next August Misaki went to Harbin where he worked directly under Ishii learning the tactics of biological warfare.

Misaki did not provide any details in his memoirs about the tactics he learned from Ishii and only touched on them in his resumé. The memoirs begin with the landing of his division on Luzon in the Philippines in September 1944. His major task there, he claimed, was the prevention of malaria among the Japanese forces, but he briefly mentioned that he was involved in what he called the "cholera strategy" late in 1944. The proposal was to contaminate with cholera one of the islands immediately before Japanese withdrawal in the event of defeat in the Philippines. There is no evidence that the strategy was ever implemented.

However, the Allies were certainly aware of the plan. Documents captured on Luzon in March 1945 concerning the cholera strategy were translated and circulated as "ATIS Enemy Publication No. 381." The following is an excerpt:[23]

b.  Methods of attack
    (1) Spraying bacterial solutions by airplane
    (2) Spraying powdered bacteria
    (3) Dropping ampoules containing bacteria
    (4) Dropping infected insects, animals, animal tissues
    (5) Dropping bombs filled with bacteria
    (6) Firing shells and bullets containing pathogenic organisms
    (7) Leaving pathogenic organisms behind when retreating
    (8) Spreading bacteria by agents

It is probable that there were medical men like Misaki, trained in biological warfare by Ishii, stationed throughout the Pacific (see Map 5.1).

Like Misaki, they may well have been involved in the detailed planning of specific biological warfare operations. A number of Japanese doctors became prisoners of the Allies and admitted under interrogation the existence of Unit 731 and the role of the medical schools of Japanese universities in collaborating with it.[24]

## POWs in Rabaul and Medical Experiments

There is strong evidence that medical experiments were also carried out on prisoners of war in the Southwest Pacific. The United States began investigating this possibility in April 1947, initially targeting the Japanese naval hospitals of the 4th Fleet on Truk and the 8th Fleet on Rabaul.[25] In the course of the investigation it was found that U.S., Australian, and New Zealand POWs were subjected to experiments by Captain Hirano Einosuke, head of the Malaria Prevention Section of the 24th Field Epidemic Prevention and Water Purification Department stationed on Rabaul. The documents arising from this investigation, which began in April 1948, are now available, as are the memoirs of a number of survivors of Hirano's experiments. Before I discuss the experiments, I sketch briefly some wartime events in Rabaul to explain how Allied troops fell into Japanese hands.

Rabaul had two airfields and a well-located port (see Map 5.2). At the outbreak of the war it was defended by 500 Australian troops in the city itself and another 1,000 troops stationed in the vicinity. The Japanese attack on Rabaul began on January 4, 1942, with air raids. On January 22 ground forces landed at Simpson Bay near Rabaul without facing a major counterattack and the next day captured the city and the nearby airfield. Of the 1,500 Australian troops, 400 retreated immediately along both the east and west coasts of New Britain to New Guinea. Most of the remaining 1,100 were captured by the Japanese. On June 22, 1,050 Australian POWs, most of them members of the Australian 2/22 Battalion, were loaded onto the *Montevideo Maru* together with 200 civilians, mostly Australians. On July 1 while sailing northward, perhaps to Japan or Hainan, the *Montevideo Maru* was torpedoed by a U.S. submarine; there were no survivors. Also in early July, 60 Australian officers, 6 Australian military nurses, and 13 Australian women civilians were transported to Japan by a freighter, the *Naruto Maru*. No POWs remained in Rabaul by early July 1942.[26]

However, Rabaul steadily gained a sizable population of POWs, as all Allied men captured either on New Britain or in eastern New Guinea were sent to Rabaul for interrogation and incarceration. Most of the POWs were pilots whose planes had been shot down. They were held either by the 6th Field Kempeitai (military police force) of the 8th Army or

146

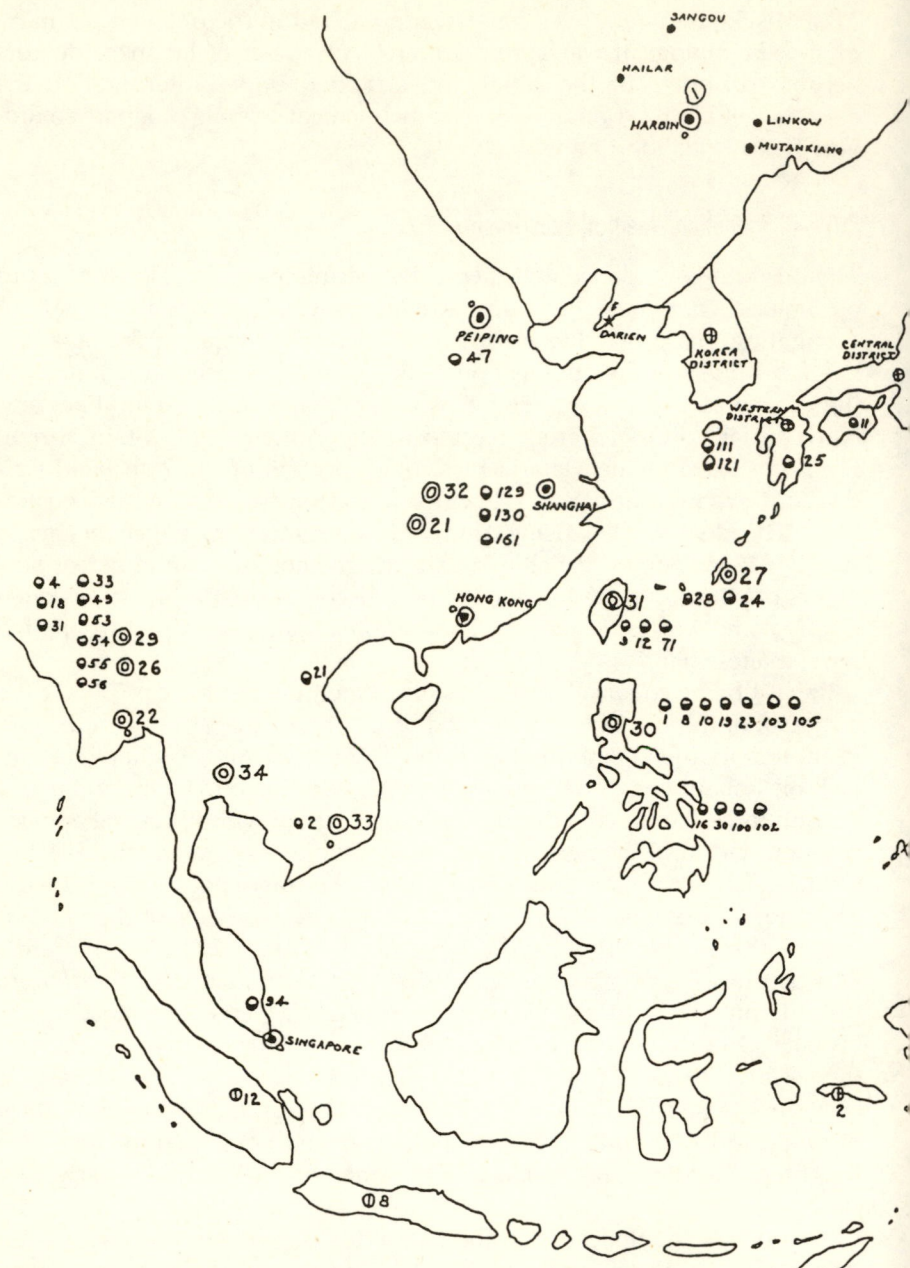

Map 5.1 *Distribution of the Epidemic Prevention and Water Purification Department (or Water Purification Unit—W.P.U.). Source: Sketch map contained in report prepared by Lieutenant Colonel Murray Sanders, U.S. Army Science and Technical Advisory Section; U.S. National Archives Collection, RG112/2/330.*

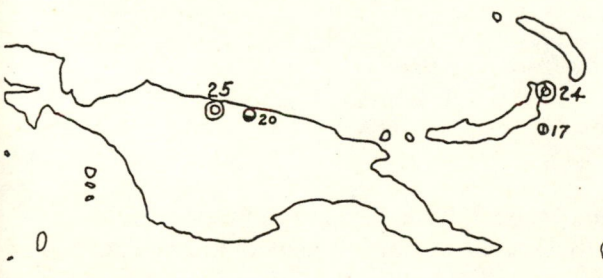

NORTHERN DISTRICT

NORTHEASTERN DISTRICT

EASTERN DISTRICT

TOKAI DISTRICT

⊚⊝ 42

## LEGEND

1. ⊙ PERMANENT FIXED W.P.U. (5)
    ⊕ FIELD W.P.U. (ARMY) (13)
    ⊝ DIVISIONAL W.P.U. (33)
    ① DIVISIONAL W.P.U. (4)
    ⊕ ARMY DISTRICT W.P.U. (7)
    • BRANCH OFFICE OF PERMANENT W.P.U.

2. NUMERAL ADJACENT TO ⊕ INDICATES NUMBER OF W.P.U. ⊝ INDICATES NUMBER OF DIVISION TO WHICH W.P.U. IS ATTACHED. ① INDICATES NUMBER OF W.P.U., NOT DIVISION TO WHICH IT IS ATTACHED. ⊙, ⊕ INDICATE NAMES OF PERMANENT UNITS.

3. 18, 31, 33 (DIVISIONS) ADJACENT TO ⊝ INDICATES UNITS REACTIVATED.

4. 1, 8, 10, 28, ADJACENT TO ⊝ INDICATES THAT PARTICULAR UNIT WAS NEVER ACTIVATED.

D

⊝⊕ 103

◎ 23

25

⊕ 24

⊙ 20

① 17

① DIRECTLY UNDER COMMAND OF KWANTUNG CO. DETAILS NOT WELL KNOWN & S.Q.
★ DARIEN SPECIAL - FORMERLY PART OF SOUTH MANCHURIA R.R. (RESEARCH CENTER).

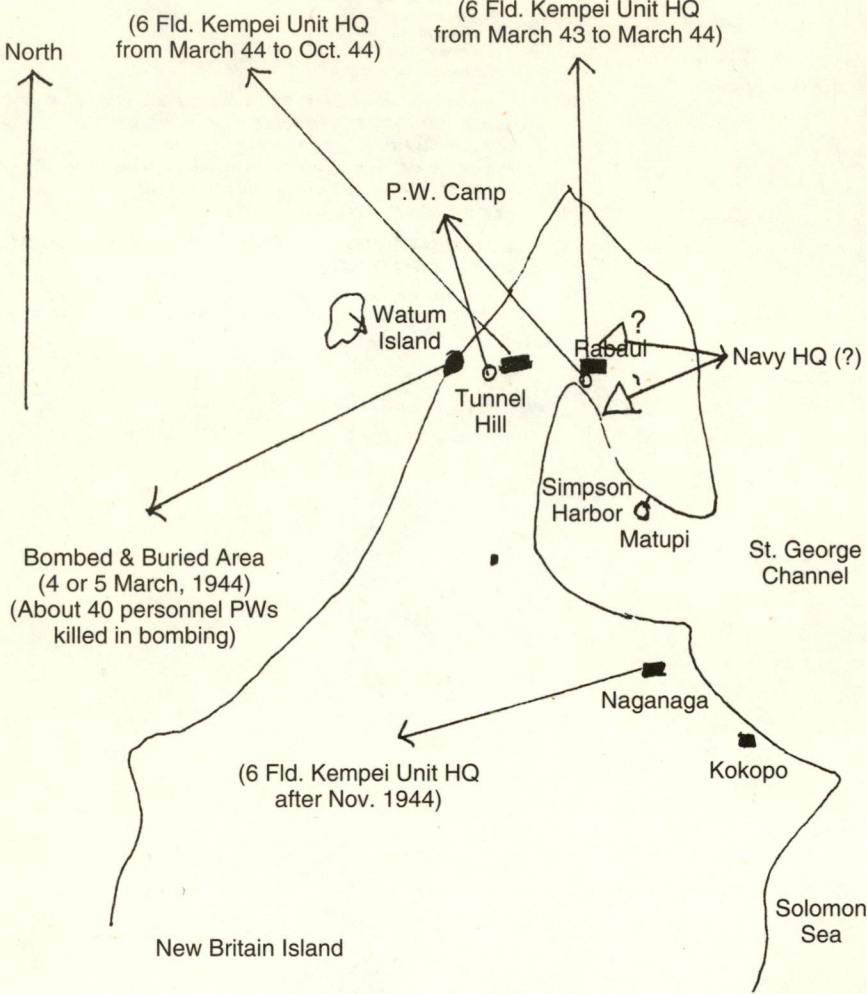

Map 5.2   *Location of Tunnel Hill POW camp.* Source: *Sketch map contained in interrogation of Major Matsuda Seiji; Australian National Archives Collection: MP742/1/336/1/1955.*

the 81st Naval Garrison Unit of the 8th Fleet. Around 20 POWs were held by the 81st, but, for reasons that will be explained, none of them survived to the end of the war.

There were 69 POWs held by the Kempeitai, 10 of whom were transported to Japan at various points in time.[27] The 59 POWs who remained in the hands of the Kempeitai in Rabaul were never used as forced labor, unlike those at Sandakan or on the Burma-Thailand railway, and, after their initial interrogations at least, were not subjected to the brutality experienced by many POWs held in other Japanese POW camps. However, all were definitely neglected, and many died from lack of proper food or medical treatment. Others died not merely from neglect but from the experiments carried out on them by Hirano. Only 8 of the 59 survived until the end of the war.

Here it is appropriate to examine the testimony of the 8 survivors. The following is an extract from the testimony of an American pilot, Second Lieutenant Jose Holquin, who was captured by the Japanese in July 1943.[28]

On the 2nd of March 1944, the Japanese guards loaded us into a truck and we departed from the area of 6th Field Kempeitai Headquarters Prisoner of War Camp, Rabaul, New Britain. The truck arrived at Tunnel Hill Prisoner of War Camp Cave, Rabaul New Britain, about 19:15 hours on the 2nd of March 1944. We unloaded, the blind-folds were removed and we were marched to the Tunnel Hill Prisoner of War Camp Cave, about a distance of two hundred yards, where we answered roll call and were then ordered into the Tunnel Hill Cave while still handcuffed. We remained in this confinement for approximately two weeks. We were first fed after arrival about 09:30 hours on the 3rd of March 1944. We were each provided with a ball of rice about the size of a tennis ball and a can of water which was shared by three men. The dimensions of the cave prison were about eight feet high, thirty feet long and five and one-half feet wide. The conditions under which we were confined would best be described as like being packed like sardines in a tin can.

According to another American POW, First Lieutenant James McMurria, about 60 POWs were confined in the cave, which was barred with a lattice of planks. Because there was insufficient space for all of the men to lie down at once, they had to take turns to sleep. According to McMurria, the prisoners were not given food and water for three days.[29] This conflicts with Holquin's account, but whatever the details, there is no doubt that the prisoners were badly treated. They were relocated from the prison in Rabaul to the cave at a time when Rabaul was subject to heavy aerial bombardment; under interrogation after the war, Kempeitai members claimed the prisoners were confined in the cave to protect them from the air raids. (In fact, the Japanese moved their headquarters at that time, the Army and Kempeitai to Tunnel Hill and the 8th Fleet to Mount Matupi.) They also claimed that the buildings to which the POWs were later relocated were under construction at the time.[30]

On March 3, 1944, at 8:00 P.M., several Kempeitai guards arrived at the cave and called out about 20 POWs. These POWs were handcuffed and blindfolded, then taken away. On the following day another 20 POWs were taken away in the same manner. Holquin gave the following testimony:[31]

I do not know as to where these two groups of prisoners were bound nor do I know as to what became of them. However, shortly after each group was removed from the Tunnel Hill Prisoner of War Cave, I heard several shots and, to the best of my knowledge, the shots sounded like or [were] best described as rifle fire. The reason for this is unknown to me. Each group was handcuffed and blindfolded when they departed. . . . I never saw any of the prisoners who departed again.

Holquin's testimony and reports by other survivors suggest that these 40 men were massacred by the Kempeitai. Major Kikuchi Satoru, commander of the 6th Field Kempeitai, Lieutenant Matsuda Saiji, who had direct charge of the POWs, and many other Kempeitai members were interrogated after the war and gave a very different account of the fate of these 40 men. Their accounts will be discussed later.

### The Diet Experiment on POWs

About 20 men were left in the cave until March 15, when they were transferred to a hut not far from the cave. Because of malnutrition and disease, only 13 were alive by early October.[32] Not long after, the Japanese commenced a diet experiment on the POWs. The experiment seems to have been a collaborative effort conducted by Lieutenant Fushida of the Kempeitai but with some involvement from Captain Hirano of the Epidemic Prevention and Water Purification Department. According to an Australian POW, John Murphy:[33]

In September 1944, or the beginning of October of that year the Japanese began to feed us on a diet of boiled cassava root. . . . The medical officer with the detachment guarding us at that time was Lieutenant (later Captain) Fushita (HQ 6th M.F.P.U.). At the time in question he came to our prison with weight scales and two medical orderlies. Each Allied prisoner was weighed naked and his weight recorded in a book. . . . The doctor then told us he was going to feed us entirely on cassava root—660 grams peeled per meal. He said it would be better for our health as we were not used to rice.

We received this ration for 30 days—the only addition being about 1/4 pint of thin, bodiless soup or vegetable water and 1/2 pint of water per meal. There were no other items such as meat, fish, salt, vegetables or fruit.

At the end of thirty days, two had died and the rest were weighed again and their weights recorded. A new ration scale was commenced—660 grams weight unpeeled. This was continued for 30 days under the same conditions and we were again weighed. . . . At the conclusion of the cassava course our rations resumed the old starvation standard—less than 1/2 lb cooked rice per day with a pint of soup; or, for some days, 1 small sweet potato or 1/2 coconut per meal: Nine survivors.

In mid-1944 the Japanese forces in Rabaul were suffering from an acute shortage of supplies because of the Allied bombings, and the Japanese high command introduced a policy of "self-sustainment." The POWs were evidently used to investigate the likely effects on the Japanese troops of having to adopt such a diet. Of course, the POWs were in poor shape at this time because of long-term malnutrition and lack of medical care, so it is scarcely surprising that four of them died during the experiment. According to the testimony of other surviving POWs, Hirano was disappointed to find that the POWs did not gain any weight during the cassava experiment.[34]

Murphy also mentioned another experiment. One day, for no apparent reason, the prisoners were given what they were told was a turtle liver. This came at a time when the prisoners had not received meat rations for a long time. Murphy wondered whether the liver came not from a turtle but from one of the Indian laborers, who were virtually prisoners of the Japanese.[35] In Rabaul, as in New Guinea, many Indians were enslaved by the Japanese forces.

### The Malaria Immunization Experiment

The nine remaining POWs faced another experiment in July 1945. Around April 15, 1945, Dr. Hirano went to the Tunnel Hill camp and took blood samples from them. He returned in July to conduct an experiment on malaria. The following is an extract of Jose Holquin's testimony concerning this experiment:[36]

On or about 19 July 1945, he came back with a Japanese Sergeant that spoke some English. One of the guards came and told five of us that we were to report to a hill across the road from that particular prison (Tunnel Hill Road). We were escorted one by one to this hill where there were shacks similar to those constructed by the natives of Rabaul. These buildings were permanent for that particular area and Doctor HIRANO used these particular buildings for his experimental injections. Ensign ATKISS and Gunners Mate LANIGAN; Lieutenant MASON and Lieutenant McMURRIA, each said later that they were given some kind of an injection by HIRANO which they protested and to the best of my knowledge was without their consent. Of the five men who reported to Doctor HIRANO, I was the last to see him. Doctor HIRANO stated that when he had made a previous visit in April 1945, that the prisoners of war were all tested for malaria and that he had found that five of the prisoners of war did not have malaria in their blood, and contended that there was such a thing as immunity against malaria contrary to the findings of the French [sic] Biologist Koch. HIRANO said that before he could prove that there is such a thing as immunity against malaria, he would have to expose me as well as the forenamed who were subjected to the malaria experiment. He said that he had five Japanese soldiers who were accompanying him and said to have had malaria in advance degrees of severity and that he was going to inject some of their blood into me to see what would happen. I told him that I had been interned as a prisoner of war for about two years and had never had malaria, and I protested to such an experiment. The Sergeant who was assisting Captain HIRANO then tied my arm and Captain HIRANO used a needle containing approximately ten cc's of blood which was obtained from one of the Japanese soldiers. Two days went by and on or about 21 July 1945, the five men who had been subjected to this experiment began to feel painful headaches and severe shivers, although not too severe at first. Lieutenant McMURRIA and I did not have the same type of case as the other three men. They suffered day after day with each day aggravating the attacks. Lieutenant McMURRIA's attacks of malaria and mine would last for approximately six hours and then we would get over it. The other three men had constant fever and they had no appetite. The men kept getting weaker and they got worse. During this time the Sergeant who had assisted Captain HIRANO would take temperatures, pulses and samples of blood readings which he recorded in a book. Nothing was done towards treating the men who were subjected to the tests and it was apparent that more interest was in the outcome or in the final results of the test. At about 10:00 o'clock on the night of 29 July 1945, Gunners Mate LANIGAN died and about 3:00 o'clock in the morning on 30 July 1945, Ensign ATKISS died. No medical assistance or aid was provided by the Japanese authorities to prevent the death of these two men. Lieutenant MASON suffered considerably and almost died during this period.

Not long after this experiment, Hirano commenced another one using two POWs he had identified through blood tests as malaria carriers. The two men were Captain John Murphy and First Class Airman Palmer of the U.S. Army Air Force. The following is an extract from Murphy's testimony:[37]

Next Palmer and I were taken up on two occasions each. Each occasion was separated by a week's interval and on each occasion we were injected in the gluteal muscles with 10 c.c's of a pale amber fluid taken from a bottle. Dr. HIRANO told us that we had Malaria and the serum he injected into us was an attempt to purge it from our blood and make us immune. Dr. HIRANO left then but the medical orderly remained still taking pulse rates, temperatures and blood slides.

Hirano reported under interrogation that he made serum from the blood of local people who were apparently immune from malaria.[38] Luckily, neither Murphy nor Palmer developed any illness as a result of being injected with the serum.

Corporal Nishikawa Masao, the man the prisoners referred to as Hirano's orderly, was also interrogated. Here is his account of the earlier experiment:[39]

He did not give me any specific instructions before he left, except to inspect daily the health of the prisoners of war. About 2 days later the 5 or 6 American prisoners of war began to show signs of having contracted malaria. By the following day 2 of them had become particularly sick from malaria they had contracted. I recall that one of them was an officer by the name of Lanigan and the other was a non-commissioned officer whose name I now cannot remember. It was on this particular day that Captain HIRANO arrived at the Military Police detachment; however, he did not go and inspect any of the prisoners of war. As soon as he arrived I reported to him the fact that some of the prisoners of war were suffering from malaria, and that 2 of them were suffering from a more serious attack than the others. Captain HIRANO replied by saying that I was on no account to give any of the prisoners suffering from malaria any medical treatment. As this was an order I simply said "Is that so." Captain HIRANO gave no specific instructions about the 2 aforementioned prisoners of war, and after he had checked my records he immediately returned by truck to 67 Line of Communications Hospital.

Two days later the condition of the two ill POWs worsened. Nishikawa went to the hospital to receive Hirano's instructions. Hirano was absent at the time, so Nishikawa left a message with one of Hirano's staff that two of the POWs were seriously ill. No instructions came from Hirano, who finally turned up at the camp only after the two POWs had died. Hirano also showed no interest in the surviving POWs apart from the data obtained from them.[40]

For both the Japanese and the Allies, malaria was a severe problem in the South Pacific battle zones. In January 1947, ATIS published a research report that included an analysis of the problems the Japanese faced with malaria. According to this report, the number of Japanese casualties from malaria in the Buna campaign (in eastern New Guinea) was estimated to be 16 times the casualties from combat. In Lae 80 percent of the 51st Division were suffering from a tropical disease, in most cases malaria. In the Admiralty Islands 82 percent of the sick soldiers were suffering from malaria, and a similar figure obtained in western New Britain. In the

Philippines an estimated 50–60 percent of all Japanese troops were suffering from malaria.[41]

The situation was probably similar in Rabaul. The malaria prevention unit in Rabaul was under the command of the 8th Army; Hirano was in charge of the unit. After the end of 1943, when Allied bombing cut off supplies to Rabaul, the stocks of antimalarial medicine gradually diminished. By early 1945 there was an urgent need for an alternative to antimalarial drugs, and thus in March the 8th Army set up the Malaria Immunization and Treatment Research Squad and appointed Hirano as its head. Dr. Fushida of the 6th Field Kempeitai also joined the squad. According to Hirano, Japanese patients at the 67th Communications Hospital were used for the squad's research.[42]

From Hirano's interrogation the following facts are clear concerning what he called the "treatment" of POWs. Hirano noticed that the natives, called Kanaka, had a very low incidence of malaria, despite the fact that the region was infested with malaria-carrying mosquitoes. He presumed these people were immune to the disease. He selected 15 Kanaka individuals who had never had malaria and made serum from their blood. This serum was injected into Japanese malaria patients at the 67th Communications Hospital. The effect of the serum, if any, was very weak, so Hirano was forced to rely on the ever diminishing stocks of antimalarial drugs to treat these patients.[43] Hirano probably remained interested in the possible value of serum from immune local people as a treatment and, perhaps in consultation with Fushida, decided to experiment on the prisoners.

Murphy and Palmer were probably selected for this particular purpose because they were already malaria carriers. In the case of the other five, who were injected with whole blood from five infected Japanese soldiers who had received the serum treatment, Hirano was evidently interested in whether the serum had any impact on the infectiousness of the pathogen. Hirano instructed Nishikawa not to give any of the prisoners antimalarial drugs in order to avoid any confounding variables in the experiments.

Murphy testified that Hirano had told him the serum was made from sheep blood and was safe to use.[44] Hirano denied this during interrogation, although he claimed he indeed had sheep for experimental use at department headquarters. Incidentally, Hirano himself became ill with malaria; however, he treated himself with conventional antimalarial drugs rather than the immunization he claimed to have developed.[45]

## Suspected Massacre of POWs and Experiments with Poison

In this section I discuss the fate of the 40 POWs who were removed from the cave in early March 1944. As indicated previously, the accounts of survivors suggest that these 40 men were massacred. The War Crimes Section of the Australian military thoroughly and repeatedly interrogated members of the Kempeitai who may have been responsible, but all denied that any such massacre had taken place.

The men interrogated claimed that 31, not 40, POWs were removed from Tunnel Hill and that they were removed to alleviate the extremely crowded conditions in the cave. The 8th Army had supposedly decided to transport the men to Watom Island, not far from Tunnel Hill, which the Allies would be unlikely to bomb. According to the accounts of Kempeitai members, the POWs were held in a hut on the Tanoura coast to await the arrival of a boat to ferry them across to Watom. The Kempeitai explained that between 8 and 9 o'clock on the morning of March 5, they heard an air-raid siren from the east and consequently put all of the prisoners in an air-raid shelter and hid themselves in another air-raid shelter some 30 meters away. The Kempeitai claimed that the prisoners' shelter was directly hit by two bombs and completely destroyed and that all but five POWs were killed, whereas their own was damaged but there were no casualties. It was claimed that the five POWs, who were all seriously injured, were returned to Tunnel Hill and treated by Fushida in one of the air-raid shelters but that all five died within 24 hours. Supposedly, all of the dead were cremated and their ashes were buried under a tree by the coast. After the Japanese surrender, the Australian forces were presented with six boxes of ashes, which the Japanese claimed were the remains of these men.[46]

The War Crimes Section of the Australian military found the Kempeitai accounts to be suspect. All of them bore a marked similarity, which suggested they had been rehearsed. The officer in charge at Watom Island denied that he had received any orders concerning the transportation of POWs and also claimed he heard nothing about POWs being killed by Allied bombing. Most suspect, however, was the claim about cremating the POWs and handing over the ashes after surrender. According to the War Crimes Section, the Japanese did not normally bother to recover the bodies of POWs; had the POWs been killed by direct hits to their air-raid shelter, the Japanese would most likely have disposed of their remains simply by filling it in.[47]

The commander of the 6th Field Kempeitai, Kikuchi Satoru, went to 8th Army Headquarters before the alleged bombing and discussed the transfer of the POWs with Lieutenant General Katō Rimpei. At the interrogation after the war, Kikuchi claimed that he had received an order to remove all POWs to Watom Island and had conveyed this order to his junior, Wakabayashi Zenichi, to carry out the transfer. However, the commander of the 8th Army, General Imamura Hitoshi, testified that although a plan to remove POWs from Rabaul to Watom Island was proposed, he did not issue the order because of the lack of shipping.[48]

Strangely, according to the accounts of the surviving POWs, the healthiest POWs were left in the cave and the 40 men who were removed were all sick and weak. It was also odd that the POWs should have been removed in two groups and at night rather than in daylight hours.

In order to sort out the conflicting accounts and to confirm the probable falsehood of the suspect ones, the War Crimes Section resorted to using a lie detector. However, the apparatus had no effect on the stories of the Kempeitai members; they stuck resolutely to their previous accounts.[49] It is now too late to find out the truth; however, the Kempeitai members, being well versed in the methods of interrogation and torture themselves, might be expected to stand up fairly well under interrogation and be able to persist with a false story.

In the course of the investigation, the War Crimes Section came across a local resident, Toniuea, who claimed to have witnessed the massacre of POWs at a place called Matupi, southeast of Rabaul. Toniuea claimed that 40 men were anesthetized, then buried alive at Matupi.[50] Initially it was thought that this account might provide the answer to the fate of some or all of the POWs who had been removed from Tunnel Hill. The remains of 24 men were dug up at the site where the massacre was alleged to have occurred. It was determined that the Matupi area had been guarded by the 81st Naval Garrison Unit and not by the 8th Army or Kempeitai. The War Crimes Section interrogated the former commander of the unit, Captain Kiyama Tatsuo, as well as other junior members of it. According to their statements, there had been at least three executions of POWs during the war: in the latter half of 1942, in June 1943, and at the end of 1943. There had also been executions of Australian, Swiss, and Finnish civilians in April 1944. After this time there were no longer any Allied men or civilians in the hands of the Navy in Rabaul. Kiyama admitted that he had ordered these executions. He claimed the executed men were either bayoneted or decapitated. Kiyama initially claimed that the orders for the executions had come from the intelligence officer of Southeast Fleet Headquarters. The Australian War Crimes Section determined that this claim was a lie and that the orders had in fact come from Kiyama himself without any communications with his superiors. When this came to light, Kiyama committed suicide.[51]

Although Toniuea's testimony that 40 men were executed proved incorrect, his claim that POWs were anesthetized and buried did have some basis in fact. The War Crimes Section obtained information from Kiyama's juniors in the 81st Naval Garrison Unit. According to Kubo Saichirō, at the end of 1943, some men were ordered to dig two large holes. About 10 POWs were brought to the place by truck and divided into two groups. POWs in one group were decapitated by an officer, and the others were given lethal injections.[52] The following is the testimony of another of Kiyama's juniors, Hosaka Katsumi:[53]

The executions were carried out by bringing one prisoner at a time to the front of the hole, making him lie flat on his back, opening his shirt and giving him an injection in the arm.

As I remember, there were three or four medical officers present at the executions. One would apply the injection while another observed the prisoner's reaction with watch in hand.

I am not familiar with medical matters, but I think most of them took about 15 minutes to die. I remember that one survived as long as 25 minutes. When one PW was dead, he was dropped into the hole and the next man was given an injection. This process was repeated until the executions were completed. By the time the executions by injection were completed, the decapitations had already been finished.

I do not know anything about the nationalities, ranks or names of the prisoners, nor do I know the names of the medical officers, who, I think, were lieutenant commanders, or thereabouts.

It seems that these POWs were injected with various poisons in order to test their effectiveness. Neither Kubo nor Hosaka knew who the doctors were or where they had come from. If the doctors had been from the 8th Fleet Naval Hospital, Kubo and Hosaka should have recognized them. The War Crimes Section interrogated hospital staff but was unable to obtain any information concerning these executions. Thus, it seems a strong possibility that the doctors were from the 24th Field Epidemic Prevention and Water Purification Department and that they had arranged with Kiyama to use POWs for experiments. Kiyama was not interrogated about the matter before he committed suicide, and, strangely, the War Crimes Section apparently did not investigate further.

## Australian Responses to Experiments on POWs

Australian POWs were used for another set of medical experiments, the scale of which seems to have been much larger than was the case at Rabaul. These experiments were carried out on a group of POWs at Ambon camp on Ambon Island in the Banda Sea, to the west of what is now Irian Jaya. Lieutenant John van Nooten of the Australian forces gave evidence about these experiments in his testimony to the Tokyo War Crimes Tribunal.

According to van Nooten, the experiment began in April 1945. Sixty patients from approximately 70 in the POW hospital were selected for the experiment. Between 30 and 40 other relatively healthy POWs were also selected. The men were divided into nine groups, with all members of each group being in similar physical condition (for instance, all members of one group were suffering from beriberi). The men were periodically given injections of an unknown substance over the course of a month.

Initially the Japanese told van Nooten that the injections were of vitamin B$_1$ and casein. However, van Nooten was familiar with the smell of vitamin B$_1$ and was sure that the injections were something else. A few days later van Nooten was told that the injections were inoculation against typhoid and paratyphoid.[54]

During this period a diet experiment was also conducted. Some groups were given 150 grams of sweet potato each day in addition to their normal rations, and some were given 200 grams of sago. Most of the POWs who were being used in the experiment and were not in the camp hospital continued to do hard labor, such as road work and trench digging. In the course of the one-month experiment, 50 POWs succumbed to malnutrition and tropical disease.[55] The 50 were not direct casualties of the experiment because casualties were also high before and after it, but two survivors, George Williamson and Jack Pannaotie, said they felt much weaker after being given these injections and sometimes were unable to walk.[56] This suggests that the experiments would have made a significant contribution to the deaths of the 50 men who died during its course.

Presumably this experiment was intended to provide information relevant to protecting the lives of Japanese troops on the battlefield when food supplies were cut off and they were dependent on local supplies. Both the Rabaul and Ambon experiments were conducted in 1945 when the Japanese were facing imminent defeat and must have known it. Why conduct these experiments, which clearly contravened the Geneva Convention, in such circumstances? Perhaps, though, that very desperation led the Japanese to take such action, in the belief that it could help them to survive and delay defeat. In order to help their own men, the Japanese military doctors did not hesitate to end the lives of the POWs they experimented on.

Although the Ambon experiment came to light at the Tokyo War Crimes Tribunal, the Rabaul experiments did not. Even in the Ambon case, however, there does not seem to have been a thorough investigation by the War Crimes Section of the Australian military in order to determine what happened and who was responsible.

The largest-scale experiment on POWs was carried out on 1,485 U.S., British, Australian, and New Zealand POWs in Mukden, Manchuria. According to the diary of a British officer, Robert Peaty, which he secretly kept in the prison camp, between January 1943 and March 1945, the prisoners were given a series of injections, which they were told were typhoid-paratyphoid, cholera, and dysentery inoculations. The men were periodically visited by groups of doctors who checked their health. Toward the end of the war the number of injections the prisoners were given increased.[57]

According to one former member of Unit 731, the prisoners were made to drink liquids infected with various pathogens. Autopsies were later carried out on those men who succumbed to disease. The same man claimed that there was a balloon-bomb factory in Mukden that used cholera and typhoid.[58] There seems little doubt that the POWs at Mukden were used by Unit 731 to test the virulence of pathogens for use in biological weapons.

An Australian doctor who was held at Mukden, B.J. Brennan, claimed that at one stage 150 American POWs were suddenly removed from the camp, never to return. He was unable to find out any information about their fate but suspected these men were used for experiments conducted by Unit 731.[59] Once again, there apparently was no detailed investigation of the Mukden experiments.

After Japan surrendered, MacArthur sent the first occupation forces to Yokohama one week before he arrived. The first contingent included a number of intelligence officers, among them Murray Sanders, who was assigned the task of finding out as much as possible about the activities of Unit 731. Sanders used Lieutenant Colonel Naitō Ryōichi, a hematology specialist who had been close to Ishii, as an informant. Sanders asked Naitō whether any POWs had been used by Unit 731 for experiments; Naitō insisted that had never occurred. Ishii and other senior staff of Unit 731 approached Sanders through Naitō and proposed that they would share all of their knowledge of biological warfare in return for immunity from prosecution for war crimes. Sanders conveyed the proposed arrangement to MacArthur, who instantly agreed to it. Soon after that deal was made, Sanders was told by an unknown Japanese informant that Unit 731 had definitely used POWs in human experiments on bacteriological bombs. Sanders conveyed this information to MacArthur, who did not repudiate the deal with Ishii and his co-workers but instead ordered that there should be no investigations into experiments carried out on POWs.[60]

The Soviet Union was also aware of the activities of Unit 731 and was able to obtain information from Japanese POWs captured by the Red Army in Manchuria. Soviet authorities approached the U.S. War Crimes Section and proposed a joint investigation into Unit 731. U.S. authorities rejected the request, claiming it was unnecessary, and also rejected Soviet requests to prosecute Ishii and members of his staff at the Tokyo War Crimes Tribunal. Soviet officials reported to the United States in January 1947 that many Japanese POWs they had interrogated admitted that Allied and Chinese POWs were used as guinea pigs in experiments on biological weapons. It must have become apparent at this time that the scale of these experiments was much greater than U.S. investigators had previously supposed. Consequently, Ishii and many of his colleagues were interrogated again but without resulting prosecutions. The United States apparently made further demands for information on biological warfare. None of this information was ever divulged to the other Allied powers; instead the U.S. government maintained a monopoly over the knowledge it had obtained.[61]

In April 1947 the United States suddenly began an investigation into experiments on POWs in the South Pacific. This was doubtless prompted by the information obtained from the Soviet Union about experiments in Manchuria. It is very odd that the War Crimes Section of the Australian military made no attempt to apprehend those responsible for experiments on POWs, with the notable exception of Hirano, despite having ample evidence of the gravity of the crimes committed in Rabaul and Ambon. Ultimately no one was prosecuted. It is surprising that even Hirano was not charged.[62] One might speculate on the possible connections between the lack of action of the Australian authorities and the deals that had been made between U.S. authorities and those responsible for biological warfare in Japan during the war.[63]

## The Ethics of Japanese Military Doctors and "Doubling"

The Allies paid some attention to Japanese medical ethics during the war. ATIS-SPA published a report in January 1945 entitled *Infringement of the Laws of War and Ethics by the Japanese Medical Corps*. Two sections dealing with the killing of patients and atrocities by Japanese doctors are representative of the Allied view of their ethics. ATIS documented evidence from interrogations of Japanese POWs that, it claimed, revealed the Japanese doctors to be totally lacking in the ethical principles that Westerners take for granted as necessary for practicing medicine. The report gave the impression that the lack of ethical treatment of POWs by Japanese doctors stemmed from Japanese military ideology, in which capture or surrender was shameful and prisoners could legitimately be treated as disposable. The ATIS report referred to such grisly events as the vivisection of conscious prisoners.[64] The report listed 12 conclusions, more than half of which dealt with the ethics of Japanese military doctors:[65]

1. The JAPANESE arm their medical corps men. Such arming is not only for self-protection or self-destruction, but if the occasion arises they use them as combat troops.
2. Even JAPANESE medical personnel have little regard for human life. Many incapacitated soldiers, with a good chance of recovery, have been disposed of on the grounds that they are useless to the Emperor.
3. A 17 Division Order commands medical officers to dispose of any sick and wounded who become a liability.
4. The term "euthanasia" cannot be applied to these killings.
5. A prisoner of war states that JAPANESE medical officers give instructions to healthy troops on methods of committing suicide should capture be imminent.

6. While Western medical equipment has been ably copied by JAPANESE they have retained their native ethical standards.
7. JAPANESE medical personnel are as guilty of atrocities as other branches of the Army.
8. JAPANESE hospitals in forward areas are usually camouflaged and rarely have Red Cross markings. These hospitals are rarely distinguishable from the air as non-operational installations.
9. The JAPANESE have often used insignia similar to standard Red Cross marking, apparently seeking immunity from Allied attacks.
10. Hospital ships have been used to transport armed medical personnel and combat personnel as well as non-medical department supplies.
11. The JAPANESE have not always conformed to standard markings for hospital ships.
12. It is claimed that an unarmed ambulance plane has shot down two Allied fighters in self-defense.

Items 8 through 12, which deal with such matters as the failure of Japanese hospitals in forward areas to carry Red Cross insignia and the use of hospital ships to transport ammunition, perhaps are an attempt to exculpate the Allies for acts such as the bombing of Japanese hospitals. However, the validity of the claims in items 1 through 6 seems beyond question. There is no doubt that medical doctors were commonly involved in the execution of injured and sick prisoners who were deemed a burden on the Japanese war effort.[66] The treatment of POWs as disposable was not, however, peculiar to the Japanese military doctors. The attitude held throughout the Japanese military, but the Japanese war leaders also had much the same attitude toward their own men, treating them as readily replaceable cannon fodder.

For the moment, though, we should set aside the issue of Japanese military ideology and ask how it is possible that any doctor could become involved in taking lives rather than saving them. It should be noted that here I am talking about taking lives that could be saved or the lives of perfectly healthy people and not about euthanasia of terminally ill patients, which is a separate ethical issue. The doctors in Unit 731 can be used for dealing with this question.

For most of us it is nearly impossible to understand how the doctors in Unit 731 could have done things that would be unthinkable in most circumstances. Should we conclude that these doctors, most of whom were eminent in their fields, were insane? In a 1992 interview, Yamaguchi Toshiaki, editor of the journal *Japan's War Responsibility*, asked Koshi Sadao, a member of the transport section of Unit 731, whether members of Unit 731 became mad as a result of their activities. Koshi responded:[67]

No, there were no such persons. Among the members of Unit 731, no one became mad or wild. We believed that the "maruta" who were brought by the
Kempeitai would be executed anyway and that it would be better to use
them for research which would save our people. At that time there was no
feeling that we were doing the wrong thing, although, looking back now, it
was horrific.

It is clear from Koshi's testimony that the members of Unit 731 went
about their work in an orderly way and were apparently unaffected by psychological problems. From this and much other testimony, it is also clear
that the members of Unit 731 had little or no sympathy toward their victims. This lack of feeling is clear in the testimony of another member of
Unit 731, Ueda Yatarō, who was directly involved in experiments with the
plague: "What was important for me was not the deaths of 'maruta' but the
fresh blood taken from them. To get even 10 cc of blood was my pleasure
and calling. The pain of the 'maruta' was not worth paying attention to."[68]
This comment gives a hint of the psychological processes that enabled
the doctors to rid themselves of any feelings of guilt or pain they might
have initially experienced. They were able to create a logic of sorts that
justified their actions. Once this logic was created, men like Ueda were
able to deal with maruta dispassionately. Maruta were no longer human
beings but a means to the end of gaining knowledge. That knowledge
was supposed to help save the lives of Japanese people. In sum, there was
the conviction that valuable lives saved outweighed any concern that
worthless lives might be lost—a conviction that made the process seem
thoroughly justifiable. This, of course, means that the willingness to dispose of certain lives did, in fact, coexist with the desire to save the lives of
others. This coexistence of conflicting desires is what Robert Jay Lifton
called "doubling."[69] For those working in Unit 731 there was nothing extraordinary about this; their extraordinary tasks and organization helped
to make this possible. The organization of Unit 731 created a coherent
group with a shared view that left no space in which individuals could
question the morality of their actions.
Similar doubling was also characteristic of the Nazi doctors, who were
involved in all kinds of medical experiments on prisoners, in particular
Jewish ones at Auschwitz, Dachau, and Buchenwald. By creating what
Lifton called an "Auschwitz self," doctors were able to experiment on
and eventually kill prisoners without experiencing guilt. Outside their
work in the concentration camps, these doctors remained humane in their
conduct toward others. They did not seem to feel any conflict between
their conduct when they were at work experimenting on prisoners and
their humane conduct the rest of the time. Josef Mengele is the most famous example of a Nazi doctor whose "Auschwitz self" doubled with his

"normal self." This doubling even occurred within his workplace. Mengele was very kind most of the time to the twins on whom he occasionally conducted grotesque and sadistic experiments. Neither Mengele nor other Nazi doctors showed any signs of suffering from major psychological disorders.[70]

The same was true of the doctors in Unit 731. They were able to go about their work in an orderly way, then at the end of each day return to their comfortable living quarters without experiencing any discomfort from what they were doing. There was evidently a "Unit 731 self" that was in all significant respects the same as the "Auschwitz self."

The doctors of Unit 731 must have begun their medical studies with the aim of saving lives rather than taking them. That they were able to take lives without remorse does not mean that they lost all conscience, however. They clearly maintained a conscience but were concerned with their moral responsibilities to others, not to the people they experimented on. Doubling enabled them to see experimenting on prisoners as consistent with the high moral causes of saving Japanese lives and demonstrating their loyalty to the emperor. The criteria of good and bad became dependent on the "Unit 731 self" and not the previous self, so the guilt that might be expected never arose. Without the burden of guilt they were able to conduct themselves as if they were normal doctors doing normal work and did not appear to be suffering from any major psychological disorders.

Other ways in which the doctors of Unit 731 were able to numb themselves psychologically included calling the prisoners "maruta" and referring to them by numbers instead of their names. In this way the prisoners were dehumanized in the eyes of their captors. The psychological distance thus created prevented the doctors from empathizing with their victims.

The Nazi doctors also used words in unusual ways to create psychological distance between themselves and their victims or to deny what they were really doing. Sometimes they would use military terminology, describing human experiments as "warning shots" (*Rampendienst*), or would combine medical and military terminology, like "medical warning shots" (*artzlicher Rampendienst*). On other occasions they used language that made the situation seem benign and attributed agency to the prisoners, such as by saying that a particular prisoner should come for a medical checkup (*Arztvorstellern*) when that prisoner had been chosen to be experimented on. Most notorious of all was the description of the Holocaust as "the final solution to the Jewish question" (*Endlosung der Judenfrage*).[71]

There are other interesting parallels between the German and Japanese doctors. Both groups had an external figure—the emperor and the führer—

to help them deal with whatever feelings of conflict might arise. Their work was an expression of their loyalty to the emperor or the führer, god-like figures who could solve any problems. Ultimately, any internal conflicts could be resolved by understanding that they were doing what the emperor or the führer would want. The Japanese doctors also had a commitment to purity of the Yamato race that paralleled the German doctors' commitment to the German Volk. Like the Germans, the Japanese were concerned that alien races might contaminate their own. Although this never led Japan on a course of genocidal efforts to annihilate an entire people, it had the capacity to legitimate otherwise unthinkable actions in the service of nation or the emperor.

I have mainly referred to the doctors of Unit 731 in this section, but I am sure that similar conclusions would apply to the doctors at Ambon and Rabaul. It should also be noted that the doubling phenomenon is not limited to wartime. The plutonium experiments that occurred in the United States in the Cold War period are surely an example of this. In these experiments approximately 1,000 civilians were given radiation doses of various kinds for experimental rather than therapeutic purposes. In Nashville, Tennessee, 750 pregnant women were given pills that were 30 times more radioactive than background. In Oregon, the genitals of 131 prisoners were exposed to large doses of X rays. In Boston, Massachusetts, 49 intellectually disabled children living in an institution were fed radioactive breakfast cereal for 10 years. In Memphis, Tennessee, 7 newborn babies were injected with radioactive iodine. In San Francisco, California, 18 terminally ill patients, including children, were injected with plutonium.[72] Most of those who were experimented on were black or working-class whites—the kind of people whose lives some wealthy white doctors (many of them graduates of the most prestigious medical schools) might not value very highly. In the context of the Cold War, these doctors might have thought it legitimate to risk lives they did not value in order possibly to save the lives of those they did. It would not be surprising to find that these doctors experienced few if any psychological disorders as a result of their actions.

The Nuremberg War Crimes Tribunal produced an International Code on Human Experiments. This code stipulated that regardless of the nature of the experiment, the informed agreement of any volunteers must be obtained following an explanation of the nature and consequences of the experiment. The code also stipulated that every possible protection should be implemented to minimize the chances of injury, disability, or death. The United States, which contributed to the formulation of this code, clearly ignored it to the extent that its government had knowledge of the plutonium experiments.

It must be concluded that any doctor has the potential for doubling, in much the same way that any man who is made a soldier has the potential to commit atrocities. Doctors are also capable of dehumanizing their enemies or prisoners. Perhaps doctors have even more potential; in the very process of learning medicine one tends to become more callous. Students dissecting corpses and vivisecting animals become accustomed to death. They also learn to separate the body of a patient from the person who inhabits it. The "doctor's self" that arises is a benign form of doubling. The narrow social networks of medical students might contribute to a lack of awareness of these changes in their sense of self. Good doctors are able to control the doctor's self and maintain their empathy. Perhaps, then, the issue of wartime medical experiments provides important serious lessons for how medicine should be taught today in Japan, in the West, and throughout the world.

# 6

# Massacre of Civilians at Kavieng

## The Japanese Invasion of Kavieng

On December 8, 1941 (December 7 in the United States), Japan attacked Pearl Harbor. On the same day, 20,000 Japanese soldiers landed on the Malay Peninsula and began moving south to capture Singapore, a vital British naval port. In mid-December Japanese forces invaded Borneo and occupied the west coast towns of Seria and Miri, securing their oil fields and establishing military headquarters at Kuching. Around the same time, Japanese military forces also landed on Luzon Island in the Philippines and began advancing toward Manila. In addition, a combined Japanese naval and army force attacked Guam in the South Pacific, occupying it on December 10. Soon after this, the same force occupied Tarawa and Makin Islands and on December 23 invaded Wake Island.

The leaders of the Japanese forces, seizing on the opportunity provided by their overwhelming success, brought forward the implementation of special plan "R Invasion Operation." This plan was specifically aimed at attacking the Bismarck Islands, now part of New Guinea (New Ireland, New Britain, Bougainville, and other smaller islands in the region). The Japanese South Sea Army and the naval R Operation unit were responsible for this maneuver and began bombing Rabaul on New Britain on January 4, 1942. Japanese forces landed at midnight on January 22, occupying the town and airfield by midday the following day. In addition, 52 Japanese planes attacked Kavieng on New Ireland on January 21, destroying its airfield and Australian military facilities. At midnight on the next day, approximately 1,000 Japanese soldiers arrived in Kavieng port and began landing a few hours later. However, when they entered the town, they discovered few enemy soldiers or civilians.[1]

When the Japanese started bombing Kavieng, 160 Australian soldiers of the First Independent Company of the Australian Army, whose commanding officer was J. Wilson, were stationed there. A few hours later the company saw the low-flying search plane scouring the bay for mines (of which there were none), and Wilson realized that a Japanese landing was imminent. He ordered about 20 soldiers to stay and destroy the military facilities while he escaped south with the rest of the company.[2] On January 28 Japanese forces landed in the middle of New Ireland at Uluptur and subsequently moved into Namatani, only to find that the Australian forces had moved farther south and eventually escaped.[3]

Few Australian soldiers were captured by the Japanese on New Ireland, and these POWs were soon sent to Rabaul to join up with POWs captured in New Britain. However, there were roughly 200 Allied civilians spread over New Ireland just before the Japanese invasion. Most of these were Australians, either coconut plantation owners or agricultural workers.[4] At that time, New Ireland was an Australian territory and supported many large-scale coconut plantations. Soon after the Kavieng bombing, most of these civilians also escaped south, except for those whose plantations were so isolated that they failed to hear the news in time.

The previous August the Australian government, concerned about the possibility of a war in the Pacific, had surveyed New Ireland to assess defense facilities, fuel storage, road conditions, and the resident Australian population.[5] The purpose was to determine how many Australian civilians were left on the island and how many were captured by Japanese forces. The survey established that approximately 40 Australian civilians and at least 10 German missionaries were living on the island at the time.[6] However, when Australian forces returned to New Ireland immediately after the war, none of these individuals could be found. There were rumors among the locals that the Japanese had killed them, but no evidence or witnesses could be located.

At the end of the war, the 14th Naval Base Force, consisting of 4,699 Japanese soldiers commanded by Rear Admiral Tamura Ryūkichi, was in the Kavieng area.[7] This force consisted of the 83rd Naval Garrison Unit and 89th Naval Garrison Unit (see Chart 6.1). The 83rd was headquartered in Kavieng and headed by Tamura. The 89th had its headquarters in Namatani, about 200 kilometers south of Kavieng. The Australian military forces who came to Kavieng questioned Tamura about the location of the missing 40 civilians. The following is an extract from the interview:[8]

Q. At what date did you assume command of all naval units in New Ireland?
A. On the departure of Rear-Admiral Ōta, I assumed command on 10th February, 1944. . . .

Q. How many Europeans, Internees or prisoners were in Kavieng prison on 11th February, 1944?

Chart 6.1   The 83rd Naval Garrison Unit (as of March 1944)

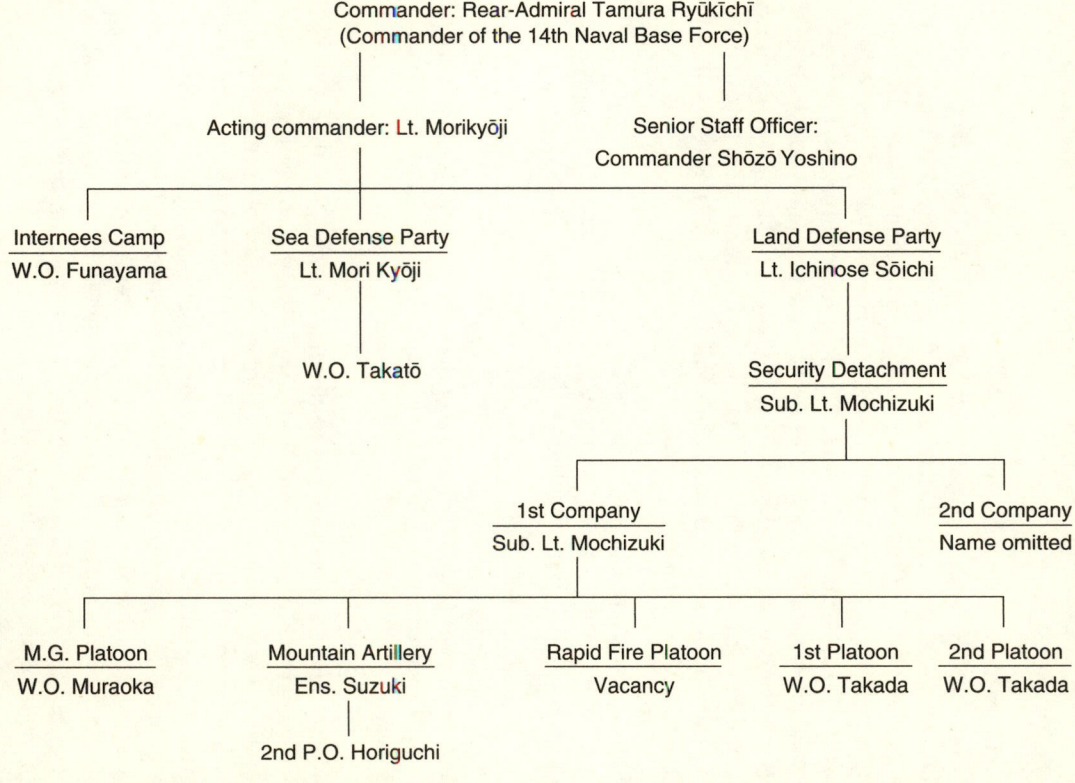

Commander: Rear-Admiral Tamura Ryūkīchī
(Commander of the 14th Naval Base Force)

Acting commander: Lt. Morikyōji

Senior Staff Officer:
Commander Shōzō Yoshino

Internees Camp
W.O. Funayama

Sea Defense Party
Lt. Mori Kyōji

Land Defense Party
Lt. Ichinose Sōichi

W.O. Takatō

Security Detachment
Sub. Lt. Mochizuki

1st Company
Sub. Lt. Mochizuki

2nd Company
Name omitted

M.G. Platoon
W.O. Muraoka

Mountain Artillery
Ens. Suzuki

Rapid Fire Platoon
Vacancy

1st Platoon
W.O. Takada

2nd Platoon
W.O. Takada

2nd P.O. Horiguchi

Source: *Australian National Archives Collection, CRS B 4175, Box 2-A6(14).*

A. There were European Internees in Kavieng. There were 23 prisoners.
They were housed in two houses in the bush near Chinatown, Kavieng. One
house was for neutral civilians and the other for Allied civilians.

Q. Are you sure that there were 23 internees, or could there have been more?
A. There were 23 Allied civilians and 9 civilians from neutral countries. I am
sure there were 32.

Q. Where are those 32 civilians now?
A. The bombing became so severe that on February 16th 1944, after consult-
ing the Supreme Commander in Rabaul, I sent the 32 civilians to Rabaul.
They were sent by barge to Doi Island, about 60 miles from Kavieng, where
the Japanese ships in convoy on their way from Japan to Rabaul were shel-
tering from aerial bombardment. The 32 civilians were put safely aboard. I
cannot definitely name the ships in the convoy, there were two and their
names were something like "Kowa Maru" and/or "Koa Maru." My signalman was listening in on the radio and he by accident heard from Rabaul that
the ship named above arrived safely. This would be two or three days after
the 32 prisoners had embarked.

Q. Did you receive a receipt for the 32 prisoners?
A. No, I did not receive a receipt for the 32 prisoners because communications were cut off between Rabaul and Kavieng by sea and air. . . .

Q. Don't you think this was of sufficient importance to warrant some comment or acknowledgement from Rabaul?
A. It is a very important matter because of the safety of their lives. I did not
make any further enquiries because my signalman had heard of the ship's
safe arrival.

As I explained, Australian authorities had information that Allied civilians detained at Kavieng numbered approximately 40, not 32 as claimed
by Tamura. The Australian military forces had also obtained information
from local people that a group of Allied civilians had been taken by the
Japanese to a small island off Kavieng called Nago and executed and
buried there. The Australians dug up the island and found 13 corpses,
which were identified as European. It was later determined that the bodies were of victims of two executions conducted by Japanese naval forces
between September 1942 and April 1943.[9] However, the location of the
rest of the civilians was still a mystery.

But Tamura was not commander of the 14th Garrison Force at that
time; in fact, he did not arrive at Kavieng until October 2, 1943. Thus
he could not be held responsible for these executions. It is probable that
the 13 were executed because they were conducting some sort of anti-
Japanese activities. The person in charge of the Kavieng detention camp,

Chief Petty Officer Funayama, had died during the war, so the Australians could not assign responsibility.

## Discovery of the *Akikaze* Massacre

In order to discover whether the 32 Allied civilians had in fact been sent to Rabaul, the Australian War Crimes Section investigated the movement of all ships between Rabaul and Kavieng during the war (Map 6.1). It also asked U.S. forces to provide information about Japanese ships sunk by them during this time. As a result, investigators determined that a ship called *Kowa Maru*, as Tamura claimed, had left Rabaul for Japan but had been sunk by an American plane 30 miles west of Hanover Island on February 21, 1944. U.S. information indicated there were no survivors. If the *Kowa Maru* sailed near Kavieng before it went to Rabaul, Tamura's claim regarding the time the civilians were sent to Rabaul seems to be correct. Captain Sanagi Tsuyoshi, staff officer at Southeast Area Fleet Headquarters in Rabaul, also claimed that he gave Tamura permission to place these civilians on the *Kowa Maru* and send them to Japan via Rabaul. The Australians released Tamura because there was no concrete evidence to contradict his claim, and he left Rabaul for Japan on November 6, 1946, on the Japanese destroyer *Hanazuki*.[10]

Tamura's attitude during his interview, however, seems to have aroused the suspicions of the Australian authorities. They speculated that the civilians might have been taken away by a different ship, so they continued to investigate shipping movements between Rabaul and Kavieng. After interviewing former crew members of the destroyer *Akikaze* in December 1946, they found that a group of Europeans had been executed on board that ship en route to Rabaul from Kavieng sometime in March 1943. The variance in dates between the testimonies of the *Akikaze* crew and Tamura was considerable, but the Australian authorities still had suspicions that it was the same group of civilians and continued to investigate. They located additional *Akikaze* crew members who had already returned to Japan and interrogated them between January and April 1947.[11] As a result of these interrogations, they established the following information and course of events.

The northeast region of New Guinea was a German colony until 1918, when it became an Australian territory at the end of World War I, so there were many German clergymen still working there with a strong influence among the local people. Because the clergymen were German civilians, soon after the occupation of Wewak in mid-January 1943, the Japanese moved them to Kairiru, although they were free to move around the island. However, Allied pilots whose planes had been shot down when attacking Wewak were hiding in the jungle of this region and had

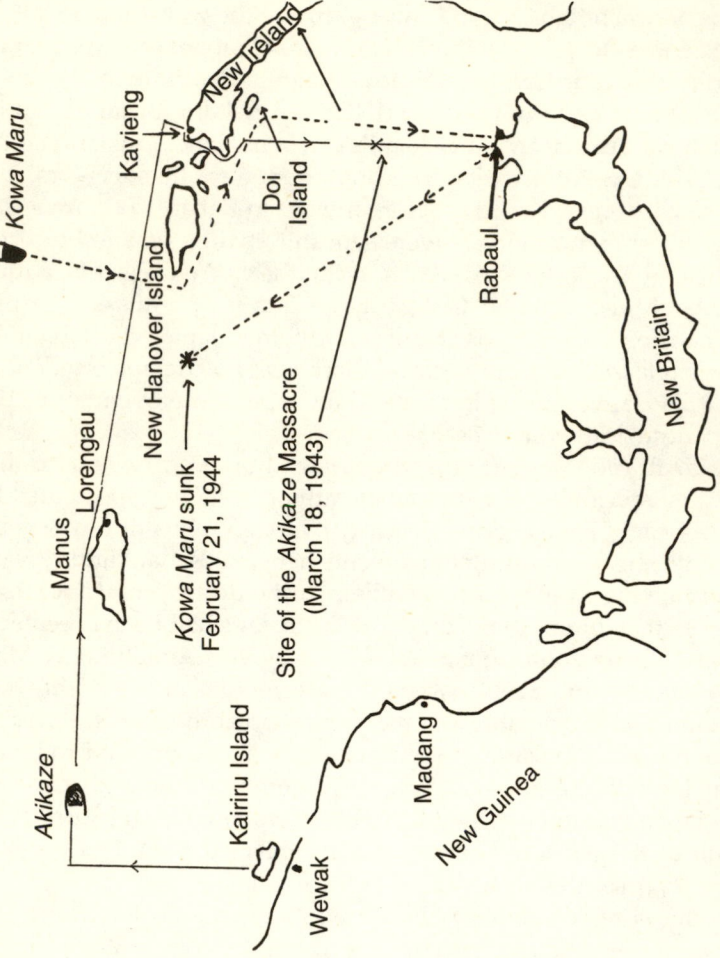

Map 6.1 *Courses taken by the ships Akikaze (solid line) and Kowa Maru (dashed line). Source: Australian National Archives Collection: MP742/1/336/1/1444.*

attempted to make contact with the German civilians through local people who harbored an anti-Japanese sentiment, to acquire food and medicine.[12] Although the German clergy were citizens of a nation allied to Japan, the pilots may have reasoned that they would be at least neutral, perhaps even sympathetic, not only because of their religious background but because they too were Westerners. They may have also reasoned that the Germans were far from their homeland and therefore not under heavy Nazi influence.

The Japanese forces also regarded these German clergymen in the area of New Guinea and the Bismarck Islands as neutral. For example, Rear Admiral Tamura referred to Germans in Kavieng as "neutral civilians"; other Japanese also called them "citizens of the third country" or "neutral civilians" but never used the expression "Allied civilians." Moreover, the Germans shared a close relationship with the local people and were familiar with local geography. Presumably the Japanese failed to secure any cooperation from the Germans and conversely feared their collaboration with those local people who were actively anti-Japanese.[13]

The 2nd Special Naval Base Force was stationed at Wewak in New Guinea during the war. In March 1943 the *Akikaze* visited Wewak in order to supply food and medicine. It then sailed to Kairiru, a small island off Wewak. Around 11:00 A.M. on May 17, about 40 civilians were delivered to the *Akikaze* by a Japanese officer and five soldiers on a landing boat. Most of the civilians seem to have been German clergymen and nuns, but there were also Chinese civilians who acted as their servants. Two Chinese infants, probably orphans, were also carried on board by the nuns. These people were moved from Kairiru because of repeated requests to 8th Fleet Headquarters by the 2nd Special Naval Base Force, which perceived that they posed a threat to the Japanese forces.[14]

The *Akikaze* left Kairiru about noon and sailed toward Manus Island, located roughly halfway between Kairiru and New Ireland. The 40 passengers were initially treated very well, and the ship's captain, Lieutenant Commander Sabe Tsurukichi, even ejected his crew from the rear cabin so that the civilians could be accommodated there and protected from attack by enemy planes. The passengers were also provided with tea, water, and bread, and those who suffered from seasicknesses were treated by the ship's doctor. It is clear that these people were treated as neutral civilians, not as enemy POWs.[15]

At that time, a small Japanese naval force consisting of 20 soldiers was stationed at Lorengau in the northeast of Manus Island, and the commander of this group was Chief Petty Officer Ichinose Harukichi. There were approximately 20 neutral civilians on the island, German clergymen for the most part but also one Hungarian missionary and a few Chinese. Six were women. They were free to move around and lived at various

locations. Ichinose was sent to Manus on April 19, 1942, and probably because at this stage the island was far from the battle zone, he established a
close relationship with the local clergymen and women. He often gave
them food and invited some of them to his house, where he provided
Japanese sake and dinner.[16]

In March 1943 Ichinose received a joint order from the chief of staff of
the 8th Fleet and the headquarters of the 81st Naval Garrison Unit to prepare for the removal of the neutral civilians to Rabaul in the immediate
future. Unlike the officers of the 2nd Special Naval Base Force, Ichinose
had never regarded the presence of the civilians as a threat or requested
their removal, so initially he did not treat the order with much urgency.
However, two or three days after the original order, he received another
telegram from Rabaul informing him that the *Akikaze* was due to arrive at
Manus in two days to pick up the civilians. Ichinose used a local as a mes-
senger boy and sent him to various places across the island in order to call
the 20 civilians to Lorengau to await the arrival of the *Akikaze*.[17]

Around five in the evening of March 17, 1943, the *Akikaze* anchored
about six or seven kilometers from Lorengau, and Ichinose took the civilians on a boat to meet it. He handed a list of their names to the ship's captain, Lieutenant Commander Sabe Tsurukichi, and asked him in which
part of the ship these people would be accommodated. Sabe told Ichinose
that they would be put in the same cabin as the German clergymen from
Kairiru. Ichinose found the cabin hot and crowded and estimated that it
would be very unpleasant if an extra 20 people were added to those already there. He asked the captain to provide an alternative cabin for these
20, so one of the front cabins was designated for their use. One of the Germans in this group had a fever, so Ichinose asked the ship's doctor to look
after him. As soon as Ichinose left the ship, the *Akikaze* sailed from
Manus.[18]

Throughout the night, the *Akikaze* traveled toward Kavieng. Because the
civilians had taken over their cabin, crew members were forced to sleep on
the deck. The ship's doctor continued to treat those civilians suffering from
sickness. At 11:00 A.M. the following day, the *Akikaze* anchored just out of
Kavieng port, but curiously no one disembarked or boarded the ship. A
small boat, however, did approach the ship, and a message was delivered
to the captain. Shortly after, the *Akikaze* sailed toward Rabaul.[19]

It seems unlikely that the *Akikaze* traveled all the way to Kavieng from
Manus just to receive this message. It is possible that it sailed to Kavieng
to pick up the civilians detained there, but for some reason the plan was
canceled. This may be why the ship left the island without receiving any
personnel or cargo.

Not long after the *Akikaze* left Kavieng, Lieutenant Commander Sabe
assembled all officer-class crew, along with Sublieutenant Kai Yajirō from

the 2nd Special Naval Base Force, who had boarded the ship at Wewak and was acting as an interpreter. Looking pale and worried, Sabe told them that he had received an order from 8th Fleet Headquarters to dispose of all neutral civilians on board. He said that the order was regrettable but was an order nonetheless and had to be carried out. The order gave no explanation as to why the defenseless civilians should be executed.[20]

Sabe instructed the officers to prepare for the executions immediately (Figure 6.1). Sublieutenant Kai was instructed to move all the civilians stationed in the rear cabin to the front cabin on the pretense of cleaning the rear cabin.[21] A plank was placed on the rear deck with matting on top of it, and a wooden structure was erected whereby each victim could be hung by the wrists from a rope and pulley and shot while the ship was sailing at a high speed. In this way, the force of the wind and the bullets would push the victim overboard, a procedure that would easily dispose of the body and minimize bloodstains on the ship's surface. The matting also served the purpose of soaking up any blood. A white sheet was hung across the breadth of ship to shield the executions from the eyes of the other civilians. All these preparations were completed in less than an hour.[22]

The civilians were led out of the cabin one by one and taken to the bridge. Each was asked his or her name, age, nationality, and other details by the interpreter, possibly to give the impression that this was a routine survey. Two soldiers then escorted the civilian to the middle of the ship where he or she was blindfolded. The civilian was then taken to the plank and strung up by the rope and pulley and shot by four soldiers using rifles and a machine gun under the command of Sublieutenant Terada Takeo, who was standing above them on the gun battery (Figure 6.2). As each execution got under way, the next civilian would be led out and undergo the same procedure. Just before the executions began, the ship's speed was raised to maximum (third battle speed), approximately 24 knots per hour. After the war, a crew member interrogated about the incident claimed that because of the loud noise of the engine, wind, and waves created by the ship's speed, the civilians at the front of the boat would have been unable to hear the shooting at the rear and so did not suffer unduly psychologically.[23]

The civilian men were executed first, then the women. The two Chinese children were taken from the arms of the nuns and thrown overboard. It took three hours to execute all 60 civilians and dispose of their bodies. After cleaning the blood from the deck, the officers conducted a funeral ceremony for the deceased. At the ceremony, Lieutenant Commander Sabe instructed all his officers not to mention the executions to anybody. The *Akikaze* returned to Rabaul at about 10:00 P.M. on March 18.[24]

176

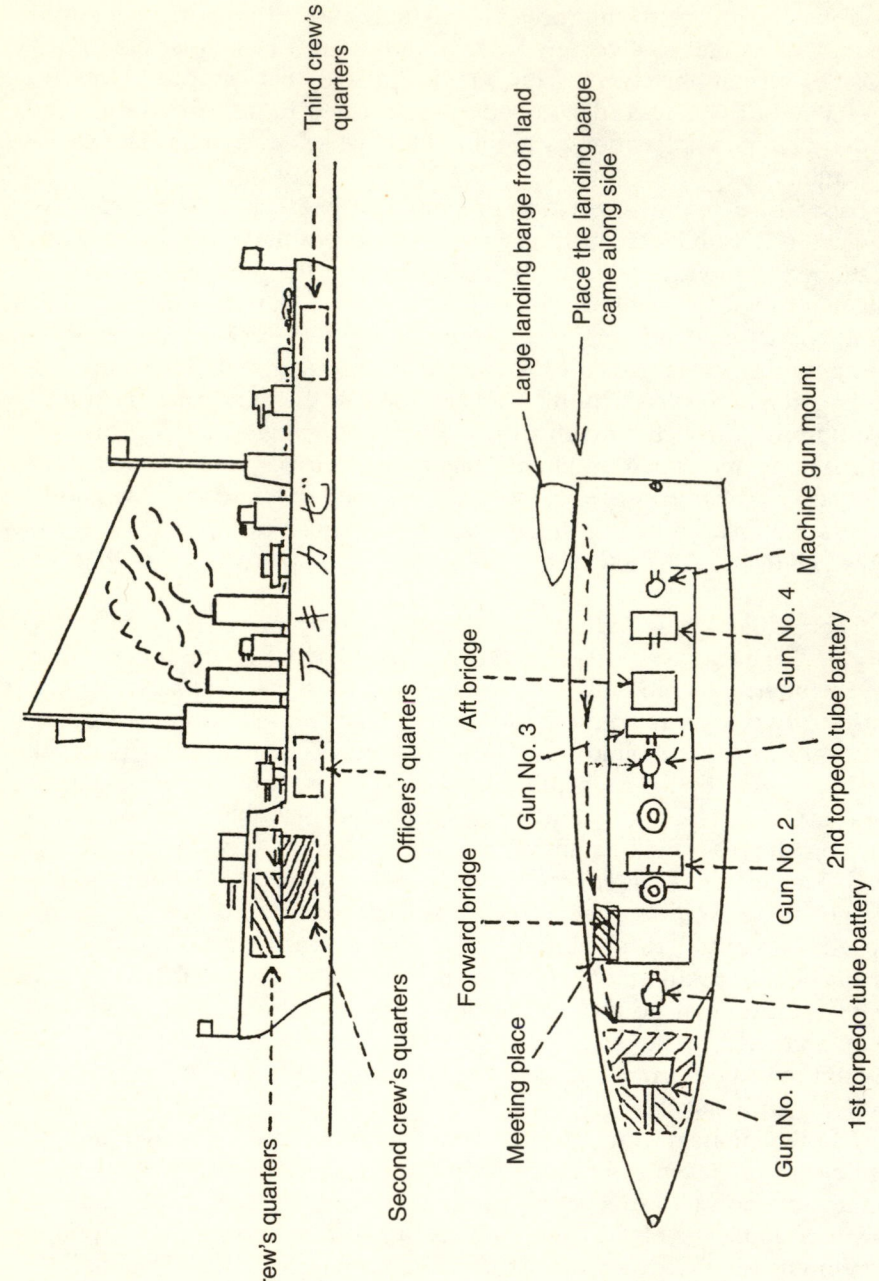

Crew's quarters

Second crew's quarters

Third crew's quarters

Officers' quarters

Aft bridge

Gun No. 3

Forward bridge

Meeting place

ブキカセ

Large landing barge from land

Place the landing barge came along side

Machine gun mount

Gun No. 4

2nd torpedo tube battery

Gun No. 2

1st torpedo tube battery

Gun No. 1

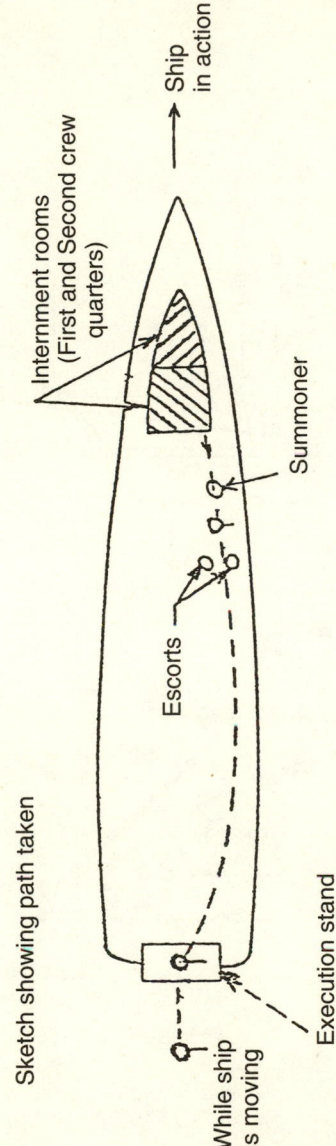

Figure 6.1  *Layout of the Akikaze and sketch of execution method. Source: Australian National Archives Collection: MP742/1/336/1/1444, "Report on Interrogation: Takahashi Manroku."*

178

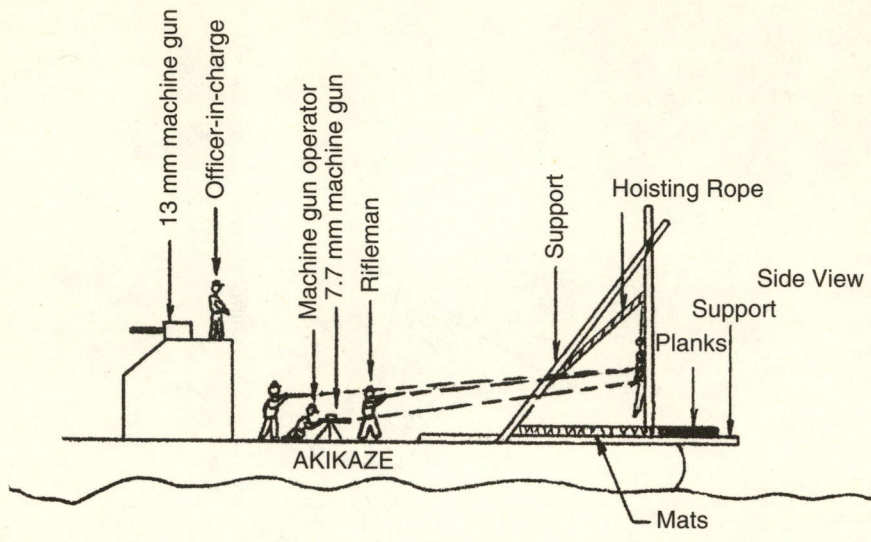

Side View

13 mm machine gun

Officer-in-charge

Machine gun operator
7.7 mm machine gun

Rifleman

Support

Hoisting Rope

Support

Planks

AKIKAZE

Mats

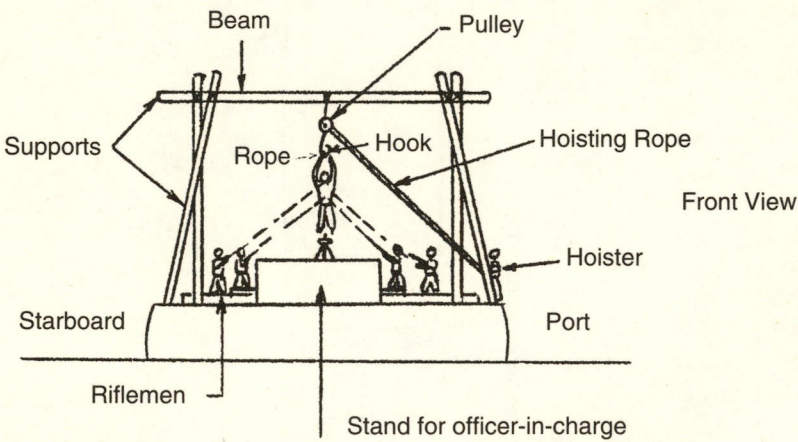

Beam

Pulley

Supports

Rope

Hook

Hoisting Rope

Front View

Hoister

Starboard

Port

Riflemen

Stand for officer-in-charge

Figure 6.2 *Detailed sketch of the execution: side view (top); front view (bottom).* Source: *Australian National Archives Collection: MP742/1/336/1/1444, "Report on Interrogation: Takahashi Manroku."*

## Responsibility Under the Australian War Crimes Act

Staff members of the Australian War Crimes Section who investigated the massacre on the *Akikaze* tried to discover who issued the order for the executions, which was clearly against the Geneva Convention, and who was ultimately responsible. According to Sublieutenant Kai, who acted as interpreter, he and Sabe had visited Lieutenant Kami Shigetoku, a staff officer at 8th Fleet Headquarters in Rabaul, and had reported to him that the order had been carried out. Kami had told the men to keep the execution of the civilians a secret and asked Sabe to secretly dispose of all their belongings.[25] The Australian War Crimes Section realized that this order could not have been issued by a single and relatively low-rank staff officer and believed the source was several senior staff of 8th Fleet Headquarters. They interrogated Rear Admiral Ōnishi Shinzō, who was at that time chief of staff at 8th Fleet Headquarters, as well as Vice Admiral Mikawa Gunichi, then the commander in chief of the 8th Fleet.

Ōnishi initially tried to avoid any responsibility by claiming that the *Akikaze* did not belong to the 8th Fleet but rather the 11th Fleet. However, in the course of the investigation, Ōnishi realized that the Australian War Crimes Section had already obtained substantial knowledge about the *Akikaze* and admitted that it belonged to the 8th Fleet, but he said the order for the disposal of the civilians had come from Kami without any approval. Ōnishi claimed that Lieutenant Kami orally reported to him and Vice Admiral Mikawa that a "small number of German missionaries" had been executed on a destroyer at the end of March 1943 and that this was the first and last time he had heard about this execution.[26]

Vice Admiral Mikawa, who was commander in chief of the 8th Fleet between the end of July 1942 and the end of March 1943, claimed that he had never seen or even heard of the *Akikaze* and that it had never been under his command. Yet he also claimed that Kami had come to see him and Ōnishi and reported the execution of some civilians on a destroyer on March 26, 1943.[27] If, as Ōnishi and Mikawa claimed, the *Akikaze* did not belong to the 8th Fleet, then it was impossible that Kami could issue the order for the executions, even without approval. In any case, Mikawa also said he did not issue the order to move the civilians in the first place, let alone to execute them, and denied any responsibility for the incident. He claimed he had been shocked when he had heard of the executions from Kami but was unable to investigate because he was soon sent back to Tokyo to take up a new position.[28]

In the course of the interrogation by the Australian War Crimes Section, Mikawa put forward the following explanation as to why Kami might have issued the order without proper approval: From the end of 1942 to the beginning of 1943, the military situation on Guadalcanal worsened for the Japanese, and the Allies knew the movement of the 8th Fleet's ships exactly and could often accurately target them. Some members of the 8th Fleet believed that local people and neutral civilians living in the Bismarck Islands and northeast parts of New Guinea harbored anti-Japanese sentiments and were secretly sending information about movement to the Allied forces, using radio equipment and transmitting either from the jungle or the coast. Mikawa received many requests from local commanders to take some sort of action to suppress these activities, but he lacked manpower to do so and dissatisfaction spread among his staff. Mikawa believed that Lieutenant Kami issued the order to dispose of the civilians without getting his or Ōnishi's approval because of Kami's overreaction to complaints by those members who held such suspicions. Mikawa also indicated that another staff officer in charge of civilian affairs, Commander Andō Norisaka, might have collaborated with Kami to issue the order.[29]

This is Mikawa's version of events. However, it is important to set against it an examination of the procedures for issuing orders in the Japanese Navy. In relation to ship movements and other secret matters, any order form was required to have the signature of the staff officer, if he originated the order, as well as the signatures of both the chief of staff and commander in chief. The order form containing these three signatures was then delivered via the staff officer in charge of signals to the staff cipher officer. The order was then encoded and sent to each ship's captain, the commander of the naval base force, and the naval garrison unit.[30] Therefore, if Mikawa's claim is correct and the order issued by Kami and Andō to move the civilians from Kairiru and Manus and execute them on the *Akikaze* was given to the staff officer in charge of signals, then Kami could not have passed it on to the staff cipher officer because he did not have the signatures of the chief of staff and the commander in chief. If, for some reason, the staff officer in charge of signals had handed over the order to the staff cipher officer, knowing that the form was missing the two signatures, then in turn the cipher officer could not—or should not— have been able to encode the order.

The Australian War Crimes Section could not ensure that the testimonies of Mikawa and Ōnishi were true because Kami, Andō, the staff officer in charge of signals (Commander Mori Torao), and the staff cipher officer (Sublieutenant Maeda Minoru)—in short, anyone who could verify the claims—were all dead.[31] There is a strong possibility that Mikawa and Ōnishi collaborated and blamed their subordinates in order to avoid prosecution. In the opinion of Captain Albert Klestadt, a Japanese-speaking member of the Australian War Crimes Section who was investigating the case, even if their claims were true, they had to accept responsibility as senior officials for being unable to prevent the war crimes committed by their subordinates.[32]

However, the Australian authorities did not prosecute anyone, despite the fact that they investigated the case thoroughly. One reason for this may be that the *Akikaze*'s captain, Lieutenant Commander Sabe, and Sublieutenant Terada both died in action during the war. But more important, in terms of the failure to proceed against Mikawa and Ōnishi, there were no Australian civilians among the victims of the massacre. Because most victims were Germans—civilians of a nation allied to Japan—this case was not considered top priority for the Australian authorities, who were attempting to determine the fate of the Australian citizens in Kavieng.

A "victim of war crimes" is defined in the Australian War Crimes Act of 1945 in the following manner:

The provisions of this Act shall apply in relation to war crimes committed, in any place whatsoever, whether within or beyond Australia, against British subjects or citizens of any Power allied or associated with His Majesty in any war, in like manner as they apply in relation to war crimes committed against persons who were at any time resident in Australia.[33]

Because of this definition, the Australian War Crimes Section did not focus on prosecuting Japanese soldiers who had committed crimes against German citizens, even though these citizens had been living on Australian territory.

However, this interpretation of the law did not hinder the Australian government from making exceptions where expedient. For instance, it took the illogical step of prosecuting Japanese soldiers who had committed war crimes against the Indian National Army (a puppet army under Japanese control) during the war, despite the fact that these Indian soldiers were fighting against the British and Australian soldiers. However, at the time of the war crimes trials, India's independence movement was gathering momentum, and it was important that the Australian government be seen to be "evenhanded" so as to avoid any propaganda value the Indian nationalists might make out of apparent colonialist indifference. But in the case of the *Akikaze* massacre, the Australian government stood to gain nothing by prosecuting the Japanese. Therefore, the decision not to prosecute stemmed not only from the definition of the law but also from political reasons.

Although the massacre on the *Akikaze* did not fit the legal definition of "war crime," Albert Klestadt's personal opinion was that it was a case of first-degree murder and a serious crime against humanity. The German civilians had been living in an Australian territory for a long period and had established friendly relations with Australian missionaries working there. Although the Germans were legally citizens of an enemy nation, they had far better relations with Australia than did the soldiers in the

Indian National Army. However, because of political considerations, the *Akikaze* massacre was officially disregarded.

## A Clue to the Discovery of the Kavieng Massacre

The investigation into the massacre on the *Akikaze* confirmed that no Australian civilians were murdered in that incident, and Australian authorities had to begin their investigations into the Kavieng massacre from scratch. Fortuitously, they had established through the interrogation of a man called Ōtsu Yoshio, the sole survivor of the *Kowa Maru*, that no Europeans were on board that vessel when it sailed from Kavieng.[34] Ōtsu's testimony, combined with information provided by Ōse Toshio, the captain of the *Kokai Maru*, which was sunk in the same attack by U.S. planes, enabled the Australians to build a detailed picture of the events preceding the sinking of the *Kowa Maru*.

On February 12, 1944, the *Kowa Maru*, a 1,106-metric-ton transport ship, was part of a convoy from Truk Island that included the *Kokai Maru*, another transport weighing 3,000 metric tons, the *Sumiyoshi Maru*, two escort destroyers, one patrol boat, and a submarine chaser. The purpose of the convoy was to supply Japanese forces in Rabaul with food and ammunition. After only one day out of Truk they were attacked by Allied forces but escaped. On February 15 they were followed by American planes all day and bombed that night but again managed to escape. At approximately 8:00 A.M. on February 16, just off New Hanover Island, the *Sumiyoshi Maru*, the patrol boat, and the submarine chaser left the convoy in order to assist another ship nearby that had also been attacked by Allied forces. The *Kowa Maru*, the *Kokai Maru*, and the two destroyers continued on toward Rabaul but were again followed by American aircraft. After sunset they returned to New Hanover Island to deceive the Americans and stayed there for several hours. Fortunately for the Japanese, there was heavy rain that night, making it difficult for them to be seen. Ōtsu stated that he could not even see the *Kokai Maru*, which was anchored very close to the *Kowa Maru*. At around 2:00 A.M. on February 17, the ships got under way again and arrived safely in Rabaul in the evening.[35]

If any Australian civilians were on the *Kowa Maru*, they would have had to board during the few hours the ship was anchored off New Hanover. However, as Ōtsu claimed, there was heavy rainfall that night, and it would have been extremely difficult to transport any civilians in a small boat from Kavieng to New Hanover.[36] Indeed, Ōtsu testified that there was no such activity: "When the ship was anchored near New Hanover Island, I was on deck for night watch duty, but I never saw any boat arrive at the ship, nor did we receive any communication regarding any passengers."[37]

At 2:00 P.M. on February 20, a convoy of five ships—*Kowa Maru, Kokai Maru, Nagaura,* a special destroyer, and a submarine chaser—left Rabaul for Japan via Truk. The *Kowa Maru* and the *Kokai Maru* were carrying 400 Japanese soldiers (of the 751st Air Force Unit) and civilian workers, but there were no POWs or civilian detainees among the passengers. Just before the convoy left Rabaul, Ōtsu was put in charge of passenger cabin allocation, and he found no foreigners' names on the lists. The ship was extremely crowded and all available space was used, so there was no possibility that any foreign passengers could have been accommodated without Ōtsu's knowledge.[38] Captain Ōse of the *Kokai Maru* also stated that at the captains' meeting before leaving Rabaul, there had been no discussion regarding POWs or civilian detainees. If POWs or civilian detainees were on board ship, it was usual to receive instructions as to their treatment and accommodation.[39]

At 5:00 A.M. on February 21 the convoy was spotted by an enemy search aircraft, and just after midday a formation of 12 B-25s began bombing. The *Kowa Maru* was seriously damaged and many passengers and crew were killed or injured. About an hour later, the 50 surviving Japanese abandoned ship and were rescued by the *Nagaura,* which had also been seriously damaged but was still operational. The *Kokai Maru* was also heavily attacked and had caught fire but managed to sail on for a few hours. However, that evening the surviving passengers and crew abandoned ship. These survivors, including Captain Ōse, scrambled into a lifeboat, some clinging to the sides, and managed to reach New Hanover the evening of the following day. Eventually they were rescued by a group of Japanese soldiers who had come to New Hanover from Kavieng. But at 8:00 P.M. on February 22, on the way to Palao, the *Nagaura* was sunk by American warships. Therefore, of the combined passengers and crew from the *Kowa Maru* and the *Kokai Maru,* only 50 survived, the only survivor from the *Kowa Maru* being Ōtsu. During this whole ordeal, no one actually sighted any foreigners.[40]

The Australian War Crimes Section was convinced that there were no Australian civilians from Kavieng on the *Kowa Maru* and started the reinterrogation of former members of the 14th Naval Base Force and the 83rd Naval Garrison Unit who had returned to Japan. In January 1947 they were called to the Tokyo offices of the Australian War Crimes Section, but the Australians knew it would be difficult to elicit a confession from them, as they would have almost certainly conspired to fabricate a false account of the incidents. For this reason, the Australian War Crimes Section placed Captain Albert Klestadt in charge of interrogation because of his knowledge of the Japanese language.

Captain Klestadt was one of the few staff members who could speak fluent Japanese. He had lived in Japan for six years (1935–1941) working in the trading business in Kobe and had acquired Japanese as a second language. He entered the Australian military forces in 1943 and because of his Japanese-language knowledge was recruited to work in intelligence. After the war he was transferred to the War Crimes Section, where he was highly valued because he could interrogate Japanese without an interpreter as well as pick up on any inconsistencies or subtleties in their testimonies.[41]

Captain Klestadt chose 70 former members of the 14th Naval Base Force and the 83rd Naval Garrison Unit and reinterrogated them one by one over the next few months. However, every testimony was the same as Rear Admiral Tamura's testimony—that 23 Australian civilians and 9 German missionaries were safely sent in two boats to the *Kowa Maru*, which was anchored near Doi Island on February 17, 1944. Klestadt was suspicious, however, because every person gave exactly the same testimony down to the smallest detail, which was unusual, as there are normally gaps in memory or small inconsistencies in such interrogations. He was even more convinced that they were fabricating the story.[42]

In order to break through this deadlock, Klestadt decided to concentrate his interrogations on those soldiers who displayed a weak character or nervous mannerisms. One of these soldiers, Jitsukawa Kinjirō, was the assistant engineer on the second barge of the 83rd Naval Garrison Unit. Under Klestadt's insistent interrogations, Jitsukawa was unable to stick to his original testimony and eventually admitted that he had been lying. On June 24, 1947, he provided the following account of the fate of the missing Australian civilians.[43]

On February 11, 1944, Kavieng suffered heavy bombing by the Allied forces. A few days later, the crew members of the first and second barges received an order to proceed to the south wharf at Kavieng. In the evening, when they returned to the barge, they found between 15 and 20 heavy concrete blocks on deck as well as a roll of wire. A steel loop was attached to each concrete block. As instructed, the crew went to the south wharf at sunset and waited. Two officers from the Land Defense Party, together with a small group of soldiers, came to the wharf. Although the sun was setting, it was not completely dark, and Jitsukawa could see the Japanese officers and soldiers. He also saw one white man brought to the wharf by some soldiers, but he did not see what happened to him, as he soon went into the engine room to prepare the barge for departure. While he was there, he heard much stomping of feet and English voices and ascertained that a number of white men had been brought on board. But at the same time, he could hear white men screaming as if they were being beaten.

After a while, the departure bell rang and Jitsukawa began the engine. About 15 minutes later, there was another signal to stop the barge. The barge drifted for about 20 minutes, but Jitsukawa stayed in the engine room and did not witness what was going on above deck. However, he could hear very heavy objects being dragged along the deck and thrown into the sea.

When the barge returned to Kavieng and Jitsukawa emerged from the engine room, he realized there were no white men on board any longer. He asked his colleague what sort of work had been carried out during the voyage and was told that each detainee had been bound to a concrete block with wire and that while the barge was floating between Nago and Edmago Islands, the block was pushed into the water. Jitsukawa later was told by crew members of the first barge that they had carried out the same procedure.

## Reconstruction of Events at Kavieng

Captain Klestadt obtained Jitsukawa's confession six months after starting interrogations in January 1947. He showed the confession to Jitsukawa's seniors, such as the chief engineer of the second barge, Yamao Unoharu, and the chief petty officer, Takatō Jūtarō, whom Jitsukawa claimed had prepared the concrete blocks and wires, and demanded their confessions.[44] Realizing that they could no longer stick to their original story, both men started recounting the true story. Klestadt later found that Jitsukawa's testimony was not strictly accurate because he did not witness the executions, but he provided the initial evidence that the massacre of the Australian civilians did in fact occur. (Jitsukawa probably confused the date of the execution with the fabricated date and said that the execution took place on March 17, 1944. The actual date was a month earlier.)

Rear Admiral Tamura Ryūkichi, who was bedridden in Kamakura, was arrested and transferred to the 31st U.S. Occupation Forces Hospital in Tokyo. On August 14 Klestadt visited Tamura in the hospital and showed him the sworn statements of Jitsukawa and others. Tamura freely admitted that they had murdered Australian civilians and German clergymen in Kavieng.[45] Based upon these confessions, Klestadt drew up a list of six people who were responsible for the murders and finished reinterrogating them by mid-September. The following account of the Kavieng massacre is based on the documents he prepared for the Tokyo War Crimes Tribunal and on tribunal proceedings.

At the end of 1943, the 23 Australian plantation owners and workers who had been unable to escape the Japanese invasion of New Ireland in January 1942 were in a detention camp in Kavieng, and the 9 German clergymen were imprisoned in a separate camp 5 or 6 kilometers away. Except for a 14-year-old boy, the 32 detainees were all adult men.[46]

In early 1944 the military situation in the Southwest Pacific was deteriorating for the Japanese, and Kavieng had suffered Allied air attacks since early February. The bombing on February 11 was the most severe, and headquarters of the 14th Naval Base Force and of the 83rd Naval Garrison Unit were directly hit. New headquarters for each force were quickly established adjacent to one another five kilometers away from the port in the bush near the airfield. On February 17 Kavieng suffered its first naval bombardment; more attacks followed on February 20, February 27, and March 21.[47]

The Japanese forces in Kavieng thought the aircraft bombings were precursors to a landing by the Allied forces, and the naval bombardment strengthened this suspicion. At this time, there were only 1,500 Japanese soldiers stationed at Kavieng under Tamura's command, and they knew there was no possibility of winning a land battle. Therefore they were prepared to fight to the end and die honorably. In this desperate situation, the one problem that worried the acting commander of the 83rd Naval Garrison Unit, Lieutenant Mori Kyōji, was what to do about the detained civilians, who were his responsibility.[48]

On March 4 Lieutenant Mori approached the staff officer of the 14th Naval Garrison Force, Commander Yoshino Shōzō, and sought his advice about the treatment of the Australian civilians and German clergymen. At this time, they were being guarded by only five soldiers from the 83rd Naval Garrison Unit, and Lieutenant Mori believed these soldiers would be more useful preparing for the Allied landings. Yoshino did not feel he could make a decision about the civilians, so he consulted his colleague, staff officer Lieutenant Commander Hiratsuka, and reported Mori's request to Tamura. However, neither Hiratsuka nor Tamura responded, and Yoshino did not reply to Mori's request.[49]

After the failure of the Torokina battle, Allied bombing of Kavieng became fierce beginning March 12. There were few civilians left in Kavieng; the locals had escaped into the bush.[50] Given the increased enemy attacks, the officers of the 14th Naval Base Force thought Allied forces would begin landing in a few days. On March 15 Yoshino received a phone call from Mori and was again asked what to do about the Australian civilians and German clergymen. This time Mori wanted permission to take the detainees to Rabaul or "take some other action." Yoshino replied that Mori should follow existing policy for the time being and thus avoided making a decision. Yoshino again consulted Hiratsuka and Tamura but received no clear instructions. Yoshino personally thought it would be impossible to send these people to Rabaul or any other Japanese-occupied territories because transportation from Kavieng had been completely cut off by the Allied forces. He also thought that "disposing" of the civilians was inhuman and therefore believed that the 83rd Naval Garrison Unit should continue to guard them. In a letter he advised Tamura that because Tamura was the ultimate commander of the 83rd

Naval Garrison Unit, he should instruct Mori as to why this policy should continue to be implemented. On the same day Yoshino submitted this letter, he met Tamura and verbally reiterated his position. Tamura replied that he had thought about the civilians but had not come to any conclusion.[51]

Two days later, just after nine in the morning on March 17, Yoshino again received a phone call from Mori, who told him that because the situation was getting worse, he could no longer take any responsibility for guarding the detainees. An hour later Yoshino passed this message on to Tamura.[52] It is necessary to consider the relationship between Mori and Tamura. As commander and deputy commander, they met every other day for briefing, so it is surprising that they did not discuss the treatment of the detainees. Strangely, Mori always expressed his opinion through Yoshino and did not directly consult with Tamura. At the War Crimes Tribunal after the war, the prosecutor also thought this was strange and asked Mori why he did not consult directly with Tamura. Mori's answer to this question was deliberately obscure.[53] Thus their relationship apparently was strained, probably for some personal reason. This conclusion is not wholly conjectural because during the tribunal Mori directly accused Tamura of ordering the executions.[54]

Tamura, who received Mori's message through Yoshino, was forced to make a decision and told Yoshino to pass on to Mori that in the face of the Allied landing everyone should be prepared to die and that Mori should dispose of the detainees secretly. Yoshino asked Tamura whether it was possible for the 83rd Naval Garrison Unit to continue to guard the detainees but could not change Tamura's mind.[55] Tamura gave several reasons why he could not avoid the disposal of the detainees.

First, Tamura had already asked Southeast Area Fleet Headquarters to transfer the detainees to Rabaul or Japan but had been rejected. Indeed, Tamura made this request soon after he came to Kavieng as commander of the 83rd Naval Garrison Unit in October 1943 because he thought Kavieng would soon become a battle zone. But there was no reply to Tamura's request. He also made the same request through a staff officer from fleet headquarters who had come to Kavieng on inspection. In February 1944 he made the same request through Rear Admiral Ōta, his predecessor as commander of the 14th Naval Base Force, when he returned to Japan. This request was sent to the Bureau of Naval Affairs in Tokyo, but he never received any instructions.[56] It is not surprising that Tamura thought his request had been rejected.

The second reason Tamura gave was that the Allied forces by then held regional control on the sea and in the air, and it was impossible to send detainees out of New Ireland, even with permission. Alternatively, if these detainees were to be transferred to somewhere within New Ireland, it would take at least two weeks to build new accommodations and transport the detainees. This would also require a large amount of manpower. Tamura said he could not afford to proceed with this option because the Allied landing seemed imminent.[57]

His third reason was that if the detainees were released, they could inform on the Japanese because they were very familiar with the terrain of the island and friendly with the local people. Tamura concluded that strategically there was no option other than to dispose of the detainees.[58]

Yoshino, who could not change Tamura's mind, passed the order of the "secret disposal" of the detainees on to Mori by telephone. Tamura again gave his deputy an order through a staff officer, which was very unusual. Ordinarily, Tamura should have given the order directly to Mori. It was even more unusual in that the two men were headquartered only 150 meters apart.[59] Although Tamura personally thought the disposal should be carried out as soon as possible, he did not give detailed instructions as to when and where the executions should occur; he simply told Yoshino to pass on to Mori the order that the detainees should be secretly disposed of.[60]

It is possible that both Mori and Tamura believed it was impossible to avoid the disposal of the detainees, but it seems likely each was waiting for the other person to initiate the action. This probably explains why they intentionally did not discuss the issue, despite the fact that they met every other day. It also explains why Tamura in the order for the executions did not go into any detail. It is clear that Yoshino did not want to be involved either and therefore just passed on the messages. All three were obviously trying to avoid any responsibility for the executions.

Mori, who received the order from Yoshino, did not ask for any details about the executions either. He had finally received the order he wanted and therefore was intent on carrying it out as quickly as possible before the Allied landing began. He had been placed in a desperate situation and was anxious to be rid of the troublesome matter of the detainees so that he could focus on confronting the Allied landing with his limited number of soldiers.

Mori himself did not want to execute the detainees and ordered his junior officer to carry it out. He called Lieutenant Ichinose Sōichi, head of the Land Defense Party of the 83rd Naval Garrison Unit, to his office on March 17 and ordered him to carry out the executions that day. However, Ichinose probably wanted to avoid taking any responsibility also and suggested that the executions should be conducted by his juniors.[61]

At about half past one, Mori called Sublieutenant Mochizuki Shichitarō, head of a security detachment under the control of the Land Defense Party, and made Ichinose repeat Mori's original order to him. Mochizuki asked Mori about the method and place of the execution. Mori thought that it was better to execute the detainees on Nago Island, just off Kavieng port, where Allied bombings had left many large craters that could be used as graves after the detainees were shot. Ichinose replied that the local people would hear the shooting, and therefore they could not carry out the executions "secretly." He suggested the detainees be strangled. Mori agreed with Ichinose, and Ichinose advised Mochizuki that the most suitable place of execution would be the south wharf of Kavieng port. Mori instructed Mochizuki that the bodies should be tied to heavy weights and dumped into the sea on the west side of Nago Island. Mori said that he would arrange for the barges, weights, and wires to be supplied by the Sea Defense Party and stated that the time of the executions would be just after sunset at around half past five.[62]

The executions were to be carried out by members of the Land Defense Party; had Mori asked the Sea Defense Party, he would have had to be involved because he was acting as head of the group. Mori did not mind supplying the equipment but did not want to participate directly. Though Mori had been anxious to get the order for the disposal of the detainees, once he received it, he was reluctant to have any personal involvement. His decision to use the Land Defense Party for the executions is clear evidence of his dilemma.

Similarly, Mochizuki, who was ordered to carry out the executions, seemed to want to avoid being at the actual place of execution. At about three in the afternoon, he summoned three platoon leaders—Suzuki, Takada, and Muraoka—from his company and instructed them in the details of the method of execution and disposal of the bodies. Muraoka, who was a judo expert, took responsibility for strangling the detainees. Takada's duty was to guard the other detainees as each individual was executed. Suzuki was to supervise the entire proceedings. Mochizuki told these men that he could not attend because of illness. Mochizuki further instructed them that they should select five soldiers from each platoon; five others selected from two other platoons brought the total to 23 soldiers present at the executions. These soldiers were ordered to carry ropes and assemble at 5:00 P.M. outside the Land Defense Party.[63]

Soon after Mori finished his discussion with Ichinose and Mochizuki, he rang Fleet Chief Petty Officer Takatō Jūtarō and instructed him to prepare two barges by five o'clock at the south wharf and to load the 5-meter-long wires and 20 concrete blocks onto each barge. Despite the fact that Takatō probably asked, Mori did not explain for what purpose these wires and blocks would be used. Takatō instructed his juniors to prepare the blocks and wires and load them onto the first and second barges. Takatō then instructed the barge captains, Kanbe Ryōhei and Miyamoto

Haruo, to take the barges to the south wharf by half past five. Therefore, the crews of these barges did not know what sort of work they would be engaged in, as Jitsukawa testified.[64]

At around five o'clock, Mochizuki addressed the soldiers gathered in front of the Land Defense Party, saying only that soldiers should follow the orders of Suzuki, Takada, and Muraoka. He then disappeared inside the office. Acting Sublieutenant Suzuki Shōzō detailed the instructions and allocated 10 soldiers to Muraoka for the purpose of strangulation, five to Takada to guard the detainees, and the rest to himself. These soldiers were responsible for blindfolding the detainees and taking them to the middle of the wharf. Suzuki then instructed Chief Petty Officer Horiguchi Yoshio to receive each blindfolded civilian at the middle of the wharf and hand the individual over to Muraoka. Suzuki further instructed these soldiers to tell the civilians they were being transferred to Rabaul and that the soldiers should never mention the execution. After this briefing, the soldiers boarded two trucks. One drove to the Australian civilians' camp, the other to the German clergymen's, where they picked up the detainees and brought them to Kavieng port.[65]

The detainees were informed that they were being transferred to Rabaul and were not suspicious. They hurriedly packed their possessions into suitcases and boarded the trucks, as instructed. The trucks drew up at the side of the road, 50 meters away from the south wharf. The detainees were told to wait there as they got off the trucks. At the War Crimes Tribunal, Horiguchi claimed that the detainees were told to squat behind a large buoy that stood on the wharf to prevent them from witnessing the executions.[66]

The executions began at six o'clock. The detainees were told that they would be taken one by one to a barge that would in turn take them to a boat off Kavieng port. A few soldiers were responsible for taking each person to the middle of the wharf, and another would follow carrying the person's suitcase. In the middle of the wharf, the detainee was blindfolded and handed to Horiguchi, who instructed the detainee to carry his own suitcase. Horiguchi then took him by the hand and led him to Muraoka. Muraoka told each detainee that the barge was waiting under the wharf and that for safety's sake he should sit on the edge of the wharf with his legs dangling over the side and his suitcase next to him. As soon as each victim sat on the edge of the wharf, Muraoka gently put two nooses over the detainee's head—one from each side—and his men, who were holding the end of each rope, would pull violently. Muraoka would then make sure the detainee was dead by listening for a heartbeat, remove the ropes, and throw the body onto the barge two meters below the wharf. Some of Muraoka's men were on the deck of the barge and tied each body to a concrete block with wire cable. The detainee's suitcase was taken to the opposite side of the wharf and thrown onto a pile. Suzuki, as supervisor, moved around among Muraoka, Horiguchi, and Takada and ensured that the whole operation went smoothly.[67]

When half of the detainees had been executed and their bodies loaded onto the second barge, the first barge took its place. After the executions had been completed, Muraoka and his men boarded one barge, Takada and his men the other, and the barges left for Nago Island. They dumped the bodies on the west side of the island where the water was deepest.[68]

The executions on the wharf were completed between nine and half past nine in the evening.[69] Thus it took approximately three and a half hours to execute 32 people, at the rate of approximately six and a half minutes per person—an extremely quick operation. Therefore, it is obvious that the operation was extremely well planned and that the Japanese soldiers carried it out with efficiency.

Suzuki, who saw off the barges, instructed some other soldiers to take the suitcases away and burn them. At around 10:00 P.M., he visited Mochizuki to inform him that the executions had been completed. The following day, early in the morning, Mochizuki went to see Ichinose and Mori and relayed to them the same information. Soon after, it is reported that Mori went to the headquarters of the 14th Naval Base Force. However, he again avoided seeing Tamura. He attempted to see staff officer Yoshino, but he was absent. Therefore, Mori asked staff officer Hiratsuka to pass the message on to Yoshino that the executions had been carried out.[70]

Two days after the executions, on March 19, Mori happened to bump into Tamura on the path between the headquarters of the 14th Naval Base Force and the 83rd Naval Garrison Unit, but Mori did not mention the executions at all. Hurriedly, Tamura asked him whether the executions had really been carried out, to which Mori simply replied "Yes." Naturally, Tamura did not report the executions to Southeast Fleet Headquarters in Rabaul, as they were undertaken without permission.[71]

The long-awaited landing of the Allied forces in Kavieng never happened, and the war ended in August of the following year. Once the war was over, the future war crimes tribunals that would be conducted by Allied forces suddenly became a crucial issue to the Japanese forces scattered around the Asia-Pacific region. Therefore, those with guilty consciences made enormous efforts to cover up their crimes—destroying evidence and fabricating alibis well before the Allied forces arrived.

Southeast Fleet Headquarters in Rabaul was no exception. Immediately after the Japanese surrender, senior officers called Commander Yoshino to Rabaul and asked him whether any serious war crimes were committed by the Japanese forces in New Ireland and, if so, whether it was possible to cover them up. Yoshino first mentioned that some Australians and Germans were executed without permission in March 1944. In the light of this information, the staff officer of headquarters, Captain Sanagi Tsuyoshi, asked his juniors to assist Yoshino in fabricating an alibi. Yoshino and these officers made up the story that the Australian and German civilians were killed when Allied forces attacked and sank the ship on which they were traveling. They studied a record of shipping movements around March 1944 and selected the most suitable incident—the sinking of the *Kowa Maru* a month before. Sanagi approved of this fabrication and told Yoshino that if he was forced to undergo questioning by Allied forces, he should tell them Sanagi had given Tamura orders to move the civilians from Kavieng onto the *Kowa Maru*. Yoshino returned to Kavieng and explained the details of the arrangement to Tamura and Mori, who called together all those soldiers of the 83rd Naval Garrison Unit who participated in the executions and instructed them as to what to say if they were questioned in the future. They carried out mock interrogations repeatedly so that the soldiers would memorize the entire scenario.[72]

The preceding account of the Kavieng massacre is based on the reports made by Klestadt and the court proceedings of the War Crimes Tribunal. However, I have some suspicions about the statements of Suzuki and Horiguchi, who were present at the executions. One of these is that the detainees may have realized what was happening because they were only 50 meters from the execution site. There were no buildings around the area, and even though the executions occurred after sunset, they still would have been visible. Horiguchi stated that the detainees were placed behind a big buoy, but it is unlikely the buoy could obscure the vision of more than 30 people.

Even if we accept Horiguchi's statement, it is unlikely that these people were not suspicious about being taken one by one onto the barge over the course of three hours, a long and drawn-out process for boarding. Suzuki also stated that none of the detainees realized what was happening until the last moment, which he asserted was a very considerate method of execution. But Suzuki's statement contradicts that of Jitsukawa, who was in the engine room of a barge. Jitsukawa stated that he had heard the screams of the detainees from above. Furthermore, Jitsukawa and Mori Yahichi, a crew member from the first barge, both stated that the crew spent several hours cleaning blood off the deck when they returned to Kavieng port from Nago Island.[73] It may be, therefore, that some detainees noticed what was happening and attempted to resist the soldiers and were bayoneted as a result. At the court, the prosecutor could not pursue this issue, as by that time both Muraoka, who carried out the executions, and Takada, another witness, were already dead. Both Suzuki and Horiguchi said they could not remember the names of any of the twenty-odd soldiers who had participated in the executions, which makes it possible that Suzuki and Horiguchi had collaborated to cover up any hint of undue violence.[74]

On December 17, 1947, the court handed down its verdict. The commander of the 14th Naval Base Force and 83rd Naval Garrison Unit, Tamura Ryūkichi, was sentenced to death by hanging. Others involved received prison sentences: the deputy commander of the 83rd Naval Garrison Unit, Mori Kyōji, 20 years; Yoshino Shōzō, staff officer of the 14th Naval Base Force, 15 years; Mochizuki Shichitarō, 7 years; Suzuki Shōzō, 12 years; and Horiguchi Yoshio, 4 years. There is no record of the prosecution of Ichinose Sōichi, who was head of the Land Defense Party and who suggested execution by strangulation, probably because he could not be located by the Australian War Crimes Section after the war. Tamura, although accused by his juniors Mori and Yoshino, accepted full responsibility for the decision to execute the civilians and asked the judge to be lenient with the other soldiers implicated in the executions.[75]

## Japanese Soldiers, International Law, and *Gyokusai*

It is significant that the War Crimes Tribunal hearing the Kavieng massacre prosecuted the Japanese only for the murder of 23 Australian civilians, not for the murder of the 9 German clergymen. As with the *Akikaze* massacre, responsibility for the deaths of the Germans was not taken into consideration. These cases serve to highlight the limitations of war crimes tribunals as a form of prosecution because the prosecuting country focuses on cases involving its own citizens or citizens of allied nations. In view of these limitations, one cannot expect war crimes tribunals to carry out full justice.

At the tribunal for the Kavieng case, the prosecutor brought up the question of just how much knowledge Tamura and other Japanese naval officers had of international law. Both the Hague and Geneva Conventions impose a duty on military forces to guarantee the security of a detainee's life, private property, and freedom of religion. Tamura, when asked at court about his knowledge of international law, stated that he briefly studied it at the Japanese naval academy at Edajima but had forgotten most of the content. Surprisingly, Tamura did not know that the Japanese government had ratified the Hague Convention until just before his court appearance. He also testified that he had never heard that the Japanese government had made an announcement that it would apply the principles of the Geneva Convention, even though it was not a signatory. Yoshino also testified that he had received a lecture on international law at the naval academy but was never given detailed information about the Hague Convention. He stated that he had read the Hague Convention only once. Mori was one of the judges of the Japanese court-martial while he was stationed in China from February to November 1939. Nevertheless, he stated that he did not know anything about international law, although he knew it existed. Mochizuki was not only unaware of international law but also quite ignorant of Japanese naval disciplinary provisions.[76] Therefore, if officers were lacking in such basic knowledge of international law, it is obvious that the ordinary Japanese soldier would have had little if any knowledge of it at all.

At the Japanese naval college, an international law course had been included in the curriculum from its inception. Especially between the Sino-Japanese War (1894–1895) and the Russo-Japanese War (1904–1905), the Japanese naval college made a great effort to educate the officers about international law.[77] The Japanese naval academy, founded twenty years before the college, began teaching international law during the Russo-Japanese War. However, as time passed, the subject at both institutions came to be regarded as expendable. In the 1910s and 1920s, when Tamura and Yoshino graduated from the academy, lecturers would have briefly mentioned the existence of international law but would not have explained the details. At the advent of the Pacific War, hours of teaching at the academy were shortened and the few lectures on law were further cut. For example, in 1941 students at the naval academy who were non-commissioned officers received only five hours of lectures on law, during which they studied the Japanese constitution, naval law and disciplinary provisions, and international law.[78] Therefore, it is estimated that the students received only one hour of teaching on international law during their time at the academy. When Mori graduated from the naval academy in 1936, the situation was no doubt similar. Even this limited exposure to the subject was better than at the military academy, where they received virtually no instruction on international law at all.[79]

It can be said that the massacres of civilians on the *Akikaze* and at Kavieng were the result of the Japanese naval officers' lack of knowledge of international law. However, the killing of innocent civilians, including women and children, is not just a matter of law but of basic human rights. Tamura visited the detainees' camp several times during his tenure at Kavieng and amiably asked about their living conditions and health. Yoshino, who had been to Melbourne, Australia, before the war on a training exercise, found a person from Melbourne among the detainees and had enjoyed a few friendly conversations with him.[80] Tamura seems to have been a very warm-hearted person. There is an anecdote that once, before the war, he gave his daughter's classmate money to go on a school excursion, as her family was poor.[81] So the question is, how could such a person give the order to execute civilians, some of whom he had met several times?

In answering this, one must not forget the extremely tense psychological pressure endured by Tamura and other Japanese soldiers in Kavieng. Their situation was desperate: They were convinced that the landing of the Allied forces was imminent, there was no communication with Rabaul, and there were no supporting forces to assist them. Therefore, for many weeks they endured the psychological position that there was no other option but *gyokusai*, or "glorious self-annihilation." As is well known, Japanese soldiers were not allowed to surrender and had to fight until the end. It was their duty to inflict as much damage as possible on the enemy, even if there was no hope of winning the battle, and then to die. The idea of *gyokusai* was to force a Japanese soldier to destroy his most precious possession—his own life. In other words, a person who must face *gyokusai* was forced to recognize how dispensable his life was. For this reason, a soldier had to find his own profound meaning for his death in order to commit the act. He gained a false sense of immortality through his belief that his life would continue through the spirit of the emperor or *kokutai*, "the national body." It is ironic that the more desperate the situation Japanese soldiers were in, the more fiercely they would fight and show strong loyalty toward the emperor so that their spirit might live on.

However, no matter how one rationalizes the meaning of one's life, this concept of immortality is basically flawed. Often, a soldier tried to rationalize his actions with fanatical nationalism, but he could not erase the unconscious fear that his life was about to be terminated. Because the soldier was forced to eliminate his own life by a violent organization of military forces that he could not resist, a natural and easy psychological "rationalization" would have been for him to regard the lives of other people as dispensable also. Therefore, for the soldier, the most important question was how to make his own death a meaningful consequence—that is, how to achieve immortality. This became his obsession, so that the lives of prisoners, detainees, and the like meant nothing to him.

At the tribunal, Tamura said that "strategically" the executions were unavoidable.[82] However, the only strategic option they had at that time was *gyokusai*, so it was up to Tamura and his men to make the act as meaningful as possible. The fact that Mori repeatedly requested Tamura to make a decision as quickly as possible clearly demonstrates the psychology of *gyokusai*, whereby the lives of detainees were regarded as obstacles toward the successful completion of glorious self-annihilation. In this sense, Mori and Tamura were both victims of the *gyokusai* ideology as well as perpetrators of a horrendous act.

The problem, therefore, is not just a question of the failure to teach Japanese soldiers international law. What must be examined is why the concept of basic human rights, in particular respect for individual lives, was lacking among the Japanese soldiers, and how this is strongly related to the concept of *gyokusai*. Thus the key is to examine the historical process that created this unique ideology, found only in the Japanese military forces during the Asia-Pacific War.

# Conclusion: Understanding Japanese Brutality in the Asia-Pacific War

## The Japanese Concept of Basic Human Rights

The extreme ill-treatment of POWs by the Japanese was a historically specific phenomenon that occurred between the so-called China Incident and the end of World War II. By making this claim, I am not denying that mistreatment of POWs, along with the other horrors of war, is a universal problem. Since the end of World War II, there have been constant recurrences of the same kinds of atrocities that were perpetrated by the Japanese. At the time of writing, the most notable ongoing conflicts (in Bosnia-Herzegovina, Rwanda, and Chechnya) have all been marked by frequent reliable reports of atrocities. Needless to say, atrocities committed against prisoners have figured prominently among them. However, to say that these problems are therefore exactly the same in any war at any time and place would unduly distort the picture, because there are important historical and cultural differences to take into account.

Prior to the China Incident, Japanese POW policy and practice were comparatively humane. Even the Chinese, who were the most brutally treated during the Asia-Pacific War, had been treated with relative respect in previous military encounters.[1] In order to understand how such drastic changes could occur within a few decades, at most, it is necessary to examine more closely some underlying developments. It is especially important to understand more about the changes that occurred in Japanese military ideology from about 1910 onward, how these affected the organizational structure of the Japanese military forces, and how both affected Japanese POW policy.

As was explained in detail in Chapter 2, Japanese POW policy and practice during the Meiji and Taishō periods were scrupulously in accordance with the international law of the time. However, it is undeniable that the Japanese military structure had within it the potential for brutality right from the creation of Japan's modern military forces in the early Meiji period. That potential was evident in the harsh treatment the military imposed on its own officers and soldiers. A case in point is the order given by the commander of the First Army of the Japanese imperial forces, General Yamagata Aritomo, during the first Sino-Japanese War of 1894–1895 that Japanese soldiers must commit suicide rather than surrender to the enemy.[2] This order marked the beginning of a modern reconstitution of *bushidō*, the ancient martial code of conduct. Yamagata's order remained in effect over the next half century. Thus, the military leaders' disregard for life and the new ethic that underpinned that attitude were taking shape long before the Asia-Pacific War. By the time of the China Incident, the military leadership's attitude of disregard for human life extended beyond its own men to encompass POWs as well. This development can be seen as an almost inevitable result of the changes in Japanese imperial ideology during that time.

The core of any military force is the soldiers themselves. No matter how sophisticated their weaponry, if there are not enough disciplined and able-bodied soldiers to utilize it, military power is diminished. Therefore, for any modern military force, a critical consideration in planning its strategies should be how to minimize casualties while still carrying out an operation effectively. However, modern Japanese military forces, which were established in the latter half of the nineteenth century and developed quickly over a short period, tended to undervalue the strategic importance of minimizing casualties. This tendency increased as the emperor ideology gained hold over the minds of the Japanese people and reached its peak during World War II, when the *gyokusai* ideology emerged. *Gyokusai* held that a soldier was expected to fight to the end for the emperor. Even when the situation was becoming hopeless for a Japanese victory, the Japanese military command, instead of trying to minimize casualties, forced *gyokusai* on its soldiers, thereby further diminishing its manpower. Instead of acknowledging imminent defeat, the military leaders became caught up in an escalating cycle of such desperate and counterproductive tactics as *kamikaze* (suicide attack by an aircraft) and *kaiten* (suicide attack by a submarine).[3] Suicidal attack is not a phenomenon peculiar to the Japanese. Suicidal attacks have occurred among both Western and Islamic military forces but as a spontaneous act rather than as part of a strategy. In this sense, the Japanese *gyokusai* is of a different nature.

It is the duty of any soldier to kill the enemy in war. Of course, soldiers violate the basic human rights of others by killing them, and in this sense the Japanese and Western forces were no different. However, in wartime, killing can be legitimized by the rationalizations that a soldier must kill others in order to defend himself and that his actions serve the higher purpose of defending his nation. These legitimizations, in combination with any military force's imposition of a rigid command structure that places the soldier's duty of obedience to his superiors as paramount, further compound the military's tendency to undervalue the basic human rights of the individual.

Despite this common element, Japanese forces were unusal in the extent to which they undervalued their soldiers. In order to discover why the Japanese committed such cruel war crimes upon detainees, POWs, and civilians in occupied territories during the Asia-Pacific War, we also need to understand more deeply why there was disregard for the basic human rights of the Japanese soldier. The answer to this question cannot be confined to the Japanese military because all sectors of Japanese society supported the imperial ideology. Therefore, we must examine what sorts of concepts of human rights the Japanese had before, during, and after the war.

This question is difficult to answer, and it is insufficient to debate the question on an abstract level. A comprehensive treatment of the issue would be a large undertaking (not even a whole book would suffice). For the moment, I will simply provide a thumbnail sketch of the trajectory of events that mark the evolution of the dominant concept of human rights in Japanese society from the Meiji restoration to the end of the war.

Japan created its first state constitution—the Meiji constitution—in February 1889. Between 1890 and 1898, a body of five laws—civil law, commercial law, criminal law, civil procedure, and criminal procedure—was established. The Meiji government borrowed from French and German legislation and, in less than ten years, created a body of law of comparable complexity and comprehensiveness. The reason for the Meiji government's comparatively hasty establishment of a constitution was not out of urgent concern for the protection of the basic human rights of the Japanese people or the need for clarification of legal duty. The constitution was adopted principally as a device to establish the power of the Japanese imperial state in the face of challenges to its authority by the "unequal treaties" the Tokugawa regime had signed with the Western powers. These treaties guaranteed Western powers legal jurisdiction over their own citizens who committed crimes on Japanese soil and made them immune from existing Japanese law. The ratification of the Meiji constitution was intended to demonstrate to the West that Japan had a systematic, nationwide body of rational laws, thereby creating the basis for ending extraterritoriality. The motive for adopting the constitution was thus primarily a response to external political forces rather than internal ones.[4]

The Meiji constitution imposed a body of laws on a society in which a demand for such laws had not developed organically. Thus a significant gap remained between the codified law and the everyday understandings of lawful and moral conduct as practiced by the populace. Nowhere was this more obvious than in the confusion surrounding the notion of *kenri,* or "rights." The very word *kenri* was an invention of the Meiji constitution; there had previously been no word for the concept of political rights in Japan.[5]

Of course, this does not mean the Japanese had no concept of rights prior to the adoption of the Meiji constitution; property and contractual rights were highly developed.[6] But there was little or no concept of universal political rights, such as those included in the U.S. Bill of Rights. The ratification of the Meiji constitution did not sweep away the historically inherited network of feudal conventions that constituted the Tokugawa regime; rather, the Meiji constitution was a superimposition of modern legal and political forms onto a continuing feudal structure, most clearly evident in the retention of the emperor. Thus Japan has no history of political rights gained by large-scale mass revolution of the common people, as is the case in Western Europe and the United States. In Japan, political rights were established mainly by the state in advance of their adoption or understanding by the common people.[7]

The Meiji constitution ostensibly enshrined a range of rights then established in Western Europe, but these rights could be circumscribed or even overridden by specific legislation. Thus the system contrasted with that of the United States, for instance, where the constitution takes precedence. For example, Chapter 2 of the 1889 constitution (Rights and Duties of Subjects) contained 15 articles that covered and ostensibly protected the range of political rights. However, the majority of these articles were framed in such a way as to make it easy for them to be overridden. An example is Article 29: "Japanese subjects shall, *within the limits of the law,* enjoy the liberty of speech, writing, publication, public meetings and associations." [Emphasis added.]

The Meiji government used provisions of this nature to make laws that flouted the spirit of the constitution but remained within the letter. Indeed, the government emphasized the concept of duty over and above the concept of rights in its practice. For example, the relatives of a man killed by a fire engine were denied compensation by the government on the grounds that the driver of the fire engine was engaged in public duty at the time of the accident. When the Itabashi ammunition depot near Tokyo exploded, destroying several houses, the owners were denied compensation on the grounds that the depot was of great importance to Japanese defense and thus it was part of public duty to live with the danger of such an installation. And when the negligence of a professor of medicine at Kyoto Imperial University resulted in the crippling of a patient on whom he operated, he was exempted from paying compensation on the grounds that, as an employee of the public education system, he was engaged in public duty at the time.[8]

However, it would be a mistake to believe that there was widespread public outrage at such official conduct. The Meiji constitution had been imposed on a feudal value structure, and significant features of that value structure persisted in the early period of Japanese modernity. Much of the populace seems to have placed a higher value on the concepts of duty and fealty to the nation than on the concepts of rights and liberties. To claim one's "rights" was seen as egocentric, individualistic, and destructive of the social fabric. The organic model of the nation—with the state as a family and the emperor as the "nation's father"—persisted as the dominant model of national life for the vast majority of Japanese.[9]

## Japanese Moral Concepts and the Emperor Ideology

The absence of a developed liberal concept of universal human rights in Japanese society had a corresponding effect on the everyday Japanese concept of the rights of others as individuals. The "other" was conceived of in national, social, and organic terms as a "sibling," owing similar duties to the national family-state. Responsibility was conceived in terms of a pyramidal model. Duties were always to one's superior: the duty of a family to the father, of the father to the state, and of the state to the emperor. The chain of responsibility was conceived of as predominantly unidirectional, from subordinate to superior.[10]

Responsibility was effectively unlimited; there was no concept of "inalienable rights" to serve as a bulwark against the demands of the state. Duty was always seen in highly sentimental terms—up to and including one's duty to die for the emperor. The terms of such duty could be highly arbitrary. Apart from duty to one's superiors, there were no clear guidelines as to whom one owed responsiblity. Nor was it clear what demands could be made on an individual—in the name of duty—by the different people in the hierarchy. Thus the notion of "national duty and responsibility" in general led to a collapse of responsibility in particular. The specific and habitual duties of citizens, and the reasonable limits to such, were never clarified. Universal responsibility thus laid the groundwork for a comprehensive irresponsibility in individual conduct.[11]

The clearest example of such an abrogation of individual responsibility for one's actions is undoubtedly the conduct of Japanese soldiers and officers during the course of the Asia-Pacific War, especially in their treatment of POWs. The military doctrine of unquestioning obedience to superior officers was heightened by the fact that such orders were explicitly given "in the name of the emperor"; the chain of duty was thus made explicit at each stage, and the responsibility for acts was transferred up the chain to the emperor. Consequently, the Japanese soldiers who were defendants in the war crimes trials denied responsibility for their acts—and did so in good faith: They honestly believed that responsibility rested with the military, the state, and ultimately their highest allegiance, the emperor.

Such a displacement of responsibility was a factor even in the defense of the A Class war criminals, such as Tōjō, who claimed that as prime minister he was nothing more than the most senior servant of the emperor.[12] Another example of a means to avoid personal responsibility was the doctrine of *ichioku sōzange*—the notion that the entire population of Japan was responsible for losing the war and should apologize to the emperor. Thus the political leaders of Japan avoided particular responsibility for their conduct of the war and absolved the emperor of personal responsibility by apologizing on behalf of the nation. In contradiction to Tōjō's defense, a myth grew that the emperor was a victim of the war leaders and, having no real power to make or effect political decisions, he did not bear any responsibility for Japan's war crimes.

The absence of a notion of personal responsibility for political acts has had an enduring impact on Japanese cultural construction of the Asia-Pacific War. The current generation of Japanese still do not have a clear concept of the responsibility of their parents and grandparents in relation to the war. This is an entirely different situation from what exists in, for example, Germany, where an acute awareness of the role of the German people in World War II and genocide of Jews and Gypsies continues to be a major factor in political life and memory.

Indeed, in Japan the whole framework of ethics was not seen as emanating from individuals or even from a collective cultural base. Instead it was seen as coming downward from the emperor to the people as a framework for understanding their duties, and these duties went upward from the people to the emperor. In both cases, the state acted as the conduit and the effective framer of the details—the emperor thus becoming a symbolic national father who legitimized state power. Thus the document defining social relations and citizenship known as *Kyōiku Chokugo,* which was introduced into Japanese schools as a basis for developing good Japanese citizenship, was known as the "Imperial Rescript on Education" and was presented as having come (whether literally or metaphorically) from the emperor himself. Such a framework for ethics gives rise to a conflict between the universalizing tendency of modernity, with its aim of founding morality in rationally discoverable rules for the personal conduct of any individual, and the older feudal ideal of a morality that was fused with authority, which emanated from the emperor and over which abstract demands for legitimation had no purchase.[13]

The authoritarian basis of Japanese morality in this period can be seen very clearly in the habitual ill-treatment of Japanese soldiers by their officers. Discipline was conducted through *bentatsu* (the routine striking and bashing of soldiers), which was presented as an "act of love" by the officers for the soldiers. Even in the Japanese Navy—which was far more Westernized in its conduct than the Army[14]—adopted a practice of harsh discipline known as *tekken seisai* (the iron fist) in the wake of the Russo-Japanese War.[15] It was often called the *ai-no-muchi*, or "whip of love." Not surprisingly, this manner of conduct was extended to Allied POWs during the Asia-Pacific War. Violence against POWs by Japanese guards was routinized and made psychologically easy for the perpetrators, as it occurred within a legitimizing framework.

Within such an authority-based system of morality, the worth of individuals was conceived in terms of their proximity to the emperor. Despite the fact that the constitution ostensibly guaranteed equality to citizens beneath the emperor, the everyday reality was that those who carried out the emperor's wishes—the state bureaucracy and the military, in particular—were represented as the most worthy and valuable citizens.[16] The "untouchable" class (*burakumin*)—the slaughtermen, cremators, and tanners—and those involved in entertainment and theater were, by virtue of their livelihoods, represented as the furthest from the emperor and the least worthy of all the Japanese people.[17]

This value system, in which human worth was anchored in proximity to the emperor, became accepted and embedded in Japanese culture to such a degree that it did not require active efforts by the state to make it hold. However, in the colonies it was a different story. The anchoring of responsibilities and rights in the authority of the emperor was not readily accepted by the colonized peoples and had to be imposed by a combination of military force and ideological inventions such as "the Asian Co-Prosperity Sphere" and *hakkō ichiu* ("the whole word under one roof," i.e., under the emperor). Within Japan's expansive empire, the emperor-as-supreme system was intended to apply to whole nations. The worth of nations was to be judged by their proximity to the emperor as represented by the Japanese nation.[18]

The Japanese notion of "world peace"—a phrase used frequently by Japan on the world stage in the 1930s—was at variance with the Wilsonian concept of "a world peace achieved by the democratic relationship of states" within the League of Nations, although in reality, the Wilsonian concept also served the interests of powerful nations (in this case, Britain and the United States) rather than weaker ones. The Japanese concept of world peace was one in which "peace" was anchored in the submission of many nations to imperial domination. In the Asian sphere the dominant nation was to be Japan. This resistance to the dominant notion of a liberal democratic framework for international relations extended to Japan's attitude to international law, which it saw as an illegitimate imposition on its anchored legal-value system.

The value system of proximity to the emperor created a contradiction in the self-regard held by Japanese enlisted men. Within the borders of Japan they were of relatively low status, yet in the colonies, among the subjected peoples, they were representatives of the emperor and their status rose greatly. This led in many cases to unbalanced psychological states: extremes of self-abnegation in relation to the Japanese domestic hierarchy alternating with excessive self-regard in relation to colonial non-Japanese subjects. The repressed resentment of the former was often expressed in violence toward the latter.[19] This was exemplified by the 1937 Nanjing massacre, in which large numbers of Chinese civilians were raped or murdered or both.

Undoubtedly POWs were also the target of such transferred anger and frustration. In literal terms, Japanese soldiers were obviously the physical perpetrators of such atrocities. In psychological and ideological terms, they were also the victims of an emperor system that legitimized such atrocities in the name of serving the emperor. The wartime propaganda used by the Allied nations portraying the Japanese people as "schizophrenic"—gentle at home yet violent outside their own country—was therefore by no means groundless. Yet any imperial nation contains the double standard of one set of morals for use within the nation and another for use outside. But in the Japanese case, the gap between these two moral standards was probably wider than that of Western imperialism. The reason for this can be found in the emperor system, which has the specific ideology and the structure of oppression.

However, like any ideology, the emperor ideology was constituted so that its oppressive elements were not easily recognized by the general populace. The concept of the emperor's paternal love toward his subjects is one such example. This feudal notion of family ties was used to cover up the political control exerted over the Japanese people. Thus, just as the familiar notion of a father's love for his children was exploited and expanded in the concept of the emperor's love for his subjects, so too was the notion of trust and obedience of the child toward the father reiterated in the concept of the subject's loyalty toward the emperor.[20] Another element was the Shinto philosophy incorporated in the emperor ideology. Because Shinto is not formulated in any readily expressed doctrines and does not have any sacred texts, it can potentially absorb a vast range of ideas so long as they are not antiauthoritarian.

As the emperor ideology strengthened, the emperor, as head of the Shinto religion, became associated with a range of political ideas and attitudes, some of which are, from a rational standpoint, contradictory or incompatible.[21] Therefore, the emperor ideology had a tendency toward totalitarianism from the beginning, but this tendency was veiled with mysticism, and as a result the illusory concept of the harmony of the nation was established. The two concepts of a familial love among all Japanese people and harmony within the nation served to disguise the oppression of the Japanese people by their rulers. Thus, in the minds of many, the emperor became the key figure in maintaining national harmony. It seemed natural to demonstrate strong loyalty to him in return for the "social welfare" he provided.

Although I have portrayed the Japanese as strongly in the hold of the emperor ideology, I certainly do not want to give the impression that there was never any organized opposition. Especially during the period of the "Taishō democracy"—which spanned 1915 to the early 1920s—there was lively political debate in Japanese society, and such strongly antiemperor ideologies as anarchism, feminism, and communism gained significant numbers of adherents, even if they always remained minorities. However, the 1920s brought the beginning of a clampdown on political dissent. Organized opposition was targeted by the police and military for violent treatment. For example, in the wake of the 1923 Kantō earthquake, the military used the ensuing disorder as a cover for rounding up prominent political activists, some of whom were executed extrajudicially. Among those executed were four famous anarchist political activists: Ōsugi Sakae, Itō Noe, Kaneko Fumiko, and Pak Yeol.[22]

The modern Japanese state, based upon the emperor system, was not established overnight. According to influential political scientist Ishida Takeshi, the point of full development of the concept of the family-state was reached around 1910. Ishida's analysis is based upon changes in school textbooks on morals, theories of the state produced by the leading Japanese philosophers of the time, and the rhetoric of grassroots nationalist political organizations.[23] We can certainly treat Ishida's claim as reliable and can therefore say something more about politics during the Taishō democracy. After 1910 the emperor ideology was sufficiently well formed to be a recognizable target for opposition. The brief flourishing of left-wing politics in the period of the Taishō democracy can be understood as a rearguard action against the emerging fascism that was motivated in large part by the emperor ideology.

Maruyama Masao, another influential political scientist, analyzed the historical development of Japanese fascism based on a concept similar to Ishida's notion of the family-state. Maruyama identified the period between the end of World War I and the Manchurian incident (1920–1930) as the preparatory stage of the Japanese fascist movement. The movement developed fully in the period between Japan's seizure of Manchuria in 1931 and the February 26 Incident (a failed coup d'etat on February 26, 1936). The period between 1936 and August 1945 following the entrenchment of fascism was the high point of the movement.[24] In other words, the emperor ideology, based upon the family-state concept, gradually penetrated the Japanese mind from around 1910, became strongly entrenched during the 1920s, then fed into Japanese fascism from the 1930s.

## The Corruption of *Bushidō*

While the emperor ideology was taking form and gaining a hold on the Japanese people, related changes were occurring within the ideologies and ethical codes of the military. One of the most important changes was the reinterpretation—or more plainly, corruption—of the ethical code of *bushidō* ("the way of the warrior") in order to subordinate it to the emperor ideology and the new military ideology. The inculcation of trainee officers in the emperor ideology at the military college gave them a very distorted understanding of *bushidō*. In the early Meiji period, the military code of conduct was still strongly influenced by *bushidō*, yet by 1920 the true spirit of *bushidō* had vanished from the armed forces. What remained was a mere husk of what *bushidō* had been in previous times—whatever superficial features that could be appropriated for the emperor ideology while dispensing with the substance.

An example of how *bushidō* had previously influenced military conduct during the Meiji period can be seen in a book written by the philosopher Nishi Amane, *Heika Tokugyō* (The Moral Virtue of the Soldier), first published in 1879. Nishi argued that it was necessary to set up a Western-style military that was mechanical in its organizational form in order for Japan to be able to fight a modern war. However, Nishi also strongly emphasized the need to maintain the traditional Japanese values of benevolence and right conduct—values that are the essence of *bushidō*.[25] During the early Meiji period the spirit of *bushidō* could still be seen in the rituals of military discipline. High-ranking officers were expected to commit *seppuku* (ritual suicide) for serious offenses, whereas ordinary soldiers were subject only to minor forms of corporal punishment.[26] In their willingness to place higher demands on themselves than those under their command, officers demonstrated their commitment to *bushidō*. This forms a stark contrast with the conduct of officers during the Asia-Pacific War, when the court-martials were used to punish the rank and file harshly for disobeying orders, no matter how absurd, and to cover up the wrongdoings of officers. Self-discipline was clearly no longer a value of the senior ranks in the Asia-Pacific War.

It is often held that the inhumane conduct of the Japanese during the Asia-Pacific War arose from within *bushidō* itself. The Japanese Field Service Code, *Senjinkun*, which among other things required that soldiers commit suicide rather than surrender, and the Imperial Code of Military Conduct, *Gunjin Chokuron*, which demanded absolute loyalty to the emperor, were both held to carry the essence of *bushidō*. All Japanese soldiers as well as Formosan and Korean prison guards were required to memorize them, and much of their understandings of *bushidō* would have come from these codes. Prisoners of the Japanese also often believed that the cruelty of their captors stemmed from *bushidō*.

Does *bushidō* justify cruelty? To answer this question it is necessary to look at the details of the code, which consists of seven essential elements.

The first element is righteousness: commitment to justice and duty and despising of cowardice. The second element is courage: the will to do right and an indomitable spirit in the face of adversity. The warrior should be concerned about nothing, including death, as an obstacle to doing right. To die for a just cause is the highest honor, although to die for a trivial cause is despised. Dying for a trivial cause is called *inujini*—"a dog's death." The third element is humanity: love, tolerance, and sympathy for others. Humanity is seen in *bushidō* as a particular requirement for leaders. Humanity toward the weak or the defeated is seen as a most honorable way for a warrior to conduct himself; therefore the ill-treatment of POWs is completely opposed to this element. The fourth element is propriety: the realization of humanity in acts of kindness. The fifth element is sincerity: the respect for truth and the avoidance of lying. The sixth element is honor: the realization of one's own duty and privilege. The honorable warrior can do no wrong without feeling great shame. The seventh element is loyalty: obedience to one's seniors but never blind obedience.[27]

In summary, it can be seen from the elements of the code that *bushidō* requires great self-discipline together with great tolerance toward others. So how and why were the demands for tolerance and compassion in *bushidō* forgotten?

The Imperial Code of Military Conduct, which was issued in 1882 by Emperor Meiji, emphasized five elements that every Japanese soldier must respect: loyalty, propriety, courage, righteousness, and simplicity. The code held that sincerity underlay all five elements. Justice and morality were also emphasized. It is clear that the code was heavily influenced by *bushidō*. This is not at all surprising, as Nishi Amane participated in drafting the conduct code, and he had the highest regard for *bushidō* as a moral code. Nothing in the conduct code could possibly be taken as justification for the cruel treatment of POWs. In Article 3 requiring the soldier to respect courage, it was stated that violent and impetuous acts can never be acts of courage. It was also stated that the courageous soldier must treat others with love and respect.[28]

However, as time passed, the real content of the conduct code was forgotten, and the code became a mere prop for ritualism. The booklet itself took on the status of a sacred object. Soldiers were given the task of memorizing the content (at least the words), but they no longer learned what the words really meant. In the period leading up to the Asia-Pacific War, an absurd situation developed: Officers who made mistakes in reciting the code would see themselves as having committed a shameful act and commit ritual suicide.

The Field Service Code was formulated in 1941 for the purpose of preventing crimes by Japanese soldiers, such as those that occurred in the Nanjing massacre in 1937, by tightening the definitions of how soldiers should conduct themselves. Army Minister Tōjō Hideki issued the code to all battalions of the imperial forces. It made specific reference to POWs and their humane treatment. However, it also specifically stated that Japanese soldiers should not allow themselves to become POWs. This no-surrender policy was emphasized, and the other directives concerning POWs were forgotten. As explained in Chapter 1, Tōjō himself violated the Field Service Code by planning the exploitation of POWs as forced laborers for the Japanese war effort.[29]

Therefore it should be clear that the ethic in which the ill-treatment of POWs was justifiable did not originate from within *bushidō* but rather from the corruption of it. The single greatest corruption was in the demand for blind loyalty to the emperor. This demand became an essential element of the new Japanese military ideology. Article 1 of the Meiji code emphasized loyalty, but this loyalty was toward the nation or state rather than to the emperor. The object of Article 1 had been to foster nationalism among the soldiers of the imperial forces. Article 2 clearly stated that soldiers should obey any order from a senior as if that order had come from the emperor himself, but it also stated that senior officers should never despise their juniors and should never behave in an arrogant manner. Therefore Article 2 emphasized propriety and demanded cooperation and mutual respect among all men in the armed forces.[30] During the Asia-Pacific War, however, the demand for obedience to senior officers was stripped of its original context of mutual respect and cooperation. The phrase "to obey orders as if they came from the emperor himself" became a slogan that was constantly used by officers. Soldiers were punished severely for disobedience, no matter how absurd the orders, and the slogan was quoted as justification.

In this way the type of loyalty emphasized in the Meiji code was replaced by blind obedience. Soldiers attempted to demonstrate their loyalty by carrying out all and any orders and to prove their courage by reckless violence toward the enemy. The new military ideology—which placed so much weight on the concepts of no surrender, loyalty through blind obedience, and honor in dying for the emperor—spread throughout the Japanese armed forces with little apparent resistance. The brutal treatment of POWs by the Japanese can be seen as a way this ideology was put into practice. To despise men who had surrendered rather than fight to the death became a first step toward justifying reckless violence against them.

Yamagata Aritomo, who invented the no-surrender policy, had a very different concept of what loyalty meant. He was typically harsh in the treatment of his own men, but Yamagata never believed in blind obedience. In 1878 he published a pamphlet entitled *Gunjin Kunkai* (Admonition for Soldiers) in which he stated that if an order is illogical, soldiers should be allowed to appeal to a higher authority, even if only after carrying it out.[31] Unfortunately, Yamagata's proposed brake on unreasonable demands for obedience was far from practical on the front lines. During the Asia-Pacific War there was no real possibility of successfully appealing illogical orders, and acts of questioning or disobedience invariably led to court-martial.

The fact that such corruption of *bushidō* brought about a major change in Japanese military ideology from around 1910 is also evident from various revisions made to the existing military regulations and methods of training in the same period. In 1908 there was a revision of army regulations on internal affairs, and revision of drill books took place for the infantry (1909), the artillery (1910), machine gunners (1910), and the cavalry (1912). Moreover, in 1913 the ordinance of military education was created, and the ordinance of field duty was created in 1914. By revising the drill books and establishing new regulations, the Japanese forces fundamentally changed their existing military strategy and methods of training based upon the French and German models. As a result of these reforms, the most prominent change was the emphasis placed on "fighting spirit" and the concept of victory at any cost. The importance of devotion to the state and emperor was reiterated in these new regulations. At the same time, in order to enhance loyalty toward the state and emperor, the family-state ideology was reintroduced into the military forces by the demand that the soldier show obedience to his superior officers as a son shows obedience to his father.[32]

This important change within the Japanese military forces is closely related to the fact that most of the older military leaders, who had been samurai prior to the Meiji restoration, retired immediately after the Russo-Japanese War. The replacement of the old military leaders contributed to the distortion of *bushidō* and thus the creation of the new character of the Japanese forces. Until the Russo-Japanese War, Army leaders had been former samurai from the Chōshū region, and Navy leaders former samurai from Satsuma. These former samurai, who had seized the high command, had not only the tradition of *bushidō* to draw upon but also their previous dual roles as politicians and military leaders. These men had conducted the civil war, which culminated in the Meiji Restoration, at a time when Japan was under threat of Western colonization. In such circumstances they had to be concerned with much more than accomplishing their immediate military objectives; they had to understand the value of compromise and they did. In other words, they proved they had wisdom concerning how to conduct a war in accordance with the political conditions of the time. In the feudal period before the civil war, it was also important for the samurai leaders to understand how to conduct limited conflicts. For instance, they often lacked the material resources to conduct prolonged conflicts, and consequently they were always prepared to stop a war in order to accomplish their political objectives. The priority of politics over warfare in the thinking of Japanese military leaders in the early Meiji period was evident in their policies during the Russo-Japanese War. Men such as General Ōyama Iwao and Rear Admiral Yamamoto Gonbei as well as Prime Minister Katsura Tarō, who was also a general in the Japanese Imperial Army, showed their ability to compromise while still obtaining their political objectives.[33]

However, because these former samurai, who had been brought up with a strong fighting ethic, all retired after the Russo-Japanese War, their wisdom was lost to the military. The new military leaders were either their sons or sons of middle- and upper-class civilians, but in both cases they apparently had little concept of *bushidō*. Most were graduates of the newly established military college, where they were inculcated with the emperor ideology and a corrupted version of *bushidō*. For these new senior officers, a major war was regarded as a collection and expansion of smaller battles rather than as a complex political situation that demanded new ways of thinking. These new leaders had been in the front line of the Russo-Japanese War. Proud of their victory in their first war experience, they arrogantly saw *themselves* as the emperor's military forces.[34] From that time on, the special Japanese "fighting spirit" was heavily emphasized in their rhetoric, and they considered it more important than military technology as a means to victory. The revision of the Japanese military code and the penetration of the emperor ideology based upon the family-state concept were therefore closely related to the fact that with the retirement of the former samurai, the means by which the military tradition could be transmitted was lost.

In 1910 both the Japanese Army and Navy decided to expand their forces, and the number of drafted soldiers suddenly increased dramatically. In 1905, immediately after the Russo-Japanese War, 68,720 men were drafted. The number jumped to 103,784 in 1912 and reached 135,948 in 1921.[35] Most of the drafted men came from poor rural areas. They were mainly the sons of tenant farmers, who were exploited by their landlords and suffered from the economic depression created by the Russo-Japanese War. In contrast to the professional warrior class, these men did not have a strong existing loyalty toward either the state or the military. As a consequence, loyalty toward their senior officers, the state, and ultimately the emperor had to be inculcated in them, often by violence.[36] Thus, the "familylike relationship" within the military forces became a sham, and the emphasis on fighting spirit promoted by the military leaders became increasingly dogmatic.

It is highly likely that the dramatic change in Japanese POW policy coincided with the preparatory period of fascism in the 1920s, a period marked by the corruption of *bushidō* and the development of the emperor ideology. This ideology reshaped the Japanese people's idea of the emperor as well as their attitudes toward other countries, and such changes were reflected in Japanese POW policy. If we compare the attitudes of soldiers involved in the Russo-Japanese War with those of soldiers in the Asia-Pacific War, we can see a clear difference in their ideas about the emperor and the state. Letters home from soldiers in the Russo-Japanese War show that they entertained few illusions about their own glorious self-annihilation, and few expressed fanaticism for the state. These men were nationalists, but their idealization of the emperor was lacking within their nationalism.[37] In this sense, they were clearly different from the Japanese soldiers who fought so tenaciously against the Allied forces in the Asia-Pacific War. This difference is clear in the wills written by Japanese war criminals from all ranks who were sentenced to death. Many of these show the degree to which these men genuinely believed they were dying in order to save their country and to maintain the integrity of the emperor, although undoubtedly there were those who were not committed to fighting for the emperor and the state.[38] Further evidence of the general belief that it was necessary to die for the state comes from the example of Okinawan people. Many Okinawan civilians fought with the Japanese against the U.S. forces in the battle of Okinawa and died because of the nationalistic indoctrination that they should fight for the state until death, despite the fact that they distrusted the Japanese as a result of racial discrimination they had experienced for many generations.[39]

There is also a large difference between the Russo-Japanese War and the Asia-Pacific War not only in the treatment of POWs by Japanese forces but also in the Japanese people's attitudes toward Japanese soldiers who became POWs themselves. For example, in 1906 the Japanese soldiers who had been POWs in Russia stopped in Singapore on their way back to Japan. The Japanese residents in Singapore welcomed them warmly, and they enjoyed the same reception when they arrived in Kōbe. These soldiers were taken to Tokyo by train, and whenever the train stopped at a station, local people would shower the men with gifts. Some of the officers who became POWs were investigated by a special military investigation committee and accused of the "shameful act" of becoming POWs, but all were let off lightly. None were court-martialed; in fact, some were awarded medals.[40] It is difficult to imagine the leaders of the Japanese military behaving in such a generous manner toward their men who became POWs during the Asia-Pacific War.

## Toward Further Research

It clearly is insufficient to examine only military organizational structure and ideology in order to reach an understanding of Japanese military war crimes during the Asia-Pacific conflict. Also required is an understanding of how emperor ideology was consolidated in the minds of the Japanese during the 1920s and 1930s and how this affected the nation's military structure and ideology. Japanese themselves have not yet truly examined the interrelationship among ideology, ethics, and war crimes, but the task is crucial and not only for historical reasons.

After the war, the Meiji constitution was abolished and the so-called democratic constitution replaced it. Human rights were unconditionally guaranteed, and the emperor was stripped of his divinity and of any administrative political power. The death of emperor ideology seemed assured. Again, however, a constitution was imposed from above—this time by the Allied occupation forces—rather than arising from the struggles and sentiments of the Japanese people. As with the Meiji reforms, the concept of human rights was not (and has not been) thoroughly internalized by the people as a living, day-to-day code of behavior, even though it is well understood in theory.

This gap between theory and practice is evident in various forms of discrimination found in Japanese society today. It is well known that minority groups such as those of Korean origin, the *burakumin* (Japan's "untouchables"), the Ainu (Japan's aborigines), and the Okinawans all suffer from discrimination in such fundamental aspects of everyday life as marriage and employment.[41] Many in postwar Japan have been arrested and jailed for years at a time without sufficient evidence to be convicted in a legitimate trial.[42] Similarly, the struggle of the people of Minamata to gain compensation for the devastating effects of industrial pollution can be seen as part of a historical continuum with antecedents in the Itabashi ammunition depot explosion mentioned earlier. Guest workers in Japan from the Philippines, Thailand, and China, for example, most of whom do dirty, difficult, and dangerous jobs ranging from construction work to prostitution, also suffer numerous forms of discrimination and hardship.[43]

There are many other examples in Japanese society today of people's failure to link the theory and practice of human rights. The recent controversy over whether the Japanese government should pay compensation to wartime comfort women (*ianfu*) extends beyond the issue of war crimes to encompass exactly how the Japanese view the concept of human rights.

The Japanese government's superficial grasp of human rights does not, however, mean that the degree of human rights abuse is greater in Japan than in the West. It is true that Western cultures were the source of much of what constitutes the loose rubric of "human rights" stemming from the Judeo-Christian tradition. John Locke and Immanuel Kant developed the most influential theories of an individual's rights to freedom and equality, for which the biblical premise that all human beings are equal in the eyes of God is a basic tenet. Furthermore, many Western revolutions, most notably the French Revolution of 1789, had as their object the attainment of freedom and equality. Although both of these examples aimed at universality, in reality they were limited by class, principally to the bourgeoisie. This is clearly seen in the failure to take seriously the rights of workers, especially in the early stages of capitalism, and in the exploitation of indigenous peoples in colonized regions.

"Respect for human rights" in Western society is an idealistic rather than realistic concept. In this sense it is similar to the Japanese concept of "national harmony" under the emperor. The West's vision of respect for human rights has been exploited by politicians and promoted as reality, despite its illusory status for many people. The use of the myth of "freedom and equality" as a political slogan is typified by the invasion of Vietnam by the United States and its allies under the pretext that the authorities (i.e., governments) are protecting the freedom and equality of all in the "free society." Discrimination, both racial and sexual, continues to exist in various guises in most if not all Western societies.[44]

Another important issue that needs to be considered when examining the brutality of the Japanese forces during the war is the study of these acts from the viewpoint of the perpetrators. Until now, critical Japanese historians have concentrated on the discovery and detailed examination of the historical facts of Japanese war crimes and have usually relied on oral history. However, the sources for these histories generally have been the victims rather than the perpetrators. This investigatory method is successful for discovering exactly what sort of war crimes were committed, but it offers no way of uncovering how or why Japanese people became capable of committing such horrific acts. Japanese historians need to broaden the scope of oral history to include the perpetrators, principally to follow their psychological development closely.

Some historians have recently focused on the confessions and diaries of former Japanese soldiers, and this has been helpful in reconstructing the events of various war crimes. However, these scholars seem satisfied with using the information from the perpetrators to confirm events; they fail to examine the important psychological process involved that would be at least partially accessible in the confessions and diaries.[45]

For obvious reasons it is very difficult to interview perpetrators of war crimes. However, perhaps because of these difficulties, it is a matter of urgency that a method for obtaining the oral histories of perpetrators be developed, all the more so now that so many Japanese perpetrators are well into old age or have already died. Successful methods have been developed for obtaining oral histories from those involved in war crimes committed by Nazis in World War II and Americans during the Vietnam War. We can learn much from that work about how better to enable and encourage Japanese perpetrators of war crimes to tell their stories.

Although I feel there is a lack of research into the psychology that leads an individual to commit or otherwise be involved in a war crime, I am not advocating this as the primary level of investigation. Psychological approaches to crime almost invariably concentrate on the individual and ignore or even obscure the relationships between the individual and his or her social context. In the case of war crimes, we must always place the psychological processes of the individual within the context of the particular circumstances of war, military structure, and dominant forms of ideology of the time. In other words, we must always keep in mind what broader social currents can make a human being a perpetrator. It is through such a method that we can discover more about how war turns ordinary people into both criminals and victims.

As I explained in the Introduction, popular thinking in Japan remains strongly linked to the feeling that responsibility for the war lies overwhelmingly in the hands of the war leaders who deceived a gullible populace and led citizens into a war no one would want to see repeated. Consequently people at large were made to feel they were victims. This is a much weaker kind of antiwar thinking than can be found among German people. It should probably be called a "dislike-of-war sentiment" rather than "antiwar thinking." Contributing factors are undoubtedly the absence of an equivalent to the Jewish Holocaust, the bombing of Hiroshima and Nagasaki,[46] and the exculpation of Emperor Hirohito and his portrayal as a victim of the war manipulated by military leaders.[47]

As previously mentioned, Maruyama Masao took popular thinking about victimhood into account and attempted to undermine it. He began the task in the late 1940s by accepting that the Japanese allowed themselves to become victims of the war leaders and then asked what kind of weakness existed in the Japanese people and their social structure to make this possible. Maruyama's proposition was strikingly appealing. Since then many progressive scholars and writers have repeatedly pointed out this weakness in Japanese people who fail to see themselves simultaneously as perpetrators and victims.[48] Unfortunately, the account Maruyama initiated was never elaborated into one that made it possible for most Japanese people to see that they also bear responsibility for the war. What seems to be lacking in Japanese history writing is the kind of work that can bring home to readers how much continuity there is between life during wartime and everyday life here and now. By contrast, this is brilliantly done by some German historians, such as Detlev

Peukert, the author of *Inside Nazi Germany: Conformity, Opposition, and Racism in Everyday Life*.[49]

What is needed is a clear indication that the extraordinary atrocities and crimes in wartime have a closer connection with the everyday life of ordinary people than we might want to acknowledge. It is also necessary to help Japanese people understand that by failing to acknowledge that they were deceived and dragged into the war by the military leaders, citizens at large eventually *supported* the war and as such bear responsibility. Seen from this viewpoint, they are thus incapable of making correct political decisions. If ordinary people are unable to examine their past unequivocally, I believe such people are also incapable of the clear self-analysis needed to grasp and confront current political and social problems. For scholars, therefore, studying our responsibility for the war is not simply an intellectual historical exercise but a profound analysis intertwined with a close self-examination of our own everyday life and thinking.

# Notes

## Introduction

1. Chaen Yoshio and Shigematsu Kazuyoshi, *Hokan Sensō Saiban no Jissō* (Fuji Shuppan, 1987), pp. 7–8.

2. For details of the Tokyo War Crimes Tribunal, see, for example, A.C. Brackman, *The Other Nuremberg: the Untold Story of the Tokyo War Crimes Trials* (Fontana/Collins, 1989); and Awaya Kentarō, *Tokyo Saiban Ron* (Ōtsuki Shoten, 1989).

3. These sentences were later commuted, especially after the San Francisco peace treaty was signed in 1951 between Japan and 49 countries, including the former Allied nations with the exception of the Soviet Union. By the end of 1958 virtually all Japanese war criminals were released from jail. Such a drastic change in the attitude of the Allied nations toward the war criminals was of course closely related to the growing political tension between the West and the East, that is, the beginning of the Cold War. The United States and its Western allies granted commutation to all war criminals as a political strategy to gain Japanese support for the anticommunist campaign. The Soviet Union and the People's Republic of China held their own war crimes tribunals at which a large number of Japanese POWs were tried, but no one received the death sentence. The details of the Russian trials are still unknown, but it is said that about 10,000 Japanese were tried. China showed a surprisingly generous attitude to Japanese war criminals. Self-criticism by the war criminals rather than forced confession was adopted as the principal method of dealing with them. Eventually, only 45 of 1,108 were prosecuted, and the rest were released and returned to Japan by September 1956. See Sumiya Yukio, Akazawa Shirō, Utsumi Aiko, Ogata Naokichi, and Otabe Yūji (eds.), *Tokyo Saiban Hando Bukku* (Aoki Shoten, 1989), pp. 128–131, 218–225.

4. Even the eleven judges of the Tokyo War Crimes Tribunal differed in their opinions about how the tribunal should be conducted and about its final verdict. Sir William Webb from Australia, the president of the tribunal, Delfin Jaranilla from the Philippines, B.V.A. Roling from Holland, Henri Bernard from France, and Radhabinod Pal from India each issued a "concurring opinion," which was in disagreement with various points of the final verdict endorsed by the majority of the judges. Pal's opinion was particularly distinctive, as he fundamentally dismissed the legality of the tribunal. Richard Minear, author of *Victor's Justice* (Princeton University Press, 1971), basically supported Pal's opinion, whereas Ienaga Saburō, author of *The Pacific War: 1931–1945* (Pantheon, 1978), was concerned with the exploitation of Pal's opinion by right-wing Japanese intellectuals for the purpose of discrediting the tribunal. My personal view on this issue is that the trial was unfair

because the Allies did not deal with any war crimes committed by Allied forces; the most obvious example of war crimes committed by the United States was the dropping of the atomic bombs on Hiroshima and Nagasaki. Of course, the unfairness of the tribunal itself does not invalidate the criminality of the various atrocities that the Japanese forces committed during the Asia-Pacific War.

5. Awaya K., op. cit., pp. 285–288.

6. Kosuge Nobuko, "Horyo Mondai no Kihonteki Kentō: Rengō-gun Horyo no Shibōritsu to Gyakutai no Haikei," *Report on Japan's War Responsibility*, No. 3, 1994, p. 20.

7. "Horyo Saishū Ronkoku Fuzokusho B," *Tokyo Saiban*, No. 337. According to information in *The Australian Encyclopedia* (Grolier Society of Australia, 1983), the number of Australian POWs was 22,376, of whom 8,312 died, a death rate of 35.9 percent.

8. *Kyokutō Kokusai Gunji Saiban Sokkiroku* (Yūmatsudō, 1968), Vol. 10, p. 766.

9. Hugh Clarke, *Australians at War: Prisoners of War* (Time-Life Books Australia, 1988), p. 153.

10. More than 60,000 Allied POWs and a greater number of Asian laborers were mobilized for the construction of a 412-kilometer railway from Kanchanaburi in Thailand to Thanbyuzayat in Burma. It is said that 12,000 POWs died because of ill-treatment, sickness, and starvation during the 16-month construction work between July 1942 and October 1943. The number of deaths of Asian laborers is unknown. For further details, see Gavan McCormack and Hank Nelson (eds.), *The Burma-Thailand Railway: Memory and History* (Allen and Unwin, 1993).

11. Many books and journal articles have been published on this issue in the last few years, most of which are works by either critical historians or feminists. However, even Japanese feminists tend to see this problem as a peculiarly Japanese one. See, for example, Suzuki Hiroko, "Jūgun Ianfu Mondai de Towareteiru no wa Nanika," *Sekai*, No. 572, September 1992, pp. 32–39; and Nishino Rumiko, *Jūgun Ianfu: Moto Heishi-tachi no Shōgen* (Akashi Shoten, 1992).

12. Ezra F. Vogel, *Japan as Number One: Lessons for America* (Harvard University Press, 1979); Karel von Wolferen, *The Enigma of Japanese Power: People and Politics in Stateless Nation* (Knopf, 1989).

13. Gavan Daws, *Prisoners of the Japanese: POWs of World War II in the Pacific* (William Morrow, 1995).

14. For example, John Dower, *War Without Mercy: Race and Power in the Pacific War* (Faber and Faber, 1986); and Mark Selden, "Sumisonian Genbakuten no Shippai," *Shūkan Kinyōbi*, No. 85 (August 4, 1995), pp. 19–20. The same article in English, "From the Fire Bombing of Tokyo to Hiroshima," appeared in *Japan-Asia Quarterly Review*, Vol. 26, No. 2, 1995. See also Mark Selden, "Sengo 50 nen: Tokyo Dai-kūshū kara Hiroshima e," *Shūkan Kīnyōbi*, Nos. 73, 74, and 75, May 1995. Another article by Selden, "Before the Bomb: The 'Good War,' Air Power, and the Logic of Mass Destruction," *Contention*, Vol. 5, No. 1, is also an excellent example of comparative analysis of war crimes.

15. See, for example, Nakamura Akira's work *Daitōwa Sensō e no Michi* (Tentensha, 1990). Nakamura is a leading conservative intellectual who publicly claims that the Japanese government should not apologize to neighboring Asian nations and former Allied nations for the atrocities committed by Japanese forces. He be-

lieves that Japanese atrocities such as the Nanjing massacre are heavily distorted by critical historians and that the Allied forces also committed equally serious war crimes against the Japanese. In February 1995 he and his colleagues organized a political rally in Tokyo to demand that Japanese parliamentarians not pass a resolution commemorating the 50-year anniversary of Japan's World War II surrender. This resolution was intended as an official apology for wartime atrocities committed by the Japanese. It was passed in June 1995, but it is only a token apology and implies that Japan was just one of many nations to engage in such conduct.

16. Especially historians (e.g., Fujiwara Akira, Yoshida Yutaka, Hayashi Hirofumi, and Yoshimi Yoshiaki) who belong to the group called "Okinawa-sen to Nankin Gyakusatsu Kenkyū-kai" (A Group Researching the Okinawan Battle and Nanjing Massacre) are actively criticizing the interpretations of major Japanese war crimes by nationalist historians.

17. During one month between December 1937 and January 1938, a large number of Chinese soldiers and civilians were massacred in Nanjing by the Japanese Army. The exact death toll is unknown, but according to findings at the Tokyo War Crimes Trbunal, about 200,000 Chinese were killed and 20,000 women were raped by the Japanese. For further details, see Chapter 3.

18. C.R. Browning, *Ordinary Men: Reserve Police Battalion 101 and the Final Solution in Poland* (HarperCollins, 1992), p. xix. For different attitudes to their own war crimes held by the Japanese and Germans, see Ian Buruma's recent work, *The Wage of Guilt: Memories of War in Germany and Japan* (HarperCollins, 1994); and Gavan McCormack, *Emptiness of Japan's Affluence* (M.E. Sharp, 1996), Chapter 5.

19. Oda Makoto, *Nanshi no Shisō* (Iwanami Shoten, 1991), pp. 41–99. One might refute Oda's argument by claiming that killing others in self-defense is unavoidable in certain circumstances. However, this is the very problem Oda tried to deal with by establishing the principle of "absolute peace," because this principle cannot be attained unless both sides adhere to it. Thus the principle seems to belong to an imaginary realm rather than reality. In order to solve this problem and make this principle practical, Oda suggested the following: "We have to continuously recognise our own experience as a perpetrator (or the possibility of becoming one) as well as the experience of others as perpetrators. Conversely, in order to achieve this truly universal principle, we must continue to criticise others as perpetrators at the same time as ourselves" (ibid., p. 81). I believe this is the only way to achieve mutual recognition of the basic human rights of others rather than to insist on the right to kill others for the purpose of self-defense.

20. An opinion survey conducted in September 1994 by one of the major Japanese newspapers, *Asahi Shimbun,* indicates that 34 percent of those surveyed think Japan should take an active military role in world political affairs, while 57 percent still object to such an opinion. In 1992 only 21 percent of those surveyed supported the expansion of Japanese military activities overseas, while 71 percent of people were against. See *Ashahi Shimbun,* September 22, 1944. According to recent NHK (Japan Broadcasting Corporation) TV news, an opinion survey conducted by NHK in January 1995 indicates that more than 50 percent of those surveyed believe that Japan should be involved in more peacekeeping activities in various parts of the world. NHK conducted the same opinion survey in March

1995 in which 80 percent of those surveyed strongly supported the idea of sending Japanese forces to United Nations missions overseas.

21. Yoshida Yutaka, "Nipponjin no Sensō-kan: Rekishi Ishiki wa Henka shita ka," *Sekai,* September 1994, p. 25.


## Chapter 1

1. Hugh Clarke, Colin Burgess, and Russell Braddon, *Australians at War: Prisoners of War* (Time-Life Books Australia, 1988), p. 118.

2. Ibid., p. 105; Gavan McCormack and Hank Nelson (eds.), *The Burma-Thailand Railway* (Allen and Unwin, 1993), p. 1.

3. *The International Military Tribunal for the Far East* (Tokyo, 1946, hereafter IMTFE), pp. 13,344–13,453.

4. Tim Bowden, an ABC journalist, interviewed Owen Campbell, Nelson Short, Dick Braithwaite, and Keith Botterill in 1983. Braithwaite subsequently died; only three of the six original survivors are still alive. I obtained permission to use typed manuscripts of these interviews, which run for more than 300 pages (hereafter ABC Interview). These records are extremely useful because they contain the survivors' personal feelings about their ordeals, which do not vividly appear in the transcripts from the war crimes tribunals.

5. Harada Katsumasa (ed.), *Shōwa: Niman Nichi no Zen Kiroku, Vol. 6, "Taiheiyō Sensō"* (Kodansha, 1990), pp. 142–143.

6. In fact, soon after the Pacific War started, Japanese Imperial Headquarters, in consultation with Yamada Masaharu, a staff officer in charge of air force affairs at the headquarters of the Borneo Garrison, decided to build an airfield not only in Sandakan but also in Labuan, Api, and Tawao. However, the Sandakan airfield was regarded as the most important strategically. This information was obtained during my interview with Yamada in April 1995.

7. H. Clarke, C. Burgess, and R. Braddon, op. cit., p. 70; Australian War Memorial (hereafter AWM) Collection, AWM54/554/3/2, "Information Regarding Allied PW: Sandakan, Jessellton, Ranau," p. 2.

8. Ajia Minshū Hōtei Jumbi Kai (ed.), *Shashin Zusetsu: Nippon no Shinryaku* (Ōtsuki Shoten, 1992), pp. 216–217.

9. ABC Interview: Keith Botterill (Second Interview), pp. 52–53.

10. It was Yamada Masaharu, a staff officer of the Kuching Headquarters, who went to Changi to get POWs and take them to Sandakan. According to Yamada, the ship that carried POWs from Singapore to Sandakan via Kuching was not the *Ubi Maru* but the *Umi Maru* (ship of the ocean). It is quite possible that the POWs mispronounced the ship name and memorized it incorrectly. Yamada believes that it was not originally a Japanese ship and that it could have been confiscated by the Japanese somewhere in Southeast Asia. This was mentioned during my interview with Yamada in April 1995.

11. ABC Interview: Dick Braithwaite (First Interview), p. 5.

12. Ibid., p. 7.

13. This information was obtained during my interview with Yamada Masaharu in April 1995.

14. ABC Interview: Keith Botterill (First Interview), p. 4.

15. ABC Interview: Owen Campbell, pp. 16–17.

16. Chaen Yoshio (ed.), *Horyo ni Kansuru Sho-hōki Ruishū* (Fuji Shuppan, 1988), p. 264.

17. Ibid., pp. 340–342.

18. Ibid., pp. 189–198.

19. For details of these new regulations, see ibid., pp. 24–29, 36–39.

20. Ibid., p. 51.

21. IMTFE, pp. 13,349–13,350; Australian National Archives (hereafter ANA) Collection, A471/1,80777, "War Crimes Opening Address: Trial of Captain Hoshijima," p. 1, and "Testimony by WOI Stiepewich," p. 14.

22. Chaen Y., op. cit., pp. 24–35.

23. Utsumi Aiko, *Chōsenjin BC-kyū Sempan no Kiroku* (Saegusa Shobō, 1982), pp. 116–117.

24. Chaen Y., op. cit., pp. 264, 299, 301.

25. IMTFE, p. 13,345; ABC Interview: Nelson Short, p. 8.

26. AWM Collection, 54/1010/4/174, "Testimony by QX9538, WOI Hector Stiepewich," p. 1; ABC Interview: Nelson Short, p. 8. Much later, a group of eight Australian POWs from E Force who came to Sandakan in 1943 escaped while E Force was still detained on Bahara Island in Sandakan Bay. E Force spent a few months on Bahara Island until huts in the Sandakan POW camp were completed. These eight POWs were rescued by Philippine guerrillas and taken to Tawitawi Island. This was the only successful case of escape from the Sandakan area, and no one succeeded in escaping once the POWs moved from Bahara Island. For details of the escape of the eight POWs, see Hank Nelson, *Prisoners of War: Australians Under Nippon* (Australian Broadcasting Corporation, 1985), pp. 110–117.

27. Don Wall, *Sandakan Under Nippon: The Last March* (private publication, 1988), p. 16.

28. For details of this event, see ANA Collection, A471/1, 80777, "Trial of Hoshijima: Witness for Defence (Capt. Hoshijima Susumu)" p. 43; IMTFE, pp. 13,347–13,348; ABC Interview: Dick Braithwaite (First Interview), pp. 13–14.

29. Chaen Y., op. cit., pp. 308–310.

30. Ibid., p. 24.

31. Ibid., p. 55.

32. Ibid., p. 24.

33. For details of this first case of the execution of a POW in Japan, see Hayashi Eidai, *Jūsatsu Meirei: BC-kyū Sempan no Sei to Shi* (Asahi Shimbun-sha, 1986).

34. Utsumi A., op. cit., p. 118.

35. Ibid., p. 119.

36. ANA Collection, A471/1,80777, "Trial of Hoshijima: Hoshijima Taii Horyo Gyakutai Benron Yōshi," pp. 2–3.

37. Harada K., op. cit., pp. 222–223; Barrie and Frances Pitt, *The Chronological Atlas of World War II* (Macmillan, 1989), pp. 77, 79, 81, 85, 87.

38. AWM Collection, S4 554/3/2, "Information Regarding Allied PW: Sandakan, Jessellton, Ranau," p. 2; IMTFE, p. 13,360.

39. ANA Collection, MP742/1,81/1/801, "Report on the Activities of 'B' Forces for Period July 1942 to July 1943 Written by Lieut. R.G. Wells," p. 1.

40. Ibid., p. 2, and "Appendix 'A': Civil Organizations."

41. Ibid., pp. 1–2.

42. Ibid., pp. 4–5.

43. Ibid., p. 5.

44. Ibid., p. 6.

45. Ibid., p. 7.

46. Ibid., pp. 7–8.

47. For details of the official history of the Kempeitai and its duties, see Zenkoku Kenyūkai Rengōkai (ed.), *Nippon Kempei Seishi* (Hara Shobō, 1978), pp. 24–48, 123–131. A former member of the Kempeitai, Sadashi Yamada, revealed in his autobiography, *Kempei Nikki* (Shinjimbutsu Ōrai-sha, 1982), various methods of surveillance and torture.

48. Zenkoku Kenyūkai Rengōkai, op. cit., p. 1,051; ANA Collection, MP897/1, 156/19/152, "War Crimes, Borneo: Ill Treatment of Prisoners of War by Members of the Kempeitai at Sandakan"; ANA Collection, MP742/1, 336/1/1943, "Ill Treatment and Torture of Australian PWs at Sandakan by the Kempeitai."

49. ANA Collection, MP742/1, 81/1/801, "Appendix 'D': Japanese Military Police Interrogations and Conditions of Custody"; ANA Collection, MP897/1, 156/19/152, "Statement by A.G. Waynton."

50. For details of the Haga and Pontianak incidents, see Izeki Tsuneo, *Nishi Boruneo Gyakusatsu Jiken: Kenshō "Ponteana Jiken"* (Fuji Shuppan, 1987). Izeki was a businessman who resided in Pontianak during the war, but he was forced to act as an interpreter by the Naval Special Police Force during the interrogations. See also Gotō Kenichi, "Ponchanakku Jiken no Shiteki Kōsatsu," in Tanaka Hiroshi (ed.), *Nippon Gunsei to Ajia no Minzoku Undō* (Ajia Keizai Kenkyū-sho, 1983), pp. 21–40.

51. Zenkoku Kenyūkai Rengōkai, op. cit., pp. 1,052–1,053; Hara Fujio, "Nippon no Kita Boruneo Tōchi to Api Jiken," in Tanaka H., op. cit., pp. 41–80.

52. Pat Burgess, *Warco* (Richmond, 1986), pp. 155–163.

53. ANA Collection, MP742/1, 81/1/801, "Appendix 'E': Conditions at Kuching Military Gaol and the Death of Spr. Keating."

54. ANA Collection, MP742/1, 81/1/801, "Appendix 'B': Details of P.O.W. arrested by the Japanese in Borneo."

55. ANA Collection, A471/1, 81957, "War Crimes: Trial of Yamawaki and One Other."

56. For details of the judicial system of the Japanese court-martial, see Hanazono Ichirō, *Gumpō Kaigi* (Shinjimbutsu Ōrai-sha, 1974); and Yamanaka Hisashi (ed.), *Zaiman Gumpō Kaigi Shokei Tokushu Hanzai-shū* (Fuji Shuppan, 1989), especially pp. 1–9. Hanazono Ichirō, a law graduate from Tokyo University, acted as a judge of the special court-martial at Bougainville between March and August 1945; his critical analysis of the Japanese court-martial system based upon his experience is quite sharp and persuasive.

57. Yamanaka H., op. cit., pp. 4, 18.

58. Kita Hiroaki (ed.), *Gunritsu Kaigi Kankei Shiryō* (Fuji Shuppan, 1988), p. 84.

59. ANA Collection, MP742/1, 81/1/801, "Appendix 'D': Japanese Military Police Interrogations and Conditions of Custody."

60. ANA Collection, MP742/1, 336/1/2084, "Trial of Yamawaki Masataka, Tsutsui Yōichi, and Watanabe Haruo."

61. ANA Collection, A471/1, 81956, "War Crimes: Trial of Yamawaki and Others."

62. ANA Collection, MP742/336/1/2121, "Trial of Yamawaki Masataka and Others"; ANA Collection, A471/1, 81956, "War Crimes: Trial of Yamawaki and Others."

63. Hanazono I., op. cit., pp. 181–191.

64. Ibid., p. 192. The kin of those Japanese soldiers, who were illegally court-martialed after the war and consequently executed, are not entitled to receive survivors' benefits because of the "criminal" status of the soldiers. It is said that 50,000 men were categorized as "criminals" in this way because they had fled the battlefield. Many people, especially the wives and children of these soldiers, suffered not only from financial difficulties but also from social discrimination as the kin of "criminals" for a long time in the postwar era. For details of their hardships, see Uryū Ryōsuke and Hirotsuka Masashi, *Shōgen Kiroku Tekizen Tōbō: Ikiteiru Rikugun Keihō* (Shin Jimbutsu Ōrai-sha, 1974).

65. There are eight files on Yamawaki Masataka in the Australian National Archives Collection. For a long time they were closed as "classified materials," but two of them were opened in 1975 and others in 1986 and 1990. It is rather unusual that it took so long for a Japanese war crimes record to be declassified in Australia, although there are a few special exceptions such as those on cannibalism, which is discussed in Chapter 4.

66. AWM Collection, S4 554/3/2, "Information Regarding Allied PW: Sandakan, Jessellton, Ranau," p. 3.

67. IMTFE, p. 13,361.

68. Ibid., pp. 13,351–13,354; ANA Collection, A471/1, 80777, "Trial of Hoshijima: Testimony by WOI Stiepewich," pp. 21–22, and "Trial of Hoshijima: Witness for Defence (Capt. Hoshijima Susumu)," pp. 45–46.

69. ANA Collection, A471/1, 80777, "Trial of Hoshijima: Testimony by WOI Stiepewich," pp. 18–19.

70. Article 12 in *Rikugun Chōbatsu Rei* (Hitofumi-kan, 1941), p. 2.

71. ANA Collection, A471/1, 80777, "Trial of Hoshijima: Witness for the Defence (Capt. Hoshijima Susumu)," pp. 47–50, and "War Crimes Opening Address: Trial of Captain Hoshijima," pp. 4–5.

72. AWM Collection, AWM 54/1010/4/174, "Testimony by QX9538, WOI Hector Stiepewich," p. 3.

73. ABC Interview: Keith Botterill (First Interview), pp. 8–12.

74. ANA Collection, A471/1, 80777, "Trial of Hoshijima: Witness for Defence (Capt. Hoshijima Susumu)," p. 49.

75. Articles 54–59 of the Geneva Convention. For details of these articles, see Chaen Y., op. cit., pp. 309–311.

76. *Rikugun Chōbatsu Rei* (Hitofumi-kan, 1941), p. 10.

77. ABC Interview: Dick Braithwaite (Second Interview), p. 27.

78. ANA Collection, A471/1, 80777, "Trial of Hoshijima: Testimony by WOI Stiepewich," p. 22.

79. Utsumi A., op. cit., pp. 101–111.

80. Ibid., pp. 121–140.

81. Ajia Minshū Hōtei Jumbi Kai, op. cit., pp. 114–119.

82. Yi Hak-Nae, "The Man Between: A Korean Guard Looks Back," in G. McCormack and H. Nelson, op. cit., pp. 120–126. Yi was a Korean guard at the Burma-Thailand railway site and was accused as a war criminal for ill-treatment of POWs. At the Australian War Crimes Tribunal in Singapore he received the death sentence, but later it was commuted to 20 years' imprisonment. His experience typifies the position of Korean and Formosan guards at Japanese POW camps during the Pacific War.

83. ANA Collection, A471/1, 80777, "Trial of Hoshijima: Testimony by WOI Stiepewich," p. 22.

84. ANA Collection, A471/1, 80776, "Trial of Japanese War Criminals: S/Maj. Murozumi Hisao and Others: Witness for Defence (Toyoda Kōkichi)," p. 22, and "Statement by Toyoda Kōkichi," p. 35.

85. ANA Collection, MP742/1, 336/1715, "Re Toyoda Kōkichi—Formosan—War Criminal Compound by K. Botterill (1 June 1946)"; ANA Collection, AWC 843, "Formosan Toyoda Kōkichi: Sentenced War Criminal (15 July 1946)."

86. ANA Collection, A471/1, 80777, "Trial of Hoshijima: Cutting Ratio of Chief Rations," p. 240, and "Testimony by WOI Stiepewich," p. 15.

87. ANA Collection, A471/1, 80777, "Trial of Hoshijima: Witness for the Defence (Col. Takayama Hikoichi)," p. 99, and "Witnets for the Defence (Arai Yoshio)," p. 108.

88. ABC Interview: Keith Botterill (Second Interview), p. 32.

89. ANA Collection, A471/1, 80777, "Trial of Hoshijima: Witness for the Defence (Col. Ōtsuka Mitsugi)," p. 91; ABC Interview: Dick Braithwaite (Second Interview), p. 25–26.

90. ANA Collection, A471/1, 80777, "Trial of Hoshijima: Statement of Nakano Ryōichi," p. 92.

91. ANA Collection, A471/1, 80777, "Trial of Hoshijima: Testimony by WOI Stiepewich," p. 20.

92. ANA Collection, A471/1, 80777, "Trial of Hoshijima: Cutting Ratio of Chief Rations," p. 240; D. Wall, op. cit., p. 57.

93. ANA Collection, A471/1, 80777, "Trial of Hoshijima: Testimony by WOI Stiepewich," p. 18.

94. ANA Collection, A471/1, 80777, "Trial of Hoshijima: Hoshijima Taii Horyo Gyakutai Benron Yōshi," p. 3.

95. ANA Collection, A471/1, 80777, "Trial of Hoshijima: Testimony by WOI Stiepewich," p. 18.

96. ANA Collection, A471/1, 80777, "Trial of Hoshijima: Witness for the Defence (Fujita Hirouchi)," p. 118.

97. ABC Interview: Dick Braithwaite (First Interview), p. 19–20; ANA Collection, A471/1, 80777, "War Crimes Opening Address: Trial of Captain Hoshijima," p. 2; AWM Collection, AWM 54/1010/4/174, "Testimony by QX9538, WOI Hector Stiepewich."

98. ANA Collection, A471/1, 80777, "Trial of Hoshijima: Witness for the Defence (Ogawa Hiroshi)," p. 103, "Witness for the Defence (Arai Yoshio)," p. 117, and "British and Japanese Medical Stores Held by the Japanese at Sandakan, Checked 17–18 Oct. 1945," pp. 225–227.

## Chapter 2

1. Zenkoku Kenyūkai Rengōkai (ed.), *Nippon Kempei Gaishi* (Zenkoku Kenyūkai Rengōkai Honbu, 1983), pp. 1,286–1,287.

2. Don Wall, *Sandakan Under Nippon: The Last March* (private publication, 1988), p. 64.

3. Australian War Memorial (hereafter AWM) Collection, 54/1010/6/59, "Trial of Japanese War Criminals: Capt. Yamamoto Shōichi, Capt. Abe Kazuo etc.: Interrogation of Capt. Yamamoto (24 Sept. 1945)."

4. Ibid., "Interrogation of Capt. Yamamoto (24 Sept. 1945)" and "The Statement of Capt. Yamamoto Shōichi." In fact, a few weeks before the march started, the deputy commander of the Yamamoto battalion, Lieutenant Iino Shigeru, was sent to Kuching headquarters by plane to request a longer period for the march as well as more food and medical provisions along the way. However, Iino met the harsh attitude of Manaki Takanobu, chief of staff of the 37th Army, who showed no sympathy for the Yamamoto battalion and insisted on the order being carried out immediately. This information was obtained during my interview with Iino in April 1995.

5. Australian National Archives (hereafter ANA) Collection, A471/1, 8077, "Trial of Captain Hoshijima: Hanketsu o Uketaru-go no Shokan."

6. Transcript of interview with Nelson Short conducted by Tim Bowden, an Australian Broadcasting Corporation journalist, in 1983 (hereafter ABC Interview), p. 31.

7. AWM Collection, 54/1010/6/59, "Trial of Japanese War Criminals: Capt. Yamamoto Shōichi, Capt. Abe Kazuo etc.: The Statement of Capt. Yamamoto Shōichi."

8. Ibid., "The Statement of Capt. Yamamoto Shōichi," "Statement by W.C.138 Abe Kazuo," and "Interrogation of Lt. Abe."

9. Ibid., "Interrogation of Officers and NCOs Who Came Over in the First Ranau March in February 1945: W.C.589 Iino Shigeru" and "Second Witness for Prosecution (Keith Botterill)."

10. Ibid., "The Statement of Lt. Hirano Yukio" and "Third Witness for Prosecution (W.D. Moxham)."

11. Ibid., "Second Witness for Prosecution (Keith Botterill)."

12. Ibid., "Second Witness for Defence (Iino Shigeru)."

13. Ibid., "Second Witness for Prosecution (Keith Botterill)" and "Interrogation of Capt. Yamamoto (24 Sept. 1945)"; ABC Interview: Keith Botterill (Second Interview), p. 44.

14. AWM Collection, 54/1010/6/59, "Trial of Japanese War Criminals: Capt. Yamamoto Shōichi, Capt. Abe Kazuo etc.: Second Witness for Prosecution (Keith Botterill)."

15. Ibid., "Third Witness for Prosecution (W.D. Moxham)."

16. Ibid., "Second Witness for Prosecution (Keith Botterill)."

17. Ibid., "The Statement of Lt. Abe Kazuo."

18. Ibid., "The Statement by Endō Hiraki." "Hiraki" is not typically a Japanese given name. It seems that "Hiroaki" was mistyped as "Hiraki" in the original document.

19. Ibid., "Second Witness for Prosecution (Keith Botterill)."

20. Ibid., "Interrogation of Capt. Yamamoto (24 Sept. 1945)" and "The Statement of Capt. Yamamoto Shōichi"; ABC Interview: Keith Botterill (First Interview), pp. 18–21; AWM Collection, 54/4/3/2, "Information Regarding Allied P.W. Sandakan, Jesselton, Ranau," p. 4.

21. ABC Interview: Keith Botterill (First Interview), p. 21, (Second Interview), pp. 24–26; *The International Military Tribunal for the Far East* (Tokyo 1946, hereafter IMTFE) pp. 13,375, 13,422–13,424.

22. ANA Collection, A471/1, 8077, "Trial of Captain Hoshijima: Hoshijima Taii Horyo Gyakutai Jiken Benron Yōshi," p. 16.

23. D. Wall, op. cit., p. 83.

24. ANA Collection, A471/1, 80771, "Trial of Japanese War Criminals: Capt. Takakuwa Takuo, Capt. Watanabe Genzō: The Prosecutor's Address," p. 2.

25. According to Masaharu Yamada, a former staff officer at Kuching headquarters, Hoshijima actually expressed to headquarters his opposition about the second march by saying that he would stay on at the camp and thus protect the POWs. This was mentioned during my interview with Yamada in April 1995.

26. ANA Collection, A471/1, 80771, "Seiso-jō: Hikoku Rikugun Taii Takakuwa Takuo, Rikugun Taii Watanabe Genzō," pp. 1–2.

27. Ibid., p. 2; AWM Collection, 54/1010/4/174, "Affidavits by Japanese Personnel in Connection with Charges Arising from Sandakan-Ranau Death March with Comments by WO HW Stiepewich Covering Prelude to March: Fourth Witness for Defence (Iwashita Manabu)," p. 32.

28. ANA Collection, A471/1, 80771, "Trial of Japanese War Criminals: Capt. Takakuwa Takuo, Capt. Watanabe Genzō: The Prosecutor's Address," p. 2; IMTFE, pp. 13,364–13,366.

29. ABC Interview: Dick Braithwaite (First Interview), pp. 41–44; AWM Collection, 54/1010/4/174, "Affidavits by Japanese Personnel in Connection with Charges Arising from Sandakan-Ranau Death March with Comments by WO W.H. Stiepewich Covering Prelude to March: The Statement of W.H. Stiepewich," p. 6.

30. ANA Collection, A471/1, 80771, "Trial of Japanese War Criminals: Capt. Takakuwa Takuo, Capt. Watanabe Genzō: Second Witness for Defence (Watanabe Genzō)," p. 14.

31. Ibid., "Extract from Statement of W.H. Stiepewich," p. 41.

32. Ibid., "Evidence Taken Before Justice Mansfield at 1st Aust. Base Sub. Area on 19 October 1945: The Statement of W.H. Stiepewich," p. 46; IMTFE, pp. 13,367–13,368.

33. ANA Collection, A471/1, 80771, "Trial of Japanese War Criminals: Capt. Takakuwa Takuo, Capt. Watanabe Genzō: Extract from Statement of W.H. Stiepewich," p. 42.

34. Ibid., "Joint Statement Made by Chen Kay, Chin Kin, and Lo Tong Who Reside Near the 15.5 Mile Post, Sandakan." This is a statement made by three local Chinese residents who witnessed the murder of POWs by the guards in the jungle.

35. Ibid., "The Prosecutor's Address," p. 2, and "Second Witness for Defence (Watanabe Genzō)," pp. 14–15.

36. Ibid., "Statement by Takemoto Isao, W.C. 547, Suga Butai," p. 64.

37. Ibid., "Statement by Nakayama Tamao, a Former Member of Suga Butai," p. 72.

38. Ibid., "Statement by Matsuba Shōkichi, W.C. 527, Suga Butai," p. 79.

39. Ibid., "The Prosecutor's Address," p. 3.

40. Ibid., "Evidence Taken by Justice Mansfield at Sydney on Friday 16 November 1945: Pte. N.A.E. Short"; IMTFE, p. 13,385.

41. ANA Collection, A471/1, 80771, "Trial of Japanese War Criminals: Capt. Takakuwa Takuo, Capt. Watanabe Genzō: The Prosecutor's Address," p. 3; IMTFE, p. 13,371.

42. ANA Collection, A471/1, 80771, "Trial of Japanese War Criminals: Capt. Takakuwa Takuo, Capt. Watanabe Genzō: Statement by Capt. Takakuwa Takuo."

43. ABC Interview: Owen Campbell, p. 31.

44. ANA Collection, A471/1, 80771, "Trial of Japanese War Criminals: Capt. Takakuwa Takuo, Capt. Watanabe Genzō: The Prosecutor's Address," p. 3.

45. ANA Collection, A471/1, 8077, "Trial of Captain Hoshijima: Witness for Defence (Col. Takayama Hikoichi)," p. 97.

46. ANA Collection, MP375/14 WC19, "War Crimes: Sandakan, Borneo: Murder of Unknown POW: Interrogation of Nishikawa Yoshinori."

47. ANA Collection, A471/1, 80776, "War Crimes, Proceeding of Military Tribunal, Murozumi H. and Others: Precis of Evidence, Minute Paper"; AWM Collection, 54/1010/4/174, "Affidavits by Japanese Personnel in Connection with Charges Arising from Sandakan-Ranau Death March with Comments by WO W.H. Stiepewich Covering Prelude to March: Statement by Murozumi," p. 418.

48. According to Stiepewich's testimony, the only surviving Japanese soldier of this final march to Ranau was interrogated in Api after the war (see IMTFE, pp. 13,385–13,386). However, I have been unable to locate the relevant document at either the Australian National Archives or the Australian War Memorial.

49. ANA Collection, A471/1, 80776, "War Crimes, Proceeding of Military Tribunal, Murozumi H. and Others: First Witness for Defence (S/M. Murozumi Hisao)," p. 10.

50. Ibid., p. 9.

51. Ibid., "Third Witness for Defence (Gotō Yoshitarō)," p. 15, and "Statement by Toyoda Kokichi, Suga Butai (12 December 1945)."

52. Ibid., "First Witness for Defence (S/M. Murozumi Hisao)," p. 10; ANA Collection, MP375/14 WC19, "War Crimes, Sandakan, Borneo: Murder of Unknown POW: Interrogation of S/M. Murozumi Hisao (16 July 1947)."

53. ABC Interview: Keith Botterill (First Interview), p. 21.

54. ANA Collection, A471/1, 80771, "Trial of Japanese War Criminals: Capt. Takakuwa Takuo, Capt. Watanabe Genzō: Extract from Statement of W.H. Stiepewich," p. 43.

55. Ibid., p. 44; ABC Interview: Nelson Short, p. 18.

56. IMTFE, pp. 13,376–13,378; AWM Collection, 54/100/6/5, "War Crimes, Trial by Military Court: Fukushima Masao of Sandakan PW Camp: First Witness for Prosecution (W.D. Moxham)."

57. ABC Interview: Keith Botterill (First Interview), pp. 28–34, (Second Interview), pp. 1–12.

58. ANA Collection, A471/1, 80771, "Trial of Japanese War Criminals: Capt. Takakuwa Takuo, Capt. Watanabe Genzō: Extract from Statement of W.H. Stiepewich," pp. 43–44.

59. IMTFE, pp. 13,382–13,383.

60. ANA Collection, A471/1, 80771, "Trial of Japanese War Criminals: Capt. Takakuwa Takuo, Capt. Watanabe Genzō: Extract from Statement of W.H. Stiepewich," p. 45.

61. Ibid., "The Prosecutor's Address," pp. 17–18, and "Statement of Okada Toshiharu," pp. 73–74; ANA Collection, A471/1, 336/1/268, "Massacre at Ranau: Trial of Gotō, T. and Others."

62. ANA Collection, MP375/14 WC19, "War Crimes, Sandakan, Borneo: Murder of Unknown POW: Statement by Wong Hiong," pp. 127–128.

63. Ibid., p. 128.

64. Ibid., "Interrogation of Wong Hiong (16 January 1947)."

65. Ibid., "Telegram from Sandakan to War Crimes Section, Melbourne, Australia."

66. Ibid., "Affidavit by Wong Hiong (30 April 1947)," p. 1.

67. Ibid., "Telegram from Sandakan to War Crimes Section, Melbourne, Australia."

68. Ibid., "Interrogation of Murozumi Hisao and Others."

69. Ibid., "Statement by Ali Asa."

70. ANA Collection, A471/1, 8077, "Trial of Captain Hoshijima"; ANA Collection, A471/1, 33/1/707, "Trial of Capt. Hoshijima, S."; ANA Collection, (CRS)B5569, "Hoshijima Susumu"; AWM Collection, 54/1010/6/59, "Trial of Japanese War Criminals: Capt. Yamamoto Shōichi, Capt. Abe Kazuo etc."; ANA Collection, A471/1, 80771, "Trial of Japanese War Criminals: Capt. Takakuwa Takuo, Capt. Watanabe Genzō"; ANA Collection, A471/1, 80776, "War Crimes, Proceeding of Military Tribunal, Murozumi H. and Others"; ANA Collection, A471/1, 336/1/258, "Sandakan Death March: Trial of Nagahiro, M. and Others"; ANA Collection, A471/1, 336/1/268, "Massacre at Ranau: Trial of Gotō, T. and Others"; Chaen Yoshio (ed.), *BC-kyū Sempan Gōgun Rabauru Saiban Shiryō* (Fuji Shuppan, 1990), pp. 108–109.

71. ANA Collection, MP742/1, 336/1/1180, "Sandakan-Ranau Death March: Lt. Gen. Baba Masarō."

72. ANA Collection, A471/1, 8077, "Trial of Captain Hoshijima: Witness for Defence (Col. Takayama Hikoichi)," pp. 97–98.

73. This information was obtained during my interview with Yamada Masaharu in April 1995.

74. Ibid.

75. The total number of Japanese soldiers in North Borneo in July 1944 was 23,000, but by the end of the war more than 13,000 were dead. Most of them died

of a combination of tropical diseases and malnutrition during the march from the east coast to the west coast of North Borneo. For details of the extremely harsh conditions of the march and the high death toll, see, for example, the memoir of a former member of the Iemura battalion, Ueno Itsuyoshi, *Kita Boruneo no Mitsurin: Shi no Kōgun 600 kiro no Shinjitsu* (private publication, 1984).

76. Zenkoku Kenyūkai Rengōkai (ed.), *Nippon Kempei Seishi* (Hara Shobō, 1978), p. 1,055; ANA Collection, MP742/1, 336/1/1180, "Sandakan-Ranau Death March: Lt. Gen. Baba Masarō."

77. ANA Collection, MP742/1, 336/1/1416, "War Crimes Borneo: Lt. Gen. Yamawaki Masataka," p. 1.

78. *Kyokutō Kokusai Gunji Saiban Sokkiroku* (Yūmatsudō, 1968), Vol. 10, p. 766; "Horyo Saishū Ronkoku Fuzokusho B," *Tokyo Saiban*, No. 337.

79. Hugh Clarke, Colin Burgess, and Russell Braddon, *Australians at War: Prisoners of War* (Time-Life Books Australia, 1988), p. 153.

80. Awaya Kentarō, *Tokyo Saiban Ron* (Ōtsuki Shoten, 1989), pp. 286–287.

81. Chaen Yoshio (ed.), *Horyo ni Kansuru Sho-hōkiruiju* (Fuji Shuppan, 1988), pp. 20–21.

82. Awaya K., op. cit., p. 291.

83. Hon Jun-Muk, *Taimen Tetsudō: Aru Chōsenjin Horyo Kanshiin no Shuki* (Ponsonfa Henshu-bu, 1988), pp. 20–21.

84. Chaen Y., *Horyo ni Kansuru Sho-hōkiruiju*, pp. 1–2; Hata Ikuhiko, "Nippongun ni Okeru Horyo Kannen no Keisei," *Gunji Shigaku*, Vol. 28, No. 2, 1992, pp. 9–10. According to another source, during the Sino-Japanese War, 988 Chinese POWs were brought to Japan and detained in various locations such as Nagoya, Hiroshima, and Osaka. However, in August 1895, less than four months after the war, 976 POWs safely returned to China. It is not clear what happened to the other 12, but they were probably too sick to travel at that time. It is said, however, that a large but unknown number of Chinese soldiers and civilians were massacred in Lushun by Japanese soldiers between November 22 and 24, 1894. Nevertheless, in general, the Japanese treatment of Chinese POWs and civilians in this war was relatively humane, and two prominent Japanese military leaders, Yamagata Aritomo and Ōyama Iwao, respectively issued a special order to their soldiers not to ill-treat POWs and civilians. See Kanda Fumito, "Dai-ichiji Taisen mae no Nippon no Horyo Shogū to sono Tenkan," *Yokohama Ichiritsu Daigaku Ronsō*, Vol. 45, No. 1, 1994, pp. 163–166. See also Olive Checkland, *Humanitarianism and the Emperor's Japan, 1877–1977* (St. Martin's Press, 1994), Part 2, pp. 45–94.

85. Utsumi Aiko, "Ikensho: Kokusai Kanshū ni Hansuru Nippon-gun no Horyo Seisaku no Sekinin o Katagawari Saserareta Chōsenjin Kanshiin" (unpublished paper), pp. 7–8; Chaen Y., *Horyo ni Kansuru Sho-hōkiruiju*, pp. 3–4.

86. For details of the life of German POWs in Japan and the friendship they formed with local residents, see Hayashi Keisuke, *Bandō Horyo Shūyōjo: Dai 9 Kōkyō-kyoku no Rūtsu* (Nankai Bukkusu, 1978); and Chaen Y., *Horyo ni Kansuru Sho-hōkiruiju*, p. 7.

87. Chaen Y., *Horyo ni Kansuru Sho-hōkiruiju*, p. 341.

88. Ibid., p. 18.

89. Ibid., p. 7.

90. John Dower, *War Without Mercy: Race and Power in the Pacific War* (Faber and Faber, 1986), pp. 11–12.

91. *Account of Forgotten Army* (BBC documentary film, 1993), written and produced by Neil Cameron.

92. Katsumata Hideo, "Rabauru Sempan no Shinsō" in Chaen Y., *BC-kyū Sempan Gōgun Rabauru Saiban Shiryō*, p. 189.

93. This particular incident is mentioned in the diary written by Lt. Commd. Suzuki Nao-omi, commander of the Japanese naval force on Ocean Island during the war. Suzuki's diary contains various descriptions of ill-treatment of Japanese by Australian forces. See his diary, which is held at the Australian War Memorial (AWM 54/253/8/1).

94. Katsumata H., op. cit., p. 201.

95. Many books by former POWs in Siberia are now available that reveal the extremely harsh living conditions, forced labor, and malnutrition that resulted in a large number of deaths. See, for example, Maeno Shigeru, *Soren Gokusō Jūichinen*, Vols. 1–4 (Kodansha, 1979); and Shida Yukio, *Shiberia Yokuryū o Tou* (Saegusa Shobō, 1984). Maeno spent 11 years and Shida spent 10 years at a POW camp in Siberia.

96. J. Dower, op. cit., p. 11.

97. Robert J. Lifton, "Home from the War: The Psychology of Survival," in Walter Capps (ed.), *The Vietnam Reader* (Routledge, 1990), p. 60.

98. William Broyles Jr., "Why Men Love War," in W. Capps, op. cit., p. 76.

99. Virginia Woolf, *"A Room of One's Own" and "Three Guineas"* (Oxford University Press, 1992), p. 158.

100. W. Broyles Jr., op. cit., pp. 68–69.


# Chapter 3

1. *International Military Tribunal for the Far East* (Tokyo, 1946, hereafter IMTFE), p. 4467.

2. Ibid., pp. 4526–4527.

3. Ibid., pp. 3904–3943, 4459, 4464–4466, 4476, 4479, 4526–4536, 13638–13652; A.C. Blackman, *The Other Nuremberg: the Untold Story of the Tokyo War Crimes Trials* (Fontana, 1989), pp. 20–21.

4. For example, see Dō Tomio (ed.), *Nitchū Sensō Shiryō*, Vols. 8 and 9 (Kawade Shobō, 1973); Nankin Jiken Chōsa Kenkyū Kai (ed.), *Nankin Jiken Shiryō-shū* (Aoki Shoten, 1992); Honda Katsuichi, *Chūgoku e no Tabi* (Asahi Shimbun-sha, 1972).

5. IMTFE, pp. 13454–13476.

6. Harada Katsumasa et al. (eds.), *Shōwa Niman-nichi no Zenkiroku: Dai 6 Kan "Taiheiyō Sensō"* (Kodansha, 1990), pp. 134–135.

7. Peter Charlton, *War Against Japan 1941–42* (Time-Life Books Australia, 1988), pp. 28–81.

8. Hank Nelson, *Prisoners of War: Australians Under Nippon* (Australian Broadcasting Corporation, 1985), p. 71.

9. Catherine Kenny, *Captives: Australian Army Nurses in Japanese Prison Camps* (University of Queensland Press, 1989), p. 21.

10. Australian National Archives (hereafter ANA) Collection, MP741/1, 336/1/1976, "Report Prepared by the British Land Forces, Hong Kong."

11. C. Kenny, op. cit., p. 21.

12. ANA Collection, MP742/1, 336/1/1976, "Testimony of Major W.A. Tebbutt."

13. Ibid.

14. H. Nelson, op. cit., p. 74.

15. IMTFE, pp. 13454–13457.

16. Ibid., pp. 13457–13464; ANA Collection, MP742/1, 336/1/1976-152, and MP742/1, 336/1/1976.

17. Interview with Vivian Bullwinkel in *Survival: Tape 3* (Social History Unit, Australian Broadcasting Corporation); H. Nelson, op. cit., pp. 74–75.

18. H. Nelson, op. cit., p. 76.

19. C. Kenny, op. cit., pp. 33–34.

20. ANA Collection, MP742/1, 336/1/1976 IJIM, "Interrogation of Maj-Gen Tanaka Ryōsaburō"; MP742/1, 336/1/1976, "War Crimes: Preliminary Report by K.M. Dixson, No. 12 Team on Major War Crimes Against Australians—Murder of Australian Nurses on Banka Island" and "Report by Major Tebbutt, AIF: Evacuation Nurses on Banka Island"; MP742/1, 336/1/772, "In the Matter of Japanese War Crimes and in the Matter of the Ill Treatment of Prisoners of War." The officer's name is replaced by the initials "O.M." for protection of privacy.

21. ANA Collection, MP742/1, 336/1/1976, "Memorandum for the Secretary, Department of External Affairs, Canberra A.C.T.: Alleged Japanese War Criminals—O.M."

22. Ibid., "Report Sent by HQ Land Forces, Hong Kong, to GHQ Far East Land Forces."

23. Ibid., "Australian Mission in Japan, Memo No. 570: War Crimes Suspect a Suicide."

24. ANA Collection, MP742/1, 336/1/1289, "Statement Made by VX39347 Sister James, H."

25. Jessie E. Simmons, *In Japanese Hands: Australian Nurses as POWs* (William Heinemann, 1954), pp. 34–35.

26. ANA Collection, MP742/1, 336/1/1288, "Statement Made by VX39347 Sister James, H."; MP 742/1, 336/1/1976–152, "Australian War Crimes Board of Inquiry: Sister Vivian Bullwinkel."

27. Ibid.

28. Ibid.

29. Ibid.

30. Betty Jeffrey, *White Coolies* (Angus and Robertson, 1954), pp. 89–90.

31. Ibid., p. 85; "POWs Fight Comfort Women Rumours," *The Australian*, July 25, 1992.

32. J. Simmons, op. cit., p. 63.

33. *Asahi Shimbun*, July 21 and 22, 1992.

34. *The Age*, December 11, 1992.

35. Interview with Doug Davey, August 1992.

36. Utsumi Aiko, Koshida Ryō, Tanaka Hiroshi, and Asukada Yūichi (eds.), *Handobukku Sengo Hoshō* (Nashinoki-sha, 1992), p. 37; Yoshimi Yoshiaki (ed.), *Jūgun Ianfu Shiryōshū* (Ōtsuki Shoten, 1992), p. 26.

37. Yoshimi Y., op. cit., pp. 28–29.

38. Yoshida Seiji, *Watashi no Sensō Hanzai* (Sanichi Shobō, 1983).

39. Yamada Sadashi, *Kempei Nikki* (Shinjimbutsu Ōrai-sha, 1982), pp. 160–172; Nogi Harumichi, *Kaigun Tokubetsu Keisatsutai: Anbon-tō BC-kyū Senpan no Shuki* (Taihei Shuppan, 1975), Chapter 9.

40. Centre for Research and Documentation on Japan's War Responsibility, *"Jūgun Ianfu Mondai no Shiteki Narabi ni Hōteki Kenkyū"* (unpublished paper, 1994), p. 9.

41. This idea is clear from the instructions for dealing with Chinese civilians, which were issued on June 27, 1938, by Okabe Naozaburō, chief of staff of the North China Area Army, to all subordinate units. For details, see Yoshimi Y., op. cit., pp. 209–210.

42. Centre for Research and Documentation on Japan's War Responsibility, op. cit., pp. 9–10.

43. A report prepared by the medical section of the North China Area Army in February 1940 warned that a soldier suffering from venereal disease required an average of 86 days' hospitalization; thus the spread of such a disease would weaken the strength of the Army considerably. For details of this report, see Yoshimi Y., op. cit., p. 237. On the concern of the military about the potential effect on Japanese public health of venereal disease brought home by soldiers, see a report prepared by a senior officer of the Ministry of the Army on June 18, 1942, reproduced in Yoshimi Y., op. cit., pp. 171–172.

44. Centre for Research and Documentation on Japan's War Responsibility, op. cit., p. 17.

45. Ibid., pp. 37–38. The fact that 7 of 19 comfort women interviewed by the Centre for Research and Documentation on Japan's War Responsibility had suffered from venereal disease also indicates a high rate of venereal disease among the comfort women.

46. Yoshimi Y., op. cit., p. 354.

47. In contrast with Nazi Germany, the bulk of medical opinion in Japan during the war was that infectious diseases, such as tuberculosis, were the most significant problem to be dealt with and that genetically based illness was a lesser threat to the nation. Thus, there were far fewer victims of eugenics in Japan than in Nazi Germany. Only 454 of 17,085 people categorized as genetically inferior were sterilized. For details of Japan's eugenic policy during the Asia-Pacific War, see Matsunaga Ei, "Nippon no Yūsei Seisaku: Nachisu Doitsu to no Hikaku," and Yonemoto Shōhei, "Yūseigaku: Nippon to Doitsu to no Hikaku," in Kanagawa University (ed)., *Igaku to Sensō* (Ochanomizu Shobō, 1994), pp. 24–43, 137–154.

48. Centre for Research and Documentation on Japan's War Responsibility, op. cit., p. 12. For evidence that some minors from colonies and occupied territories were forced to become comfort women, see Yoshimi Y., op. cit., pp. 102–103, 135–137, 304.

49. Centre for Research and Documentation on Japan's War Responsibility, op. cit., pp. 13–15.

50. Ibid., pp. 22–24.

51. This instruction appears in the telegram sent by Tōgō to the head of foreign affairs in the government-general of Taiwan on January 14, 1942. It is reproduced in Yoshimi Y., op. cit., p. 143.

52. Ibid., p. 146. An open question is whether Emperor Hirohito also bore responsibility because of his position as grand marshal, the highest position in the Japanese Imperial Forces, even if he was not informed on this matter.

53. Centre for Research and Documentation on Japan's War Responsibility, op. cit., p. 17.

54. Yoshimi Y., op. cit., pp. 365–375: Shigemura Minoru, "Tokuyōin to iu Na no Butai," *Bungei Shunjū*, Vol. 1, 1955, pp. 224–225.

55. Yoshimi Y., op. cit., pp. 83–84.

56. Hayashi Hirofumi, "Marei Hantō no Nippongun Ianjo," *Sekai*, May 1993.

57. Kankoku Teishin-tai Mondai Taisaku Kyōgikai (ed.), *Shōgen: Kyōsei Renkō Sareta Chōsenjin Gun-ianfutachi* (Akashi Shoten, 1993), p. 125.

58. Utsumi A. et al., op. cit., p. 37.

59. Yoshimi Y., op. cit., p. 232.

60. Ibid., p. 229.

61. Unpublished private memoirs written by a former soldier of the Kantō Army, which I obtained a few years ago, clearly testify to such action. However, the author's name is not disclosed here for the sake of privacy.

62. Yoshimi Y., op. cit., p. 232.

63. Jewish Black Book Committee (ed.), *The Black Book: The Nazi Crime Against the Jewish People* (New York, 1946), pp. 301, 329, 340, 342, 366, 436.

64. Paul Hilberg, *Destruction of the European Jews* (Quadrangle, 1961), p. 28; William Shirer, *The Rise and Fall of the Third Reich* (Simon & Schuster, 1960), pp. 430–431.

65. Susan Brownmiller, *Against Our Will: Men, Women, and Rape* (Secker and Warburg, 1975), p. 52.

66. Ibid., p. 52.

67. Ibid., p. 52.

68. Ibid., pp. 51, 53–54, 64; Nora Levin, *The Holocaust* (Thomas Crowell, 1968), p. 150; R.J. Minney, *I Shall Fear No Evil: The Story of Dr. Alina Brewda* (William Kimber, 1966), pp. 141 ff.

69. *Trial of the Major War Criminals Before the International Military Tribunal*, Vol. 7 (Nuremberg, 1947), pp. 456–457.

70. Ibid., Vol. 6, pp. 404–407.

71. Cornelius Ryan, *The Last Battle* (Simon & Schuster, 1966), pp. 26–33, 484–493.

72. Theodore Schieder (ed.), *Documents on the Expulsion of the Germans from Eastern Central Europe*, Vol. 1 (Bonn, 1953).

73. S. Brownmiller, op. cit., p. 67.

74. Tanigawa Mitsue, *Onna-tachi no Harukanaru Senjō: Jūgun Kangofu-tachi no Nagakatta Shōwa-shi* (Kojin-sha, 1989), p. 196.

75. Ibid., pp. 184–188.

76. Ibid., pp. 204–209.

77. Cynthia Enloe, *Does Khaki Become You? The Militarization of Women's Lives* (Pluto Press, 1983), pp. 27–28.

78. Ibid., p. 28.

79. Bernard Fall, *Street Without Joy* (Schocken, 1972) p. 133; Yamada Meiko, *Senryō-gun Ianfu* (Kojin-sha, 1992) p. 29.

80. However, there are many anecdotal testimonies by Okinawans about rape committed by U.S. soldiers during the Okinawa battle between March and August 1945. For example, according to Ōshiro Masayasu, an eminent Okinawan historian who recorded much information on this battle, almost all the women of a village on Motobu Peninsula on Okinawa were raped by a troop of U.S. marines. See his book, *Okinawa-sen: Minshū no Me de Toraeta Sensō* (Kobunken, 1988), pp. 171–173. The Japanese forces brought many Korean comfort women to Okinawa well before the battle started, but accurate numbers of these women are unknown. Research indicates that some of these Korean women were forced to serve Americans after the Japanese forces were defeated. For details, see Yamatani Tetsuo (ed.), *Okinawa no Harumoni* (Bansei-sha, 1992), p. 169.

81. Yamada M., op. cit., pp. 34–36.

82. S. Brownmiller, op. cit., p. 77.

83. Yamada M., op. cit., pp. 90–91.

84. A. Clifton, *Time of Fallen Blossoms* (Cassell, 1955), in particular pp. 141–148, 174–182.

85. Ibid., p. 141.

86. Harada Katsumasa (ed.) *Shōwa Niman-nichi no Zenkiroku: Dai 7 Kan "Haikyo kara no Shuppatsu"* (Kodansha, 1989), p. 136.

87. Ōshima Yukio, *Genshoku no Sengo-shi: Sengo o Nipponjin wa dō Ikita Ka* (Kodansha, 1986), p. 166; Yamada M., op. cit., pp. 25–27.

88. Yamada M., op. cit., pp. 7, 42–43.

89. B. Fall, op. cit., pp. 132–134.

90. S. Brownmiller, op. cit., pp. 94–95.

91. For details of rape and massacre in My Lai, see Michael Bilton and Kevin Sim, *Four Hours in My Lai: A War Crime and Its Aftermath* (Viking, 1992), especially Chapter 4.

92. Slavenka Drakulic, "Good People Must Not Keep Quiet This Time," *The Age*, December 23, 1992; Catherine Bennett, "Ordinary Men Can Rape," *The Age*, January 27, 1993.

93. W. Broyles Jr., "Why Men Love War," in Walter Capps (ed.), *The Vietnam Reader* (Routledge, 1991), p. 79.

94. S. Brownmiller, op. cit., p. 107.

95. Ibid., p. 32.

96. C. Enloe, op. cit., p. 15.

97. Recently a number of cases of rape and sexual harassment within the military have been reported in Australia. In the United States, too, there have been reports of this phenomenon, which increased noticeably during and after the Gulf War. For example, at a U.S. Navy convention held at the Hilton Hotel, Las Vegas, in September 1991, which celebrated the Gulf War victory, 90 sexual assaults were reported. The victims in 83 cases were women, either female officers or wives

who accompanied their husbands to the convention. About 5 percent of 4,000 participants were female naval officers. Some male officers were wearing T-shirts that had "Women Are Property" written on the back and "He-Man Women Haters' Club" printed on the front. For details of sexual harassment at this convention, see *Tailhook Report: The Official Inquiry into the Events of Tailhook 1991* (St. Martin's Press, 1993).

98. Virginia Woolf, *"A Room of One's Own" and "Three Guineas"* (Oxford University Press, 1992), pp. 151–414.

99. S. Brownmiller, op. cit., p. 11.

## Chapter 4

1. Australian National Archives (hereafter ANA) Collection, M1418/1, 517, Telegram No. 388.

2. Ibid., Cable, December 10, 1946.

3. Chaen Yoshio (ed.), *BC Kyū Senpan Gōgun Manusu Saiban Shiryō* (Fuji Shuppan, 1991), p. 37.

4. Ōoka Shōhei, *Fires on the Plain* (Charles E. Tuttle, 1967). In this novel, starving Japanese soldiers in the Philippines start killing each other fighting over "monkey's meat," a euphemistic expression the soldiers used for human flesh. Ōoka himself was sent to the Philippines as a member of the Japanese forces and was taken prisoner in the 1945 defeat.

5. Hara Kazuo (dir.), *Yuki Yuki te Shingun* (Imamura Production, 1987).

6. Ogawa Shōji, *Kyokugen no Naka no Ningen: Shi no Shima Nyūginia* (Chikuma Shobō, 1983), pp. 166–167.

7. Ogawa Shōji, *Tōbu Nyūginia Sensen: Suterareta Butai* (Tosho Shuppan-sha, 1992), p. 196.

8. Ibid., p. 196.

9. Nogi Harumichi, *Kaigun Tokubetsu Keisatsutai: Anbon Shima BC Kyū Senpan no Shuki* (Taihei Shuppan-sha, 1975), p. 207. It seems there were many cases of Japanese cannibalism during the battle on Leyte Island in the Philippines in late 1944 in which U.S. soldiers and the locals also became victims. U.S. forces investigated this matter in April 1945 when Leyte, Luzon, and Mindoro came under U.S. control. The following is an extract from testimony given by an American Pfc., Richard Charles Rusell, that appears in the investigation report (U.S. National Archives [hereafter USNA] Collection, RG 331 SCAP 1066, F–96): "At about 4 o'clock on the afternoon of December 12th or 13th, 1944, my battalion, the 3rd Battalion of the 511th Parachute Regiment, 11th Airborne Division, 8th Army, withdrew from a hill we were occupying about half way in the interior of Leyte between the cities of Tacloban and Ormoc. A few of our soldiers failed to withdraw with the balance of the regiment. Upon again advancing and occupying this hill the next morning at about 11 o'clock, the mutilated bodies of Pfc 'S' [the original document contains a full name, but initials only are used here for the sake of privacy] and four or five other American soldiers were found. All flesh was cut from the bodies of these men, apparently with a knife. The legs had been removed

and the meaty flesh cut from the calves and thighs. The cheeks had been cut from the faces of the men, and in fact, all fleshy portions of their bodies had been sliced from the bodies. . . . We were opposed by the 16th and 26th Japanese Divisions and the Japanese who committed this act were no doubt members of these divisions. . . . It was almost impossible to recognize any of the dead men because of the way in which the flesh had been sliced from their bones and I recognized only 'S.'"

10. Ogawa S., *Kyokugen no Naka no Ningen*, p. 167.

11. ANA Collection, MP729/8, 12/431/5; 02762, "Report on Japanese Atrocities to Australian Personnel."

12. USNA Collection, 775011, RG331, Box 943, "Japanese Cannibalism and Atrocities."

13. ANA Collection, MP729/8, 12/431/5; 4607, "Report: Japanese Atrocities."

14. USNA Collection, 775011, RG331, Box 943, "Japanese Cannibalism and Atrocities."

15. The Australian War Memorial (hereafter AWM) Collection, 54/1010/9/116. Of all the Australian documents on Japanese cannibalism I have found, this 127-page document contains the largest number of cases on cannibalism, of which all the victims were Australian soldiers. It contains reports on over 80 cases and gives evidence that about 100 Australians were victims of this crime.

16. ANA Collection, MP742/1, 336/1/1263, "War Crimes Wewak New Guinea: Cannibalism of Australian Airman."

17. Ibid.

18. Ibid.

19. Gavan McCormack and Hank Nelson (eds.), *The Burma-Thailand Railway* (Allen and Unwin, 1993), pp. 1, 64.

20. AWM Collection, 54/1010/9/94, "Interrogation of Lt-Col Tanaka Kengorō, Staff Officer of 18 Army H.Q.," and "Interrogation of Cap Araki Kankichi."

21. Ibid., 87, Box 12: A–1, a Japanese document entitled "Rikukai-gun Genkyō ni Kansuru Shuyō Sūryō."

22. Ibid., 54/1010/9/94, "Statement of No. 20531 L/Nk Hatam Ali."

23. Ibid.

24. ANA Collection, A476/1, 80794, "Record of Military Court: T.T. and Others."

25. Ibid.

26. USNA Collection, NG 343(G–37), "Cannibalism—Kumusi River."

27. Ibid., NG 313(F–61), "Mutilation of Bodies—Maffin Bay."

28. ANA Collection, MP729/8, 12/431/5, "Statement of Wimbap."

29. Ibid.

30. Ibid., MP742/1, 336/1/1129, "Interrogation of Lt F.M."

31. Ibid., MP729/8, 12/431/5, "Alleged Atrocities by Japanese."

32. Ibid., "VX5383."

33. G.M. Byrnes, *Green Shadows* (Queensland Corrective Commission, Brisbane, 1989), pp. 1–2.

34. Mentioned by Dick Collins during my interview with him September 18, 1992.

35. G. Byrnes, op. cit., p. 167.

36. W. Arens, *The Man-Eating Myth* (Oxford University Press, 1979), p. 20 in the Japanese edition published by Iwanami Shoten, Tokyo.

37. Ogawa S., *Kyokugen no Naka no Ningen*, p. 167.

38. For example, see some reports included in AWM Collection, 54/1010/9/116.

39. ANA Collection, MP742/1, 336/1/1323, "Abstract of Evidence: Etiringae of Irorkor."

40. USNA Collection, NG 315(F63), "Cannibalism at Guhu, New Guinea."

41. ANA Collection, AA1978/67/1, "A Report on Japanese Atrocities and Breaches of Rules of Warfare (March 1944)."

42. AWM Collection, 54/1010/4/168, "Mutilation of Dead and Cannibalism."

43. ANA Collection, A471/1, 80713, "Record of Military Court: First Lieut T.T."

44. ANA Collection, MP729/8, 12/431/5; 44/rlj, "Prisoner of War Preliminary Interrogation Report."

45. Ibid., "Information from Captured Document No. 80,107."

46. Bōei-chō Bōei Kenshūjo Senshi-shitsu (ed.), *Senshi Sōsho: Tōbu Nyūginea Hōmen Rikugun Kōku Sakusen* (Asagumo Shimbun-sha, 1968), p. 188.

47. Peter Charlton, *Australians at War: War Against Japan 1942–1945* (Time-Life Books Australia, 1989), p. 68.

48. Bōei-chō Bōei Kenshūjo Senshi-shitsu, op. cit., pp. 189, 275–276.

49. Ogawa S., *Tōbu Nyūginia Sensen*, pp. 12–22.

50. Bōei-chō Bōei Kenshūjo Senshi-shitsu, op. cit., pp. 276–277.

51. Ogawa S., *Tōbu Nyūginea Sensen*, p. 240.

52. *Argus*, April 24, 1945.

53. ANA Collection, MP729/8, 1945–1957, 43/431/6, "Chief Publicity Censor: FPC/1548."

54. Ibid., "War Cabinet Minute, No. 4187."

55. The first two reports prepared solely by Webb are *A Report on Japanese Atrocities and Breaches of Rules of Warfare* (March 1944) and *A Report on War Crimes by Individual Members of the Armed Forces of the Enemy Against Australians* (October 1944). The third report, *Australian War Crimes Board Inquiry Report on War Crimes Committed by Enemy Subjects Against Australians and Others, Vols. 1–3* (1945–1946), was a joint work by Webb and two other judges. These reports are now available to the public, but all details related to the victims (names, locations where the bodies were found, unit names, etc.) have been deleted from the documents.

56. Chaen Yoshio and Shigematsu Kazuyoshi, *Hokan: Senso Hanzai no Jissō* (Fuji Shuppan, 1987), pp. 105, 109, 111, 122, 152.

57. Brian McKinlay, *Australia 1942: End of Innocence* (Mead and Beckett, 1985), pp. 96–97.

58. John Dower, *War Without Mercy: Race and Power in the Pacific War* (Faber and Faber, 1986), p. 71.

59. Tim Bowden, *One Crowded Hour: Neil Davis Combat Cameraman, 1934–1985* (Angus and Robertson, 1987), pp. 293–303.

60. Key Ray Chong, *Cannibalism in China* (Longwood Academic, 1990).

61. Hanazono Ichirō, *Gunpō Kaigi* (Shinjimbutsu Ōrai-sha, 1974), pp. 16–21.

## Chapter 5

1. U.S. documents on the activities of Unit 731 as well as Japanese biological warfare activities during the Asia-Pacific War are now held in the U.S. National Archives. Documents on these subjects total about 8,000 pages. A Japanese historian, Tsuneishi Keiichi, selected about half of these documents and translated them into Japanese, available in book form. See Tsuneishi Keiichi (ed.), *Hyōteki Ishii: 731 Butai to Bei-gun Chōhō Katsudō* (Ōtsuki Shoten, 1984). The English translation of large amounts of original Japanese medical reports on various human experiments conducted by Unit 731 are now housed in the U.S. Army Dugway Laboratory in Utah. Some original Japanese documents on various types of human experiments were also in the possession of a former member of Unit 731, Inoue Yoshihiro, who died in 1969. In 1983 Dr. Inoue's relatives sold these documents to a waste-paper recycling merchant, who then sold them to a secondhand bookshop in Kanda, Tokyo. Eventually they were found by researchers at Keio University and purchased by the university library. These documents and other originals found elsewhere are now available in book form. See Tanaka Akira and Matsumura Takao (ed.) *731 Butai Sakusei Shiryō* (Fuji Shobō, 1991).

2. Tsuneishi K., op. cit., pp. 10–11; Peter Williams and David Wallace, *Unit 731: The Japanese Army's Secret of Secrets* (Hodder and Stoughton, 1989), pp. 5–12. The United States commenced research on biological weapons in 1943 at Camp Detrick in Frederick, Maryland. In June 1944 the Special Project Division was set up to promote further research in this field, and three additional research facilities were built in Mississippi, Indiana, and Utah. At this stage, the Special Project Division had a staff of 3,900 (including 100 academics at various universities) with an annual budget of $12 million. See Tsuneishi K., op. cit., pp. 22–23.

3. For details of the organizational structure and the various research activities of Unit 731, see "Sanders' Report" and "Thomson's Report" in Tsuneishi K., op. cit., pp. 215–376.

4. Ibid., pp. 331–334; Miyazaki Akira, "Impei to Kaimei to: 731 Butai Kenkyū no Rekishi o Tadotte," *Report on Japan's War Responsibility* No. 2, 1993, p. 35. For details of Unit 731's activities in Singapore and Malaysia, see Takashima Nobuyoshi, "Marei Singapōru no Saikin Butai: Pekin no Saikinsen Butai o Fukumu Nippon-gun Himitsu Butai no Jittai," *Report on Japan's War Responsibility* No. 2, 1993, pp. 36–51.

5. P. Williams and D. Wallace, op. cit., pp. 63–65.

6. Ibid., pp. 25–27.

7. Yoshimi Yoshiaki and Ika Toshiya, "Nippon-gun no Saikin-sen: Akiraka ni natta Rikugun Sōgakari no Jissō, *Report on Japan's War Responsibility* No. 2, 1993, pp. 12–13.

8. Ibid., p. 17.

9. P. Williams and D. Wallace, op. cit., pp. 31–50.

10. Ibid., pp. 42–44. The original medical summary report on details of frostbite experiments written by Yoshimura Hisao is included in Tanaka A. and Matsumura T. op. cit., pp. 225–288. Dr. Yoshimura, who was head of the frostbite research team of Unit 731, became a member of the Special Committee on the

Antarctic Expedition set up by the Science Council of Japan in 1972 in order to advise the Japanese expedition team on the problem of frostbite.

11. For details of the production, research, and use of chemical weapons by the Japanese forces during the Asia-Pacific War, see Yuki Tanaka, "Poison Gas: The Story Japan Would Like to Forget," *Bulletin of the Atomic Scientists,* Vol. 44, No. 8, 1988, pp. 10–19; and Tanaka A. and Matsumura T., op. cit., pp. 1–42.

12. The newly discovered documents are 111 volumes of *Gyōmu Nisshi* (Records of Military Plans and Operations) written by four army officers: Lieutenant Colonel Imoto Kumao and Major General Sanada Jōichirō in the Chiefs of Staff and Colonel Kanahara Setsuzō and Colonel Ōtsuka Fumiro in the Bureau of Army Medical Affairs. These records contain various plans for biological warfare, some of which were carried out during the Asia-Pacific War. Some records were hitherto virtually unknown to researchers. The records are held by the Research Library of the Japanese Defense Agency, but until Ika Toshiya and Yoshimi Yoshiaki analyzed them late in 1993, their details had not been thoroughly examined. See Yoshimi Y. and Ika T., op. cit., p. 8.

13. Ibid., pp. 15–16.

14. Ibid., pp. 17, 22–23.

15. Ibid., p. 24; Tsuneishi Keiichi, *Kieta Saikin Butai* (Kaimei-sha, 1981), pp. 249–250; Hata Ikuhiko, *Shōwa-shi no Nazo o Ou* (Bungei Shunjū, 1993), pp. 249–250.

16. Of course, most on-the-ground intelligence gathering concerning the Japanese would have been done by U.S. and Australian forces. See Australian National Archives (hereafter ANA) Collection, MP729/8, 9/431/107, "Memorandum on B.W. Intelligence up to 1st September, 1944."

17. Ibid.

18. Allied Translator and Interpreter Section Southwest Pacific Area (hereafter ATIS-SWPA), *The Japanese and Bacterial Warfare* (July 24, 1944), p. 17.

19. ANA Collection, MP729/8, 9/431/107, "Minutes of the Tenth Committee Meeting" Appendix, pp. 3–5.

20. ATIS-SWPA, ATIS Enemy Publications No. 96: Bacterial Culture Media—issued June '41 by No. 1 Section of Sasaki, Ko Force.

21. Tanaka Nobuyoshi, "Gun-i Gakkō Atochi no Jinkotsu Jiken sono go," *Gijutsu to Ningen,* Vol. 22, No. 7, 1993, p. 41.

22. "War Memories of Misaki Yōichi," in English translation, has not been published, but the Australian War Memorial holds a typescript. Australian War Memorial (hereafter AWM) Collection, 010545.

23. ATIS-SWPA, ATIS Enemy Publication No. 381: Defense Against Bacterial Warfare.

24. AWM Collection, 54/737/5/1, "Historical Division, GHQ, AFPAC 'Biological Warfare' AG385, 16 Oct., 1944."

25. It is not clear why these two hospitals were initially targeted for investigation; no existing documents give any reason for this decision. See the documents dated between April 2 and July 31, 1947, which are in the file of ANA Collection, MP742/1, 336/1/1398–155C.

26. Hugh Clarke, Colin Burgess, and Russell Braddon, *Australians at War: Prisoners of War* (Time-Life Books Australia, 1988), p. 115. Zenkoku Kenyūkai

Rengōkai (ed.), *Nippon Kenpei Gaishi* (Zenkoku Kenyūkai Rengōkai Honbu, 1983), pp. 1227–1228.

27. ANA Collection, MP742/1, 336/1/1398, p. 1.

28. Ibid., "Capt. Jose Holoquin's Affidavit," p. 8.

29. Ibid., "Affidavits of 1st Lt. James A. McMurria and S/Sgt. Escoe E. Palmer," p. 4.

30. Zenkoku Kenyūkai Rengōkai, op. cit., pp. 1233–1234, 1242.

31. ANA Collection, MP742/1, 336/1/1398, "Capt. Jose Holoquin's Affidavit," p. 14.

32. Ibid., pp. 8–9.

33. Ibid., "Statement by Mr. J.J. Murphy," pp. 1–2.

34. Joseph G. Nason and Robert L. Holt, *Horio: You Next Die* (Pacific Rim Press, 1987), pp. 184–185. Joseph Nason was one of eight POWs in Rabaul who survived until the end of the war. Two other books by surviving POWs are *Trial and Triumph* by James McMurria (private publication) and *Missing in Action over Rabaul* by John B. Kepchia (Palace Printer, 1986).

35. Mentioned by J. Murphy during the 1983 interview conducted by Tim Bowden, an Australian Broadcasting Corporation (ABC) journalist.

36. ANA Collection, MP742/1, 336/1/1398, "Capt. Jose Holoquin's Affidavit," p. 11–12. Biologist Koch mentioned in this affidavit was not French but German.

37. Ibid., "Statement by Mr. J.J. Murphy," p. 3.

38. ANA Collection, MP742/1, 336/1/1398–155C, "Interrogation of Dr Hirano Einosuke," p. 6.

39. Ibid., "Interrogation of Nishikawa Masao," pp. 3–4.

40. Ibid., pp. 4–8.

41. ATIS-SWPA, *Research Report: Survey of Japanese Medical Units* (January 18, 1947), pp. 1–3.

42. ANA Collection, MP742/1, 336/1/1398–155C, "Interrogation of Dr Hirano Einosuke," pp. 3–5.

43. Ibid., p. 6.

44. ANA Collection, MP742/1, 336/1/1398, "Case Analysis," p. 5.

45. ANA Collection, MP742/1, 336/1/1398–155C, "Interrogation of Dr Hirano Einosuke," pp. 9–10, 12.

46. ANA Collection, MP742/1, 336/1/1955, "Interrogation of Wakabayashi Zenichi."

47. Ibid., "War Crimes—Rabaul Area Written by Director of Prisoners of War and Internees (September 27, 1948)."

48. Ibid., "Statement by Ogata Kahachi, Formerly CO of Watom Island," "Interrogation of Kikuchi Satoru," and "Interrogation of Imamura Hitoshi."

49. Wakabayashi complained bitterly about "psychological torture" with the lie detector as well as physical ill-treatment by the staff of the Australian War Crimes Section. See his complaint written in Japanese on December 22, 1948, in ANA Collection, MP742/1, 336/1/1955.

50. Ibid., "Summary of Material Held on Praed Point Matupi File."

51. Ibid., "Statement by Kiyama Tatsuo," "Sworn Statement by Sanagi Sadamu," and "Report on Death of Kiyama Tatsuo."

52. Ibid., "Sworn Statement by Kubo Saichirō."

53. Ibid., "Sworn Statement by Hosaka Katsumi."

54. *The International Military Tribunal for the Far East: Record of Proceedings* (Tokyo, 1946), Vol. 48, pp. 13961–14005.

55. Ibid., p. 13962.

56. Mentioned by George Williams and Jack Pannaotie during the ABC interview conducted by Tim Bowden in 1983.

57. P. Williams and D. Wallace, op. cit., pp. 53–55.

58. Ibid., pp. 57–59.

59. Ibid., p. 56.

60. Ibid., pp. 133–134; Tsuneishi K., *Hyōteki Ishii*, pp. 377–435.

61. Sheldon H. Harris, *Factories of Death: Japanese Biological Warfare 1932–45 and the American Cover-up* (Routledge, 1994), pp. 190–223. In December 1949 the Soviet Union independently held a war crimes tribunal in Khabarovsk to prosecute 12 former members of Unit 731 who were among the Japanese POWs captured by the Red Army in Manchuria. They were sentenced to various terms (2 to 25 years) of forced labor. The Soviet government published the details of the trial proceedings in Russian in 1950; the Japanese translation is available as *Kōhan Kiroku: 731 Saikin-sen Butai* (Fuji Shobō, 1982). The U.S. government virtually ignored this trial. For more details on U.S. and Japanese reactions to it, see P. Williams and D. Wallace, op. cit., Chapter 16.

62. Surviving POWs are still angry that no one was prosecuted for such horrific medical experiments. See, for example, J. Nason and R. Holt, op. cit., p. 251.

63. As far as I know, there are two cases of U.S. prosecutions of Japanese medical doctors who experimented on American POWs. The first was of doctors at Kyūshū University who experimented on eight B-29 bomber crews while they were anesthetized and ultimately dissected them. The second was of staff of the naval hospital on Truk Island, including the head of the hospital, medical officer Captain Iwanami Hiroshi, who killed 10 POWs altogether on three separate occasions. In these two cases, however, those who were convicted were not associated with Unit 731 at all. They were ordinary doctors of hospitals that were not under the unit's control, and they were never involved in developing and testing biological and chemical weapons. In particular, the experiments on POWs at the Truk hospital were not really medical experiments in the strict sense but rather acts of revenge against the American pilots who bombed the hospital and thus killed many Japanese patients. For details of these two cases, see the U.S. National Archives documents, RG 153, Entry 143, Boxes 1062–1073 and 1362–1363.

64. ATIS-SWPA, *Research Report: Infringement of the Laws of War and Ethics by the Japanese Medical Corps* (January 26, 1945), p. 4. It seems that dissection of live prisoners for the purpose of medical training was widely practiced by Japanese military doctors throughout the Asia-Pacific region. Dr. Yuasa Ken's rare and honest account of such conduct seems to support this claim. According to Dr. Yuasa, who participated in these operations several times at an Army hospital in Manchukuo, the practice was common at military hospitals in Manchukuo. Normally, the Kempeitai supplied Chinese prisoners for this purpose. See Yoshikai Natsuko, *Kesenai Kioku: Yuasa Guni Seitai Kaibō no Kiroku* (Nitchū Shobō, 1981), pp. 65–93.

65. ATIS-SWPA, *Research Report: Infringement of the Laws of War and Ethics by the Japanese Medical Corps*, p. 9.

66. Ibid., pp. 1–3. This ATIS research report uses much information obtained from Japanese POWs on the behavior of Japanese doctors on the battlefield.

67. "Tōjō Shushō Mizukara Butai Honbu o Shisatsu: Moto Tai-in ga Akasu 731 no Senritsu," *Report on Japan's War Responsibility* No. 2, 1993, p. 65. This is a reproduction of an interview with Koshi Sadao conducted by Yamaguchi Toshiaki in Nagano on October 10, 1992.

68. "731 Butai to wa Nani ka," *Report on Japan's War Responsibility* No. 2, 1993, p. 54.

69. For details of Robert Lifton's concept of doubling, see his book *The Nazi Doctors: Medical Killing and the Psychology of Genocide* (Basic Books, 1986), in particular, Chapter 19, "Doubling: the Faustian Bargain." His book coauthored with Eric Markusen, *The Genocidal Mentality: Nazi Holocaust and Nuclear Threat* (Basic Books, 1990), is also useful to an understanding of his argument on this issue.

70. R. Lifton, *The Nazi Doctors*, pp. 269–302, 420–421. For details of Josef Mengele's doubling character, see the collection of testimonies by twins who were experimented on by Mengele in L.M. Lagnado and S.C. Dekel *Children of the Flames: Dr. Josef Mengele and the Untold Story of the Twins of Auschwitz* (Pan Books, 1991).

71. R. Lifton, op. cit., p. 445.

72. See various articles on this topic that have appeared in *The Albuquerque Tribune* (November 15, 16, 17, 19, 22, and 23, 1993; December 7, 1993; January 5 and 14, 1994; February 4, 8, 12, and 23, 1994; March 5, 8, 9, and 22, 1994; August 17, 1994). See also Phillip McCarthy, "Poisoning Their Own: U.S. Experiments on Citizens to Keep Cold War Edge," *The Age*, January 1, 1994.

## Chapter 6

1. Bōeichō Bōei Kenshūjo Senshi-shitsu (ed.), *Senshi Sōsho: Nantō Hōmen Kaigun Sakusen*, Vol. 1, *Ga-tō Dakkai Sakusen Kaishi Mede* (Asagumo Shimbun-sha, 1971), pp. 26–73.

2. Australian National Archives (hereafter ANA) Collection, MP158/98, "Attacks on Kavieng, 21st January, 1942—Report by District Officer J.H. Macdonald."

3. Bōeichō Bōei Kenshūjo Senshi-shitsu, op. cit., p. 73.

4. Australian War Memorial (hereafter AWM) Collection, 54/831/3/93, "Reconnaissance Report."

5. AWM Collection, 54/419/1/8, "Reconnaissance Report."

6. ANA Collection, MP742/1/336/1/160, "Missing Civilians: Suspected Murder Kavieng."

7. ANA Collection, MP158/98, "An Intelligence Report on New Ireland."

8. ANA Collection, MP137/93, "Statement of Rear Admiral Tamura Ryūkichi."

9. Ibid., "Nago Island: Fate Allied Airmen and Civilians."

10. ANA Collection, MP742/1/336/1/1444, "Civilians in New Britain and New Ireland" and "Interrogation of Naval Capt Sanagi Sadamu"; MP137/93, "New Guinea: Missing Personnel."

11. ANA Collection, MP742/1/336/1/1444, "Report on Interrogation: Baba Takashi," Missing Australians and Foreign Nationals: Akikaze Massacre," and "Translation of a Statement of Kai Yajirō."

12. Ibid., "Report on Interrogation: Baba Takashi."

13. Ibid., "Translation of a Statement by Mikawa Gunichi."

14. Ibid., "Translation of a Statement by Takahashi Manroku" and "Translation of a Statement by Ishigami Shinichi."

15. Ibid., "Translation of a Statement by Takahashi Manroku" and "Translation of a Statement by Ishigami Shinichi."

16. Ibid., "Report on Interrogation: Ichinose Harukichi."

17. Ibid., a Japanese document entitled "Ichinose Harukichi Sensei-sho."

18. Ibid., "Ichinose Harukichi Sensei-sho."

19. Ibid., "Report on Interrogation: Oimoto Yoshiji" and "Translation of a Statement by Takahashi Manroku."

20. Ibid., "Translation of a Statement of Kai Yajirō" and "Report on Interrogation: Oimoto Yoshiji."

21. Ibid., "Translation of a Statement of Kai Yajirō."

22. Ibid., "Report on Interrogation: Takahashi Manroku."

23. Ibid., "Report on Interrogation: Takahashi Manroku," "Report on Interrogation: Oimoto Yoshiji," and "Report on Interrogation: Takahashi Shigeo."

24. Ibid., "Report on Interrogation: Oimoto Yoshiji," "Translation of a Statement of Kai Yajirō," and "Report on Interrogation: Oguchi Shigeru."

25. Ibid., "Translation of a Statement of Kai Yajirō" and "Report on Interrogation: Yagura Satoshi."

26. Ibid., "Report on Interrogation: Ōnishi Shinzō."

27. Ibid., "Translation of a Statement by Mikawa Gunichi."

28. Ibid., "Translation of a Statement by Mikawa Gunichi."

29. Ibid., "Report on Interrogation: Mikawa Gunichi."

30. Ibid., "Missing Australians and Foreign Nationals: Akikaze Massacre" and "Report on Interrogation: Yamazumi Teijirō."

31. Ibid., "Report on Interrogation: Maeda Shigeru."

32. Ibid., "Comments in the Report on Interrogation: Mikawa Gunichi."

33. The Australian War Crimes Act of 1945, No. 48, Article 12. For details of this law, see Chaen Yoshio (ed.), *BC-Kyū Senpan Gō-gun Rabauru Saiban Shiryō* (Fuji Shuppan, 1990), p. 171.

34. ANA Collection, MP742/1/336/1/160, "Report on Interrogation: Ōtsu Yoshio" and a Japanese document entitled "Ose Toshio Sensei-sho"; ANA Collection, MP742/336/1/1444, a Japanese document entitled "Ōtsu Yoshio Sensei-sho."

35. ANA Collection, MP742/1/336/1/160, "Report on Interrogation: Ōtsu Yoshio."

36. ANA Collection, MP742/1/336/1/1444, "Ōtsu Yoshio Sensei-sho."

37. ANA Collection, MP742/1/336/1/160, "Report on Interrogation: Ōtsu Yoshio."

38. Ibid., "Report on Interrogation: Ōtsu Yoshio."

39. Ibid., "Ōse Toshio Sensei-sho."

40. Ibid., "Report on Interrogation: Kuriyama Shigeru" and "Civilians in New Britain and New Ireland and Movement of *Kowa Maru*."

41. ANA Collection, MP742/1/336/1/1444, "Proof of Evidence: VX128203 Captain Albert Klestadt." Albert Klestadt, a refugee from Germany under Hitler, went to Japan in 1935. When it became clear that Japan was about to enter the war, he moved to the Philippines. He escaped from Manila soon after Japanese forces invaded in January 1942 and went to North Sangboy. From there he sailed to Australia on a small boat with a crew of seven Filipinos without any navigation instruments. Almost seven months later he reached Darwin in northern Australia. For details of this voyage, see Albert Klestadt, *The Sea Was Kind* (Kangaroo Press, 1988).

42. ANA Collection, MP742/1/336/1/1444, "Comment in the Report on Interrogation: Hiratsuka Seiichi."

43. Ibid., "Summary of Examination on Jitsukawa Kinjirō." AWM Collection, 54/1010/6/134, PT2, a Japanese document entitled "Jitsukawa Kinjirō Senseisho."

44. ANA Collection, MP742/1/336/1/1444, "Report on Interrogation: Takatō Jūtarō," "Summary of Examination of Takatō Jūtarō," "Takatō Jūtarō Sensei-sho," "Translation of Statement by Yamao Unoharu," and "Summary of Examination of Yamao Unoharu."

45. Ibid., "Sworn Statement by Tamura Ryūkichi."

46. Ibid., "Report on Interrogation: Suzuki Shōzō" and "Report on Interrogation: Horiguchi Yoshio."

47. AWM Collection, 1010/6/134/, PT1, "War Crime Trial: Admiral Tamura Ryūkichi and Others," pp. 38, 103.

48. Ibid., pp. 39, 71. Lieutenant Mori, whose official title was deputy commander, acted as commander for the 83rd Unit after February 10 when Tamura took on additional duties as commander of the 14th Naval Base Force.

49. Ibid., pp. 67–68; ANA Collection, MP742/1/336/1/1444, a Japanese document "Yoshino Shōzō Sensei-sho."

50. AWM Collection, 54/1010/6/134, PT1, p. 71.

51. Ibid., p. 68.

52. Ibid., p. 69.

53. Ibid., pp. 106–107.

54. Ibid., pp. 120–121. At the tribunal Mori implied that Tamura was solely responsible for the execution of detainees. However, from Mori's statement it is clear that he was avoiding any responsibility.

55. Ibid., pp. 68–69.

56. Ibid., pp. 36–37, 83; ANA Collection, MP742/1/336/1/1444, "Yoshino Shōzō Sensei-sho."

57. AWM Collection, 54/1010/6/134, PT1, pp. 40–41, 43.

58. Ibid., p. 70.

59. Ibid., p. 101.

60. Ibid., p. 42.

61. Ibid., p. 108.

62. Ibid., pp. 108–109, 140–142.

63. Ibid., pp. 145–146, 160–165; ANA Collection, MP742/1/336/1/1444, "Sworn Statement by Suzuki Shōzō" and "Report on Interrogation: Horiguchi Yoshio."

64. ANA Collection, MP742/1/336/1/1444, "Report on Interrogation: Takatō Jūtarō," "Summary of Examination of Takatō Jūtarō," and "Takatō Jūtarō Sensei-sho."

65. AWM Collection, 54/1010/6/134, PT1, pp. 165–167.

66. Ibid., pp. 167–168, 189–191.

67. Ibid., pp. 167–168.

68. Ibid., pp. 176–178.

69. Ibid., p. 168.

70. Ibid., pp. 110–111, 142, 152, 168.

71. Ibid., pp. 57–58, 92–94; ANA Collection, MP742/1/336/1/1444, "Yoshino Shōzō Sensei-sho."

72. ANA Collection, MP742/1/336/1/1444, "Yoshino Shōzō Sensei-sho," "Sworn Statement by Suzuki Shōzō," and "Report on Interrogation: Horiguchi Yoshio"; AWM Collection, 54/1010/6/134 , PT1, pp. 57, 144.

73. ANA Collection, MP742/1/336/1/1444, "Translation of Statement Concerning POW made by Mori Yahichi," "Summary of Examination of Mori Yahichi," and "Summary of Examination of Jitsukawa Kinjirō."

74. Ibid., "Report on Interrogation: Suzuki Shōzō" and "Report on Interrogation: Horiguchi Yoshio"; AWM Collection, 54/1010/6/134, PT1, p. 171.

75. AWM Collection, 54/1010/6/134, PT1, p. 2, and "Petition Against the Finding and/or Sentence of the Military Court by Tamura Ryūkichi." In fact Tamura expressed his gratitude to Albert Klestadt for the fair trial after being sentenced. This information was obtained during my interview with Albert Klestadt in June 1995.

76. Ibid., pp. 53–54, 58–59, 78–79, 117, 147.

77. Kita Yoshito, "Kyū Kaigun Shogakkō ni okeru Kokusai-hō Kyōiku," in Chaen Y., op. cit., pp. 260–263.

78. Ibid., p. 267.

79. Kita Yoshito, "Kyū Rikugun no Shōkō Yōsei Kikan ni yoru Kokusai-hō Kyōiku," in Chaen Yoshio (ed.), *BC-Kyū Senpan Beigun Shanhai-to Saiban Shiryō* (Fuji Shuppan, 1989), pp. 150–166.

80. AWM Collection, 54/1010/6/134, PT1, pp. 36, 81.

81. Ibid., "Statement in Mitigation Re Tamura Ryūkichi by Reiko Osawa." It is apparent from various petitions and character references put forth in support of Tamura that he was a warm and sincere person. This episode was described by his oldest daughter in her character reference about him.

82. Ibid., pp. 40–42, and "Petition Against the Finding and/or Sentence of the Military Court by Tamura Ryūkichi."

## Conclusion

1. Although it is almost certain that during the Asia-Pacific War the Chinese were seen as inferior by the Japanese (and by white people as well), it is difficult to define when the Japanese actually adopted such discriminatory ideas and

attitudes toward the Chinese (and the Koreans). Soon after the Meiji restoration, Japanese political leaders quickly developed the idea that international relationships with other nations were determined principally by the strength of military power. Based upon such a notion, they believed that Korea should be subordinated to Japan immediately and that Japan would subjugate China in the near future when Japan's military power superseded that of China. Therefore, the basic element for racial discrimination against other Asian races already existed in the very early years of the Meiji period. However, it seems that the general population in Japan at this time did not have a fixed image of neighboring countries and races. For details of the views of Japanese political leaders about China and Korea in this period, see Shibahara Takuji, "Taigai-kan to Nashonarizumu" in Shibahara Takuji, Ikai Tadaaki, and Ikeda Masahiro (eds.), *Nippon Kindai Shisō-shi Taikei Dai 12-kan: Taigai-kan* (Iwanami Shoten, 1988), pp. 458–534.

2. Chaen Yoshio (ed.), *Horyo ni Kansuru Sho-hōkiruiju* (Fuji Shuppan, 1988), p. 18.

3. For details of how various methods of suicidal attacks were planned and carried out, see, for example, Morimoto Tadao, *Tokkō: Gedō no Tōsotsu to Ningen no Jōken* (Bungei Shunjū, 1992).

4. Kawashima Takenori, *Nipponjin no Hō Ishiki* (Iwanami Shoten, 1967), pp. 2–3; Inoue Kiyoshi, *Jōyaku Kaisei* (Iwanami Shoten, 1955), pp. 129–170.

5. Kawashima T., op. cit., p. 16. The word *kenri* was developed by Japanese scholars of Dutch (the most prominent Western language in Japan in the Tokugawa period) as a neologism to translate the Dutch word *regt* (rights). It was first officially used in the Meiji constitution.

6. Ibid., pp. 16–19.

7. However, I am not claiming that popular movements such as those by peasants (e.g., *ikki* in the Edo period) or the democratic rights movement (e.g., *minken undō* in the early Meiji era) had no influence upon the advancement of political rights of the common people in Japan.

8. Kawashima T., op. cit., pp. 51–55.

9. Ibid., p. 32; Ishida Takeshi, "Kokka-shugi no Shisō to Undō," in Maruyama Masao et al. (eds.), *Nippon no Nashonarizumu* (Kawade Shobō, 1953) p. 118. The restored emperor system in the Meiji era was not, of course, the system of feudal practice simply continued from the Edo period. Many revisions and inventions were added to the existing emperor system in order to adjust it to the modern political and socioeconomic environment. In particular, new methods to enhance the emperor's symbolic power were invented in order to control mass ideology. On this point, see, for example, Taki Kōji's excellent work *Tennō no Shōzō* (Iwanami Shoten, 1988).

10. Maruyama Masao, *Nippon no Shisō* (Iwanami Shoten, 1961), p. 47.

11. Ibid., pp. 31–32, 39.

12. Ibid., p. 37–38; Maruyama Masao, *Gendai Seiji no Shisō to Kōzō* (Mirai-sha, 1956), p. 123.

13. Maruyama M., *Gendai Seiji no Shisō to Kōzō*, p. 11–16.

14. The Japanese naval academy had been founded in 1870. In 1872, 34 British naval officers were invited to take up positions as instructors. For details of British influence on the Japanese navy in the early period of its history, see

Nomura Minoru, "Kaigun Hei-gakkō Enkaku-shi: Sono Eikō to Kunō," in *Bessatsu Rekishi Dokuhon: Edajima Nippon no Kaigun Kyōiku* (Shinjimbutsu Ōrai-sha, 1992), pp. 40–43.

15. Kamisaka Yasushi, "Saigo no Sotsugyōsei 75-ki," in *Bessatsu Rekishi Dokuhon: Edajima Nippon no Kaigun Kyōiku*, p. 82.

16. Maruyama M., *Gendai Seiji no Shisō to Kōzō*, pp. 13, 19.

17. For details of the cultural and ideological link between *burakumin* and the emperor system, see Kan Takayuki, *Senmin Bunka to Tennōsei* (Akashi Shoten, 1986); Kobayashi Sueo, *Sabetsu to Tennōsei* (Shiraishi Shoten, 1986).

18. Maruyama M., *Gendai Seiji no Shisō to Kōzō*, p. 23; Shibahara T., op. cit., pp. 464–467.

19. Maruyama M., *Gendai Seiji no Shisō to Kōzō*, p. 22.

20. Ishida T., op. cit., p. 134.

21. Maruyama M., *Nippon no Shisō*, pp. 33–36.

22. Okuma Miyoshi, *Kantō Daishinsai: Sono Jissō to Rekishiteki Igi* (Yūzankaku, 1973), pp. 217–273. For details of various political ideas and movements during the Taishō democracy, see Matsuo Takayoshi, *Taishō Demokurashii no Kenkyū* (Aoki Shoten, 1966).

23. Ishida T., op. cit., pp. 115–141.

24. Maruyama M., *Gendai Seiji no Shisō to Kōzō*, pp. 27–28.

25. Nishi Amane, *Heika Tokugyō*, reproduced in Yui Masaomi, Fujiwara Akira, and Yoshida Yutaka (eds.), *Nippon Kindai Shisō Taikei Dai 4-kan: Guntai Heishi* (Iwanami Shoten, 1989), pp. 149–162.

26. Fujiwara Akira, "Tōsuiken Dokuritsu to Tennō no Guntai," in Yui M., Fujiwara A., and Yoshida Y., op. cit., pp. 477–502.

27. For details of the spirit of *bushidō*, see, for example, Takahashi Tomio, *Bushidō no Rekishi*, Vols. 1 and 2 (Shinjimbutsu Ōrai-sha, 1986); Nitobe Inazō, *Bushidō: The Story of Japan* (Charles E. Tuttle Company, 1969); and Adachi Sumio, "Traditional Asian Approach: A Japanese View" in Queensland Ex-POW Repatriation Committee (ed.), *Nippon Very Sorry—Many Men Must Die: Submission To the United Nations Commission of Human Rights* (Boolarong Publications, 1990), pp. 12–17.

28. *Gunjin Chokuron*, reproduced in Yui M., Fujiwara A., and Yoshida Y., op. cit., pp. 173–177.

29. Chaen Y., op. cit., pp. 17–18.

30. Articles 1 and 2 of *Gunjin Chokuron*, in Yui M., Fujiwara A., and Yoshida Y., op. cit., pp. 174–175.

31. Article 2 of *Gunjin Kunkai*, reproduced in ibid., p. 166.

32. Fujiwara Akira, *Nippon Gunjishi: Jōkan Senzen-hen* (Nippon Hyōron-sha, 1987), pp. 127–132.

33. Maeda Tetsuo, *Nippon no Guntai: Jō Kōgun-hen* (Gendai Shokan, 1994), pp. 68–69.

34. Ibid., p. 70.

35. Ōe Shinobu, "Tennōsei Guntai to Minshū," in Tōyama Shigeki (ed.), *Kindai Tennōsei no Tenkai* (Iwanami Shoten, 1989), p. 72.

36. Between 1910 and 1920, it became popular throughout Japan for families who had young boys to visit Shintō shrines and pray that these children would

not be drafted into the military forces. At the same time, many incidents occurred at various army camps in which soldiers deserted in a group because they could not bear the ill-treatment by their officers. Such phenomena clearly indicate that veneration for the emperor and loyalty toward the military by the general populace were still weak in this period. For details, see Fujiwara A., *Nippon Gunji-shi: Jōkan Senzen-hen*, pp. 132–133; and Ōe S., op. cit., pp. 73–99.

37. Ōe Shinobu, *Heishi-tachi no Nichirō Sensō: 500 tsu no Gunji Yūbin kara* (Asahi Shimbun-sha, 1988), p. 304.

38. Such romantic ideas and nationalistic sentiment are also clear in some of the last letters written by the soldiers who died from *gyokusai* or by those who committed suicide after defeat in battle during the Asia-Pacific War. See, for example, Fukutake Takeshi and Fukushima Jurō, *Jiketsu to Gyokusai* (Chōbun-sha, 1993).

39. For details of the general attitude of Okinawans during the battle of Okinawa, see, for example, Shōji Sakakibara, *Okinawa: Hachijūyon-nichi no Tatakai* (Iwanami Shoten, 1994), pp. 202–225.

40. Hata Ikuhiko, "Nippon-gun ni Okeru Horyo Kannen no Keisei," in *Gunji Shigaku*, Vol. 28, No. 2, 1992, p. 15.

41. For details of various discrimination problems that minorities in Japan are facing, see, for example, G.A. de Vas and W.O. Wetherall, *Japan's Minorities: Burakumin, Koreans, Ainu, and Okinawans* (Minority Rights Group, 1983).

42. The case of Sakae Menda is a good example. Sakae was suspected of murder and was arrested and imprisoned for many years without trial. Subsequently he was proved innocent and released. For details of his ordeal and other similar cases, see Gavan McCormack, "Crime, Confession, and Control in Contemporary Japan," and Igarashi Futaba, "Forced to Confess," both in Gavan McCormack and Yoshio Sugimoto (eds.) *Democracy in Contemporary Japan* (M.E. Sharp, 1986), pp. 186–214.

43. See, for example, Tezuka Kazuaki, *Gaikokujin Rōdōsha* (Nippon Keizai Shimbun-sha, 1989), in particular Chapter 2; and *Japan-Asia Quarterly Review*, Vol. 19, No. 4, 1988, pp. 2–21.

44. Although the analyses by Maruyama Masao and Ishida Takeshi of the emperor ideology were extremely incisive, both idealized Western society in terms of democracy and human rights. It is interesting that very few scholars in the field of Japanese political science have tried to critically analyze and develop the concepts that Maruyama and Ishida constructed more than 40 years ago. On Maruyama's concept of democracy, see Andrew Barshay, "Imagining Democracy in Postwar Japan: Reflections on Maruyama and Modernism," in *Journal of Japanese Studies*, Vol. 18, No. 2, 1992, pp. 365–406.

45. One reason for such tendency in the research by progressive historians seems to lie in the particular type of debates on war crimes between these historians and nationalist scholars in Japan. Progressive historians constantly face nationalist historians' efforts to dispute the occurrence of specific events such as the Nanjing massacre. In order to counter such attacks, they tend to concentrate their efforts on discovering historical documents that can corroborate Japanese atrocities and war crimes.

46. John Dower's recent article on the relationship between the bombing of Hiroshima and Nagasaki and the failure by Japanese people to acknowledge responsibility for the war is quite appealing. His approach to this problem through analysis of the Japanese government's postwar policy to promote science education and of the corresponding popular thinking is novel and persuasive. See his article, "The Bombed: Hiroshima and Nagasaki in Japanese Memory," *Diplomatic History*, Vol. 19, No. 2, 1995, pp. 275–295.

47. On the role Emperor Hiorohito played in decisionmaking at various stages of the Asia-Pacific War and the myth created after the war to conceal such active conduct, see, for example, Fujiwara Akira, Awaya Kentarō, Yoshida Yutaka, and Yamada Akira, *Tettei Kenshō: Shōwa Tennō "Dokuhaku-roku"* (Ōtsuki Shoten, 1991); Herbert Bix, "The Shōwa Emperor's 'Monologue' and the Problem of War Responsibility," *Journal of Japanese Studies*, Vol. 18, No. 2, 1992, pp. 295–363; Herbert Bix, "Japan's Delayed Surrender: A Reinterpretation," *Diplomatic History*, Vol. 19, No. 2, 1995, pp. 197–225.

48. See, for example, Takeuchi Yoshimi, "Chūgoku-jin no Kōsen Ishiki to Nippon-jin no Dōtoku Ishiki," *Chisei*, May 1949; Hashikawa Bunzō, "Nippon Kindai-shi to Sensō Taiken," in *Gendai no Hakken*, Vol. 2, ed. Hashīkawa Bunzō (Shunjū-sha, 1959); Arai Shinichi, "Kiki Ishiki to Gendai-shi," in *Gendai no Hakken*, Vol. 6, ed. Hashīkawa Bunzō (Shunjū-sha, 1960); Irokawa Daikichi, *Aru Shōwa-shi* (Chūō Kōron-sha, 1975); Yasumaru Yoshio, *Nippon no Nashonarizumu no Zenya* (Asahi Shimbun-sha, 1977); Yoshida Mitsuru, *Senchū-ha no Shisei-kan* (Bungei Shunjū-sha, 1980); Watanabe Kiyoshi, *Watashi no Tennō-kan* (Henkyō-sha, 1981); Yoshizawa Minami, *Watashi-tachi no naka no Ajia no Sensō* (Asahi Shimbun-sha, 1986).

49. D.J.K. Peukert, *Inside Nazi Germany: Conformity, Opposition, and Racism in Everyday Life* (Harmondsworth, 1989).

# About the Book and Author

This book documents for the first time previously hidden Japanese atrocities in World War II, including cannibalism; the slaughter and starvation of prisoners of war; the rape, enforced prostitution, and murder of noncombatants; and biological warfare experiments.

The author describes how desperate Japanese soldiers consumed the flesh of their own comrades killed in fighting as well as that of Australians, Pakistanis, and Indians. Another chapter traces the fate of 65 shipwrecked Australian nurses and British soldiers who were shot or stabbed to death by Japanese soldiers. Thirty-two other nurses, who landed on another island, were captured and sent to Sumatra to become "comfort women"—prostitutes for Japanese soldiers. Tanaka recounts how thousands of Australian and British POWs died in the infamous Sandakan camp in the Borneo jungle in 1945. Those who survived were forced to endure a tortuous 160-mile march on which anyone who dropped out of line was immediately shot. Only six escapees lived to tell the tale.

Based on exhaustive research in previously closed archives, this book represents a landmark analysis of Japanese war crimes. The author explores individual atrocities in their broader social, psychological, and institutional milieu and places Japanese behavior during the war in the broader context of the dehumanization of men at war—without denying individual and national responsibility.

Yuki Tanaka is a Visiting Research Fellow at the Australian National University.

# Index